Reflections of Amma

Reflections of Amma

Devotees in a Global Embrace

Amanda J. Lucia

UNIVERSITY OF CALIFORNIA PRESS

Berkeley · Los Angeles · London

University of California Press, one of the most
distinguished university presses in the United States,
enriches lives around the world by advancing
scholarship in the humanities, social sciences, and
natural sciences. Its activities are supported by the UC
Press Foundation and by philanthropic contributions
from individuals and institutions. For more information, visit www.ucpress.edu.

University of California Press
Berkeley and Los Angeles, California

University of California Press, Ltd.
London, England

© 2014 by The Regents of the University of California

Cataloging-in-Publication data is on the file with the
Library of Congress.

ISBN 978-0-520-28113-4 (cloth : alk. paper)
ISBN 978-0-520-28114-1 (pbk. : alk. paper)

Manufactured in the United States of America

22 21 20 19 18 17 16 15 14 13

10 9 8 7 6 5 4 3 2 1

*For Jonas and Zoe, whose hugs keep everything
in perspective*

Contents

Illustrations

Acknowledgments

In 2006 I asked Amma directly if I might have her blessing to write my dissertation on her and her movement. Amma seemed surprised and playfully amused at first, and then with seriousness she said yes and encouraged me to read all of the books at the "bookstore" in the back of the darshan hall. She then gave me a special sandalwood *ṭīkā* with the ring finger of her right hand and her classic darshan embrace. Without this gracious blessing, I would have been in a dilemma. While receiving Amma's blessing for my academic project would not have been of consequence to many scholars (and for some it may even function detrimentally), for devotees it was all that mattered. Amma's blessing became a virtual passport that I carried with me throughout my fieldwork, and for that I am most grateful.

Devotees invited me into their homes and their lives, embracing me as friend, sister, auntie, and niece. I was consistently overwhelmed by the warmhearted kindness of Balan, Lakshmi, Vinita, and Krishna, Molly and Suresh, Manju and Praveen, Preet and Raman, Dhananjay and Dhanashree, Jay and Sunitha, Latha and Harish, Pradeep and Reena, Santosh and Bindu, Saveen and Sindhu, Milind and Meetali, Gulbinder and Vinoo, Viji and Ramesh, Gangadhar and Madhusmita, Kasi and Annam, Raj and Sudha, Alok and Lorena, Beena, Madhu, Mridula and Sethu, and AYUDH (Amma's youth group). Each taught me the meaning of "satsang family." Puneeta, Jayan, Eric, Gail, Hanuman, Shakti Prasad, Barbara, Tanushree, Radha, Stevik, Kalavati, and Aaron were exceptionally welcoming and taught me how to sing without shyness in small groups of my peers. In later years I was consistently buttressed by meaningful conversations with earnest devotees, too many to name here, but I especially would like to thank Priya, Ron, Temba, Nirmalan, Mithilesh, Renuka, Kathy and Linda, Lina, C. C., Shiva Rae, Sridhar, Harsha, Rema Devi, Venilla, Neelima, Jodi, and Amma's tour staff. I am so thankful for the dozens of anonymous devotees who often shared their most intimate feelings with a stranger with openness, patience, and loving kindness. I also owe a sincere debt of gratitude to the ashram staff at Amritapuri and in San Ramon, in particular, Janani and Sachin for their advice, guidance, and patient assistance with illustration permissions. Last, I am most grateful for the assistance of Swami Amritaswarupananda Puri, Swami Ramakrishnananda Puri, Br. Shantamrita, and, most significantly, Br. Dayamrita Chaitanya, who graciously provided interviews and logistical support.

In my earliest days of fieldwork, I tacked between devotional communities in the Chicago suburbs and my academic home at the University of Chicago, where I relied on a wealth of expertise and support for my research. Of those who were at the University of Chicago at that time, I am indebted to Malika Zeghal, Catherine Brekus, Christian Wedemeyer, Bruce Lincoln, Tanika Sarkar, Martin Riesebrodt, Dipesh Chakrabarty, Rochona Majumdar, and Omar McRoberts, all of whom offered significant suggestions and intellectual adjustments to my thinking. Steven Collins raised poignant questions over many long lunches and coffees, for which I only now realize what a privilege that time was. Similarly, Wendy Doniger has always shown unflagging support and her own intellectual style of maternal care in pedagogy, letting me run free and tightening the reins with impeccable pacing and only as needed, as any good horsewoman would.

Before and after Chicago, I have been fortunate to be surrounded by intellectual excellence in my colleagues, friends, and mentors, who have all provided insights that I have incorporated into the text in various forms. I would like to thank, in particular, David Haberman, Rebecca Manring, James Hart, Pamela Winfield, Ron Mourad, Todd Penner, Hugh Urban, Deepak Sarma, Peter Gottschalk, Hanna Kim, John Nemec, David Shulman, Laurie Patton, Purushottama Bilimoria, Sheldon Pollock, and Joanne Punzo Waghorne. At the University of California, Riverside (UCR), I have gratefully accepted intellectual support from and stimulating conversations with my colleagues, in particular, Vivian Nyitray, Pashaura Singh, and Ivan Strenski. I also have benefited immensely from discussions that took place at the Institute for the Study of Immigration and Religion at UCR and with my codirectors, Jennifer Hughes and Michael Alexander. My cohorts and friends continue to assist me in developing my thoughts; particular thanks go to Jen Sandler, Romi Mukherjee, Lucas Carmichael, Benjamin Schonthal, and Jeremy Morse.

This book has benefited greatly from audience responses at the American Academy of Religions (2012), the Society for the Anthropology of Religion (2011), the University of Wisconsin, Madison, South Asia Conference (2010), and the American Anthropological Association (2009). In addition, invited presentations at the University of Chicago's conference "Hindus in India and America" (2010), the Art Institute of Chicago (2011), and Asia Week at Austin College (2011) helped formulate my thoughts on Swami Vivekananda. Thoughtful engagement with students at University of California, Riverside has improved the manuscript, specifically in response to my graduate seminar on the North American encounter with religious "Others" and my undergraduate course "Gurus and Saints," wherein students raised intelligent questions that pushed my own work further. I am grateful to Jessica Rehman for her logistical assistance with final edits to the manuscript. The two anonymous reviewers at the University of California Press provided excellent suggestions and careful commentary that made this book a much better one; I thank them deeply for their very hard work. I am wholly grateful for the staff at the University of California Press, particularly Lissa Caldwell, Stacy Eisenstark, Michele Lansing, and Reed Malcolm, who supported me throughout the publication process with vision and smart professionalism. Of course, despite such insightful interventions and careful commentary, I am wholly accountable for that which is presented herein.

In addition, I benefited from the financial support of the Divinity School and the Committee on South Asian Studies at the University of Chicago, the American Institute of Indian Studies, the Foreign Language and Area Studies Program, and a UCR faculty research grant. Furthermore, I am deeply indebted to my friends and family whose personal connections enabled me to complete my fieldwork. Debra Bernard graciously loaned me her house and her car so that I could conduct my research at the San Ramon ashram. Mark Singleton offered to drive me out to the Santa Fe ashram, and countless others facilitated my research in wonderful and practical ways. I am also grateful to Ramu Pandit and Max Katz, who first recounted their stories of Amma and encouraged me to look into her movement in more detail.

I am forever grateful to my mother, who reads drafts when asked and always (regardless) tells me that I am wonderful. This book would not have been possible without her constant encouragement and her child care support in the field (Boston, Dallas, Los Angeles, and Amritapuri) and at home. I am fortunate to be enfolded in family across the United States, all of whom encourage my work and offer loyalty, love, and support, including my father, whose careful and patient ear on the world of academe has become invaluable. But most of all I am indebted to Andrew, who has suffered through my absences and picked up the financial slack with patience and constancy. To my children, Jonas and Zoe, who know much more about Hindus, gurus, and hugs than most American children their age—may they grow up to know the purity and power of unconditional love.

Note on Language

All quotations without correlative citations in this book derive from my conversations and digitally recorded interviews with Amma devotees. Three-quarters of my interactions in the field were conducted in English, with the remaining quarter spliced between Hindi, Malayalam, and "kitchery bhasha," meaning a mixed language combining Hindi-English or Malayalam-English. Sanskrit was the dominant devotional language of scripture and prayer recitation. I was consistently grateful in the field for my competency in Hindi, my ability to read and recite Sanskrit, and my playful flirtation as an eager student of Malayalam, which encouraged many within the Malayalee devotional community to adopt my language pedagogy as a pet project.

Nearly all of Amma's literature and devotional materials are available in English. In fact, the majority of published materials are intentionally made available in dozens of languages in an effort to increase potential readership. In a similar effort to make this book more readable for audiences, I have eliminated diacritics for words that have already been incorporated into the English language (e.g., guru, mantra, yoga). When referencing less frequently occurring Indic terms (e.g., *iṣṭadev* [favored deity]) and Sanskrit texts (e.g., *Śrī Lalitā Aṣṭottara Śatanāmāvali*), I generally keep these words and phrases in italics with diacritics in an effort to help readers with pronunciation. For Indic terms more conventionally used in English, I have simply followed English pluralization norms (e.g., gurus, mantras, bhajans).

Situating Amma as Female Guru in the Context of North American Multiculturalism

The Servant of Everyone
Do you ask why the sun shines, or the river flows?
It is Mother's nature to love—her embrace
expresses that love.

An unbroken stream of love flows from Mother
to every being in the universe.

Mother does not give expecting
anything in return.

What nourishes Mother
is the happiness of her children.

Mother is the servant of everyone.
I have no home of my own—
I live in your hearts.[1]

—Messages from Amma

VARKALAM, KERALA 1996

A hawkish young man approaches me on Varkalam beach in Kerala, a premier tourist destination in South India. "Sah-un-gley-sses," "Sah-un-gley-sees," he calls out in my direction, vigorously motioning to me. He carries a stanchion that offers an array of sunglasses for purchase; he wears a dynamic pair himself, modeling their fashion potential. I am an easy target. My white skin gleams beneath my Indian clothing, which does little to mask my status as a foreigner. I squint in the relentless blazing sun, its shimmering reflection dancing on the waves of the Indian Ocean. As he draws near, I notice a smiling female visage dangling about his neck, similar to the guru pendants that I have seen devotees wear in North India. Before now, each pendant I have seen has been the image of a male guru. Though I am away from my research among Banarasi Hindu ascetics, I cannot resist asking him about the smiling woman. He says simply, she is Amma, a local guru. He motions into the distance and tells me that her very large and beautiful ashram is somewhere on the nearby horizon.

I coast through the next several days of lovely Kerala, relieved that my seaside sanction is away from the commotion of the northern cities. Before departing, I purchase a pocket-sized book with the same smiling female visage on the cover that reads: *For My Children: Spiritual Teachings of Mata Amritanandamayi*. Six months later, after interviewing many dozens of Hindu ascetics in Banaras and in the Himalayan regions, I carefully pack this small book in my duffel bag and head home to the United States. From time to time, in curiosity, I take it off its shelf and turn over in my mind its simple teachings of love and compassion. Eight years after this first chance encounter, and despite the considerable time I had spent among ascetics and gurus in India, I experienced Amma's *darshan* not in Kerala but in Naperville, Illinois.[2]

NAPERVILLE, ILLINOIS 2004

Dusk is settling on throngs of bustling people, families with young children, girlfriends arm in arm, and individuals of all shapes and sizes as they shuttle between the glass and chrome doors opening the way into the polished pristine lobby of the four-star hotel in the suburban American landscape. The doormen professionally mask their wonder as the bright brocaded saris, scarves, kurtas, and eclectic flowing wardrobes enliven the muted color palette of the wide hallways. The rich smells endemic to South India (roses, curry, camphor, incense) overwhelm the sterile atmosphere. Monitors vigilantly guard the lobby entrances to make sure the largely barefoot crowd does not enter into the common areas without shoes, a code violation that could impinge on the good standing of Amma's return to the same venue the following year. A token queue already stretches for hundreds of yards from the ballroom entrance, a wait necessary only for those who wish to receive darshan tokens for the early hours of the program. Devotees' long afternoon of patient endurance will ensure them a full night of sleep. Attendees need not wait in line if they plan to revel in the darshan atmosphere all night long or plan to work doing *sevā* (selfless service) for the duration of the program. They can also collect their darshan tokens after prayers for world peace conclude the seated program and Amma begins to give her darshan embraces. Although attendees are encouraged to get their darshan tokens early, no one will be turned away.[3]

In time, these crowds settle into the ornately decorated and brilliantly illuminated grand ballroom. Soon a conch shell blows, and then several swamis (male ascetics) and one swamini (female ascetic) in ocher robes ensure the path is clear as Amma enters the venue.[4] These swamis begin to intone the deep, lilting melodies of Sanskrit chants. Select lay devotees stand in formation ready to perform the worship of the guru's feet (*pada puja*). Some are Indian Hindus and the rest are mostly white Americans, though all have been instructed in the intricacies of this traditional Hindu ritual during their local *satsangs* (congregational gatherings). Additionally, they rehearsed their assigned roles with Amma's tour staff *brahmacāriṇīs* (ascetic disciples) earlier in the afternoon.[5] Carefully, the devotees perform their practiced roles, dabbing Amma's feet with blessed water, sandalwood, kumkum powder, and rose petals. She stands still in silent, closed-eye meditation. A devotee adorns her with a heavy and perfumed garland of 108 fresh roses that he had crafted the night before, mentally reciting his Sanskrit mantra as he threaded each flower. Upon completion of the pada puja, Amma embraces several of the officiants; their eyes are brimming with tears of delight. Amma and her swamis then proceed to the stage. She centers herself, stands on the edge of the stage, and blesses the entire audience. She then sits on a low seat, cross-legged to begin a program consisting of spiritual addresses, silent meditation, and impassioned devotional music. Often young children accompany her on stage to sit with her. Their rambunctious and playful squirming contrasts with her calm stillness.

As Amma and her musicians conclude their last fervent and emotive notes of devotional praise, the nexus of the evening begins: Amma begins to give hugs to every attendee present. Devotees patiently wait in the darshan line, their anticipation rising as they slowly proceed toward Amma over the course of two parallel rows of fifteen to twenty chairs, until they reach her feet. In the special needs section, an older father pushes his severely disabled son who is in an expensive wheelchair

people count on her

toward her intently; hope and tears mingle in his eyes as he gazes lovingly toward Amma. A young woman clutches a photo of her daughter; she prays that her daughter will be successful in conceiving a child and carefully plans to thrust the image into Amma's hands and seek her advice when her turn for darshan arrives. A young couple with offerings of elaborate flower garlands for Amma in their laps nervously glance toward each other and then back to Amma while they wait. They plan to seek Amma's blessing that she will perform their marriage ceremony while she visibly embodies the goddess on *Devī Bhāva* darshan night. A wide-eyed young man in the darshan queue cranes his neck to catch a glimpse of the woman he has heard so much about, the woman his friend has told him will give him a hug that will be wholly transformative and overwhelming.

Closer to Amma these personal narratives intermingle with intersectional emotions—tears, smiles, laughter, and concern—as Amma listens to and advises her most ardent devotees. All the while she uninterruptedly maintains the rhythmic motion of embracing, releasing, embracing, releasing, embracing, holding, and releasing a seemingly endless stream of attendees. A fan gently blows the tendrils of hair around her face as she methodically and rhythmically turns the heads of attendees and whispers the driving chant "my daughter, my daughter, my daughter" or "my son, my son, my son" into their right ears. With a handheld counter in her left hand, she subtly clicks it for each darshan embrace. The counter runs into the thousands most nights, sometimes into the tens of thousands. Amma's subtle attention to the counter ensures that she can pace herself, engaging each and every person who seeks her darshan for the most time possible. Blessed food (*prasad*) of Hershey's kisses and flower petals transfers hands from her attendees, to Amma, to devotees in swift and calculated movements. She will not rest, eat, sleep, stretch, or even stop for a small break of any kind before all who have come to see her have had the opportunity to receive her darshan embrace. Tonight's evening program will likely last into early dawn.

Amma

Many devotees sit as close to Amma as possible without interrupting the darshan process. They sit here at the energetic nexus of the ballroom meditating and singing devotional songs along with the live musicians, but mostly they sit so close in order to watch Amma giving darshan. They watch carefully Amma's every move and her every interaction in the darshan process; this observational witnessing is also a process of darshan (seeing and being seen by God). They watch each attendee's face filled with hope, longing, excitement, and nerves for her or his momentary instant of intimate proximity to Amma. They watch for tears of joy and relief as Amma's assistants help devotees stand and move to the side after their darshan embrace. They watch for special moments when Amma dotes particularly on babies and young children and for her compassionate strokes on damaged limbs and wounded hearts. They watch for her playful jesting with young children and for her strong and confident rub on the swollen bellies of pregnant mothers. They watch for her sympathetic ear as she leans toward devotees to listen more closely to their questions and stories and for her unfailing attention to each and every attendee, her raised eyebrow, and her smiling and laughing composure. They watch mostly for the intricacies of her warm embrace from which the heavy scent of her signature sandalwood rose oil lingers long after the event has receded. They watch not only the awesome sight of such a seemingly superhuman production but also in the hope that some of her enduring love and compassion, as well as her creative power (*śakti*), will infiltrate their own realities as a catalyst for personal transformation.

Amma is a dark-skinned South Indian woman who is believed to be both guru and goddess, but most of all she is "Mother" to her millions of devotees around the world. Devotees believe her to be imbued with love, compassion, and self-sacrifice. Conforming with Hindu cultural ideals, they identify such qualities with the virtues of the mother who completely and unconditionally devotes herself to her children. Although her children may harbor doubts, have impure thoughts, make mistakes, or act selfishly, the ideal mother always attempts to fulfill even their most petty desires and showers them with her warm embrace. For many devotees, Amma's unconditional love and compassion, her attention to even their most whimsical wishes, and her warm and flower-scented embraces fill them so greatly with abundance, energy, joy, and completeness that their own love overflows and exudes from their bodies often in the form of tears.

This book approaches Amma through the crowds of devotees in hotel ballrooms and, increasingly, in Amma's ashrams across the United States, navigating the various populations of devotees who seek out her embrace. While noting unifying trends among particular demographics, it also listens to the personal stories of individuals, stories that direct us to the intimate and deeply emotional reasons that people around the world place their faith in Amma and mold their lives around her message. It is within this juxtaposition of the institutional and the personal that this ethnographic narrative unfolds.

Devotees from across the United States and from around the world shared with me stories of their experiences with Amma. Their narratives bring to the fore not only their claims to the miraculous and superhuman but the personal and emotional relationship that they believe themselves to have with her. Despite the awesome crowds who surround her, many devotees believe that Amma touches them personally in affective and transformative ways. They, in her absence, interact with her in dreams, through sympathetic magical events, signs, and symbols, and through her countless photographic images, the Internet, Amrita TV, and her periodicals *Amritavani* and *Immortal Bliss*. They eagerly anticipate her physical presence wherein she interacts with them intimately through her physical embrace during her darshan programs in major urban centers around the globe. Typically, in Hindu tradition, darshan is the experience of seeing and being seen by God, as one would view and be viewed by a *murti* (divine figurine) in a Hindu temple. When among avatar-gurus, darshan also means to be in the presence of perceived divinity, seeing and being seen by a living embodiment of the divine. Amma expands on this traditional darshan experience by presenting herself as a divine incarnation with whom devotees speak, interact, and share a most intimate physical experience: a hug.

In Amma's presence the traditional darshan experience transforms into the loving embrace of the Divine Mother. Among all of the characteristics that onlookers and devotees attribute to Amma, the most pervasive envisions her as an omnipresent and omnipotent mother. This book suggests that maternality provides the core of her religious identity. But Amma is no ordinary mother. Both her maternality and the ascription of the divine qualities of the goddess that devotees attribute to her reflect devotees' diverse, inherited cultural perspectives. Goddess worship is one of the central aspects of much of Hindu religiosity that has proliferated on the Indian subcontinent since antiquity. But Amma's movement presents goddess worship in a unique and original way. It centralizes the feminine through the symbiotic veneration of the goddess, the worship of her as a living divinity (avatar-guru), the overt centralization of maternality, and, most importantly, the superimposition of these socially sanctioned exaltations of symbolic femininity onto the lived realities of her devotees. These foundational premises of Amma's movement indicate an alternate lens through which to interpret Hindu asceticism and contemporary developments in global Hindu religiosity.

Amma was born in 1953 into a "low caste" family in the small fishing village of Parayakadavu, now Amritapuri, along the backwaters in

Kerala, a state located on the southwestern coast of India. Her hagiographies recount that even as a young child she exhibited extraordinary compassion for her fellow villagers and began to embrace and console sufferers. Because of her low caste background, her unconditional embraces radically upset the traditional boundaries of purity and pollution wherein low castes were disallowed from physical contact with those above their social station. To compound this issue, Hindu cultural idioms would strictly forbid a woman to have such overt and indiscriminate physical contact with strangers. Nevertheless, through these comforting embraces, Amma eventually developed her public persona until those who were suffering began to approach her to receive her embrace. The numbers of those who sought her embrace expanded rapidly, and many believed they found comfort, solace, peace, happiness, spiritual transformation, and/or healing through this experience. At age twenty-one Amma began to exhibit *bhāvas*, ecstatic states through which believers saw her to be revealing her superhuman nature; she first appeared as Krishna and then as Devi (initially in the form of Kali). With the increased profile brought about through these bhāvas, Amma began to attract large audiences, and in time she began to sit for hours at a time giving hugs to the crowds of people who assembled to receive them. She became famous for her supposedly transformative and even healing embraces and developed a following of devotees who believed her to be a goddess incarnate, a God-realized soul, a *mahātma*, a guru, a Divine Mother, and/or simply a loving being. As Amma achieved superhuman status in her devotees' minds, their primary experience with her (her embrace) became known as "darshan." The assembled crowds grew in number, and her darshan embraces were formalized into ritualistic darshan programs in which formalized bhāvas became a significant component.

In the late 1970s Amma established an ashram site in her childhood village, which has since developed into Amritapuri, a large ashram complex housing approximately 4,500 residents. Amritapuri is the headquarters for her operations in India (the Mata Amritanandamayi Math [MA Math] and the Mata Amritanandamayi Mission Trust [MAMT]). It consists of several high-rise dormitories for residents, a centrally located Kali temple, a demarcated sacral space for vedic *homas* (fire sacrifices), administrative offices, resident elephants, kitchens and cafeterias, an Ayurvedic store, a bookstore, a general store, a swimming pool, libraries, and an impressively large darshan hall. In addition, Amma has established satellite ashram sites throughout India, as well as her North American headquarters in the United States (the Mata Amritanandmayi Center [MA Center]) and many other global centers. Smaller devotional communities around the globe (often operating programming in devotees' homes) largely aspire to develop their particular localities into larger ashram-type satellites. Devotees feel that this intense growth trajectory is essential to their mission to spread Amma's message throughout the world. With the permission and supervision of the central authority of the MA Math, Amma's devotees have established sizable communities in India, the United States, Canada, the United Kingdom, France, Italy, Germany, Spain, the Netherlands, Finland, Sweden, Australia, Japan, Singapore, Brazil, Mauritius, Reunion, Kenya, and Chile (see figure 1).

In 2005 the United Nations conferred Special Consultative Status to the Mata Amritanandamayi Math because of its extensive humanitarian initiatives, particularly those in response to the 2004 Indian Ocean tsunami. Amma has founded numerous humanitarian and educational institutions in South India. The medical institutions that her ashram has founded include the Amrita Institute of Medical Science (AIMS hospital), a cancer hospice in Mumbai, an AIDS care home in Trivandrum, and the Amrita School of Ayurveda, Hospital and Research Center. The educational organizations that the ashram has founded include approximately thirty-eight secondary schools (Amrita Vidyayalam) and more than sixty networked educational institutions throughout India, ten branches of which belong to the umbrella organization of Amrita University (Amrita Vishwa Vidyapeetham). The ashram also operates extensive social welfare programs, including initiatives to curb farmer suicide in India, letter-writing programs to prisoners in the American penal system, tribal welfare programs, free legal services, mass marriages for those who cannot afford the cost of marriage rites, Anna Danam and Vastra Danam (The Gift of Food and Clothing), elder care, orphanages, vocational training, and self-help groups.[6] Amma's ashram has instituted major environmental initiatives through its global organization known as GreenFriends. Disaster relief is another major avenue through which Amma's organization provides humanitarian relief across the globe: Amma initially donated $23 million to tsunami relief in 2004, but she soon doubled that effort. She has also made significant financial contributions to humanitarian relief efforts in response to the earthquake in Lahore (1992), the earthquake in Gujarat (2001), the Kumbhakonam fire (2004), the flooding in Mumbai (2005), Hurricane Katrina in New Orleans (2005), the earthquakes in Kashmir (2005) and Haiti (2010), and the tsunami in Japan (2011).[7] Amma's organization

FIGURE 1. Mata Amritanandamayi Ashram, Parayakadavu (now Amritapuri), Kollam district, Kerala, India (© MA Center)

supports a printing press and has an affiliated television station in Kerala (Amrita TV), the latter supplying various types of programming (both religious and secular) available globally through the Internet.

Amma spends four to five nonconsecutive months each year in residence at Amritapuri, tending to business there in person, hosting darshan programs, performing rituals, hosting *bhajan* (devotional music) programs, giving discourses, and providing spiritual counsel. When not in residence at Amritapuri, she spends the majority of her time giving darshan programs in major urban centers around the globe. Even while away from Amritapuri, Amma closely supervises her various projects and the particular needs of her devotees who manage those projects. Devotees frequently reinforce the idea that Amma is the center of all ashram activities performed in her name, and that she is omniscient in her knowledge of the specifics of each enterprise. They often cite instances in which Amma personally performs menial tasks or insightfully questions administrators regarding the detailed practices of their particular responsibilities. These testimonies provide evidence for devotees' belief in Amma's superhuman qualities.

In 1987 Amma first came to the United States and toured the country hosting darshan programs during which she hugged all attendees who were present. The number of attendees was small (ranging from dozens to hundreds of devotees) compared to the crowds in India, where she routinely attracted thousands. In February 1989, one of her devotees gifted her a 160-acre parcel of land on which she established an ashram and a residence site, the MA Center. While the MA Math at Amritapuri functions as the epicenter of her organization, the MA Center in San Ramon, California, has developed into an influential international location as well. In the past twenty years it has developed its resources to maintain a printing house for the dissemination of publications and a distribution house for the online store (The Amma Shop). It also serves as a major distribution center for humanitarian relief efforts and supplies. As Amma's movement has attracted an increasing number of followers in the United Sates, the MA Center has also initiated karma yoga programs, retreats, religious education programs, social service and environmental initiatives, and specialized ritual and festival events.

Since her first arrival in 1987, Amma has toured the United States twice each year, in the fall and in the summer. The number of attendees at her darshan programs in the United States remains small compared to the number in India, but over time the scale of her darshan programs has grown considerably. In 2008, Amma's two days of darshan programs in

Chicago attracted 8,000–10,000 attendees. Her two-week-long darshan programs in San Ramon, California, during the summer of the
same year attracted approximately 35,000 attendees. Smaller stops on
her U.S. summer tour, such as Coralville, Iowa, attracted only 4,000–
5,000 attendees. The most ardent American devotees often travel to
multiple cities during Amma's summer tour to take advantage of the
opportunity to be in her presence as much as possible. Devotees particularly appreciate the smaller crowds in cities such as Coralville because
of the intimacy of the darshan programs and the opportunity to achieve
greater proximity to Amma there.[8] Some wealthy Indians even fly from
India to these smaller darshan programs in the United States to avoid
the massive crowds at Amma's darshan programs in Indian cities, which
regularly attract as many as fifty thousand attendees.

During Amma's annual fall tour, she visits the MA Center in San
Ramon, California, residing there for three to four weeks and offering
darshan programs every day and many evenings. She then continues
on to Dearborn, Michigan, a suburb of Detroit, close to another well-
established ashram community of Amma devotees, where she stays for
over a week hosting a similar schedule of darshan programs. Amma's
annual summer tour is much more extensive; she travels to Seattle, San
Ramon, Los Angeles, Dallas, Albuquerque, Coralville, Chicago, New
York, Washington DC, Boston, and Toronto over a period of approximately twelve weeks. Each year, in addition to her two tours in the
United States, Amma usually tours North and South India, Europe,
Australia, Asia, Africa, and South America. She is constantly expanding her already robust tour schedule to reach more people in more
countries.

Amma's message focuses on selfless service (sevā) as the solution to the
crises of modernity, articulated as the general loss of spirituality, which
results in wars, violence, poverty, hunger, homelessness, and the degradation of the environment. Her primary message, "Love and Serve,"
condenses her religious philosophy into two simple ideas, notably two
ideas that make no definitive reference to her Hindu roots. Her primary
identity statement, "Embracing the World (ETW)," branded during
the summer of 2009, centralizes her darshan embrace as her most
distinctive characteristic within a sea of contemporary guru figures, a
self-image that has caused her to be dubbed "the hugging saint" in the
American media. Her significant Internet presence creates virtual communities through which devotees and visitors can gather information
about her spiritual message, humanitarian initiatives, local activities, tour

schedule, and products available for purchase. Her websites demarcate the various interlacing devotional communities by geographical region: www.amritapuri.org focuses on South Asian and ashram happenings; www.amma.org accentuates activities for international communities (largely based in the United States); and local websites provide information about particular regional devotional communities, for example, http://chicago.amma.org.

The majority of people who come to Amma's darshan programs in the United States simply attend when she is in their vicinity and then incorporate her and her message (to varying degrees) into their extant religiosities. However, a strong minority of ardent devotees also attend monthly satsangs and devote much of their personal time to furthering the humanitarian initiatives of the movement, sponsoring devotional programs, fostering youth groups, and organizing the local logistics of hosting Amma's programs. The central network of devotees often chooses to reside at the Amritapuri ashram for some duration, contributing to the community through selfless service and relishing their proximity to Amma at the epicenter of her global activities. Beyond Amritapuri, local ashrams also host residents (both long-term and short-term), but their numbers are usually small. All devotee administrators in the North American centers of Amma's organization operate under the supervision and direction of the MA Center in San Ramon, which is in turn subordinate to the MA Math at Amritapuri.

Amma is the Malayalee (and, more generally, South Indian) term for "mother." In the Indic context, nearly all female religious leaders, gurus, and virtuosos identify themselves and are identified with maternalistic titles such as "Amma, Mata, or Ma."[9] Likewise, when Sudhamani Idamannel (Amma's given name) developed a public religious persona in her early adulthood she began to identify herself (and be identified) as "Mata Amritanandamayi," "Mata Amritanandamayi Devi," "Ammachi,"[10] or simply "Amma." While male religious exemplars employ generalized masculine honorific titles such as "sri," "guru," "swami," or "bhagvan," the identity-marking titles of female religious exemplars explicitly gender their referent. These titles not only designate female gender, but they also delineate a matrifocal identity that signifies motherhood as both a desexualized feminine identity and a culturally sanctioned avenue of authority and respect for women.

THE FEMALE GURU

Many would mark the heyday of gurus in the American scene as the moment in the late 1960s when The Beatles communed with Maharishi Mahesh Yogi in India and then George Harrison chanted the *māhāmantra* of Krishna devotionalism into the pop culture mainstream. But the first entrée of gurus into American culture occurred more than a century earlier. In 1818, Rammohan Roy delighted the Unitarians and liberal Protestants with his monotheistic interpretations of the Vedas, which were published widely in *The North American Review*.[11] Roy became such a bastion of Unitarian-style Hindu religiosity that Ralph Waldo Emerson's aunt, Mary Moody Emerson, wrote to her nephew about a visitor from India who was "studied much in the Vades [*sic*]" but was a "fixed Unitarian." Knowing full well the difficulties of the Unitarian missions in India, and perhaps predicting their ultimate failure, Ralph Waldo Emerson besmirched the idea that Roy's fame in the *Christian Register* would counterbalance the successful missionary inroads of the Trinitarians.[12] Yet, a decade later, Rammohan Roy would found the Hindu reform movement of the Brahmo Samaj, which was orchestrated around the Unitarian (and Advaita Vedanta) ideal of a universalistic aim to coalesce the eternal truths of all religions. By the 1880s the young spiritual aspirant and humanitarian fund-raiser, Narendranath Datta, was also affiliated with the Brahmo Samaj in India. In 1893 he captivated American audiences in his ocher robes and turban as Swami Vivekananda in his enchanting performance at the World's Parliament of Religions.

The entrée of Swami Vivekananda in 1893 marked the beginnings of the contemporary paradigm wherein mystic religious adepts from India attracted followers of large American audiences of spiritual seekers. At the turn of the century, yoga and Hindu philosophy had taken hold of an American subculture, one that often appealed to middle- and upper-middle-class white women. As the ideal of the mystic swami from India became an American reality, so too did the accusations of fraudulence, exploitation, and sexually lascivious behavior. Often viewed as a commercial endeavor to dupe the gullible white woman of her wealth, the populist backlash against the Indian guru swelled with Christian fervor. By the early 1900s the trope of the mystical, magical, and potentially dangerous Indian yogi/guru populated the thriving national and local presses, wherein potentially vulnerable clientele were warned against his claims of authenticity, spiritual prowess, and affections. Still, Swami Vivekananda, Swami Abhedananda, the Omnipotent Oom, and dozens of others developed considerable followings among subcultures of the devout. They would be followed by Paramhansa Yogananda in 1920, Bhaktivedananta Swami Prabhupada in 1965, and Swami Muktananda in 1970, each of whom would establish seminal institutions of Hindu-derived religiosity in the United States (Self-Realization Fellowship, the International Society for Krishna Consciousness, and Siddha Yoga, respectively).

In the 1960s and 1970s, the popular rejection of mainstream religiosity and of "the system" more generally led to a turn toward Eastern religions. Coupled with the radical reforms of U.S. immigration policy that exponentially increased the annual number of visas issued to twenty thousand select elites of the Indian populace, the demographic composition of the United States radically diversified. Populations of Indian immigrants increased 2,800 percent between 1965 and 1972, more than twice the rate of increase of any other nation.[13] As a result, more and more Indian gurus who espoused variations on Hindu religiosity entered into the American scene and developed their ideas in the architecture of American religions. Whether the Maharshi, Yogananda, Prabhupada, Muktananda, or Osho, the immigration reform policy of 1965 directly augmented the continuation of Indian gurus proselytizing to Americans on their own soil.[14] But by the 1970s and 1980s, many of these guru movements were embroiled in scandal. Regarded with suspicion from many in the American mainstream from their first entrée into American religious environments, the sexual promiscuity and hedonism of the "free love" era fueled vociferous critiques, many of which had some grounding in reality. As such, by the 1980s and 1990s, the American subculture of guru-friendly devotees was aptly primed for the entrance of female gurus, spiritual entrepreneurs from India who exemplified an asexual form of the divine feminine. Many disillusioned devotees believed that these women would escape the negative press and sexual appetites of their male predecessors. The female gurus arrived more than two decades after U.S. immigration reform in what Karen Pechilis has accurately termed the "3rd wave" of gurus in the United States, who are, in her perspective, "globalizing, harmonizing, and naturalizing Hindu-inspired tradition."[15] (Those who wish to delve deeper into the scholastic literature developed with regard to contemporary gurus should at this point turn their attention to the appendix for a more comprehensive literature review.)

But despite the widespread positive reception of female gurus in the United States, the figure of the female guru remains somewhat of an anomaly in both South Asian and diasporic contexts. Not all female ascetics (celibate renunciates) are gurus; by definition, a guru must have students/followers, and not all female ascetics do. Similarly, not all female gurus are ascetics, though sexually active female gurus are extremely rare. In most cases, female gurus are celibate (and thus, by definition, female ascetics), though some maintain asexual relations with spouses, male partners, and family members. Sometimes the female guru is a householder who has already borne and raised her children and now has chosen the role of religious adept rather than the culturally stigmatized role of widow. Many onlookers regard such women as renunciates only in name, women who have chosen to become religious adepts through the pressures of social circumstances rather than through their particular spiritual aptitude or expertise. Other women become gurus from a very young age, eagerly demonstrating their religious proclivities and spiritual prowess and often fighting against societal demands that aim to constrain them to the more traditional roles of wife and mother (strīdharma). Some of these latter types of women marry and maintain somewhat unusual relations (often celibate) with their husbands. Others never marry and choose to remain celibate religious ascetics in an effort to propagate their religious messages in the more traditional manner of the Hindu religious adept. Although these women remain celibate renunciates, they simultaneously draw on cultural understandings of traditional roles for women by presenting themselves as ideotypical mothers. These ascetic women are not biological mothers; rather, they present themselves as metaphorical mothers to their devotee children. Amma, who has neither a husband nor biological children and claims lifelong celibacy, is precisely such an ascetic mother.

Because the scriptures of Hindu asceticism privilege the supremacy of male ascetics, early scholarship on Hindu renunciation suggested that female ascetics subsist in a liminal relationship to their male counterparts. In the early foundational literature on Hindu renunciates, female practitioners are given only slight mention, if any at all.[16] In brahmanical[17] prescriptive texts that delineate the appropriate conduct for renunciates, such as the Saṃnyāsa Upaniṣads, the authors depict women as temptresses, deceivers, and decrepit reminders of the limitations and attachments of bodily existence.[18] Male renunciates are warned repeatedly to keep their distance from women, just as they would from other indulgences. Although there is evidence for the existence of female ascetics since the vedic period, these medieval instructional texts on asceticism largely ignore the existence of such a population.

But in the latter decades of the twentieth century, scholars began to acknowledge the existence of minority populations of female ascetics in India. Still, most concluded that female ascetics existed on the periphery of the field dominated by their more powerful, historically prevalent, and socially influential male counterparts. In her posthumously published work, Lynn Teskey Denton argued that an internal unity defined the Hindu ascetic field in her ethnographic field research conducted in Varanasi between 1976 and 1981. She concluded that while the field contains both male and female practitioners, "female ascetics espouse the same set of core ideals as their male counterparts, and they participate in the same institutions and are subject to the same codes of behavior."[19] Building on this idea, scholars generally accepted that while small populations of female ascetics in India exist, both males and females exhibited strategies, practices, expressions, and institutions derived from within the brahmanical mode of Hindu ascetic religiosity.

In the interim decades since Denton's seminal field research, populations of female ascetics garnered a significant increase in publicity in modern Indic politics, social movements, and academic publications. There are two primary reasons for this increased presence. First, the intellectual tides instigated by the political impulses of subaltern studies and feminism have brought forth a generation of anthropologists and scholars of religion who have actively sought out women's narratives of renunciation. Second, while it is extraordinarily difficult to gather accurate demographic information about this largely itinerant and undocumented population, both Vijaya Ramaswamy (1997) and Ursula King (1984) suggest that renunciation has become more, not less, accessible to women over the last century.[20] Westernization and globalization have introduced the rapid transformation of modern Indian society in the twentieth and twenty-first centuries. In these tumultuous times, women's issues have occupied central roles in the contestation of India's trajectory of "development." These modern forces challenge the primacy of brahmanical exclusions of women and have created new cultural spaces for a multiplicity of voices occupying positions of religious exemplars (including low castes and women). Hindu nationalist movements have also contributed by privileging women as symbols of the nation and celebrating the virtues of women idealized as self-sacrificing ascetic mothers. Such discourses have given rise to powerful religio-political female figures and women's organizations, from Uma Bharati and Sadhvi Rithambara to the Sadhvi Shakti Parishad (affiliated with the Vishva Hindu Parishad) and the Rashtra Sevika Samiti (affiliated with the Rashtriya

Swayamsevak Sangh). In sum, the increased scholarly attention, combined with augmented populations and religio-political privilege, suggests that female asceticism and the public figure of the female guru are becoming significantly more influential both within Hindu ascetic traditions and global Hindu religiosity.

Contemporary inquiries into Hindu female asceticism provide evidence that women may not be liminal appendages to brahmanical models as initially thought. In fact, Hindu female ascetics often articulate theologies and practical forms of religious expression that are often uniquely gendered. The manner in which contemporary female exemplars ubiquitously construct their identities in terms of maternality (and are constructed as maternal) suggests that female ascetics perform their renunciation in particularly gendered ways.[21] Instead of operating as parasitic attachments to a male-dominated system, these women develop their own spaces of identity articulation. As maternal ascetic figures, they draw on historical and traditionally lauded roles for women in Hindu society. They also borrow significant authority from long-standing traditions of mother goddess worship in Hindu traditions. Their personal self-identification with ascetic maternality justifies their participation in the male dominant system of renunciation by activating culturally esteemed roles for women. As such, female asceticism does not exist parasitically to a male-dominated system but, rather, it demarcates a parallel structure to male asceticism by asserting its own identity, ideology, and practice. In this gendered renunciation, women activate the existing Indic cultural reverence for both the goddess and maternality, and in so doing they performatively construct, articulate, embody, and reinforce ideotypical concepts of socially sanctioned femininity.

This performative gendering reinforces its own representation with every repetition both internally enacted by the rhetoric and practices of female ascetics and externally superimposed by the receiving public. Female ascetics reify ideotypical feminine virtues by constructing their identities in active engagement with established and esteemed social avenues for women: the apotheosis of the mother and the veneration of the goddess. They routinely represent themselves as celibate symbolic mothers who often embody goddesses, identifying with a set of fixed polythetic characteristics of the "feminine" and the "maternal." As such, they reify social understandings of what it means to be a woman, ideals of femininity, and conceptions of "natural" gendered normativity. Instead of signifying the natural qualities of womanhood, these women perform and construct the social imaginary of what women should be. Indeed, as

Judith Butler suggests, the construction of gender exists without a central referent; it is a signified without a sign.[22] She questions: "To what extent do *regulatory practices* of gender formation and division constitute identity, the internal coherence of the subject, indeed, the self-identical status of the person?"[23] This book analyzes various regulatory practices of gender formation, division, and production of one such ascetic mother and her global devotees who are encouraged to emulate her example through mimesis. It focuses in particular on the ways in which variant devotee populations react to Amma and embody her message of maternal asceticism and veneration of the goddess. Intertwining the theoretical discourses of feminism and multiculturalism, this book draws attention to the popular reception of modern Indic Hindu-inspired "spirituality" in the diasporic context of the United States.

Like gurus more generally and Amma particularly, this book is theoretically situated at a "vector between domains,"[24] engaging gender studies and the anthropology and sociology of religion in the context of the transnational dialectic between South Asia and the United States. It concentrates on perennial themes of the religious adept, engaging Max Weber's notions of charisma, prophet, and asceticism and what Emile Durkheim calls *the negative cult*. I show how Amma's darshan programs create not only Durkheimian "collective effervescence," but also show signs of Weberian routinization and bureaucratization as they have grown larger and more institutionalized. My analysis of Amma's darshan programs builds on Pierre Bourdieu's work, demonstrating how Amma marks herself with distinction not only with her hugs, but also through Devī Bhāva darshan events wherein she performatively becomes the goddess. Her performative displays of social identity enacted through culturally specific religious costuming reveals how Bourdieu's field of performative social capital translates beyond the French context into transnational, and even transhuman and supernatural realms. I also show how Bourdieu's concept of *habitus* is not static and determined, but radically shifts as devotees transform themselves and their social dispositions to embody qualities that Amma believes to be ideotypically feminine. In so doing, they adopt a behavioral and gendered transformation that conforms to what I call the *maternal ascetic habitus* of the movement.

Interlaced throughout the narrative are developments on themes in the study of Hindu religiosity, religion in the North American context, and the dialectic between the two. With regard to Hindu religiosity, I focus particularly on the ways in which Amma's movement demonstrates radical innovations, particularly with regard to darshan and women's roles in religious leadership. In this vein, I show that despite her upsetting of traditional norms of purity and pollution, ritual authority, and sanctified roles for women, Amma largely aims to, in the words of the ninth-century Kashmiri logician Jayantabatta, "rephras[e] the older truths of the ancients in modern terminology."[25] I suggest that the "modern terminology" in question is the language of democracy, individualism, and gender equality. In the North American context, I show how Amma's movement both reinforces and challenges the extant paradigm of multiculturalism; here furthering the work of Charles Taylor, Anthony Appiah, Patchen Markell, and Kelly Oliver. The bounded cultural-identity politics of multiculturalism determine that Amma's devotional communities frequently fissure along ethnic-cultural lines and independent congregational gatherings slip into what Stephen Warner terms "de facto congregationalism," the fragmentation into largely homogenous subgroups of affinity. My research among Amma devotees suggests that fragmentation and de facto congregationalism are not limited to traditional contexts (i.e., the history of racial segregation policies), but rather they are emblematic of religious communalism in the United States and, in fact, buttressed by multiculturalism to the extent that even new religious movements conform to rather than challenge their constructs.

In the study of any guru, scholars must choose which thread of the multifarious and interwoven fabric of the movement they will follow to formulate their analyses. Maya Warrier's foundational work on Amma's movement chose to focus on Amma's urban, educated, middle-class Indian devotees. Her careful research explores their religious "choices" and shows how their various "modes of self-fashioning" indicate "possibilities and potentials for new and alternative figurations of Hinduism."[26] Her argument suggests that in such forms, Hinduism becomes wholly compatible with modernity, adaptive and personalized, signifying how "individuals *construct* 'modernity' in their imagination and thereby *negotiate* its conditions."[27]

At the end of her book, Warrier provocatively juxtaposes the ideals of selfhood within Amma's movement with supporters and proponents of the often militant form of modern Hindu nationalism, the religio-political engagement known as "Hindutva." First, she notes that Hindutva supporters, particularly the Sangh Parivar, idealize Rama as a hypermasculine warrior king ready for battle, whereas Amma is an avatar of maternal love and compassion. Second, for Hindutva supporters, the "enemy" is external, often characterized as a Muslim or Western threat to Hindu dominance and security, whereas for Amma devotees the "enemy" is within, in the form of *vāsanās* (behavioral tendencies due to karmic effects). Last, Hindutva discourse and rhetoric commonly focus on the deep-running theme of the recuperation of fierce masculinity in the face of a perceived emasculation of the Hindu self. In contrast, Warrier notes that Amma's movement demonstrates an "effort of 'effeminization' (though none of my [Warrier's] informants perceive their selfhood thus in polarized gender terms) wherein they [devotees] seek to revive their emotional selves, and enhance their receptivity to the Mata's love and compassion."[28]

My own work begins here, at the question of the polarization of gender in Amma's discourses and among the commitments and constructed selves of her devotees. Unlike Warrier's inquiry into Indian middle-class devotees, I found that the North American context, one of the foundational premises of the movement, is the turn toward "effeminization," expressed through the goal of embodying the "feminine" qualities of maternal love, compassion, and self-sacrifice (just like Amma). This book focuses particularly here, delving deeply into the discourses and practices within the movement, juxtaposing human women and goddesses and devotees and their female guru, often under the rubrics of women's empowerment and feminism. In navigating this theoretical lens, I submit that devotees' reflections and interpretations of Amma's meaning and message frequently differ as a result of their inherited religio-cultural backgrounds. As a result, this inquiry segues by necessity into the politics of representation and recognition within contemporary American multiculturalism and the history of the cultural encounter between India and the United States.

It is fascinating that Warrier's informants (mostly urban, educated, Indian Hindu middle-class devotees) did not imagine themselves within the polarized categories of the masculine and the feminine. In my fieldwork among Amma devotees in the United States, I contend that the devotees of that comparable demographic (urban, educated, Indian Hindu, upper-middle class but residing in the United States) similarly preferred to construct their selfhood and their interpretations of Amma's message in terms of gender complementarity rather than polarity and mutuality rather than opposition. As such, they often balked at the term *feminism* and preferred instead to speak of Amma's message of "women's empowerment" and advaita vedantic nondualism ("all is one"). But the differences in our findings emerge from the fact that in the United States more than half of Amma's devotees are white, and women comprise approximately two-thirds of that population. Many of the devotees within this demographic have sought out Amma's movement precisely because of her emphasis on women's empowerment, the feminine, and goddess worship. I also found that the commonplace expectation that devotees embody a mimetic relationship to the guru played heavily in the gendered self-construction of devotees when combined with Amma's discourses on women's empowerment, her privileging of the "feminine" qualities of what she calls *universal motherhood*, her advocacy for goddess worship, and her position as a female avatar-guru and goddess.

Amma presents a focused attempt to rectify gender imbalances by augmenting the feminine, which is situated at the nexus of her movement and theology. She argues that women's empowerment is essential to the immediate project of crafting a better world. In her view, in order to solve the pressing crises of modernity, both women and men must further develop their feminine qualities in order to develop into moral and spiritually refined human beings. Practically, her movement aggressively challenges Hindu norms by instituting women as ritual officiants (*pūjāriṇīs*) and positioning women in central roles of religious authority. She leads as an exemplar with her own self-styled trajectory to global fame as a charismatic guru and goddess figure, instantiates women in roles of ritual leadership, and emphasizes goddess-centric Hindu texts and practices. Her solution for the crises in the modern world demands the increase of ideotypical feminine attributes, such as love, compassion, and selfless service. Furthermore, she advocates for women's rights, education, and economic independence through developing micro-businesses. Through these efforts, Amma has radically reenvisioned socially appropriate roles for women. It may not be the dominant voice in modern Hinduism, but her activism on behalf of women, juxtaposed with her woman-centric goddess theology, presents an important and popular alternative narrative.

Ardent devotees believe that Mata Amritanandamayi is an avatar-guru, a goddess incarnation who has become manifest in the material world to spread her message of universal love and selfless service. While the majority of devotees are reticent to locate her within the confines of Hinduism, Hindu devotees regard her as their most favored divinity among the many superhuman incarnations of the Hindu pantheon. Largely they worship her not as a mediating lens to divinity but as a divine goddess incarnate. Non-Hindus often obfuscate the Hinduness of her inherited tradition and envision her through a generalized conception of the goddess or simply as a maternal figure, a loving divine mother devoted to her human children. For her part, Amma supports both receptions, constructing her religious identity carefully by supplanting the religiously bounded terminology of Hinduism with the more diffuse *sanatana dharma* and the even more polysemous term *spirituality*. Instead of demanding uniformity of religious conviction, she implores her devotees to follow whichever tradition suits their personal tastes and dispositions, but to do so in the spirit of universal love and selfless service. The freedom of religious choice advocated by the movement is one of its most salient features, and devotees value highly the autonomy, personalized attention, and intimacy that they experience in community with Amma.[29]

Devotees' commitment to their belief in Amma's superhuman qualities increases in tandem with their transition from minimal to maximal involvement in the movement. But the nexus of these commitments to Amma's divinity—Amma as the goddess incarnate—is founded on different religious (and political) worldviews. This study recognizes the polyvalent reflections of Amma through the embodied experiences and received religious traditions of her various populations of devotees. It traces the variety of ways in which devotees imagine Amma by examining simultaneously their internal reinforcements through the rhetoric and practices of the movement and following their antecedents into the religio-political beliefs of devotees prior to their involvement in the movement. It is a popular refrain within the movement (and guru communities more generally) that one sees in the guru only a reflection of oneself and, likewise, the idea that the guru mirrors the spiritual maturity of the devotee (a very convenient premise, should anyone be underwhelmed by the guru). Devotees construct the identity of the guru through their personal associations, largely contingent on the religious convictions that they inhabited upon their entrée into the movement. Amma reflects devotees' spiritual development and devotees too reflect Amma through their varied cultural contexts.

The various representations and interpretations of the gendered subject of the female guru intertwined in this project cannot be disassociated from the globalizing nature of the movement. This book operates at the dialectic intersection between the local and the global, juxtaposing a Hindu vernacular of the maternalistic female guru in negotiation with the ideal type of the Hindu goddess. It analyzes Amma's positioning of the Hindu goddess as a religious exemplar for human women and probes its signification for internally diverse groups of immigrant Indian Hindus and American metaphysicals. Here I aim to show that Indian Hindus do not often equate veneration of the goddess with female empowerment, whereas American metaphysicals often idealize the goddess as a potent symbol for their feminist projects. But these clear cultural dichotomies become less distinct when all Amma devotees are encouraged to develop a mimetic relationship with Amma, whom they believe to be a living goddess. Furthermore, Amma actively suggests that society must begin to treat all women as exemplars of the goddess, as she believes they were in the vedic society of antiquity. With such statements, Amma feeds into the extant beliefs of the American metaphysicals associated with the goddess movement, but she inserts an innovative focus on the goddesses' relation to human women for many traditionalist Indian Hindus. I suggest that Hindu devotees who are drawn into Amma's movement find her message appealing not in spite of it upsetting traditional gender hierarchies but, rather, because it embraces advaita vedantic nonduality articulated through egalitarianism and democratic values.

In opposition to Amma's message, the dominant strains of contemporary Indian feminism largely minimize the importance of Hindu goddesses as exemplary role models for Hindu women. Indian feminists are palpably conscious of the ways in which the self-sacrificing behaviors exhibited by some Hindu goddesses (Sita) are difficult to rectify with the goals of a feminist political project. Furthermore, many Indian feminists see the mythologizing of women's issues to be wholly beside the point, if not detrimental to their cause. In their views, for centuries Indian women have been envisioned as goddesses with romantic and poetic language, while their material conditions in actual homes, families, jobs, and society remain underrepresented, unequal, and inadequate.[30] Western feminist critiques of the women's spirituality movement also articulate reticence to map the goddess as an ideotypical formation of female empowerment and the lived realities of women. Critics argue that such theologies serve to reify essentialist ideals of socially sanctioned heteronormative womanhood.[31] While there is significant contention and disagreement between the various feminisms in the West and in India, this is a point of agreement. A strong majority agree that feminism must focus on political action and material realities, not on suprahuman imaginings that mythologize or mysticize the very real inequities for human women acting in the material world.

But in both geographies there are vocal minorities of goddess movement activists, in the West more so than in India. These advocates argue that women can generate significant cultural and personal power through their identification with and veneration of goddesses. In India, a few feminist scholars have argued that women already generate and maintain a personal sense of autonomy, freedom, and self-worth through their devotions to and identifications with independent and powerful goddesses. They suggest that Indian feminists should intensify and utilize this existing religio-cultural feminist modality for women instead of squandering it through denial of its existence or condemnation of its positive attributes.[32] The strong contingent of goddess movement advocates in the West largely uses the mythic imaginary of premodern goddess cults to argue that prior to the influx of Abrahamic patriarchal religions women and men were coequals in society. According to this gynocentric theology, the suppression and demonization of these premodern goddesses correlate directly to the similar degradation of societal attitudes and actions toward women.[33] Among Amma devotees, the majority of Hindus identify their devotion to Amma as an extension of their existing inherited Hindu religiosity. Their devotion symbolizes the embrace of a liberal and democratic interpretation of modern Hinduism, but instead of articulating this with feminist language most use the language of human rights, democracy, and egalitarian ideals of representation. In contrast, many of the Western devotees (particularly women) envision Amma as a champion for the resurgence of the feminine and particularly their own devotion to Amma as the goddess as part of a radical rejection of a patriarchal Godhead of Abrahamic religions.

Both primary groups of devotees (whom I call *inheritors* and *adopters*) subscribe to a radically democratic understanding of personhood and access to the sacred. Hindu devotees wholly support Amma's radical upsetting of caste and gender restrictions based in traditional brahmanical norms. While her Hindu devotees represent a diversity of geographies and religious affinities, many are Malayalees who locate their caste lineages to the Nayars (with surnames of Nayar/Nair, Menon, and Pillai). Nayar castes emerge from the Indian state of Kerala and occupy the midstrata positions within caste divisions there. Perhaps because the Nayars cannot secure the highest social status of the Nambudri brahman castes, they actively support Amma's thwarting of traditional caste hierarchies. Her popularity among middle-class Indian Hindus may also signify the tensions between democratic forces in modern India and the social hierarchies inherent in conservative formulations of Hindu religiosity. Amma's radical exhibition of unconditional embraces of all persons signifies and reinforces the democratic pulse of the movement.

Such visible affirmations of individualized egalitarianism make her movement particularly suited to the democratic ideals of the American context.[34] The majority of Amma's Hindu devotees accept and promote her revision of gender and caste restrictions as an extension of their commitment to equity among all persons, regardless of gender or caste identification. On the other hand, non-Hindu devotees are much less sensitive to the culturally provocative issues at stake in Amma's unconditional darshan embraces. Instead, they see Amma activating the radical social reform of repositioning an unmediated experience of the divine through her embodiment of a female form of divinity.

THE ETHNOGRAPHER IN THE ETHNOGRAPHY

MY FIRST DARSHAN: *DEVĪ BHĀVA*, NAPERVILLE, ILLINOIS, 2004

We had purchased a sweet-smelling mango in the lobby and sat down with it in the darshan line. When our turn approached we followed the attendants onto the stage, removed our bags, wiped our faces, and knelt at Amma's side waiting our turn. The bright lights seemed to magnify the precision of the process. When the family of four in front of us had just stepped a few inches away, Amma reached forward and took the mango from my son's hand. No sooner had she done this that I felt a hand on my back as she quickly pulled us both to her chest. My head was buried in the sweet flowers of her *mālās* (garlands) and she began to chant, "Ma, Ma, Ma, Ma, Ma, Ma, Ma, Ma, Ma." With every "Ma" I felt a pulsing of energy. Between the chanting and the intoxicating smell of the flowers, when she pulled away from me my head was spinning and I gazed at her like a deer in headlights. I was shocked. I must have conveyed my stunned appearance clearly, because in response she looked back at me intently—and then she winked.

I have puzzled over that wink for years. Did I imagine it? Did Amma know my skepticism and wink at my astonishment at my visceral reactions to receiving her darshan embrace? Was it supposed to solidify the commonly held belief among her devotees that she does, in fact, see into the hearts of each and every person she hugs? In considering these questions, I recalled just how poignant the signification of the wink in particular has been for ethnographers in the field.

Clifford Geertz has immortalized deciphering the wink as emblematic of the potential efficacy and the objective of the "thick-description" style of ethnography. Citing Gilbert Ryle, he proposes the scenario of two boys contracting their right eyelids—one has an involuntary twitch, and the other winks, signaling to a friend. A third boy parodies their eyelid contractions mockingly; he signifies his parody with additional facial contortions to ensure that his observers do not mistake his parody for the real thing—a twitch or a wink. Geertz goes on to suggest that we might also question the authentic facial representations of the one twitching, to suggest that the boy is merely pretending to twitch, thus actually winking. He asserts that the object of ethnography lies between what the rehearser (twitcher, winker, parodist) is doing and the "thick description" of what he is doing ("practicing a burlesque of a friend faking a wink to deceive an innocent into thinking a conspiracy is in motion").[35] Ethnography takes as its purpose to decipher actors' (or institutions') actions through the lens of their embedded sociohistorical and cultural context. This deciphering demands a primary process of interpretation and a secondary process of explication on the part of the ethnographer. As Geertz says, "Right down to the factual base, the hard rock, insofar as there is any, of the whole enterprise, we are already explicating: and worse, explicating explications. Winks upon winks upon winks."[36]

The analytical enterprise of ethnography, then, is to sort out the structures of signification contained in the data that one collects in the field. But these data are not uniformly transparent; as Geertz says, they are winks upon winks upon winks. In the interpretive function, ethnographers use the collected data from fieldwork, contextualized within its sociohistorical and cultural milieu to reach conclusions and sustain arguments that direct their readers to ideas that push the boundaries of existing understandings of sociocultural phenomena. In this endeavor they cannot make scholarly claims about the innermost intentions of the actors in the field, as one can never experience and accurately interpret another's subjective experience of the world. Thus while I have pondered it at length, I cannot make scholarly conclusions about the intent of Amma's wink or her potentially superhuman ability to see straight into my heart—of which the wink could have been an outward signification. Instead of guessing at these unverifiable aspects of experience—thus blurring the lines between the scholarship *of* religion and the scholarship *about* religion—I choose to look at the aspects of the ethnographic data that are verifiable.

This does not mean that I am forced to bracket Amma's wink entirely but, rather, that I analyze the wink as a vital discursive component with a social function in the context of the culture of Amma's movement and in the larger sociohistorical and religious context of American religion. When I compile all of the winks that I have observed, they signify important modifications and innovations to forms of Hindu religiosity that have been heretofore underrepresented in the United States. These modifications and innovations make Amma's movement not only a noteworthy development but also a case study through which we can expand and develop our theoretical understandings as scholars of religion.

Part of ethnography's contribution lies in its provision of a methodology through which to reveal the macrocosm through the study of the microcosm. It enables scholars to read the subtext of subtle daily interactions, ritual performances, social encounters, institutions, and so on as a means to relate that which they witness to larger social, economic, and historical forces that inform and impel these events. It is particularly relevant to the academic study of religion in that careful observation of religious actors in social and ritual contexts highlights their dimensions as sociohistorical actors operating with human motivations and within human cultural structures. Through participant observation, scholars create a window through which to deconstruct religious discourses and practices and their claims to transcendent authority. Ethnographers reveal themselves and their fellow actors as human agents creating religious meaning with human means and human ends. Ethnography enables scholars to read society as a text[37] and thereby to enfold themselves in practical participatory situations through which they may probe deeper by interacting with their sources in search of subtext. In the field, one witnesses and participates in the microcosm while constantly reading the social world as text for the subtext representations of the macrocosm.

The experiential aspect of ethnography also lends itself to a better understanding of the psychological, emotional, and physical aspects of religious practice. Some anthropologists have taken this to the extreme as they analyze their own visceral and personal reactions to the field as the subject of inquiry. Others have self-reflexively declared, "I am a fieldnote,"[38] meaning that while anthropologists act in the field, the field also acts within them; their shifting subjectivities become evidence of the field. Throughout my fieldwork, I used my field notes and my personal experiences as data through which I analyzed my own thoughts, emotions, reactions, and experiences as a participant in Amma's movement. I noted the changes and acculturation that occurred therein over time and conceptualized them as semblances of what other newcomers to the movement may experience. Another practical aspect of finding the macrocosm in the microcosm in my ethnographic research followed the "extended case method," which constructs *genetic* explanations (explanations of particular outcomes that emerge *from* the field) that aim to tell us more about the sociohistorical world in which situations are embedded.[39] This approach to which I adhere analyzes the production of social relations on the micro level by embedding social actors in their sociohistorical contexts.

In addressing a transnational movement that emerges from a distinctly South Asian context, the revaluation of accustomed patterns of geographical and spatial mapping of the boundaries of the field proved essential. In Arjun Appadurai's words, "The task of ethnography now becomes the unraveling of a conundrum: What is the nature of locality, as a lived experience, in a globalized, deterritorialized world?"[40] In response, I followed ethnographers who developed the concepts of extended place theory and multisited ethnography to address the shifting localities of contemporary actors and cultures and the displacement inherent in the interlacing systems of modernity and globalization. The innovation of multisited ethnography attempts to construct a mobile ethnography that "defines for itself objects of study that cannot be accounted for ethnographically by remaining focused on a single site of intensive investigation."[41] The very nature of late capitalism and modernity demands this shift from one isolated fieldwork location to multisited fieldwork locations. In our globalized world, chains of factors work together to produce any cultural product. Multisited ethnography seeks to trace these chains in order to understand the related networks that produce meanings in social situations. This research takes as its starting point the understanding that cultural products cannot exist in isolation. In order to unearth their significations, ethnographers must analyze them within the context of the larger social networks within which the actors in the field situate and define themselves.

My technique for enacting this methodological imperative throughout my fieldwork involved, simply put, following the people. I not only attended events within Amma's movement that devotees attended (such as darshan programs, special events, and satsangs), but I also routinely attended events (alone or with Amma devotees) that were related to their religious worldviews but external to Amma's organization. For example, I attended cultural, ritual, and devotional events at Hindu temples, the programs of other gurus and religious leaders, and devotional festivals. At these events I often recognized Amma devotees in attendance and gleaned a greater understanding of the related nodes of their religious networks. I also developed long-term relationships with devotees while they traveled to different cities to see Amma. Thus my initial impressions of the field expanded to more adequately mirror the variety of religious activities and engagements in which Amma's devotees participate.

My fieldwork was also multisited in that I participated in multiple levels within Amma's movement simultaneously: local satsangs, special events, darshan programs, and retreats. I also participated in multiple geographies important to Amma's organization in the United States: Chicago, San Ramon, Los Angeles, Dallas, Coralville, Detroit, Boston, and Amritapuri. This model attempted to mirror American devotees' experiences in Amma's global movement. The subject of this ethnography operates in multiple contexts in multiple regions, reflecting the transnational impulses of the larger organization. My multisited ethnographic approach sought to follow devotees through these layers and regions in order to experience a similar transitivity as the majority of devotees who participate in these multifarious arenas. The combinative analytical strategies of sociocultural anthropology, ethnography, and history produced this text. I interlaced these strands together to approach Amma's organization on a multiplicity of levels with the aim of depicting it and engaging it through a variety of lenses.

In addition to attending darshan programs (2004–2013), I attended satsangs and special events nearly every week (sometimes two or three events in one weekend) throughout the Chicagoland area (March 2007–October 2008).[42] I also assisted in the orchestration, hosting, and staffing of Amma's Chicago programs (July 2007–2013). Because of my involvement in the Chicagoland satsangs, I was fortunate to participate in highly desired *sevās* at Amma's darshan programs in San Ramon, Coralville, Boston, and Dearborn (Michigan). Because my primary sevā was assisting at the welcome desk some distance from Amma (Chicago, 2007–2013), I was also invited to perform special sevās with closer proximity to Amma, such as *prasad* sevās (2007–2013), star gazing sevā (2009–2013), timekeeper sevā cocoordinator (Chicago, 2007),[43] *pada puja* (Chicago, 2008), *ārāti* (Chicago, 2009), decorating Amma's chair (Chicago, 2012), darshan line front (Chicago, 2012),[44] and *Devī Bhāva* stage monitor (Chicago, 2012).[45] I was also conveniently situated to witness the dream of a Chicago ashram come to fruition, from the initial scouting of properties in 2008 to its inauguration by Amma in 2012.

During satsangs, it was inappropriate in this intimate devotional setting of devotees to record or take notes. Inside darshan programs, all photography and audio recording devices were prohibited, and I followed Amma's rules. In such circumstances, I relied on my field notes, memory, and recorded conversations with devotees outside the darshan hall. After several years of participant observation, I spent the summer of 2008 conducting interviews with a representative sample of devotees who were attending Amma's darshan programs in San Ramon, Coralville, and Boston. Between 2008 and 2013, I continued to engage in the field, maintain relationships with devotees, and take particularly important interviews.[46] While interviews were vital to this project, totaling approximately forty, I viewed them as only one facet of my many interventions in the field. I learned just as much through what Elaine Peña terms "co-performative witnessing," an approach that centralizes embodied action within the field as both an object and a method of study.[47] To preserve the anonymity of participants, all names used in this text are pseudonyms, with the exception of Amma, her swamis and senior brahmacāris, and other public figures.

In the late-night hours of Amma's 2008 Chicago programs, one of the leaders of the Paloma satsang did a quick sketch of me while I read one of Amma's books while doing sevā at the welcome desk. This simple sketch brought into graphic relief the obvious, but only recently theorized, critique of ethnography that the watcher is also the watched. This reciprocity signifies the ongoing dialectic between ethnographers and their informants. In early ethnographies, anthropologists imagined themselves as translators and representatives, omnipotent in their authority of *speaking for* the natives, who were deemed unable to speak for themselves. In the 1980s and 1990s, anthropologists issued sharp critiques of this unidirectional understanding of the power dynamics of ethnography. Not only was the educationally privileged (male and presumably white) anthropologist revealed to be a direct descendant of his colonial predecessor and thereby subject to the same critiques, but the very idea of a bounded, isolated, and authentic other, who was the object of study, was shown to be an intellectual impossibility. Instead, contemporary ethnographers began to recognize that which this simple sketch visually portrayed: that the ethnographer is one of many characters acting in the field, and that while she writes the culture of her informants, they also inscribe her as a character in their lives. My own vanity-inspired uneasiness with my appearance in the sketch served as an overt reminder that subjects are not always pleased with their representations by others. The reciprocal motion of defining and inscribing, assessing and representing both self and other, characterizes the fluctuating multidirectional power dynamics between researcher and informant embedded in the ethnographic experience. Such a dialectical engagement goes beyond Geertz's call for the ethnographer to decipher and interpret the various winks enacted in the field. Instead it questions the ethnographer even more provocatively: what if the field winks at you?

While I engaged Amma's programs (satsangs and darshan programs) as a participant-observer, the exact nuances of my ethnographic method varied depending on the situation. Sometimes I participated fully and wrote down feelings and questions that came to my mind in response afterward. Sometimes I engaged individual devotees in long conversations about their experiences in the movement; and other times these conversations were casual group discussions over a shared meal. When I was at a loss for conversation partners, I often wrote real-time descriptions of my surroundings, in the vein of Georges Perec's details of the Café de la Mairie in an attempt to reveal the "infra-ordinary," those multilayered events occurring around us that remain unnoticed unless directly attended to.[48] At other times, I engaged in "deep hanging out," as Renato Rosaldo famously put it.[49] In more structured settings, I guided conversations in order to incite devotees to tell me more about particularly interesting things that they had said or to which they had alluded. I sometimes opened conversations with proximate strangers with simple questions like, "How did you meet Amma?" In the first moments of introduction with devotees at Amma's public programs and satsangs, I explained that I was writing a book about Amma and her North American devotees. Most devotees were excited about the project and saw any book about Amma as a contribution to spreading her message. I made clear my status, my shifting research affiliations (University of Chicago, Austin College, University of California, Riverside), the different shapes of my continuing ethnographic project, and how the devotional community would fit into it. As such, sometimes the book too became a character in the field as devotees sometimes joked, "Put *that* in your book!" At other times, devotees obfuscated the book and my research status in favor of building unity within the devotional community.

Not only did my ethnographic styles vary, but also my personal relation to the field changed with time. I began my field research very aware that I needed to be accepted into the satsang community in order to further my research. In the beginning, I demonstrated this concern in my dress and diligence; during satsangs I often wore long-sleeved, embroidered Indian *kamiz* shirts and jeans, or *sawar-kamiz*. I carefully chanted the Sanskrit prayers and sang bhajans wholeheartedly. I was dutiful, helpful, amenable, and friendly—and I always brought dessert. I spoke with Indian satsangees in Hindi and English and often practiced my Malayalam with them. I accentuated my familiarity with India and Hinduism among Indian Hindus and my experiences with metaphysical spirituality among non-Hindus. I became somewhat of a chameleon, blending into multiple environments.

In time I recognized that I was using conservative dress, my facility with Indian languages, and my familiarity with Hindu culture to differentiate myself from those who eclectically (and often superficially) dabble in Hindu spirituality. Indian devotees supportively reinforced this differentiating move by introducing me to their Indian friends alongside a list of my qualifications, often even directly claiming, "She is like one of us." These qualities facilitated the process of "getting in" and establishing myself in the Indian Hindu satsang community. In the non-Indian satsangs, "getting in" was a nonissue. I was immediately accepted into their loose networks of largely white, eclectically minded devotees. Over time, the relationships that I established with Amma's devotees became based on camaraderie, rapport, and a shared history instead of superficial appearances and cultural/linguistic qualifications. In essence, all of my efforts to create camaraderie and rapport between myself, as an ethnographer, and the devotees came to fruition in this statement by one of the leading members of the Paloma satsang during our interview:

> You and I, we've become good friends and I feel in the deep crevices of my mind that Amanda is not a hurtful person. I can level with her; I can reason with her; I can feel good with, you know, by sitting with her and talking with her like good friends and there is nothing malicious in your thinking or in my thinking. When that much of awareness comes to my mind then all of my reservations fall away.

My research has been a consistent effort to deserve this confidence and to represent an analytically critical, yet compassionate, view of Amma's organization. To share my research with the organization, I presented several central leaders in the Chicago devotional community and Amma herself with a copy of the dissertation (2010), which I also made freely available online. With regard to this book (a wholly different manuscript), Amritrashmi (Maribel), a senior brahmacāriṇī at Amritapuri, provided helpful edits and suggestions after reviewing an early version of the text and Pankaj (Mark), a senior brahmacārī at Amritapuri, deeply engaged a more final version. In my later interviews and conversations, I often discussed the conclusions that I was drawing in this work with various devotees. Though I am aware that some devotees will not agree with my arguments and conclusions, it is my hope that they will grant the validity of my sources, the factuality of my accounts, and the absence of malice in my intent.

STRUCTURE AND AIMS

The skeletal structure of this book mirrors the initial encounter with Amma at her North American darshan programs. Newcomers are immediately overwhelmed by the striking diversity and immensity of the crowd as they enter one of Amma's ashrams or the many different four- and five-star hotels where she hosts her public programs in the United States. Chapter 1 opens with a novel analysis of the Hindu practice of darshan by incorporating tactility into what is often represented as a visual process. Amma not only gazes at her devotees during darshan, but she physically embraces them. I propose that this physicality, while innovative, inheres already in the concept of darshan, wherein "to see" is directly related to ingestion, transformation, and the idea of physical encounter with the divine. It is, in part, the potential for the intimate physicality of a hug that draws many devotees to Amma. I argue that Amma's intimate physical embraces appeal particularly to devotees who desire to witness and be witnessed through darshan. The physicality of Amma's darshan embraces also provides an intimate tactile experience that becomes a barometer for authenticity, an evasive yet highly sought-after quality of assurance that is vital to devotees in the movement.

Usually once per city on Amma's U.S. tours (and several times in San Ramon), newcomers may encounter an entirely resplendent Amma and a highly orchestrated darshan program. No longer a simple dark-skinned woman in a plain white sari giving hugs, Amma dresses in fine silk saris, with jewels, crown, and elaborate flower garlands about her neck, all underneath a brightly sequined umbrella and amidst the glittering curtains and bright stage lights: this is Devī Bhāva. Chapter 2 details Devī Bhāva darshans, highlighting how they performatively equate Amma with the goddess. I argue that these performances provide a publicly demonstrable arena in which Amma displays her supposed superhuman qualities for devotees. Tracing their lineage, I show that these are evidences of the active processes of the routinization of charisma. Devī Bhāvas, which were once unpredictable and ecstatic experiences, have become heavily orchestrated productions that are both predictable and institutionalized. This transition from ecstatic to orchestrated also reflects the spatial transition from a local South Indian context to global arenas. I argue that this type of routinization, institutionalization, and, in this case, the taming and beautification of the once wild, ecstatic, and fearsome Hindu goddess represents an often-repeated paradigmatic shift as Hindu religiosity disseminates from the village to the urban and from the Indian subcontinent to global arenas.

It is during Amma's Devī Bhāvas that she most directly equates herself with the Hindu goddess and presents herself a mimetic role model for all of her devotees. Although Amma says that all of creation is ultimately divine, Chapter 3 provides a detailed analysis of Amma's actions and messages that view women as human representatives of Hindu goddesses and use goddess imagery to empower women. I begin with her very practical gendered innovations, which situate her female followers in unconventional (and even forbidden) positions of religious and ritual leadership. I also demonstrate how her humanitarian programs often directly seek to impact the material realities of women in India. In analyzing her theology, I focus particularly on her women-centric critique and her advocacy for the instillation of "universal motherhood" in the hearts and minds of all of her followers, whether male or female. Chapter 4 reflects on devotees' testimonies in their reactions to Amma's persona as the goddess, her advocacy on behalf of women, and her call for universal motherhood. Highlighting the narratives of devotees, this chapter intimates that the interpretations of Amma's women-centric message can be differentiated largely along cultural lines. I propose that while Indian Hindus situate such goddess rhetoric within an advaita vedantic context that aims to subordinate difference to universalized equanimity, American metaphysicals are more likely to infuse Amma's rhetoric with a feminist politics that subsists on gender differentiation.

Chapter 5 investigates further the cultural encounter between Indian Hindus, those I have termed *inheritors* to Hindu traditions, and the metaphysicals (American spiritual seekers), those I have termed *adopters* of Hindu traditions (often as one tradition among others). Herein I argue that the tensions that are sometimes present between these two primary demographic populations exhibit inherited power dynamics still remaining from orientalist attitudes and the reification of cultural stereotypes that underlie contemporary discourses of multiculturalism. I delve deeply into the particularities of this cultural encounter and its multifarious contexts, suggesting that the ingrained and institutionalized social divides between these two populations dissipate as they gain proximity to Amma. Their desire for proximity to Amma and their feelings of mutuality overwhelm the potentiality for social fragmentation as they unify in "collective effervescence," anticipating her embrace.

I draw these themes together and analyze the ways in which cultural encounter shapes the movement as it transitions from a local presence to global institutions. Amma's radical initiatives on behalf of women, particularly women's initiatives in India, suggest to many international audiences that she constructs her message within a feminist politics. But the majority of Indian Hindus and close devotees in India argue that in fact these actions represent not feminism but an advaita vedantic equanimity toward all persons. The patriarchal systems in place make such actions appear feminist, when in fact they are aimed at the equanimous dissolution of difference. For most Indian Hindus, the fact that Amma represents and embodies the Hindu goddess does not suggest a feminist politics. This is substantiated by the reality that the veneration of the goddess in India has little to do with the empowerment of the material realities of Hindu women. American metaphysicals, on the other hand, are likely to view the reclamation of the goddess as a feminist assertion of female empowerment, and they quite easily find support for such assertions in Amma's messages. They often come to Amma's movement with a proclivity toward goddess worship and a preconceived feminist politics; many believe in the primacy of matriarchal approaches to the divine. Thus when they encounter Amma representing herself as a physical incarnation of the goddess and often advocating for the empowerment of women, they easily elide this with their existing convictions and proclivities toward goddess feminism. For these devotees, Amma's practical message represents one more piece of evidence of the power of the goddess to positively transform the lives of women. While the matrifocality of Amma's movement is a common signifier among devotees, that which is signified differs according to cultural demographics.

This book aims to delve deeply into the complexity of these dialectics within Amma's organization to problematize the relationship between feminism, goddess worship, and the everyday realities of human women. It suggests that the facile interpretation that such concepts maintain inherent and linear connectivities masks the temporal and spatial variances of global Hindu religion and the multiplicity of narratives therein. I conclude with a historical inquiry into the gendered representations of Hindu religiosity and argue that Amma's presentation of a goddess-centric and matrifocal interpretation of Hindu religiosity challenges the enduring assimilationist paradigm that demanded that immigrant Indian Hindus shape their religiosity as a reflection of liberal Protestant values. Although Amma's intervention flourishes under the current dominant discourses of multiculturalism in the United States, still her movement and message have adapted to the American context in significant ways. I suggest that although the celebration of multiculturalism provides a welcome step away from assimilationist "melting pot" ideologies, its affirmations of assumedly bounded and autonomous cultural and ethnic identities unintentionally reify dominant discourses and existing cultural stereotypes. As such, they often restrict the diversity of cultural narratives that may be imported to the United States, articulating a static conception of what it means to be appropriately Hindu in the American context.

This ethnography shows that inheritor devotees create ethnically and culturally distinct congregations, performing the particularized cultural identities so valorized in American multiculturalism. But they baulk at certain appropriations of Hinduism, such as goddess worship as a feminist project. The goal of this book is to destabilize the complacency of current narratives of multiculturalism by showing complex negotiations between cultural brokers and appropriators, wherein they sometimes come together but more often sequester into distinct groups.

CHAPTER 1

A Darshan Embrace

Experiencing Authenticity and Feeling Witnessed

To Amma, whether they be a fanatic Hindu or a fanatic
Muslim or a fanatic Christian, everybody is her children [*sic*].
If tomorrow Bin Laden were to come and get a *darshan* from
Amma, Amma would hug him. Amma will not even say that,
"oh why are you being a fanatic?" For her, everybody is her
children [*sic*]. So in one sense, she embodies the compassion,
compassionate aspect of everything. And so she cannot say
that this person is wrong and this person is right. She will not
say that. Because as I said, to her, everyone is an expression of
the Divine. But that doesn't mean that she says what they
do is correct. And personally, I have seen Amma giving
advice to people saying that this is not the correct path to
follow, you should change. And so, I would say that, Amma,
it is according to each person and their ability to understand
and listen and to implement those things that Amma gives the
advice. And if they are not ready to hear what Amma says,
then Amma will not give them any advice. [It is] just like
pouring water on a cup that has been kept upside down.

—Br. Dayamrita

In 2008, in the midst of the bustling *darshan* program[1] in San Ramon,
California, a medical van arrived outside of the overflowing darshan
hall of the ashram. Personal assistants helped Jason, a severely disabled
young man with Lou Gehrig's disease, enter the sacred space. He arrived lying flat on a portable medical bed, and with the necessary medical accoutrements. Guided by the special needs assistants on the tour
staff, he was carefully wheeled to the center of the darshan hall until he

reached Amma's feet. In response, Amma stood up from her low seat for the first time after several hours of continuous darshan embraces and began to stroke his entire body with her hands. Slowly and deliberately she leaned far over and ran her hands delicately over each of his limbs, his hands and feet, and his torso. Finally, she affectionately stroked his face and attentively applied sandalwood paste to his forehead, all the while patiently and carefully murmuring over him words of affection and blessings. The assembled audience intently observed her maternal care and concern for this acute mind trapped within such a severely challenged physical body. Tears streamed down many of the observers' faces over the possibility of such unadulterated love and compassion for another. After having come to Amma's darshan in this manner many times in increasingly severe states of bodily degeneration, Jason wrote online about his first darshan experience with Amma ten years earlier. At that time he was confined to a wheelchair, which he could propel largely by himself. He recounted that initially he was determined to remain strong and not to weep in Amma's presence. He explained that it was not the unconditional love and attention that she devoted to him that first brought him to tears but instead his father's darshan experience that moved him to his core. He wrote:

> It was awesome but I didn't cry so I thought I was safe. But when I wheeled back a few feet and saw her hug my father, I lost it. To see someone treating my big, bad, tough, smart father like her little boy was pretty neat. He didn't have to be the responsible one for a minute. He could just lay in Amma's lap and get loved. Then I thought that she does this for millions of people. And not only for that minute does she take our burdens if we let her. She will take all our burdens regardless of how good or bad we think we are. She looked at me [as I was] crying with such an understanding face it melted me.[2]

In many ways, releasing one's burdens at Amma's feet defines the darshan experience. Amma enables her devotees to experience meaningful emotional release from their everyday responsibilities and sufferings by encouraging them to become like little children, sharing their problems, needs, and desires with their mother.[3] The abundant and often unexpected emotive tears that tend to accompany the darshan experience derive from this process of unburdening, a process that subsists on the qualities of surrender and relinquishing the ego.

In the Indic context, gurus throughout history have urged (or demanded) their followers to approach them with an aura of complete self-surrender and submission. The famed story of Ekalavya in the Hindu epic *Mahābhārata* exemplifies the idealized extent of a disciple's self-sacrifice as Ekalavya, a proficient archer (so proficient as to fill a barking dog's mouth full of arrows to silence him without harm), willingly surrenders that which is most essential to his archery skills, his thumb, at the guru's command. Other Indic stories from Hindu, Sikh, and Jain religious traditions describe disciples who compete with each other for primacy through their demonstrations of who can sacrifice more at the feet of the guru.[4] Despite the evident potential for abuses of power in the guru-disciple relationship, the tradition (*guru-śiṣya-parampara*) suggests that self-surrender at the feet of the guru leads the disciple toward the transcendence of the self, which is the aim of ascetic practice across the major religious traditions.

Most religious traditions would agree that the submission, sacrifice, and subordination (or even elimination) of the ego-driven self establish the primary foundation for religious experience. In ascetic traditions, the practitioner must be willing to sublimate the individuated self (and all of its accompanying desires, passions, and preferences) to an alternative cosmological goal. The ultimate religious experience, variously interpreted as the entrance into the kingdom of heaven, nirvana, self-realization, and so on, demands some form of self-subordination. Devotees' first moments of their personal transition from a materially oriented to a spiritually oriented reality depend on their becoming like little children at the feet of a spiritual master, releasing their material burdens, and surrendering their personal control (or the illusion thereof) to God. For devotees, Amma's darshan experience creates the foundation and the continued affirmation for this transition. They are bolstered by Amma's warm, fragrant, and maternal reassurances that they are "safe" in such treacherous processes of spiritual transformation, protected by the unconditional love of a mother who engulfs them in her compassionate embrace (see figure 2).

Like Jason, many devotees come to receive Amma's embrace with the glimmer of hope that she will heal their emotional, mental, or physical ailments. Some seek solace and comfort as a result of previous traumas or cataclysmic life events. Others desire to be seen, recognized, witnessed, and validated. Still others seek to alleviate feelings of melancholia or ennui brought on by the isolationism, fragmentation, and disenfranchisement that characterize much of life in modern society.[5] Whether experiencing physical, emotional, or merely bourgeois suffering, many devotees come to Amma only after they have exercised numerous other

FIGURE 2. Amma's darshan embrace (© MA Center)

available options for healing. When I asked Br. Dayamrita Chaitanya about whether Amma's darshan embraces were healing, he responded:

> Of course. That is the healing factor of love. You know . . . I talked to one of the residents at the ashram and he told me that Amma entrusted him with—at least now in the last four to five years—about fifty or so mental patients, out of which forty or so were highly suicidal and he told me that the only cure for their disease was Amma's love—the attention that Amma showered on each one of them. They are holding on just because of the love that Amma gives to each one of them. So do you think that it is healing?

The evidence of devotees' faith in the healing capacities of Amma's embraces lies in the many severely disabled people who repeatedly attend her darshan programs. Many report miraculous recoveries due to Amma's blessings. But even if the large number of parents who arrive at Amma's darshan programs with their wheelchair-bound children will not see their children walk or talk on this day as a result of Amma's embrace, they still can find comfort in this embrace as they experience a momentary release of their heavy caregiving burdens. Not only do the parents find a temporary respite, but there is always a glimmer of hope for healing and renewal.

Many devotees attend only for the novelty of the experience. Others desire the spiritual energy (*śakti*) they believe Amma embodies and the comfort and consolation that she imparts through her embrace. For many it is enough to briefly encounter a person they believe to be a *satguru* (a realized soul). These devotees tend to be more loosely affiliated with Amma, and they may have begun to attend Amma's darshan programs only recently. Other devotees are more committed to Amma in particular and stay for the entire program. These devotees aim to spend as much time as possible with Amma, absorbing her spiritual energy.

Some gurus envision darshan as an opportunity to provide devotees with the unmediated experience of divinity through direct contact with audiences. But in the practical, conventional, and immediate sense, modern gurus host darshan programs to bring together in community their followers and potential followers, to display and perform their superhuman abilities and natures, and to proselytize their spiritual messages.[6] Mother Meera hosts silent darshan programs in which she quietly gazes into attendees' eyes, one devotee after another. Sathya Sai Baba used to enter the darshan hall according to his divine whimsy (*līlā*) and then quietly gaze at the entire audience, pausing poignantly to look at particular individuals before retreating into private darshan meetings with select devotees in a separate room. Karunamayi Ma individually blesses her attendees from a raised platform by placing her hands on their temples and third-eye energy centers (chakras). Mata Amritanandamayi embraces her devotees one by one. During darshan the gurus' gaze is poignantly directed to their audiences with the goal of fostering individuated movements of visual exchange, dialogic interaction, and believed transformation. Each of these gurus offers free darshan events.

Darshan is the intimate process of seeing and being seen by a deity. Hindus describe darshan not as the detached, passive sight of aesthetic observance but with the active transitive verbs of taking (in Hindi, *darshan lena*) and giving darshan (*darshan dena*). In modern usage, the term *darshan* signifies the moment when humans view the supernatural, whether through an icon of a deity (*murti*), a sacred site (*tīrtha*), or a living embodiment of the divine (*avatār*). Through darshan, the deity and the devotee engage in a mutual seeing in "a moment of dramatic spiritual interaction."[7] This interactive process symbolizes the "desire for fusion—for the subject/object dissolution of the 'double sensation.'"[8] As Isabelle Nabokov/Clark-Decès explains, "The act of *darshan* . . . also becomes a form of absorbing, so that any objectification of a supernatural is always a form of assimilation as well."[9] It is in such moments of Hindu devotional ritual that the individual both recognizes divinity and is recognized as divinity.[10] In Hindu practice, it is through darshan that humanity gains the opportunity to experience the divine on earth. Ideally, the darshan experience dissolves the individual ego into cosmic unity with divinity. When interpreted through the advaita vedantic theological ideal of nonduality, the moment of darshan between guru and devotee provides the opportunity for the dissolution of the individuated ego, the symbolic union with divinity, and the intense physical expression of metaphysical cosmic oneness that eradicates duality. Ideally, darshan transforms the individual through these temporary suspensions of the sense of self and individuated difference that incite the recognition of the ultimate similitude between the self and divinity.

Through darshan, devotees not only see the image of the deity but infuse themselves within it in an active process of becoming. Devotees aim to absorb the gaze of the deity and in the process be transformed. As Lawrence Babb suggests, there is a parallel between the impulse behind eating blessed food (*prasad*), wherein "you become what you eat," and the process of darshan, in which "you somehow become what you see."[11] Thus darshan should not be explained in terms of being merely an aesthetic experience—something that one passively witnesses—but, rather, as an agentive interaction—something in which one actively engages, a transformative and participatory process. A devotee of Mother Meera understands her unique method of silent visual darshan in highly active terms of transformation. She says, "Along with the gaze from Mother Meera's eyes comes an infusion of light, light designed to heal wounds within the psyche and give a person sufficient power to move from the perspective of the personality to a divine perspective. . . . This is not one woman staring as the other stares back. Instead, one offers the gift of her soft, penetrative gaze, and the other offers the gift of acceptance."[12] In the Radhasoami tradition the compassionate gaze of the guru during darshan is believed to assist devotees in their spiritual development: "the *drishṭi*, the 'seeing' or 'glance,' of the guru aids the devotee in achieving deliverance."[13] Devotees of Sathya Sai Baba experience darshan as "a moment of ultimate self-transformation by which they are 'captured' spiritually and experience a 'complete immersion in Sai Baba's love.' "[14]

Amma's devotees relate similar experiences of the dissolution of individual boundaries, immersion in divine love, and cosmic awakenings. Shanti relayed a particularly powerful experience of her darshan during one *Devī Bhāva* night: "As we knelt in front of Amma, she put our heads together, cheek to cheek, and looked straight into our eyes, the right eye on me and the left eye on Caleb. I remember thinking, *Oh no! here we go!!!* I lost all track of where I was . . . there was no sense of time, the universe was swirling to life in her eye, and then I was *in* the universe and I sort of *felt*, for lack of a better word, everything that has ever been and every thing that will ever be in one second. She pulled back and it was over. I totally lost track of where I was for a second. But as soon as she disengaged I was back with no confusion." Devotees long for the darshan experience because of the potential for this type of transformative experience, the possibility of experiencing a glimpse into the cosmic reality of the divine, and the efficacy of darshan for catalyzing spiritual awakening.

Devotees pursue this possibility for transformative experience through their intimate interactions with the guru during darshan. Amma's unique offering of a maternal embrace provides temporary satisfaction to devotional communities fueled by what Tulasi Srinivas has called "proxemic desire," meaning not only the desire to be close to the guru but to be acknowledged as a good devotee.[15] In Amma's movement, devotees nearly burst with proxemic desire as they rush to catch a glimpse of her as she enters and departs from the darshan hall or crowd as close to her as possible when given the opportunity. Similarly, devotees exhibit the desire to meld with Amma's presence through star gazing *sevā* (wherein devotees sit close to Amma and watch her intently in five-minute-long shifts) and even clamor to receive and consume small distributions of special prasad, a food item that Amma has previously sampled, believed to be imbued with sacrality through the ultimate proximity of having once been so close to her mouth.

Sai Baba devotees' conceptions of self-worth were directly related to their darshan experiences, meaning that good devotees received "good darshans," and good darshans were marked by proximity to Sai Baba.[16] In Amma's movement the parallel valence between good devotees and good darshans resonates less because all attendees are granted the intimate proximity of a hug and few devotees would admit to feelings of having received "bad darshans." All darshan experiences are part of "Amma's grace" and while their efficacy may not be readily apparent, devotees believe that Amma presents precisely what is needed at that moment. Still, devotees anxiously desire more time in direct proximity to Amma, and they strive to improve themselves internally and behaviorally (to transform themselves into good devotees) in order to receive more of Amma's positive attention. This substrata correlation between good devotees and good darshans places on the shoulders of devotees the responsibility for the emotional intensity and efficacy of the darshan interaction. If one has a lackluster darshan, then one must go within to find meaning and ultimately to access more significantly transformative darshan experiences.

Many contemporary gurus provide their devotees with public darshan experiences, but they limit their accessibility and visibility to them by appearing in front of large audiences, thus having limited physical contact, or no contact at all, with them. As a result of this restricted access to the guru, devotees often rely on photographs, videos, and websites as mediators for the darshan experience. In these movements (and in the Hindu use of devotional iconography more generally), the darshan experience is necessarily dependent on visuality. Still, as Christopher Pinney rightly points out, "*Darshan's* mode of interaction . . . mobilizes vision as part of a unified human sensorium, and visual interaction can be physically transformative."[17] Similarly, Smriti Srinivas introduces Sathya Sai Baba's darshan as a "sensorium of the sacred" and centralizes the sensory and somatic nature of the encounter with divine or holy persons in South Asia.[18] Amma's movement also employs photographic images and websites to augment opportunities for devotees to experience her darshan in her absence. But when she is physically present, the somatic nature of the divine encounter increases exponentially because of the barrage of sensory stimuli from the darshan hall juxtaposed with the immediate physicality of her embraces.

TAKING AMMA'S DARSHAN

The physicality of Amma's darshan creates a multisensory event that most devotees experience as emotionally overwhelming and spiritually transformative. Amma's unique presentation of darshan in the form of a hug provides devotees with unusually intimate access to her physical body and thus creates the potential for an overwhelmingly tactile corporeal experience. The physical interaction with Amma during darshan creates the ultimate fulfillment of devotees' desire for proximity to the guru. Many devotees choose to follow Amma because of this potential for personal attention and physical intimacy. They recall their darshan experiences not only in terms of visuality but also in terms of visceral feelings and multisensory engagement, through touch, smell, sound, and emotion. As such, Amma's unique innovations to the Hindu ritual of darshan prompt a revisiting of the commonplace understanding of darshan as a visual exchange between deity and devotee.

Pinney notes that darshan, often directly translated into English as "seeing," has little to do with Western conceptions of aesthetics, usually understood to involve detached observation, the separation between the image and the beholder. Instead he proposes the term *corpothetics* to signify the "desire to fuse image and beholder, and the elevation of efficacy . . . as the central criterion of value."[19] Corpothetics (sensory corporeal aesthetics) emphasizes the bodily contingent of the darshan experience and expands the conception of darshan from its ocular restriction to the incorporation of its multisensory dimensions. In a living deity, the eye is also an organ of touch in the sense that it is used to form a connection between the guru and devotees.[20] "The perception of the guru, *pir*, or a deity emerges not only from visuality or sound but may include smell, dreams, touch, taste or tears—religious experience is also an experience of the senses."[21] In Amma's darshan, the superimposition of the tactile onto the visual assumes material form because darshan becomes not only the vision of Amma but the bodily experience of her physical embrace. As one might imagine, her devotees place little emphasis on their vision of her during darshan and instead foreground their feelings related to touch, smell, and hearing. They recall "her warmth," "her beautiful scent," and "the chanting," and they describe how these multisensory experiences catapult them into emotive states that they describe as "intoxicating," "drunk with love," and filled with "a deep peace" and "inner stillness and inner luminance."

One hour prior to the start of the darshan program, a select *brahmacāriṇī* distributes darshan tokens to the queued attendees and *sevites*[22] present (many devotees know her by name because of her administrative control over this important task). Attendees then funnel into the hotel ballroom wherein ashram recordings play Amma's acceptance speeches for one of the many international humanitarian awards she has received, and promotional videos highlight Embracing the World humanitarian activities. Spliced with Indic *bhajans* (devotional music), the auditory cacophony blends with the colorful atmosphere of throngs of bustling devotees (wearing color) and brahmacārī/iṇīs (wearing white), tables offering a variety of services (Ayurvedic readings, radiance healing, Jyotish [vedic astrology] readings, and those highlighting the humanitarian activities of the MA Math [Amritapuri], MA Center [San Ramon], and the local *satsangs*), a sevā desk, and a bounty of products for purchase at various merchandise tables, the proceeds of which support Amma's humanitarian activities—all of these things are positioned along the periphery of the central stage and altar space on which Amma will soon appear.

As Amma arrives, usually in a light-colored sedan, the most ardent devotees rush to the external doors to greet her as the tone of the conch shell reverberates through the hall and vicinity. Amma enters the space with her arms outstretched to graze the similarly outstretched hands of devotees who clamor to gain a preliminary glimpse of her. She stands in meditation while her swamis and *swaminī* chant Sanskrit prayers (*ślokas*) and select devotees perform the worship of the guru's feet (*pada puja*).[23] She then makes her way to the stage where she sits and bows to the audience with a respective greeting and prayer. All morning programs begin with a brief meditation, while evening programs consist of longer periods of spiritual talks (given by Amma and her immediate swamis, and/ or brahmacārī/iṇīs). During these preliminary portions of the program, audience members are encouraged to maintain a quiet atmosphere and to stay in their seats. Some of the audience sits on the floor space closest to Amma, while others sit in chairs, though the number of chairs in the darshan hall has increased significantly over the past ten years.[24] Although the ritualized sequence of these initial formal aspects to the darshan program shares considerable similarities with Sai Baba's darshan programs, at Amma's programs there is no reserved seating except for

FIGURE 3. Devotees pray for world peace, Amma's darshan program, Mata Amritananda-mayi Center Chicago (MACC), July 2012 (© MA Center)

those who require assisted darshan (those attendees with special needs); a small section is also reserved for VIPs. During darshan programs social hierarchies do not govern devotees' proximity to Amma: men and women are not segregated, and the only ritually marked entrance is Amma's[25] (see figure 3).

During the evening programs, at the conclusion of meditation and spiritual talks, the atmosphere lightens and Amma personally begins to lead the audience in singing bhajans, accompanied by her musicians. In 2009, she began to augment her bhajans by simultaneously projecting lyrics (in transliteration and in English translation) onto two large screens adjacent to the central stage. This addition encourages audience participation and assuages the cultural divide between the largely Indic bhajans and their American audience participants. Bhajans are offered primarily in Malayalam, Hindi, Gujarati, Tamil, Telugu, and English, while smaller numbers of bhajans are offered in Spanish, French, Portuguese, Bengali, and Punjabi. Some of the non-Indic language bhajans are translations of Indic bhajans, while others are original compositions by Amma or her devotees around the globe. Presenting devotional music in multiple languages signifies the importance Amma places on appealing to global audiences. For example, during her birthday celebrations in 2003

(*Amritavarsham50*) Amma sang the popular bhajan "Ishwar Tumhi Daya Karo" ("Lord, Shower Me with Your Compassion") in Hindi, English, French, German, Italian, Spanish, Czech, Arabic, Hebrew, Japanese, and Malay.[26] Such code switching (the concurrent use of multiple languages) during darshan programs and in Amma's publications reinforces the idea that everyone is welcome to embrace Amma and her communities. Devotees are invited to experience and perform devotional singing with Amma in their own languages as well as in Amma's native Malayalam and other Indic vernaculars. Similarly, Smriti Srinivas shows how Sathya Sai Baba used code switching and code blending to become, in Hawley and Juergensmeyer's terms, a "theological bridge-builder," appealing to various audiences by approaching them in their own "language of experience."[27] Multilingualism and the practices of code switching, code blending, and code mixing (in the terms of sociolinguistics) vitalize each movement's claim to universal applicability. Amma devotees often cite such multilingualism in Amma's routine devotional music programs as validation of her appeal to diverse cultures and of her movement's extensive and global reach.

Bhajans often develop into jubilant, energetic, and emotive audience responses to Amma's impassioned singing, uniting the audience in a communal revelatory experience of divine praise and "collective effervescence."[28] The devotional singing usually begins with calm and lilting melodies and over time escalates into repeated refrains pulsating with devotional fervor and Amma's ecstatic cries to "Ma," the goddess. Many devotees develop highly emotional responses to Amma's devotional singing and often transform their musical preferences to emphasize recordings of Amma's bhajans in response. As Pithambara, an older Indian Hindu gentleman with graying hair, kind, twinkling eyes, and a beautiful devotional voice, recounted: "The day when I saw Amma singing I was crying, but not because I was sad. I was crying because that void was filled by her music. Whatever that void that was in me that was filled that day . . . I was crying because they were tears of joy and that only came from her music. And that is when I gave up all of the filmy music and that type of thing and became devoted to bhajans." In time, Pithambara developed his love for Amma's bhajans by leading the musical endeavors of his local satsang gatherings, hosting benefit concerts for Amma's charities, and showering his devotional love on Amma through the sevā of musical performance (see figure 4).

After the emotional climax of ecstatic communal bhajans has receded, Amma immediately begins embracing individual attendees. She

FIGURE 4. Bhajans, Amma's darshan program, Amritapuri, India, August 2012
(© MA Center)

continues the rhythmic process of darshan without interruption until
each token holder has received her embrace. Live bhajan musicians
maintain their devotional music throughout the program, supplemented
by occasional cultural programs and performances. During darshan,
attendees kneel before Amma as she folds them into her embrace. Some
steal a moment to ask her personal questions (a privilege taken particularly by devotees fluent in Malayalam or Tamil, though others may also
have their questions translated by Amma's immediate attendees for a
less fluid conversation). But the majority of devotees rest their heads on
the cushion of flower garlands at Amma's breast, drinking in the experience until she leans forward and chants "My daughter, my daughter, my
daughter, my daughter [or son]" deep into their ears and places prasad
in their hands, at which point they are lifted by attendees and ushered
away. Outside of India, prasad consists of a Hershey's kiss and flower
petals for non-Indians and a Hershey's kiss, flower petals, and a small
brown packet of *vibhūti* (sacred ash) for Indians.[29] Amma also routinely
gives an apple to pregnant women and those who are embarking on
new projects. Sometimes she gives an apple without explanation, a representative signifier of her divine whimsy (*līlā*). For couples who wish to
be married or for those who have recently become engaged, she often

pulls a rose from the decorations adorning her low seat and gives it to the couple as prasad. For especially lucky (or blessed) devotees and young children, Amma places an unwrapped Hershey's kiss directly into their mouths. For special occasions and blessings, Amma dips her ring finger into fragrant sandalwood paste and applies it to the center of devotees' foreheads. Because all of the aforementioned darshans are infrequent, they incite delight and gratitude among devotees when they do occur. The prasad assistant (as well as the prasad assistant's assistant) diligently watches Amma in order to quickly and gently place the appropriate prasad in her hand after each darshan embrace.

TRANSCENDING BOUNDARIES OF PURITY AND POLLUTION

Amma's process of giving darshan in the form of an unconditional physical embrace subverts traditional Hindu norms of caste and gender hierarchies, particularly because she was born as a low-caste, dark-skinned female. The physicality of her maternalistic darshan embrace democratizes the darshan experience in two primary ways: it enables all participants to attain the most intimate proximity to the guru, and it publicly thwarts Hindu strictures of purity and pollution regarding the practices of untouchability and gender segregation. In fact, one recent book by a devotee correlates Mahatma Gandhi's rejection of the Hindu practice of untouchability with Amma's darshan embrace, arguing that, framed positively, both leaders advocate "touchability." "Touchability means removing the false sense of separation between our hearts and the rest of the Creation."[30] The author concludes that Amma "is perhaps the most touchable person on the planet. From her internal vision, she tells us: 'The universe is one, not many. Man has divided the world into fragments, not God. It is man, who, through his thoughts and actions, creates turmoil and disintegration in the natural, harmonious unity of the world. Each atom serves as a building block of this universe and is intrinsically connected to every other atom.'"[31] Amma's public darshan embrace invites a new paradigm of devotionalism that centralizes ritualized bodily contact among strangers (even those of different genders and castes) from within the confines of a culture that carefully guards physical contact and corporeal boundaries as potentially dangerous arenas for bodily pollution[32] (see figure 5).

While Amma's darshan experience of a hug forms the primary public persona of the movement, it does not result in a *communitas* of hugging

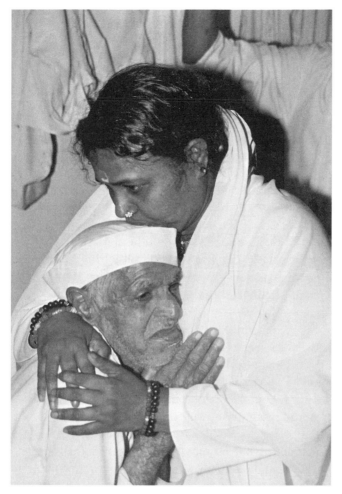

FIGURE 5. An elderly Muslim man in Amma's darshan embrace
(© MA Center)

among devotees. The increased physicality present in the guru-disciple
relationship in Amma's movement does not translate into a generalized
culture of unusually augmented physical intimacy among devotees. Instead, the movement is infused with a largely ascetic impulse toward
sevā in which devotees are encouraged to enact an ethos of loving and
compassionate behavior in their routine interpersonal interactions and
through their participation in ETW humanitarian campaigns. In the
United States, the minority population of dreadlocked countercultural
youth who follow Amma on her tour echoes her advocacy for love and

compassionate behavior by hugging each other perhaps more frequently while in her presence. But most devotees view the darshan embrace as a very particular ritually sanctified interaction with their guru, one with specific qualities and particular efficacy.

As the recent "Free Hugs" campaign (2004) demonstrates, strangers are reticent to embrace strangers, even in a Western context. Juan Mann stood holding a sign that read "Free Hugs" in a Sydney shopping mall for fifteen minutes before an elderly woman gave him a hug. Later, as his campaign increased in popularity, he was barred by the authorities because of his lack of public liability insurance. Eventually, Mann's campaign and his proposition for "free hugs" gained social acceptability but not legal latitude, despite the fact that he garnered ten thousand petition signatures and became a YouTube sensation (with 72 million views as of May 2012, due in part to the support of the band Sick Puppies).[33] In 2013, Brian, an adopter devotee in his mid-thirties arrived at Amma's Los Angeles darshan programs and stood just outside the darshan hall holding a sign that said "Free Hugs," silently soliciting free hugs from devotees. After some time Amma officials asked him to leave and he spent the remainder of the evening holding his sign in the front alley silently soliciting devotees as they entered the hotel. His expulsion signified the distinct sacrality that both devotees and Amma officials reserve for Amma's hugs. In Durkheimian fashion, Amma's tour staff carefully guarded the boundary between the sacred and the profane, Amma's sacred hugs and Brian's profane "free hugs."

In Western countries, sexuality and sex may be open topics of discourse and practice, but physical embraces among strangers (without the potential for ultimate sexual gratification) are uncommon and violate the everyday practices of social conventions. As Michel Foucault has aptly shown, the hyperverbalization about sex and sexuality in Europe (and in the United States) signifies an inherent sexual anxiety rather than its antithesis.[34] In a recent exhibition of the legacy of American Puritanism, many high school administrators in the United States have become concerned about the ramifications of students hugging in schools. To rectify this situation, a growing number of secondary education institutions in the United States have prohibited not only hugging but all touching among students.[35] The promotion of lasciviousness in media discourse and industry should not prompt the conclusion that Westerners somehow feel more comfortable with hugging strangers than their counterparts do in contemporary India. Both Indians and Westerners fold themselves into Amma's embrace and willingly surrender their socially constructed reservations against this type of physical intimacy with strangers. This process of surrender marks the first transition to the sacrifice of the individual ego at the feet of the guru.

In India, social conventions and religious prohibitions heavily govern physical contact between strangers. Simply put by Dhara, a young female inheritor devotee, "We [Indians] don't touch!" Such prohibitions are derived from long-established traditions that locate social and bodily boundaries as contested spaces through which to exert and maintain caste hierarchies. Caste hierarchies and the maintenance of female chastity are intimately related in the conventional Hindu prohibitions against bodily pollution. As Mary Douglas reminds us, "[T]hrough women the blood and purity of the caste is perpetuated. Therefore their sexual purity is all-important, and every possible whisper of threat to it is anticipated and barred against."[36] In the Hindu societal norms of a century ago, Amma, as a low-caste woman, would be relegated to relations with members of her own social station, forced to restrict herself to particular servile forms of employment, and banished from public forums and physical contact with upper castes. Though Article 17 of the 1949 Indian constitution formally outlawed the practice of untouchability (designating classes of people as impure, servile, "untouchable"), caste hierarchy and discrimination in India persists. Amma's public solicitation of hugs from strangers marks a radical usurpation of Indian societal norms for female behavior and caste relations. No other guru (let alone a low-caste female guru) engages the breadth of global populations (the healthy, sick, old, young, rich, poor, dirty, clean, mentally ill, and so on) with this level of physical intimacy.

Amma intentionally thwarts Hindu social customs with regard to restrictions on purity and pollution; her famed darshan programs publicly challenge conventional social structures on an international stage. She intentionally embraces the sick, the dirty, and the mentally ill of all castes and creeds without outward concern for her personal safety and cleanliness. At the close of darshan programs, Amma emerges wide-eyed and electrified with a broad smile as she exits the darshan hall, but the shoulder of her white sari is usually stained a medium brown with translucent edges encompassing smudges of red, pink, and black from the oils and residual makeup of thousands. Her right cheek bears a darkened impression (a callus, bruise, or both) from the thousands of hugs she delivers each day and night. While attendees encourage devotees to wipe sweat and makeup from their faces and dreadlocked attendees to cover their hair with a shawl, still the process entails that Amma embraces all of humanity, regardless of an individual's appearance, hygiene, caste, class, age, gender, or religion. One devotee praises Amma for publicly defying structures of social inequity in the Hindu tradition. She says, "In front of her outpouring of pure *Ahimsa* [non-violence], the conditioning of caste simply does not exist. Her *darshan* queue has no social distinctions. In front of her, caste is a moot point, an archaic thought form, from an era when people did not realize they were all children of the same Mother."[37] Devotees follow Amma as an international spiritual leader and humanitarian dissociated from Hindu mores, but they also simultaneously view her as a Hindu reformer who challenges historical paradigms that do not resonate with their modern liberal democratic sensibilities.

The documentary film *Darshan: The Embrace* (2006) begins with the opening scene of Amma licking and sucking the pus from the wounds of Datta, a leper who frequented her ashram at Amritapuri to take her darshan, which he believed to have healing properties. When questioned about him, Amma responded, "Mother sees him in the same way as she sees you or anybody else. He is also my child. How can a Mother feel loathing or hatred when she sees her son or daughter, however ugly or badly diseased he or she is? In fact, Mother has a lot of compassion and love for him. Mother's heart melts when she sees him."[38] Unlike Catherine of Siena, who famously drank pus in a compulsion to serve humanity through her own suffering, Amma drinks the pus of lepers to model the extremities of unconditional love while emphasizing equanimity as the means to transcend aversion and hatred.[39] In her discussion of her behavior toward Datta, she advises, "Children, let your minds open up fully and contain love with all its fragrance and beauty. Hatred and aversion will only make it look ugly. Love towards everyone gives real beauty, enhancing both the giver as well as the receiver."[40] Br. Dayamrita Chaitanya recounted his personal experience of witnessing this transgressive event:

> So then I went back to see her a second time and it was this time that I saw Amma licking a leper, the leper, you know Datta the leper, with my own eyes and that is what transformed my life, really. It was when I saw her compassion, when I saw her love I realized that I have never seen [that] in any other human being. And that to show so much compassion to another human being—through her own interactions is what drew me, changed [me], and blew my mind. And even today that is what I see in her.

The stories of Amma's interactions with Datta are famous throughout her movement. Often cited, for devotees they serve as one of the most extreme examples of Amma's unconditional love and compassion for everyone, regardless of personal circumstances and her own personal safety. From another perspective, they also demonstrate Amma's intentional thwarting of traditional Hindu conceptions of appropriate social hierarchies and the ritualistically enforced boundaries demarcating purity from pollution. Hindu concepts of purity and impurity are often closely connected to notions of bodily integrity and the boundaries of the physical self. Those substances that flow over the boundaries of the body are dangerously polluting: "Violations of the boundaries of the body, such as menstruation, elimination, wounds, and mutilation, create impurity."[41] As if Amma's unconditional darshan embraces were not radical enough, this famous public act of compassion, wherein she consumes the pus of a leper, intentionally challenges established conventions. By violating prohibitions against bodily pollution, Amma overtly confronts the historical socioreligious prescriptions of brahmanical orthodoxies that maintain caste boundaries and purity/pollution restrictions governing Hindu society. Through darshan Amma not only confronts such restrictions, but she performatively and publicly flouts them. As Selva Raj succinctly puts it, "Darshan is Ammachi's discourse on defiance."[42]

But in many ways her movement instantiates traditional Hindu divisions (historically often caste-based) that separate her followers into Indians and Westerners, whether in regard to food offerings (between Indian or Western meals and snack shops), clothing stalls (between Indian or Western clothes), or even darshan.[43] During darshan, Indians receive one prasad and non-Indians receive another. In practice, this means that the prasad assistant (and the prasad assistant's assistant) must attentively scan the line of individuals advancing toward Amma and make quick (and subjective) judgments about the ethnic identity of those waiting to receive darshan. Prasad assistants are eager to please, and they tremble at the opportunity to interface so directly with their beloved guru. One prasad assistant characterized this sevā as "an amazing experience and an intense meditation . . . utter bliss."[44] But it is also a task that must be undertaken only after proper training, and then with the utmost care and attention to detail.

As in most Chicago darshan programs, I was assigned in 2008 to take a shift as the prasad assistant's assistant. Like most devotees, I too had a few butterflies in the pit of my stomach as I approached Amma in anticipation of my minute-long shift. When I finally reached her and was about halfway through my shift, the timekeeper (an austere Indian

Hindu woman from the local satsang) abruptly chastised me for hand-
ing out only Hershey's kisses and flower petals to the prasad assistant
to give to a Latino couple who were in Amma's darshan embrace. She
quickly shoved some vibhūti (sacred ash) into my hand and silently
scolded me with fierce eyes and a stern facial expression to also place the
ash into Amma's slightly opened hand. Confused and shamed, I asked
her afterward (perhaps a bit cynically) if all brown-skinned people were
to receive vibhūti, or just Indians. She then realized that the couple was
in fact Latino and not Indian, but she shrugged off the mistake without
comment.

This momentary conflict highlights the tension in the movement's
transition from an antiquated model of an ethnic dichotomy between
whites and Indians to a global organization with complex and multifarious ethnic demographics. What once was a clear distinction between
locals and foreigners in India has become a difficult, subjective, and often
fallible process of quick, sight-based ethnic identification in the United
States and around the world. Local leaders in the movement explain
that they continue this practice because non-Indians are not usually
culturally familiar with the properties or uses of vibhūti, thus receiving
it as prasad would only confuse them. One senior ashram resident explained that many Westerners, not being acclimated to the use and ap-
plication of vibhūti, were throwing it away, while Indians consider it "a
bad omen" not to receive vibhūti from a *māhātma* like Amma. But as
more and more cosmopolitan Indians in Western clothes and non-Indian/
nonwhite populations (sometimes in Indian clothing) begin to attend
Amma's darshan programs, the process of instantly distinguishing between the complexions of Indians and non-Indians has already become
difficult. To make matters even more complex, non-Indians who are acculturated to Hindu norms often ask, or secretly desire, to receive vibhūti
because they believe in its medicinal and auspicious properties.

In this task, devotees demonstrate careful attention to pleasing Amma,
particularly when in direct contact with her. Amma has been known to
toss aside improper prasad, often with an aggravated glance at the prasad
assistant if she or he errs. Devotees view this type of direct reprimand
not only as an unfortunate public humiliation but also as contributing
to an unnecessary strain on Amma's already taxed physical body, because Amma must then turn to assemble the appropriate prasad herself.
While nearly all *mahasevites* (major volunteers) relish in the honor of
serving as a prasad assistant because of the proximity to Amma (signified by the fact that the shifts are only one or two minutes in duration),

one devotee confessed to me that she dreads prasad sevā because she gets intensely nervous with the pressure of "getting it right" so close to Amma and in the bustle of the darshan process. What was once a clear distinction between Indians and foreigners (largely white) in the local Indian context has now become a difficult, fallible, and problematic process of ethnic identification as the movement expands into more ethnically diverse territories (largely the United States, South America, and Africa).

Another difficulty with which devotees and casual attendees alike must contend emerges from the awkward scenario wherein one receives less than what she or he had anticipated from the darshan experience. Some react by withdrawing from the movement (which is often the case when there are only minimally established ties), while others justify their experiences and continue to be devoted to Amma. Let down by the darshan experience, newcomers often seem befuddled by all of the "hype" surrounding Amma as a divine persona. Many simply go home disappointed or pass the time by wandering the darshan hall and engaging in shopping, Ayurvedic readings, acupuncture, and so on. When newcomers have a disappointing darshan experience, they rarely pursue further involvement in the movement, though they often recall their experience for some time despite its lackluster effects.[45] But when this occurs among ardent devotees, they often interpret it as Amma trying to teach them some spiritual lesson, such as humility or nonattachment, or to focus on their heart instead of their intellect. This last lesson is a particularly common interpretation when devotees approach Amma for darshan while they are intellectualizing the darshan experience, questioning Amma as a guru, analyzing their place in relation to her or her movement, or focusing on getting an answer to a pressing question or concern. Their vacuous darshan experiences then serve as a reprimand for intellectualizing the "heart journey" of spiritual experience, a common theme in Amma's discourses.[46]

The frequently repeated idea that "Amma is simply a mirror reflecting the internal nature of the devotee" supplies another common sentiment used to explain these anomalous negative (or, more commonly, merely vacuous) darshan experiences. In this manner, the responsibility for the nongratifying darshan experience is placed squarely on the shoulders of the darshan taker (the devotee) instead of the darshan giver (Amma). Br. Dayamrita Chaitanya explains that even if devotees are initially unimpressed by the darshan experience, "they may think that they did not receive anything; after a while, what happens is they realize the depth of such things, that experience. It might take them time." Ardent devotees are able to balance a few unmemorable darshan experiences with their memories of uplifting darshan experiences that occurred in the past and their expectations of the same types of rewarding experiences in the future.

The emotional states, preconceived notions, and dispositions of individuals determine their perceptions of the efficacy and the related affective result from their darshan experiences. The darshan embrace that occurs while Amma is otherwise engaged reveals a polarity of interpretations among devotees. But first, to contextualize, Amma receives individuals and families in a constant procession of sequential darshan embraces, each person receiving her attention for just a few moments. However, because Amma presents herself in the public sphere largely through her darshan programs, it is during her successive darshan embraces that she gives interviews to media representatives, arranges business matters with local satsangs, and manages the major decisions of her organization. While she embraces individuals and manages these affairs, she also pays careful attention to the particular details of the program logistics in that location, often calling for particular mahasevites by name with regard to the details of particular tasks. In tandem with these administrative affairs, devotees often present Amma with significant life crises and questions during their darshan embrace. If the circumstance demands more than a simple answer, Amma often directs devotees to stand at her side, where she discusses their problem at length, as she continues to embrace people in the darshan line in front of her. These simultaneously occurring interactions result in the reality that Amma is sometimes engaged in conversations with others while attendees rest in her lap during their darshan embraces.

The darshan experience is deeply colored by individual perception, which is signified by the fact that casual and ardent devotees interpret their experiences differently, and in sometimes oppositional ways. While newcomers to the movement may be disillusioned with Amma's apparent multitasking, ardent devotees relish the lengthier darshans that they receive by simply resting on Amma's breast while she holds discussions with others. Despite the multitudes who surround Amma and demand her attention, at the end of each darshan embrace Amma gives all attendees (regardless of individual distinctions of ethnicity, class, gender, and so on) her absolute, undivided attention for a few moments with a firm grasp, a deep whisper into their ears, and an exchange of prasad. Attendees' differing interpretations of their darshan experiences may stem from the lack of recognition among newcomers that this final moment of undivided attention during darshan is in fact their darshan experience. As one senior devotee explained: "Everything else is extra."

In Chicago (2011), Laura approached me, excited that Amma had placed the top of her head (her center of intellectual activity) right on Amma's heart and held it there constantly while she discussed matters at length with another devotee. Laura was thrilled at this privilege of an extended darshan and thought it significant that Amma was subtly advising her to think with her heart instead of her scattered intellect. Similarly, early on in my research I was resting my face among the rose garlands on Amma's chest when my mind began to wander to the conversation that she was having in Malayalam with a standing devotee immediately above my left shoulder. The conversation seemed to be about the petrol and rickshaw costs at one of her secondary schools in Kerala. Curious (and ever the intellectualizing academic), I shifted my attention from the roses and lifted my head in order to watch and listen more carefully. After a few moments of this type of intellectual voyeurism, Amma looked down and frowned at me. She then quickly pushed my head back down toward the roses, chanted in my ear, and released me from her darshan embrace, sending me on my way. Like Laura, I understood this not-so-subtle reprimand to be her direct message not to neglect the emotive and spiritual aspects of the darshan experience in favor of the intellectual. Amma's message does not support a wholesale anti-intellectualism, but it is certainly an undercurrent to her discourses that focus so attentively on heartfelt love and compassion above all else.

Another devotee initially interpreted her lackluster darshan critically but then, in hindsight, rationalized the experience. "Feeling a nervous excitement, I joined the queue. When I reached Amma's arms, she whispered something into my ear and pressed her cheek to my cheek. She was talking to a man next to her at the same time, and I was put off by this seeming lack of attention. 'You should do your job with more sincerity,' I thought to myself. I was disappointed." Understood in this type of negative valence, some attendees emerge from Amma's embrace unimpressed or even disillusioned. Others, as in this particular account, conclude with a buttressing of their faith in Amma's omnipotence, thinking simulacra of the idea that, "Of course, I did not know [then] that Amma could pay attention to many people at the same time, giving each one exactly what was needed."[47] The variances in interpretation of the darshan experience often solidify the commonplace belief among devotees that the guru functions as a mirror, reflecting that which devotees present to her. Amma and the administration of the movement also support this interpretation. For example, a recent e-newsletter ran the front-page story with an exchange from the question-and-answer session during the San Ramon retreat in 2011: "One devotee asked Amma 'why does Amma gets more beautiful and younger, year after year, while we get old and ugly, as years pass by?' Amma explained that the beauty you see in Amma, is actually the reflection of the love you have for Amma."[48]

DARSHAN IN ABSENTIA

For the significant majority of attendees at Amma's darshan programs, the opportunity to release their burdens in her embrace presents itself only once or twice a year. Though a miniscule percentage of North American attendees regularly attend congregational gatherings (*satsangs*) (.01 percent), many reserve time during the lengthy darshan programs to purchase a photograph of Amma at the expansive tables where hundreds of images of Amma are sold in the posterior of the darshan hall.[49] These photographs then often become placeholders for Amma in their home altars, sacred spaces, or eclectic arrangements of spiritual ephemera. Notably, photographic images of Amma represent the visual reminder of her ideal of love and compassion, even for those attendees who may not inculcate themselves fully within the religiosity of Amma's movement and message. For other more ardent devotees, visual representations of Amma serve as lifeboats and lily pads, proximate reminders of her constant guidance and presence in their lives that sustain them until her next visit.

The twentieth-century German philosopher Walter Benjamin famously argued that the photograph reactivates the object reproduced but cannot reproduce the "aura" of authenticity of the original.[50] In this case Amma's presence is brought into devotees' living rooms, offices, vehicles, and so on through photographic representations in an effort to reactivate her presence therein. Still, such representations are at the end of the day merely representations—they cannot effectively reproduce Amma's "aura" nor an authentic, deeply personal experience of her presence. As mere representations, they suffice to remind devotees of that intimate sense of authenticity that they tactilely receive through her darshan embrace. Notably, herein the photographic image is not dislocated from its initial ritual function, as Benjamin argues it has been in the transition from paintings to photographs, but, rather, the photographic representation is reinserted as a proximate value of an embodied entity, which is often used in ritual contexts as a proxy for that entity. Devotees sacralize photographs of Amma through worship; as such, these photographs are representational placeholders for devotees who use them for their personal, emotive, and ritual efficacy as reminders of Amma.

Amma's most fervent devotees usually surround themselves with multiple photographic images and renderings of her that they place on their home altars, bodies, cars, offices, and computers, with the purpose of sacralizing these spaces and reminding them of Amma's message. Small photos of Amma's feet, linked to the well-established Hindu tradition of venerating the feet of the deity or guru, are most often found on devotees' home altars, though they appear elsewhere. Devotees often have a favorite image of Amma; the majority of ardent devotees have an enlarged photograph of that image in the center of their home altars. Photos and artistic renderings of Amma may be purchased at her darshan programs and at the online Amma shop. One can even arrange with Amma's audiovisual personnel to purchase a photograph of her or his own individual darshan experience (or interaction with Amma during special rituals [*pujas*], or moments) for a suggested donation, though this service is not advertised publicly. Amma's organization tightly regulates the dissemination of photographs of her; all cameras and audio and video recorders are strictly forbidden on Amma's ashram grounds and in darshan halls. These restrictions are in place for the general public in an effort to prevent Amma's darshan from developing into a touristic experience, wherein camera flashes would envelop the atmosphere and each attendee would have someone take a photo during her or his individual darshan experience. Notably, with Amma's permission, some members of the press and documentarians are allowed to photograph and film her. Still, while such practicalities and provisions are in place, these restrictions also enable Amma's organization to control the crafting of Amma's public image and the potential profits from the reproduction and commodification of her image.

Devotees who yearn for virtual proximity to Amma often pray to her photographic images and talk to them. Some believe Amma's presence is felt in the environment in which the photos are displayed. The imagery of Amma becomes a mediating tool in her physical absence, though the most ardent devotees would explain that Amma is never truly absent from any space because of her divine omnipresence. Nevertheless, adorning one's environment with images of Amma provides devotees with a sense of her physical presence and guidance in their everyday lives. In our conversations, some devotees recounted occasions when these iconographic images "responded" to their interactions with them by turning upside down, falling to the floor, or becoming three-dimensional. Although these events are not heavily emphasized in the movement as they are among Sai Baba devotees, for some Amma devotees they serve as validation that Amma is truly present in their lives, guiding them in their daily decisions and relationships.

For other devotees, the chance encounter with a photograph of Amma becomes an opportunity for personal transformation. Many devotees related transformative moments in their lives in which they were presented with, or stumbled across, a visual image of Amma that inspired them to learn more about her and eventually to seek her out. Bhavana Upadhyaya, in her recent doctoral dissertation on Amma, states that during a hospital visit, when she "was in a deep personal crisis and in despair about life," a nurse gave her a newspaper photo of Amma that appeared to her like a "beacon of hope."[51] Devotees often recounted similar moments in which a photo of Amma on a colleague's desk, in a newspaper, in a vehicle, or at a friend's home resonated with them to such a degree that afterward they sought out Amma in person. The devotees who related these stories to me often interpreted such events as Amma's divine intervention. They said Amma "appeared" and "called" them to experience her presence and message.

Because Amma interacts with her devotees through darshan in the tactile experience of an embrace, in her absence many devotees long for this physical contact with the guru. In response to this longing, Amma's organization created a unique form of Amma iconography: Amma dolls. Amma dolls are sold at darshan programs and at the online Amma shop; they come in three sizes (small, medium, and large) and vary in price from $45 to $180. Devotees purchase special clothing for their Amma dolls; Devī Bhāva outfits are particularly popular. The doll makers (brahmacāriṇīs residing at Amma's ashrams) hand sew each Amma doll, stuff it with Devī Bhāva rose petals, and adorn it with clothing and embellishments from materials that Amma has worn on Devī Bhāva nights. Prior to their sale, Amma specially blesses each doll. Still, many devotees bring their Amma dolls with them to Amma's darshan programs to have them specially blessed by Amma; upon the devotees' request, Amma will adorn their doll's forehead with a sandalwood dot (ṭīkā) during darshan. In addition to Amma dolls, the doll makers recently expanded their repertoire to include the production of Kali,

FIGURE 6. Amma doll (large), dressed in *Devī Bhāva* accoutrements (author photo)

Shiva, Radha, Krishna, and Jesus dolls (ranging in price from $75 to $250). Selva Raj notes, "The Amma dolls also represent the creative and innovative synthesis of Hindu image culture and American popular culture and market economy. The economic implications of this emphasis on physicality are no less significant, as these items generate sizeable revenue for the movement."[52] While photos and Amma dolls certainly generate income for Amma's organization, they are by no means its primary, or even a significant, income source (see figure 6).

Instead, devotees keep Amma dolls as mediating representatives of Amma's spiritual power and presence that become even more important in her absence. Amma dolls also provide devotees with the opportunity to care for them as if they were Amma herself. They can dote on them, dress them, place food and drink before them, and decorate them with finery. For many devotees, these dolls *are* Amma. One devotee explains:

> These little "Angels" are Mother's gift of love and healing to all who are open to their blessings. Sometimes I take her off the top of my bedroom bookshelf and meditate with her in my lap (bliss). Other times, I need only to gaze at her form to feel her with me and loving me. Sometimes, I need a hug from her and that same feeling of all-accepting love and softness is there. It is as if she is my little piece of Mother.[53]

The "first aid" tent for Amma dolls at darshan programs makes clear the extent to which devotees identify their Amma dolls with Amma herself. Early on in my field research, I walked past a brahmacāriṇī meticulously repairing an Amma doll behind a large trifold cardboard screen erected at the front of her sewing table. Boldly, I asked the seamstress, "Why do you put up the screen? Is it because people would feel funny seeing you take apart their Amma doll?" She raised her head from her sewing, looked at me as though I were completely dense, and said, "Well, of course! This is like an ICU!" I was initially surprised at her vehement reaction, but I should not have been. In Hindu traditions there are strict rules regarding how one should treat and ultimately dispose of a representation of a deity. For example, ideally, both two- and three-dimensional deity representations should be submerged in water (a river or well) to ensure that they never come into contact with human feet or other forms of impurities. In addition, in Hindu religious practice it is customary to adorn, dote on, and feed figurines (*murtis*), which are viewed as physical embodiments of deities. For devotees, Amma dolls should be treated with the same reverence and respect that would be given to other Hindu images of the divine. The practice of adorning, doting on, and even worshipping Amma dolls as proximate deity representations likely has some relation to many of the Vaisnava traditions of India, in which the religious decorate and adorn small doll-like figurines of Krishna, including the most popular, the baby Krishna (Bala Gopala), for worship, particularly during Krishna's annual birthday celebrations (Janmashtami).

The sanctity surrounding religious iconography (and Amma dolls) derives from the belief that the deity inheres in its image. Iconographic representations are believed to become increasingly powerful through the darshan process as devotees (and Amma, through her blessing) infuse them with power. Devotees believe that Amma's blessing magnifies her presence in every Amma doll, and they tend to bring their Amma dolls for individual blessings when they receive darshan. According to popular understanding in Amma's movement, the more the devotee cherishes the doll, prays to it, and worships Amma through it, the stronger Amma's presence in it will become. The Amma doll activates Amma's presence in devotees' lives. As Copeman and Ikegame rightly suggest, "The Amma doll seems not to dilute her aura [as Benjamin might have argued] but to reactivate it at home."[54] It also fulfills the tactile and corporeal void created between the experience of Amma's darshan embrace and the interaction with two-dimensional photographic representations of her that, to put it simply, devotees cannot hug.

The majority of devotees with whom I interacted sought to reactivate Amma's presence through the placement and adornment of two- and three-dimensional representations of Amma's physical body. However, other devotees superimposed their own preferred understanding of divinity onto Amma, viewing her as a black Madonna, the Sri Yantra, or a particular Hindu goddess personified, and so on. Traveling with Amma on her North Indian tour, Judith Cornell desired Amma's affirmation that Amma was in fact the Sri Yantra. Originally a tantric symbol, the Sri Yantra is an abstract symbol of the feminine energy of the universe. Convinced of this idea, she writes, "How could I explain to her [Amma] that I had been intuitively led to believe that *she* was the full embodiment of what the Sri Yantra symbol represented? As twilight waned, it took all my courage to boldly pose the intuition as a direct question. 'Amma, you *are* the Sri Yantra, is this not true?' She [Amma] bowed her head and very quietly said, 'Yes, yes, yes.'"[55] Many Śakta Tantric practitioners in the Śrī Vidyā tradition worship the goddess Lalitā through the Śrī Yantra. As I discuss in the next chapter, Amma often equates herself with—and others equate her with—the goddess Lalitā. Still, this anecdote probably tells us much more about Judith Cornell and her visions of Amma as a devotee than it tells us about Amma's identity. Remember, the commonly iterated position among devotees referenced previously is that which devotees see in Amma is in actuality a reflection of themselves.

Beyond physical embraces and representational images, many devotees also related to me that they connect with Amma through dreams and meditational states. These intersubjective states of consciousness are ripe for devotees who long for guidance in their lives, and thus they find signs and suggestions in their liminally conscious states. In Indic thought, dream states are often significant allegorical images for meditative states. Upaniṣadic texts establish four states of being: waking, dreaming, dreamless sleep (all natural states), and the supernatural, transcendent fourth state: unity with the Godhead. The two intermediary states (between waking and the transcendence of self) give the practitioner glimpses of the gods, for example, Vishnu or Rudra, who create (dreaming), or of *brahman*, who does not create (dreamless sleep).[56] In upaniṣadic thought, human error causes the perception that we are most engaged in reality when in a waking state, while we perceive the other three stages to be progressively more illusory. In contrast, the upaniṣadic authors argue, it is just the opposite. Instead, reality is the transcendence of the self in unity with the Godhead, and the remaining three stages are progressively more illusory. In this view, waking is the most illusory state, a kind of dream, whereas unity with the Godhead represents ultimate reality. The upaniṣadic philosophers point to the frequent confusion of waking, dreamless sleep, and dreaming as suggestive of their illusory unity and their ultimate disjunction from the ultimately real state of unity with the Godhead. According to this reasoning, the progression from illusion to reality is waking, to dreaming, to dreamless sleep, and finally to the ultimate reality of unity with the Godhead. Thus dreaming realities are in a sense more real than waking realities. In dreams one sees both the real (*sat*) and the unreal (*asat*); it is this liminal nature of dreaming realities that imbues dreams with such a powerful valence in Indic thought.[57]

In everyday life, dreams are significant for many devotees within Amma's devotional milieu. Many North American devotees may have absorbed such upaniṣadic ideas through the warp and woof of Indic culture, while others may be influenced by the popular intersection of American spirituality and dream analysis, with roots in Western psychology. Some devotees draw parallels between other religious traditions, such as Native American traditions, in which visions and dreaming are significant forms of supernatural communication with humanity. The strong majority of devotees with whom I interacted were not only acutely aware of their own mental and physical processes (like dreaming), but they also instilled meaning into even seemingly insignificant events. The commonplace adage "everything happens for a reason" colored their realities so completely that the probabilities of chance, chaos, or a random occurrence had little to no explanatory place value in their lives. For these devotees, events occurred because of karmic disposition, or because they are "part of Amma's divine plan," or "the universe is sending a message." These events could be as minute as finding a parking space or stubbing one's toe or as significant as acquiring gainful employment, birthing a severely handicapped child, or meeting a suitable spouse. Thus in a world in which there are no accidents, seeing Amma in a dream cannot be dismissed as a chance occurrence. There must be a message therein, and devotees (and would-be devotees) will likely seek to uncover it.

Visitation by the gods characterizes dreaming states of consciousness in Indic dream theory. Divinities of the Hindu pantheon often enter into the dream states of mortals. In fact, the goddess Kali first appears in her contemporary form in the dreams of the Pandava brothers in *Mahābhārata* (10.8.64–65). Such divine interventions may relay important and even practical messages. For example, when Swami Paramatmananda was becoming increasingly frustrated with some of the residents at the Amritapuri ashram, he had a dream, which he recounts as follows:

> I saw Ammachi looking at me with the full moon shining in the sky to her left and the sun shining to her right. She pointed at the sun and said, "Do you see the bright ray of the sun? Like that ray, try to see the ray of Divine Light in each one's eyes."[58]

Through Amma's admonitions in this dream, he recognized the futility of his frustrations with the residents' behavior. Visitations by Amma in dreams may not only deliver divine messages, but devotees believe that they may also contain glimpses of ultimate reality, signified by the transcendent experience of unity with the Godhead. Thus dream encounters with Amma are highly valued darshan experiences among devotees; many devotees routinely told me stories of dream encounters with their guru. Devotees with whom I conversed viewed dreams that included Amma not as chance occurrences, bringing their deep unconscious to liminally conscious states, but, rather, as emblematic of Amma's ability to appear metaphysically or her powers of paranormal teleportation to interact with her devotees through their dreams. Numerous gurus in the modern period, including Anandamayi Ma, Sai Baba, Srila Prabhupada, and Yogananda, also visited their devotees in dream states of consciousness, according to devotees' accounts.

Perhaps even more interesting, however, are the narratives of devotees who relate events in which the guru first appeared to them in dream states prior to their knowledge of or physical encounter with the guru. Several devotees related stories about how they first dreamed of a dark-skinned woman in a white sari and then only later recognized that dream image in a photograph or met Amma in person. While we were sitting under the night stars at the San Ramon ashram, Maya, a beautiful African American mother in her late thirties, with a bohemian style, told me about how she first met Amma. She explained, "I had a dream about Amma. She came to me in a dream. I dreamed she came to me and told me to surrender and three days later one of her devotees called me out of the blue and said do you want to go see Amma. And of course I said yeah—I want to go see Amma—and I didn't know who she was at the time." Later in the interview, she elaborated on this story:

> Amma saved my life. When I dreamt about Amma, I was suicidal. . . . I wanted to leave the planet and if it had not been for Amma I probably would have. I think on one side it was Amma and on the other side my daughter. If it hadn't been for the push-pull of the two of them—you know, like the maiden and the crone or the goddess, then I would have just fallen through the cracks really. So there is nothing anybody could say that could turn me against Amma. [See], it is not part of African American tradition to go to a psychiatrist. . . . So I had to go to that place alone and with Amma. There were many days that I just cried and cried and cried and cried. So she saved my life. I mean I saved my life, but if she had not been holding me and I hadn't had that—her to just know. Like what she says "I'll never forsake you, I'll never let you go." And I believed her. . . . And I dreamt of her during that period and in the dream she just said, "surrender my child, surrender." . . . I didn't even know what it meant. Now of course, coming here, she teaches surrender.

In Maya's narrative, her dream of Amma (prior to her initial physical encounter with her) mirrors the core impulse of the darshan experience, which encourages devotees to surrender by becoming like little children in the arms of an unconditionally loving mother. Amma encouraged Maya to release her mental and psychological burdens during this metaphysical dream state of consciousness as well as later during her first darshan experience. This metaphysical release of burdens then recurred in the physical darshan experience that Maya sought out several days after her first dream-state encounter with Amma. While the skeptics will certainly view such narratives as fabrications, psychological imaginings, or coincidences, for devotees they are nothing less than Amma's divine interventions, and, as in Maya's case, such paranormal events often instill in them an unwavering faith in Amma.

THE QUEST FOR AUTHENTICITY

While darshan experiences in absentia provide a proximate experience of Amma's darshan, devotees long for the aura of authenticity of the original, to be in Amma's presence and to feel the experience of her darshan. This longing for unmediated contact with the divinity that devotees believe to be present in Amma characterizes their desire to remain in the movement. Both Indian Hindus and American metaphysicals who follow Amma long for her darshan because they believe in the authenticity of the experience. The intimate physicality of Amma's darshan reinforces their belief that Amma is an authentic guru and divine incarnation, a quality that she demonstrates through darshan in unmediated, tactile, and emotionally overwhelming ways.

Indian Hindu diasporic communities in the United States are in many ways engaged in an endless search for authentic Indian experiences. Among the elites in Indian Hindu communities in America, weddings often aim for not only opulence but for a cultural and religious connectivity to India, the communal display of which functions as a form of social capital.[59] From another angle, many families whose children are engaged in the study of classical Indian music take advantage of the immediacy of globalized telecommunications networks by hiring Indian classical music gurus to teach their children via Skype and online audiovisual interfaces. Radha Hegde argues that these new systems of transnational virtual pedagogy are furthered through diasporic communities' desires for Indian authenticity, represented here through the process of learning from an Indian guru in India. The participants in this reinvention of the guru-disciple relationship as a transnational experience view authenticity as something they can "feel" when learning from an Indian guru. Authenticity is a feeling; for these diasporic communities, it is a feeling of Indianness.[60] The search for authenticity influences their choice of wedding music, venue, attire, decorations, and goods, as well as their choice of classical music gurus, to provide just two disparate examples.

But the search for authentic experiences is not limited to Indian diaspora populations alone. Many have argued that authenticity is an emerging desire for postmodern consumers in general. In a book offering strategies for the business community Gilbert and Pine (2007) argue that businesses must add authenticity ("authenticity of experience") to the old tripartite model of quality, cost, and availability. The back cover of the book reads, "The more contrived the world seems, the more we all demand what's real. As reality is qualified, altered, and commercialized, consumers respond to what is engaging, personal, memorable— and above all authentic."[61] Such statements appear to follow on the heels of critical theorists such as Jean Baudrillard, whose concept of the "hyperreal" attempts to capture the contemporary expression of postmodernity wherein reality becomes mere simulacra. The cacophony of simulations of reality (media images, photographs, cartography, and so on) supplants the real, creating a postmodernity in which the real is wholly replaced by its simulations. In such a postmodernity, the search for authenticity becomes a search for the real. This may be a futile search. Baudrillard suggests that there has been an eclipse of the possibility of the presence of any real behind or underneath its multiple simulations; the simulacra have effectively replaced the real to the extent that the real becomes obliterated, inaccessible.[62] Nevertheless, it is the experience of the real, the experience of the authentic, that devotees seek in Amma's embrace. If authenticity is felt through affective, visceral, and corporeal experiences, then the emotive bodily experience of the embrace amplifies the feeling of immediate access to such authenticity. Feeling the void of the simulacra surrounding them, devotees seek out real experiences of authenticity, which many believe they find in Amma's embrace.

In contemporary guru movements, the search for an "authentic" guru has additional importance because of the nefarious legacy of scandal and corruption that has plagued many transnational global movements throughout history. The majority of Amma's North American devotees have encountered such movements and charismatic leaders mired in scandal. Many have turned away from these gurus, disillusioned and skeptical about the whole arena of transnational guru movements. Even if devotees have not been disillusioned by "fake" gurus or directly impacted by guru scandals, they still exist within a religious milieu in which such occurrences are commonplace. As a result, many approach the prospect of mental and emotional immersion in Amma's movement with initial feelings of skepticism, reserved behavior, and timidity.

Darshan, usually one of devotees' primary encounters with Amma, presents devotees with an immediate, tactile experience. Devotees are encouraged to feel for themselves the experience of authenticity through Amma's embrace. For them, Amma's unconditional darshan signifies an emblematic new paradigm of Hindu religiosity as well as a utopian representation of unconditional love, one that is orchestrated in tandem with their humanistic values of the potential of all persons to experience and commune with the divine without the interventions of priestly (or brahmanical) authorities. It is through the darshan embrace itself that many devotees not only return Amma's embrace but embrace her as an authentic guru. As Dhara relates about her first darshan experience: "I was such a skeptic, not cynical necessarily, but skeptic[al]. . . . But in this experience [her first darshan] I could tell that she was real, she wasn't a charlatan." For the initially wary, like Dhara and a significant number of other newcomers, their first encounter with Amma's darshan is a barometric measure of Amma's authenticity, which they discern through their immediate, personal, affective, and bodily experience. It is usually after this first immersion experience that devotees begin to populate their environment with representational photographic images of Amma to reactivate the presencing and possibility of what they perceive to be the authentic experience with the real in their lives.

Newcomers to the movement may test Amma's authenticity during darshan, but ardent devotees experience authenticity by recognizing Amma and presenting themselves to be recognized as similarly authentic selves through the darshan experience. Herein, devotees desire acknowledgment, the acknowledgment of their own struggles and desires, interior experiences, and self-understanding. This momentary exchange of recognition is the acknowledgment of individual authenticities, an ultimate attempt to dissolve the division between individuals, forming a cosmic unity. Framing darshan in this language of recognition, acknowledgment, and authenticity suggests potentially interesting parallels within the dialectical exchanges in contemporary discourses of multiculturalism. In discourses of multiculturalism, authenticity links directly to the ideal of a social identity that one represents (and by which one is represented) in the public sphere. Herein, it is the presentation of an individual and social identity as an authentic self, derived from a romanticist ideal of autonomous identity formation and presentation. As Charles Taylor summarizes, "Being true to myself means being true to my own originality, which is something only I can articulate and discover. In articulating it, I am also defining myself. I am realizing a potentiality that is properly my own. This is the background understanding to the modern ideal of authenticity, and to the goals of self-fulfillment and self-realization in which the ideal is usually couched."[63] Locating such an individuated personal and social identity becomes essential for those who desire to participate in the multiculturalist processes of representation.

Formulated in this way, Taylor argues for a politics of recognition, in which through social encounter the individual (or state) recognizes the other in its presentation of an authentic self. But recognition also shapes our identity, as does its antithesis, *mis*recognition.[64] Critics to such formulations of multiculturalism as a politics of recognition argue against the ways in which the demand for autonomous identity has the potential to flatten and essentialize individuals and cultures into their most salient or visible features. As such, the demand for recognition of a cultural identity in particular inserts boundaries and standards that define what it means to be a member of that culture. As K. Anthony Appiah explains, "Demanding respect for people as blacks and as gays requires that there are some scripts that go with being an African-American or having same-sex desires. There will be proper ways of being black and gay, there will be expectations to be met, demands will be made. It is at this point that someone who takes autonomy seriously will ask whether we have not replaced one kind of tyranny with another."[65] Recognition implies a fixed self that recognizes, through certain qualities and attributes, the existence of the other. The often-cited and most problematic notions within the politics of recognition are this imagined fixity of autonomous, sovereign, and authentic identities and the ways in which the object of recognition must have the attributes of designated qualities in order to be recognized. As such, the politics of recognition presents the possibility of essentializing and even solidifying extant cultural stereotypes; it is "a multiculturalism that demands a performance of authenticity."[66]

One such critic, Kelly Oliver, argues instead for an alternative model of a politics of "witnessing," in which one experiences and responds to one's connection to and dependence on others while bearing witness to the ways in which injustices inform this relation.[67] The term *witnessing* holds multiple valences in legal, social justice, and Christian contexts. Here, I restrict my use of the term to follow Oliver's intent, wherein a politics of witnessing rejects the autonomy of the subject and accepts an interactive, mutually dependent, and fluctuating relationship to others in the maintenance of subjectivity. For Oliver, such witnessing intimately relates to the ideal of love, which suggests a move toward others, across differences, an openness to otherness that inherently involves a turn toward others.[68] It is precisely this loving openness between the self and the other, as well as the active process of witnessing, that characterizes devotees' experiences of Amma's darshan. I have described devotees' longing for darshan as a desire to see and be seen and as a desire for recognition, but Oliver's critique suggests that this analysis must push beyond recognition and move into the languages of love and witnessing of the other.

Within the term *recognition* lies a chasmic space between the self and the other; there is an identified autonomous self that recognizes a demarcated and bounded other. It is this process of recognition that prasad assistants are encouraged to enact as they filter the darshan queue into "Indian" and "Western" devotees. But the darshan experience, like the concept of witnessing, attempts to dissolve the distance between the self and the other. Witnessing occurs in the inevitable presence of the dependence on others and one's connection to others. As Oliver says:

> If we reconceive of recognition from a notion of vision that emphasizes the fullness of space and the connections—interdependence even—between the visible world and vision, between the seer and the seen, then we begin to move away from the Hegelian struggle for recognition and toward the acknowledgement of otherness. Starting from this alternative notion of vision, otherness or others are not forever cut off from subjects or seers, threatening alienation and annihilation. Rather the gaps or spaces between us open up the very possibility of communication and communion. Vision itself becomes a process, a becoming, rather than the sovereign of recognition. Vision becomes a circulation of energy between and among rather than an artificial and inadequate bridge between a subject and an alien world.[69]

Amma's transformation of darshan from a visual encounter between the self and the other to a tactile experience of the other animates a similar reimagining of the role of recognition and vision. The multisensory experience of darshan expands the visual into such connective regions that open to the presencing of the self in the other and the other in the self. The "circulation of energy between and among" the self and the other characterizes the darshan experience that attempts to dissolve the subject/object dichotomy. Amma's darshan signifies the performative act of connectivity and presencing that such a politics of witnessing aspires to elucidate.

CONCLUSION

My repeated encounters with hundreds of devotees in the environs of Amma's darshan experiences suggest there is something vital in precisely this experience as a "process, a becoming." During darshan, devotees long to be seen by Amma just as much as they desire to see Amma. They long for precisely this "circulation of energy between and among" in their intimate embrace with Amma. They desire to be witnessed and comforted in Amma's embrace, validated as individuals with existence, importance, and special qualities. As much as this may contradict the darshan goal of the subordination of the self in fusion with the divine, it is an extant desire expressed by many devotees, which derives from the bounded attachments and grasping nature of the ego. Devotees exhibit these ego-driven attachments in subtle mannerisms of self-congratulation and pride that they take on when Amma bestows special treasures on them through darshan (an apple, a conversation, a longer moment of connection) and their envy, jealousies, and frustrations when she does not. Many devotees are self-aware enough to see the folly in such pride, but for others it is all too easy to get wrapped up in the desire for recognition by the guru and to miss the intention of the darshan experience. The temptation to jockey for recognition through the darshan experience may derive from the suggestion that such moments of recognition fulfill a painful void instigated by the misrecognitions and nonrecognitions that occur in the routine interpersonal interactions of daily life.

Devotees again and again recounted their experiences of emotive relief at being seen, understood, and witnessed during darshan. They consistently explained with confidence that "Amma sees everything"; "She knows me better than I know myself"; and "Amma saw right into my soul." The emotive responses of many during and after their darshan experiences exhibit the intimacy inherent in this mutual seeing. In postmodern capitalist societies, the commonplace inquiry into the well-being of another has developed a level of superficiality, demanded by the quickening pace of globalization, consumer culture, and capital-driven markets, to which the individual submits and reifies as a matter of both necessity and convention. As a result, the inherent intimacy in even a few moments of direct immediate connection engenders more intense personal witnessing than many devotees experience in their mundane activities of worldly experience. The intense immediate witnessing that devotees attain (or believe themselves to attain) through the darshan experience often generates overwhelming emotions that they exhibit through tears, a sense of contentment, laughter, and love.

With that said, it is important to note that the intensity of such a visual and bodily exchange also causes unease and discomfort in those who are unprepared and/or unwilling to engage in such revealing acts of intimate connection. For some, the superficial connections of everyday interactions with others have become so routinized that the visual and physical intimacy inherent within the darshan experience demands too much connection and revelation of the inner self. Those who feel as such largely distance themselves from this intimacy by reserving emotive responses, not wholly engaging in the darshan experience, or rejecting the darshan experience. For these attendees, darshan is just a hug, a transient superficial physical connection that will not likely make them want to return to Amma's programs as devotees.

But for those who do return again and again, the intensity of their longing to be seen and witnessed intimately and wholly sustains one of the powerful intimating factors in their continued devotions. These devotees also believe darshan to be a transformative event; by repeated contact with Amma, they believe themselves to be gradually transforming into better, and more spiritual, human beings. They contend that the darshan experience brings them closer to mirroring Amma's divine persona and absorbing her spiritual power, and that the more frequently repeated, the greater the intensity of the transformation. The narratives that Amma's devotees relate about the darshan experience highlight their beliefs in darshan as a symbolic fusion between deity and disciple. Amma's unique darshan process of an embrace amplifies these feelings of the active dissolution of the subject/object dichotomy. Devotees recount that in the darshan experience "time stood still"; they "lost consciousness" of the distinctions between their two bodies; and they "melt and dissolve" feeling as though they are "diving into an endless something and losing [themselves]." The spiritual transformations invoked in these recollections suggest that devotees come to Amma for darshan embraces not only to see her but for a physical and visceral experience of mutual witnessing that transforms their realities and heightens their spiritual proclivities.

Devī Bhāva

Revelation and Performance of the Guru as Goddess

Mother is not manifesting even an infinitesimal part of her spiritual power during the Bhavas. If it were to be manifested as it is, no one could come near! . . . All the deities of the Hindu Pantheon, who represent the numberless aspects of the One Supreme Being, exist within us. A Divine Incarnation can manifest any of them by mere will for the good of the world. Krishna Bhava is the manifestation of the Purusha or Pure Being aspect, and Devi Bhava is the manifestation of the Eternal Feminine, the Creatrix, the active principle of the Impersonal Absolute. Here is a crazy girl who puts on the garb of Krishna and after some time that of Devi, but it is within this crazy girl that both exist. However, it should be remembered that all objects having a name or form are mere mental projections. Why decorate an elephant? Why should a lawyer wear a black coat or why does a policeman wear a uniform and a cap? All of these are merely external aids meant to create a certain impression. In a like manner, Mother dons the garb of Krishna and Devi in order to give strength to the devotional attitude of the people coming for Darshan. The Atman or Self that is in me is also within you. If you can realize that Indivisible Principle that is ever shining in you, you will become That.[1]

—Mata Amritanandamayi

When Amma tours the United States, her two- and three-day *darshan*[2] programs in each city conclude with *Devī Bhāva*, an elaborate, festive, celebration of the goddess, wherein Amma presents herself as the goddess adorned in goddess regalia. In San Ramon, California, during the summer tour, Amma may host two Devī Bhāva programs during her lengthier stay at her primary American ashram. Newcomers and those unfamiliar with the idea of Devī Bhāvas (or even Hindu goddesses) may only notice that on Devī Bhāva nights Amma wears a silver crown and an elaborate, gold-brocaded, vibrantly colored sari instead of her usual ascetic garb of a simple white sari. Fliers for these special public programs describe Devī Bhāva as simply "a ceremony in honor of the Divine Mother."[3] But acculturated devotees may see aspects of the goddess manifest in Amma as she performs Devī Bhāva; for example, many believe that they see a darkening of her skin, resembling Kali's blue-black pigmentation. Devī Bhāvas have a long history in Hindu religious environments and in Amma's back story beyond what is currently presented to American audiences; these are the thematic strands that this chapter aims to elucidate (see figure 7).

In *The Madness of the Saints*, June McDaniel contends "*Bhāva* [defined as "spiritual ecstasy"] is the major criterion for female saints and holy women in Bengal, for religious experience is the basis for their religious status."[4] Women often implement bhāvas (emotive states of divine inspiration and ecstasy) to create arenas in which they are able to acquire power and respect as religious virtuosos. There is significant evidence, throughout India, that female ascetics and holy women who are barred from leadership roles in traditional forums of institutionalized Hinduism often acquire religious authority through the revelation of their divine personas through bhāvas. In fact, the presence of bhāva often determines whether a person is considered to possess the charisma of sainthood.[5] Many female Hindu ascetics in India garner religious authority (at least initially) by embodying the goddess (or another deity—usually Krishna) through bhāvas, during which they transgress social boundaries and assert their assumed divine powers. The ninth-century Tamil saint-poetess Āṇṭāl was a Krishna devotee who declared herself the bride of God and identified with the *gopīs* (cowherdesses) during her ecstatic states. Lalleshwarī, the fourteenth-century saint-poetess of Kashmir, who wandered India half-naked, dancing in ecstasy, wholly identified with God in her bhāvas. In the sixteenth century, there was Mirabai, who fell in madly in love with Krishna and wandered in devotion between bhāvas and poetry. In the nineteenth century, Sarada Devi, Ramakrishna's wife and spiritual counterpart, was often worshipped during bhāvas as the mother goddess Lalitā. In the early twentieth century, Anandamayi Ma, the Bengali mystic was worshipped as Kali and

FIGURE 7. Kali *murti* with *Devī Bhāva* accoutrements, Kali temple altar, Amritapuri, India (© MA Center)

had body-defying bhāvas; and in the later twentieth century, Amma is worshipped as Kali and Lalitā and exhibits bhāvas of Krishna, Kali, and Devi. All of these women have become famous through their bhāvas, to name only a select and internationally famous few.

That is not to say that women are the only religious exemplars who enact emotive states of divine ecstasy. This is far from the case. Chaitanya, Rupa Gosvamin, and Ramakrishna are only three among many exemplary male Hindu religious adepts whose bhāvas characterize their

gendered bhavas

religious virtuosity.[6] However, the difference is that without bhāvas, men have a variety of other established avenues through which to gain religious authority, whereas women do not. The contemporary practices of bhāva are also supported by extensive textual enumerations, primarily derived from Vaiṣṇava and Śakta Tantra traditions. The *Bhaktirasāmṛtasindhu* of Rūpa Gosvāmin lays the foundation for the five bhāvas of the Vaiṣṇava tradition, while the *Mahānirvāṇa* and *Kulārṇava Tantras* do the same for the three bhāvas in the Śakta Tantric tradition.[7]

→ who gets primed to be a guru? Do you pick ur guru?

In her introduction to *The Graceful Guru*, Karen Pechilis suggests that a defining characteristic of a guru in the Hindu tradition is that "a guru is understood to experience the real continuously. Most often, the real is defined as *brahman*, which among many possible meanings, denotes the subtle, sacred essence that pervades the universe."[8] According to this contention, the continual state of consciousness of the guru differs from that of ordinary humans. Bhāvas are temporary events (often ecstatic) in which the guru reveals this higher state of consciousness, his or her actuality as a divine persona, for the witnessing public. Some suggest that the guru *as guru*, because of his or her higher state of consciousness, will be able to control such bhāvas. But the lived experiences of many famous female gurus (Gauri Ma, Anandamayi Ma, Jayashri Ma, Amma) suggest that even among such eminent figures, controlling bhāvas is a gradual, tenuous, and not inevitable process.[9] For example, when Anandamayi Ma (1896–1982) first fell into ecstatic bhāvas during *kirtan* (devotional music) performances, she turned to her host and said, "I do not know what my body is doing." The host sprinkled her with water and fanned her but soon called her relatives to take her home.[10] Many women who later developed into world-renowned gurus developed their religious personas through bhāvas that they could not initially control and that those in their immediate circles initially believed to be evidence of mental illness, possession, or erratic behavior. In many cases, but not all, it is within the transition from religious adept to codified guru that the individual develops increasing control over ecstatic states of consciousness.

1. Like many of her female contemporaries, Amma's early Kali bhāvas were an ecstatic and even violent exhibition of power resembling village goddess possession rituals. Over time, Amma transformed these wild transgressions into Devī Bhāvas, enacted through a beautified and docile representation of the goddess incarnate suited to the tastes of her middle-class bourgeois Indian and Western audiences. Amma's bhāvas

(first Krishna bhāvas, then Kali bhāvas, and then Devī Bhāvas) became effective tools through which she was able to claim divine status and validate that status through their repeated performance. Very self-consciously, Amma explains that she enacts Devī Bhāvas "in order to give strength to the devotional attitude of the people coming for Darshan."[11] Devotees believe that Devī Bhāvas represent Amma in her true nature as the goddess. Her decorated appearance in goddess regalia encourages her devotees to worship her in that form. Devī Bhāvas present a performance through which she jointly enacts and reinforces her exalted status as a goddess incarnate.

But how has this come about? Amma's claims to be a goddess incarnation mean nothing without her devotees who ascribe that status to her. Her religious authority is dependent on her devotees who believe she is what she claims to be. Bruce Lincoln's argument about nature of authority may provide some useful tools in understanding the importance of bhāvas, particularly for women, who aspire to exalted religious positions of authority. He explains, "It [authority] is best understood in relational terms as the effect of a posited, perceived, or institutionally ascribed asymmetry between speaker and audience that permits certain speakers to command not just the attention but the confidence, respect, and trust of their audience, or—an important proviso—to make audiences act *as if* this were so."[12] He explains that this effect of authority results from the combinative factors of the presentation of the agent being perceived as right (right time, right place, right speech, right staging, right speaker, and so on) according to the dispositions of the audience. The effect is that attitudes of reverence, trust, respect, docility, and submission pervade the audience, who then grants the agent authority.[13]

At their core, bhavas are a performance. Even leaving aside the potentially descriptive efficacy and the recent scholarly trend toward performance theory, in indigenous Hindu categories, the term *bhāva* can be traced to Hindu aesthetic theory.[14] In the Vaiṣṇava bhakti tradition, according to Rupa Gosvamin, bhāva is the emotional foundation from which love (*prema*) and then *rasa* flow.[15] Bhāvas, translated as the mood, emotion, or ecstasy of spiritual communion with the divine, can be achieved through either practice or unmediated revelation.[16] These revelatory experiences of the divine often consume their subjects until they exhibit wild and otherworldly characteristics, such as dancing, crying, lying on the floor, and/or performing superhuman feats (such as the cessation of breathing, mirroring death, turning darkened hues, and so on). Witnesses to these bhāvas often cannot help but be convinced that something otherworldly is occurring in these subjects. They supply the evidence of a "posited, perceived, or institutionally ascribed asymmetry" between the bhāva performer and the audience. Thus bhāvas provide the external proof, the physically visible revelation, of the presence of (G)od in a given religious adept that when witnessed by conditioned and/or faithful audiences provides the effect of authority to the religious adept and the effect of reverence to the audience members.

Amma's Devī Bhāvas began as spontaneous moments of divine inspiration, from which gathered audiences eventually perceived her to be not possessed by the goddess but revealing her true nature as a goddess incarnate. She garnered religious authority from these bhāvas and became widely recognized as a guru and goddess. As her religious authority has become more secure, Amma has diminished the importance of these practices. She ceased to perform bhāvas in India (circa 2005), though Devī Bhāvas continue to be important representational arenas in the United States. While there has been much speculation about her reasons for discontinuing these performances in India, there has been no definitive response from Amma or her central organization, the MA Math. Most ashram staff members cite the ever-increasing logistical complexities as the primary reason; Devī Bhāva programs simply got too big. Other devotees explain that it is because Amma is getting older and the goddess is usually depicted in India as a young woman. Another suggestion that follows the trajectory of my arguments here is that Devī Bhāvas are no longer necessary theaters needed to establish her religious authority in India, where she has already established her exalted position as both guru and goddess. This would also explain the discrepancy in that she is actively promoting Devī Bhāvas in the West, where she is not yet a household name. In Br. Dayamrita's words:

> The people who used to come in the olden days, they used to have this strange belief in that Amma used to embody the divinity at a particular time and that at that particular time she was manifesting the divine consciousness. They never had the belief, they did not have the outlook that Amma was a God realized soul, Amma was a master, a guru, a teacher, a spiritual teacher. All they came to Amma for was to ask for material benefits, so Amma liked to act like that at that time. But for now the people who come to her understand who she is in much better fashion, so she doesn't have to do all of those things, what she did earlier. And that is the reason why she is not doing those things.

While described in a different register, Br. Dayamrita's position supports the sociological argument that Amma used Devī Bhāvas to garner religious authority and to establish herself as a *recognized* goddess incarnation. Once she had secured her position as "a God realized soul . . . a master, a guru . . . a spiritual teacher," she no longer needed the performance of Devī Bhāvas in order to validate her claims to religious authority.[17]

But in the United States, where Amma is still developing her public persona and following, Devī Bhāva performances are flourishing. These performances are composed of rituals that seek to establish Amma as the goddess and are characterized by Amma's self-presentation in the attire and adornments of the goddess. The majority of devotees in the United States believe that Amma is a goddess incarnation and they look forward to Devī Bhāva performances because of their spiritually charged atmosphere and the potential for miraculous events. Devotees believe that the darshan experience during Devī Bhāva, in particular, brings Amma's divinity into sharp relief. Bala explains, "Devi Bhava is a[n] incredible night filled with just about the highest bliss available, no intoxicants needed, just Amma's most radiant intoxicating love who has taken form as Devi Herself."[18] Victoria writes, "During Devi Bhava, she takes on the presence of Devi, the Goddess, bringing even more powerful transformation and healing to those who are ready for it."[19] Moses explains, "This [Devī Bhāva] is when she more fully embodies the Divine Mother, and when she is at her most powerful."[20] Vishwanath writes, "The Devi Bhava[s] (bhajans) are somehow very special . . . the devotion in the air is thick and really pervades everything."[21] Amma's devotees believe that her power as the goddess can be more acutely perceived and easily transmitted during Devī Bhāva darshans. Amma buttresses their beliefs by routinely presenting herself to her audiences as the goddess and by instituting (and advocating) ritual worship practices that aim to reinforce her as a living goddess incarnation.

Amma's Devī Bhāvas actively assert her divinity in the resplendent form of the goddess. As she performs the role of the goddess, she transforms her social standing in the eyes of many of her devotees. When devotees witness this performance repeatedly, they are reassured of her exalted status and affirm their beliefs that she is, in fact, a goddess. This might lead us to the hypothesis that as Amma solidifies her status as a goddess incarnation, she will no longer need the theater of Devī Bhāvas to prove her exalted status. For now, many of her American devotees feel particularly blessed in their frequent opportunities to interact with and embrace Amma as she reveals herself as the goddess incarnate in her finest adornments.

PERFORMANCE: THE VIOLENT ADVENT AND
ROUTINIZED REVELATION OF THE GODDESS
The Violent Advent of the Goddess

In 1975 Amma began manifesting Krishna bhāva (the divine mood of Krishna), during which she would be playful and smiling in the classical mood of Krishna enacting his *līlā* (divine play) with the *gopīs* (cowherdesses) in Vrindavan. One night during Amma's Krishna bhāva a devotee approached her in tears and begged her to intercede against some nonbelieving villagers who were harassing her devotees. This is what happened next:

> Without warning, the gracious smile vanished. Sudhamani's [Amma's] entire facial expression changed and became fierce, as if the final dissolution had come. Her eyes looked like two smouldering iron balls. Burning with anger, they seemed to emit shooting flames. Her fingers were holding the Devi mudra. All present both inside and outside the temple were shocked to hear boisterous laughter issuing from her whole being. They had never heard such laughter in their lives. Seeing the sudden change in Sudhamani, those standing in the temple began trembling out of fear. Some scholars who were present began loudly chanting peace mantras and devotional songs in praise of the Divine Mother, while some others performed the ceremony of Aarathi [the waving of camphor lamps]. After much prayer and chanting of various mantras, she became calm and peaceful, but the Bhava had been transformed from that of Krishna to that of Devi.[22]

Sudhamani [Amma] later confided, "Seeing the distress of that devotee, I felt like destroying all the unrighteous people who persist in ridiculing the devotees. Unknowingly the Devi of fierce nature (Kali Mata) manifested to grant refuge to the persecuted." Swami Amritaswarupananda's commentary continues, "Thenceforth, in addition to Krishna Bhava, the Holy Mother, as we will call her now, regularly gave Darshan to the devotees as Devi. . . . This marked the beginning of the Mother's spiritual mission."[23] Her biography contains many accounts of similar instances in the early days when Amma used Devi Bhāva to exhibit the more dangerous qualities of the goddess in her fearsome form as Kali. When crossed, she would assume the persona of the goddess Kali and threaten her antagonists in that form. One wealthy fisherman who taunted her for being "a crazy girl" in need of a dowry found that his boat sank that very day and that he had incurred 75,000 rupees in damages.[24] An interloper (Amma's skeptical cousin, Satyasilan) who attempted to stab Amma with a knife during darshan soon found himself *reminded of movie*

died even w/ [illegible]

in the hospital continuously vomiting blood. Amma visited him in the hospital and consoled him; he repented for his actions, but he died in the hospital as a result of his ailments.[25] Sarah Caldwell writes that Amma's Keralan devotees told her that in her youth Amma performed an even more violent form of Kali bhāva that included cutting her arms and head with a curved iron sword. Caldwell takes this as evidence that Amma's early ecstatic experiences drew from the ancient Keralan female tradition of oracular goddess possession that occurred in Bhagavati temples.[26] Readers should note that Caldwell's assertion is tenuous, one that the contemporary organization wholeheartedly denies.

Amma's hagiographies recount that once Subhagan (Amma's skeptical brother) harassed a Muslim woman for going to see Amma. When the woman finally arrived, she cried to Amma:

> "O Mother . . . O Mother . . . is this the fate of those who come to see You?" Hearing the Muslim woman's distraught cries, the Mother's radiant and smiling face underwent an immediate transformation. With a terrifying appearance, she stood up from the sacred seat holding a trident in one hand and a sword in the other [symbols of the fearsome form of the goddess]. In a solemn and deep tone, the Mother said, "Whoever has caused this undue grief to this devotee will die after seven days." [Subhagan was told of Amma's prediction. After seven days, on June 2, 1978, he committed suicide.][27]

Here the fearsome goddess Kali served as a powerful interlocutor against those who sought to harm Amma's devotees. While later chapters will investigate the role of the goddess in relation to human women in detail, these early Kali bhāvas demonstrate that when Amma needed to exhibit her power, she turned to the vibrant religio-cultural symbol of the goddess Kali. In Kali's fearsome form, she made her will heard and ensured that others in the surrounding community recognized and respected her authority. Over time, these fierce and dangerous Kali bhāvas became routinized and institutionalized as benevolent and beautiful displays of Devī Bhāvas. Amma became renowned for her embodiment of the goddess and began to perform Devī Bhāva at regular intervals; this enhanced her fame and marked the significant expansion of her mission.

Though bhāvas are distinct from possession rituals, contextualizing Amma's early bhāvas within the cultural environment of goddess possession in Indian Hindu religiosity will shed some light on the character and significations of these events. In India, it is uncommon, but still a cultural reality, for human women to become vehicles for goddess possession. The particularities of this practice vary from region to region; several good ethnographic studies have investigated its local manifestations in Bengal, the greater Punjab region, Kerala, and Tamil Nadu.[28] According to these accounts, for many women the first encounter with possession by the goddess occurs spontaneously and can be a fearful experience. Afterward, if the goddess continues to visit and possess ("play" in) the same woman, that woman often alters her lifestyle to accommodate the goddess, and the initially spontaneous possession rituals take on a more ordered form. The Hindu women whom the goddess possesses frequently exhibit ecstatic emotions and embody characteristics of the goddess (turning a dark hue, sticking out and even lengthening their tongues, emitting wild and otherworldly laughter, and ecstatically twirling their heads in circles to loosen their long hair). These actions signify the presence of the goddess. Many Hindus approach these women as conduits to the goddess who may impart valuable information or respond to their pressing questions and concerns. The devout consider it auspicious to be in the presence of a woman exhibiting the "play" of the goddess. It is a holy opportunity to receive darshan from a living goddess. In some communities a religious adept spontaneously enacts these moments of goddess possession. In others they may be structured into night-long festivals (jagrātā) during which several women (in whom the goddess frequently plays) are ritually overcome by the goddess. For these women, the role of conduit to the goddess can become not only a valuable source of income and religious authority, but it also can be used as an acceptable justification for their refusal of traditional householder life (marriage and bearing children). Women are primarily the conduits for the play of the goddess. Many women who have risen to positions of religious authority have made their entrée into the largely male-dominated arena of religious authority by exhibiting goddess possession.[29]

However, there is a difference between goddess possession and women who are regarded as living incarnations of the goddess. By nature, goddess possession is a temporary event that often takes the form of a communal performance. In goddess possession, at least initially, the woman is a passive vehicle for the possession of the goddess. Revealing oneself to be an incarnation of the goddess, in contrast, is a state of being that persists as long as devotees ascribe that level of religious authority to the woman in question. As June McDaniel explains:

> Bhava [states of ecstasy] implies a conscious union with a deity, a merger in which the individual mind is opened to the deity's mind, and usually filled with devotional love (bhakti or prema), during this process. Bhor [trance states/possession], on the other hand, implies that the practitioner has a weaker or more primitive mind, unable to stand the surge of divine energy

that occurs during the deity's visit. When the person is in a state of *bhor* . . .
the mind disappears or sleeps, and the person is taken over by the deity
without participating consciously in the event. . . . This is unlike the active
cooperation involved in *bhava*, in which both centers of consciousness
work together within a single body.[30]

To complicate matters, female gurus (like Amma or Anandamayi Ma)
who are deemed to be continual incarnations of the goddess may also
perform temporary exhibitions of the goddess, bhāvas. In such cases,
devotees do not suggest the coexistence of two consciousnesses working together within a single body but, rather, the revelation of the guru's
true consciousness, the temporary lifting of a veil for the pleasure, benefit, and knowledge of the viewer, as is the case when Krishna reveals
his true form to Arjuna in the *Bhagavad Gītā*.[31]

When experiencing bhāvas, female gurus, like those who are passively taken over by goddess possessions, may lie as if dead for hours
(sometimes ceasing to breathe, according to devotees' accounts), dance
wildly, wield swords and sickles (the emblems of the warrior goddess),
loll their heads uncontrollably, elongate their tongues (to resemble
Kali's), and darken their skin (to resemble Kali's blue/black color). To assuage the goddess, devotees often sing bhajans, chant Sanskrit mantras,
comfort the physical body of the woman, and attempt to cool her from
the goddess's fiery comportment. Devotees perceive the revelation of
the active presence of the goddess in the incarnation as a dangerous occasion but also a fecund opportunity to interact with her. As in possession rituals, devotees are drawn to gurus as goddess incarnations during these bhāvas because they believe the goddess to be palpably present
and revealed in these exhibitions. Many consider bhāvas to be a fortu-
itous time to confront the guru for blessings, healings, and advice.

Amma's early development of her religious persona may have been
influenced by specific regional traditions of goddess incarnation and embodiment in her native Kerala. In Keralan Bhagavati temples, an oracle
(*veḷiccappāṭu*) embodies the goddess and presents her to devotees in
daily worship. Wielding a sword, the oracle moans, shakes his body,
and runs through the temple courtyard while blessing people, answer-
ing questions, and giving advice.[32] Although contemporary oracles are
men from the Nāyar caste, Caldwell argues that their actions derive from
religious traditions enacted by pre-Aryan tribal female shamans who performed similar ritual roles embodying and expressing the power of the
goddess. During goddess festivals, these women would participate in
possession trances and divination, often exhibiting the wildly transgres-

sive behavior of the goddess through orgiastic dancing, singing and drumming, eating meat, drinking liquor, and cutting their heads with swords.[33] In South Indian villages bordering the Kerala region, in Karnataka and Andhra Pradesh, *dalit* virgins are also initiated as manifestations of the goddess. The selected young girl then serves these village communities as an incarnation of the goddess, and in her moments of possession by the goddess she drinks toddy and dances in a "wild frenzy" as she runs about spitting toddy on the assembled crowd "uttering strange wild cries" and hurling obscenities.[34] Even Amma's earliest bhāvas were never as violent as these accounts of the behavior of female shamans of the tribal regions of Kerala. But her Kali bhāvas, in which she wielded swords while dancing wildly and laughing ecstatically (and, according to Caldwell, sliced herself with Kali's sword), share cognate ritual emblems with these regionally distinct modes of goddess possession and embodiment.[35]

Perceived as a living goddess incarnation, Amma differentiates her Devī Bhāvas from commonplace goddess possession rituals. She claims that her bhāvas temporarily reveal her inner superhuman state of being rather than exhibit an external assumption of a deity, who then leaves, ending the possession ritual. Amma explains, "If you were to really see Amma as She is, it would overwhelm you—you couldn't possibly bear it. Because of this, Amma always covers Herself with a thick layer of Maya (illusion). But during Devī Bhāva, Mother removes one or two of Her veils, revealing a little more of what She really is."[36] Couching her words in this language of revelation, she often explains that the goddess does not come to her or leave her but, rather, her Devī Bhāvas "are nothing but the external revelation of her incessant Oneness with the Supreme."[37]

On October 18, 1983, Amma announced to her devotees that she would no longer manifest Krishna bhāva. She reasoned that she became too detached in the play of consciousness of Krishna's divine līlā during Krishna bhāva. Instead, she explained that she preferred to relate to her devotees through Devī Bhāva. She explained, "During Krishna Bhava, Amma is totally detached. In that state of detachment everything is a play. *No authority is exercised during Krishna Bhava; whereas, in Devi Bhava, Amma does use Her authority and Her omnipotence to protect Her children.*"[38] In the early years, Amma would be spontaneously overcome by Kali bhāvas, often in response to challenging social situations in which she used the goddess as a means to respond with uncharacteristic vengeance and, in her own words, to assume greater religious authority.

THE ROUTINIZED REVELATION OF THE GODDESS

Over the years, Amma transformed what were initially spontaneous and often vengeance-inspired bhāvas into heavily routinized and highly structured rituals that suppressed the more dangerous and fearsome aspects of the goddess Kali. In general, Amma admonished her votaries against worshipping the fierce form of Kali (*bhadra Kali*). She said:

> Children, you worship while knowing and understanding the *tattwa* (essential principle) behind it. There is no harm in that. Your attitude is that Kali is *Brahmamayi* (the nature of the Absolute Pure Being), *Parashakti* (the Supreme Power), and that She is Everything. Whereas, many worship Kali considering Her only as a fierce goddess who kills the enemies. Those who worship Her in that manner will have the same fiery nature. Quarrels and conflicts will occur in such houses, which will cause harm to them who worship in that way. In fact, that is the wrong conception and the wrong way to worship Her. There is no harm if one worships while understanding the essential principle or *tattwa*.[39]

As time progressed (and she began to speak to a broader audience), Amma increasingly presented herself to her devotees as a more domesticated and beautified form of the Hindu goddess. She suppressed bhadra Kali in favor of her more amenable form as the benevolent Divine Mother, envisioned as Lalitā. It is this form that she routinely presents to her devotees during contemporary Devī Bhāvas. Amma embraces her devotees, showering them with benevolent maternal love while adorned in her resplendent accoutrements of the goddess and sitting under a glittering umbrella (signifying her exalted religious status).

Amma's contemporary Devī Bhāva darshan programs represent not only the routinization of what was once a spontaneous and ecstatic event but also the taming, purification, beautification, and even the "bourgeoisification" of Keralan village goddess possession rituals.[40] They became somewhat routinized and tamed when she instituted them as periodic events at her ashram in Kerala (circa 1975). But they have become even more structured and increasingly present the goddess as being beneficent in order to accommodate the attitudes and comportments of large Western audiences (and the regulations of secular venues) in the United States. The charisma that was once located in Amma herself has transformed into the institutionalization of Devī Bhāvas. Max Weber explains this phenomenon of routinization as "that peculiar transformation of charisma into an institution: as permanent structures and traditions replace the belief in the revelation and heroism of charismatic personalities, charisma becomes part of an established social structure."[41] Devī Bhāva performances no longer only draw attention to Amma's personal charisma in her revelation of herself as a living goddess, but their routinized performances within prescribed social structures garner credibility for the institutional authority of the movement. But with that said, Devī Bhāvas have not developed into a Weberian notion of bureaucratized charisma, as in the Catholic priesthood, in which another charismatic leader would supplant Amma's charismatic role while maintaining a similar position of institutional authority. In guru movements, the full transition to bureaucratic authority tends to emerge definitively only after the death of the guru within a guru-specified succession of leadership, and it is only rarely successful in maintaining the continuity of the movement.

While Devī Bhāvas were once Amma's wild and uncontrollable ecstatic invocations of Krishna and Kali, enacted with knives and sickles on earthen ground in South India, now they are highly orchestrated demonstrations of goddess regalia and domesticated female comportment on a rose-petal-laced raised stage in immaculate hotel ballrooms or in Amma's ashrams. The *Ātma puja* component of Devī Bhāva used to preserve traditional Hindu features (the removal of shoes, sitting on the floor cross-legged, individual camphor oil flames for each participant, and hand-poured *prasad* [blessed] water). Today, devotees are permitted to wear their shoes inside the darshan hall (changed in 2008); they sit in chairs during the Ātma puja (changed in 2009); the audience symbolically performs the *āratī* without the use of live flames (changed in 2004); and the audience receives small plastic containers already filled with prasad water. Amma implemented these changes in response to the perceived needs of Western audiences and for convenience, practicality, and safety when dealing with large crowds and public institutions in the United States (think fire codes and insurance policy costs). Still, many long-term devotees miss the traditionalism of the Ātma puja as it used to be performed.[42] Critics cite the brevity of the Ātma puja, the immense crowds, the increased documentation (constant film and video), and the incessant drive to give more hugs and increased publicity as the primary detractions from the atmosphere of modern Devī Bhāvas.

The performance of the Ātma puja differentiates Devī Bhāva from regular public darshan programs at the outset.[43] After Amma enters the hall and devotees perform the worship of the guru's feet (*pada puja*), she ascends to the stage where four large vessels of purified water are situated. There she sits before them and whispers Sanskrit prayers (ślokas) under her breath for some time. She lights a camphor oil flame and performs a small āratī with it while ringing a handheld brass bell. She then sits in meditation while brahmacārī/iṇīs and select attendees remove the vessels of water and transport them to the side of the hall where the water is divided and distributed as prasad to all attendees present. During the distribution, Swami Amritaswarupananda makes some small talk with the crowd (often humorous), telling them not to drink this water but instead to add it to another larger quantity of purified water and use it in times of need for its auspicious and rejuvenating properties.[44]

Then, after everyone has received prasad, Amma gives a spiritual talk, while Swami Amritaswarupananda translates. Swami Amritaswarupananda then guides the entire audience in a meditation (approximately ten to fifteen minutes).[45] Afterward he instructs audience members to bring their palms to their eyes and run their hands over their entire bodies three times and then to chant "Oṁ" once. Then he chants some of the names of the Śrī Lalitā Aṣṭottara Śatanāmāvali (The 108 Names of Lalitā), to which devotees are encouraged to respond to each name with "Oṁ Parāśaktyai namaḥ" while motioning their hands in rhythmic cycles of offering gestures. He instructs audience members to stand up and turn around in place three times while chanting, "Oṁ Parāśaktyai namaḥ" each time. As a last step, he instructs devotees to sit down again and leads them in a shorter meditation and the closing prayers for world happiness and peace, asking that they send their prayers out to all of humanity.[46] Amma then leaves the stage and the curtain is closed.

At this point the crowd is free to wander, and a low din of commotion fills the darshan hall. Some attendees connect with friends and fellow devotees, while others rush to the adjacent kitchens to have dinner (a choice between "Indian" or "Western" vegetarian meals). After five minutes or so, the curtain is opened again and Amma can be seen standing before an altar to the goddess. Her hair flows loosely down her back and she is wearing a white sari. She performs a ritual (puja) to the accoutrements of the goddess that she will wear, prostrates before them, and sings a bhajan venerating the goddess—then the curtain is closed again. After approximately ten more minutes, the curtain is flung open wide to the sound of the conch shell and the crash of a gong. The goddess is revealed. Amma sits on an elaborate throne dressed as Devī. The brahmacārī/iṇīs chant the Durga Suktham (from the Mahānārāyaṇa

Upaniṣad) and sing the āratī prayer (most audience members join in), and then Amma immediately begins to give darshan embraces. As Devī, Amma dresses in a formal, brightly colored silk sari with gold brocade trim, earrings, a jeweled nose ring, bracelets, a waist bracelet, and a silver crown on her head. She wears a heavy garland of 108 roses or colorful carnations and sits beneath an umbrella, usually golden.[47] Her hair is tied back into a loose low ponytail that hangs to her waist.[48] Asked about the reason for her Devī Bhāva costume, Amma says, "The world places great emphasis on outward appearance. It is because of this that Amma wears a special costume during Devi Bhava. The visual appearance of Amma in Devi Bhava serves to release you from your limited perception of the Self, and reminds you of the Supreme, which is your true Nature."[49]

Devī Bhāva draws double, if not triple, the number of attendees of regular public programs. On Devī Bhāva nights, Amma gives darshan to all attendees present (whereas other public darshan programs frequently reserve darshan for first-time and first-time-this-tour attendees). On Devī Bhāva nights, she also gives personalized mantras and spiritual names to devotees who ask for them and performs life-cycle rituals for her devotees: first feedings, first writings, and marriages.[50] Devī Bhāva nights support a particularly jovial, carnivalesque atmosphere. Late into the night the various satsangs perform bhajans and cultural programs. Sometimes Amma's staff and ashram residents perform skits, dances, and music for Amma, including a funk-rock band called "Goddess Jams" (comprised of brahmacārī/iṇīs from the San Ramon ashram). Devī Bhāva nights begin with the Ātma puja at 6 or 7 p.m. and continue until sometime between 6 a.m. and 2 p.m. the next day, depending on the size of the crowd.[51]

The life-cycle rituals that Amma performs after all of the darshan embraces at the end of Devī Bhāva are an important component for long-term devotees, many of whom have no other religious community in which they would choose to celebrate these milestones. First feedings (*annaprāśanam*) are for babies who have not yet had solid food. After the last person has received darshan, families approach Amma one by one, place a garland around her neck, and then place their baby on her lap. Amma then feeds the baby a small taste of sweet rice pudding, which (depending on the baby's reaction) incites laughter and/or sighs of affection from the audience. Amma gives the family members prasad (Hershey's kisses, flower petals, and sacred ash [*vibhūti*]), and then they step to the side of the stage to make room for the next family in line.

After the first feedings have been completed, families with preschool-age children approach Amma one by one for the traditional Hindu Malayalee ceremony of first writing (*vidyarāmbham*). Herein the family members place a garland around Amma's neck and then stand to the side while she holds the hand of each child and uses his or her pointer finger to write "*oṁ hari śrī ganapathāye namaḥ*" into a plate of uncooked rice. Again, Amma gives the family members prasad and they step to the side to make room for the marriage ceremonies.

Marriage ceremonies are events formalized not only by highly ritualistic actions but also by participants' attire. Grooms wear pressed silk *kurta pajāmas* (many purchase these from Amma's clothing booths), while brides are required to wear Amma's Devī Bhāva saris.[52] Several brides delightedly recalled how their bodies felt electrified and infused with Amma's energy while they wore these saris. In their view, the sari had absorbed the collective energy (*śakti*) of Amma and the Devī Bhāva darshan during which it was worn. During the marriage ceremony the couple sits facing each other at Amma's feet. First, together the couple places a flower garland around Amma's neck. At this point some couples exchange gifts with each other and with each other's family. Then the woman applies a red vermillion *ṭīkā* to the man, and the man applies the same to the woman. Some couples then exchange rings, or the woman receives the *mangal sutra* (the traditional Hindu necklace marking a married woman). Then the woman places a flower garland around the man's neck and the man does the same for her. Next the woman does āratī to the man by moving a camphor flame in a clockwise circle three times in front of him and then she bows to him; then he does āratī to her and he bows to her.[53] They then feed each other Hershey's kisses and turn to Amma to be showered with flower petals and to receive their darshan embrace. After their darshan, the family members shower them with flower petals and they stand up and circumambulate Amma (the wife following the husband). At this point the audience and family members applaud and cheer while many of the women ululate. The couple and their families then exit the stage to make room for the next couple. In addition to heterosexual unions, Amma also routinely performs marriage ceremonies for gay couples during Devī Bhāva.

The marriages are usually the final ritual that Amma performs while seated on the same throne where she has been giving darshan all night long.[54] The marriage ceremonies usually are completed in the early to late morning (in San Ramon, it is sometimes early afternoon). Amma then slowly rises (the first time she has stood up in fifteen to twenty hours) and walks to the edge of the stage. The musicians, led by Swami Amritaswarupananda, thrust forward with the closing bhajans that conclude every Devī Bhāva program, culminating in the high-energy bhajan "Amma Amma Tāye."[55] Audience members sing along heartily. Many are tearful and enraptured. Awestruck devotees gaze lovingly at Amma, who stands larger than life in her full goddess regalia. The powerful energy that has been building in the room throughout the darshan program culminates in these moments when Amma presents herself and gives her full attention to the audience. Prior to this she has been actively engaged in the specifics of the darshan program. Standing at the edge of the stage, she showers all of the audience members with flower petals as they circumambulate to pass in front of her. She then stands completely still, allowing the audience a full darshan. These final moments of Devī Bhāva exemplify the dynamic visual exchange of darshan. Not only does the audience see Amma as the goddess, but Amma also pointedly looks at the devotees in the audience, shifting her gaze from person to person. In this powerful darshan experience, one cannot escape her gaze. Many devotees report that personal communications and revelations occur during this moment.

It is now usually somewhere between 9 a.m. and 3 p.m. of the following day. The majority of attendees have stayed awake throughout the Devī Bhāva program, sometimes catching an hour or two of sleep in the midst. Those who wish to stay at the programs are expected to contribute to the sanctity and collective energy of the manufactured sacred space. Sleeping in the ballroom is forbidden (though this rule is not often enforced). Returning to one's room to sleep for a bit and reentering the ballroom is discouraged. The outside doors of the ballroom are usually locked at 3 a.m., as per Amma's stipulation. During the previous portions of the Devī Bhāva darshan program, attendees have passed the long night lounging, sleeping intermittently (though against the rules), wandering, meditating, chanting, reading, singing, purchasing Amma sponsored products and services, doing selfless service (sevā), and socializing. However, at this final intercession, all attention is on Amma. She will soon be gone, with the cumulative sacrality of the preceding night vigil eclipsed and the return to everyday life eminent. These culminating moments reverberate with the fixed attentions and emanating love of the devotees who are present. All eyes are on Amma's goddess splendor. Some devotees weep with tears of emotive cleansing. Some weep with joy. Some weep with overwhelming faith, their eyes overflowing with the same relished assurance of divine recognition and protection.

After approximately ten minutes of this full-frontal darshan of Amma as the living goddess, the curtains are abruptly drawn in front of her. Devi has gone. When Amma reappears after five minutes or so, she is once again dressed in her simple white sari and has reverted to her ascetic human form. The crowd hums with anticipation as excited devotees attempt to move closer to Amma's designated path of exit. She descends from the stage and with her hands held out slightly from the sides of her body she walks through the crowd, giving affectionate light touches to the devotees who rush to touch her one last time. After Amma leaves, the general audience disperses and the tour staff brahmacārī/iṇīs and local sevites begin to break down and pack up the remaining darshan program accoutrements.[56] Some devotees move toward the stage where Amma has been for the past fifteen to twenty hours, and they sit in meditation for some time.

The majority of the audience then proceeds directly to get some sleep, but many brahmacārī/iṇīs and local sevites will not be able to rest until everything is packed away and readied for the next city's or next year's program and they are traveling or safely home in their beds. An impromptu market emerges wherein kitchen staff and darshan hall staff sell and freely distribute remaining perishable items: food, Amma prasad, flowers, and plants that will not last the journey to the next city. Crowds clamor around the local welcome desk, where attendees look for rides, places to sleep, and lost items. Even in such a large and diverse crowd comprised of strangers, car keys, cell phones, credit cards, glasses, meditation pillows, cash, and jewelry are often reunited with their owners through the acts of honest people. The spirit of generosity at Amma's programs is perhaps nowhere more explicit and assumed than in the routine bustle of carpooling and drivers' services that take sleep-deprived voluntary chauffeurs far from their anticipated destinations.

For casual attendees at Amma's programs, Devī Bhāva nights are a spectacle, a carnivalesque event that is simply worth seeing. For more ardent devotees, they are an extraordinary opportunity to interact with Amma as the goddess, to be embraced by her, and to see and be seen by her. Devī Bhāva heightens the intensity of devotees' anticipation of Amma's darshan programs. They look forward to the performances and the festival atmosphere, but more particularly they anticipate the possibility that the fantastical or miraculous will occur. Those who seek healing, answers, and/or a spiritual experience come to Devī Bhāva with the expectation that the possibilities for such miraculous happenings are more likely when Amma is revealing more of her believed superhuman nature as the goddess. Many devotees also await Devī Bhāva with heightened anticipation because they wish to receive a spiritual name or mantra from Amma (normally given during Devī Bhāva) or they will be participating in one of the life-cycle rituals that Amma performs on Devī Bhāva nights. Devotees clamor to gain proximity to Amma during her regular darshan programs in order to experience the transference of the power of the goddess. During Devī Bhāva this intensity and desire for proximity are amplified exponentially. Devotees often receive that which they desire; their expectations are often met with intense spiritual experiences, revelations, cures, and answers that they experience and obtain during Devī Bhāva.

The practice of routinely revealing Amma as a divine incarnation of the Hindu goddess through Devī Bhāvas also serves an organizational purpose for Amma. Amma tells the following anecdote:

> One man was cutting down a tree which was growing by the side of the road. Another man who happened to see him doing this said, "Don't cut down that tree! It is wrong to do so, it is against the law." The man not only refused to stop cutting but also scolded him severely. The person who tried to prevent the hooligan from cutting the tree was a policeman. He departed but soon returned in his official dress. Even from a distance the mere sight of the policeman's cap was enough to make the hooligan flee without looking back. See the different impact created when he came in ordinary and then official dress. Therefore, special attire is needed to teach ignorant people. Likewise, the costumes of Krishna and Devi Bhavas [sic]. Some people who still feel dissatisfied even after talking to Mother for hours will feel fully content after conversing with her only for a couple of seconds during Bhava Darshan. They feel peaceful after having told all their worries directly to God.[57]

Much like the uniform of the police officer in this parable, Amma's dress and comportment during Devī Bhāvas reinforce her claims to religious authority. She also explains that she performs Devī Bhāvas because her devotees wish to see her assume the physical form of the goddess. This desire is overwhelmingly evident. Devotees clamor to attend Devī Bhāva darshan programs, more so than any other Amma event.

But in assessing their sociological import, I would also suggest that her continuous performance of this theater signifies the contentious and contested nature of her claims to religious authority. It reveals that these claims are tenuous enough to necessitate constant representation and reinforcement. The theoretical perspective of Pierre Bourdieu provides useful insights into the relationship between social realities, performance, and representation with which we can better understand

Amma's repeated performance of Devī Bhāva. In his discussion of the petit bourgeois' tenuous claims to social status, Bourdieu notes that "to assert his pretensions and demands, to advance his interests and upward aspirations—the petit bourgeois is inclined to a Berkeleian vision of the social world, reducing it to a theatre in which being is never more than perceived being, a mental representation of a theatrical performance (*représentation*). His ambiguous position in the social structure, sometimes compounded by the ambiguity inherent in all the roles of intermediary between the classes . . . predisposes him to perceive the social world in terms of appearance and reality."[58] The ambiguity of one's social position incites the emphasis on representation in order to further define that position through appearances, which then stand in for a more concrete reality. The visual representation of the policeman's uniform or, in Amma's case, her goddess regalia, seeks to eradicate the ambiguity of her social position by visually representing the social status that she wishes to obtain. When successful, the theater of Devī Bhāva effectively transforms her lived reality from one who exists liminally, betwixt and between, on the fringes of conventional social roles, into an exalted goddess manifestation whose social position is decidedly located within the superhuman.

CHANTING THE NAMES OF THE GODDESS

But who is this goddess that Devī Bhāva signifies? Is it Amma herself? Or is there a particular form of the goddess that Amma reveals? A pertinent clue about the goddess of Amma's Devī Bhāvas lies in the two most commonly chanted Sanskrit prayers of her movement, both of which are recited prior to the close of each of her darshan programs (both Devī Bhāva and everyday darshan programs). They are the *Śata Nāmāvali* (*The 108 Names of Mata Amritanandamayi*) and the *Śrī Lalitā Sahasranāmāvali* (*The 1000 Names of Śrī Lalitā*). These two Sanskrit prayers have been institutionalized in positions of highest prestige within the movement. From this we might imagine then that it is Amma herself or perhaps the goddess Lalitā whom Amma reveals during Devī Bhāva. But what of the *Mahiṣāsura Mardinī Stotram* (popularly known as *Ayi Giri Nandini*), which signifies the beginning of the end of every darshan and satsang program in cities around the world? The *Mahiṣāsura Mardinī Stotram* recounts the tale of how the Hindu goddess Durga slayed the buffalo demon Mahiṣa. The Sanskrit chant, consisting of twenty verses, plays with sounds and syllables to create alliterative phrases that serve to drive the melody forward. The recitation of the chant whisks the crowd into an energetic pulse during Amma's darshan programs and satsangs (to a lesser extent). The actual meaning of the chant is quite violent and bloody, as it describes the fierce battle. For example, verse 4 reads, "*ayi śatakhuṇḍa vikhuṇḍita ruṇḍa vituṇḍita śuṇḍa gajādhipate | ripu gaja gaṇḍa vidāraṇa caṇḍa parākrama śuṇḍa mṛgādhipate || nija bhuja daṇḍa nipārita khaṇḍa nipātita muṇḍa bhaṭādhipate | jaya jaya he mahiṣāsuramardinī ramyakapārdini śailasute ||* O One who split the heads (of demons) into hundreds of pieces and One who cut the trunks of great battle elephants | whose great lion is skilled in terrifying valor in tearing apart the temples of enemy elephants | One who has cut down into pieces the heads of enemy chieftains with the strength of her own arms || be victorious, be victorious, O destroyer of the demon Mahiṣa, with beautiful braided hair, daughter of the mountain Himalaya |"[59] The initial pulsating notes of the performance of *Ayi Giri Nandini* mark the climax of Amma's darshan programs. The incessant pulse of the music and the onomatopoeic repetition of the lyrics are juxtaposed to awaken drowsy attendees and infuse energy into the crowd. Many of the more vibrant attendees begin to dance and twirl at the boundaries of the crowd, while others sing and clap along with the music. Perhaps then it is the Hindu goddess Durga, or her more bloodthirsty counterpart, Kali, who exudes from Amma's small dark form beneath the jewel-toned silk and gold-brocaded Devī Bhāva sari and silver crown.

All of these prayers are recited only in Sanskrit, though many devotees, to aid in their recitations, use the archana book, which includes both the Sanskrit prayers and their translations.[60] The archana book also includes a collection of shorter prayers for distinct purposes, including a rendition of verse 32/58 of the *Guru Gītā*,[61] verse 1.3.28 of the *Bṛhadāraṇyaka Upaniṣad*, the *Gāyatrī Mantra* (*Ṛg Veda* 3.62–10), verses 1.1 and 1.12 of the *Taittirīya Upaniṣad*, verses from the *Iśavasya Upaniṣad*,[62] and verse 4.24 of the *Bhagavad Gītā*.[63] Since approximately 2008, the transliterations and translations of the archana prayers have been projected onto two large screens above the stage so that audience members can follow along, reading silently or aloud. The projected archana prayers include the *Śata Nāmāvali*, the *Śrī Lalitā Sahasranāmāvali*, the *Mahiṣāsura Mardini Stotram*, and *bhajans* (devotional music).[64] Both the archana book and a multiple series of bhajan books (*Bhajanamritam*, vol. 1–10, and annual supplements) are also available for purchase at the bookstore at the rear of the darshan hall during programs and online.

Amma encourages her devotees to chant at least the *Śata Nāmāvali* once every day, preferably before sunrise during morning puja practices. If devotees are able to commit more time to their devotional practices, she encourages them to recite the *Śrī Lalitā Sahasranāmāvali* in addition to the *Śata Nāmāvali*, again during morning puja practices, or, for the even more dedicated, during morning and evening practices. According to Amma, morning puja rituals should include burning incense, offering flowers and prasad to the image of the deity (the devotee's favored deity [*iṣṭadev*], usually Amma), chanting the *Śata Nāmāvali* (and, if time permits, the *Śrī Lalitā Sahasranāmāvali*), and meditating (Integrated Amrita Meditation or some other).[65] The recitation of the *Śata Nāmāvali* and the *Śrī Lalitā Sahasranāmāvali* is the primary devotional practice of Amma devotees. Devotees describe these two prayers as "doing archana," which they can often be seen doing periodically during Amma's darshan programs.

This raises the question of just how much devotees know what they are saying as they recite these prayers. Many devotees believe that there is something sacred in the rendition of the Sanskrit itself. The goal is not to comprehend the prayers in their entirety; rather, it is the process of recitation that creates the ritual, praises the goddess, and brings virtue to the devotee. In his commentary on the *Cāndogya Upaniṣad*, Śankara says simply, "Two persons may perform the same act, both the one who understands and the one who does not. But understanding and ignorance are different, and what one performs with understanding becomes far stronger than what one performs in ignorance."[66] Amma addresses this issue with a bit more consternation by telling a story of a priest whose cat always interrupted his puja. One day he became so annoyed that he put the cat in a basket prior to beginning the puja. Thereafter, he made this a habit that nearly became part of the ritual. After the old priest died, his son continued his practice of conducting the puja only after putting the cat in the basket. But after some time, the cat died. Frantic, the son vigorously searched for another cat to replace it so that he could conduct the puja. Finally, he bought another cat, and after putting it safely in the basket he conducted the puja. He had never understood the reason for putting the cat in the basket but instead had merely mimicked his father's actions.[67] Amma says, "Rituals shouldn't be like that; we should perform acharas [observances] only after grasping the principle behind them. Only then will we benefit from them; otherwise, they will deteriorate into mere routine."[68] Perhaps it is for this reason that Amma's materials, archana books, prayers, and so on are translated and made available in so many different languages.

Those who have facility in Sanskrit likely understand these prayers; the better their Sanskrit, the better their understanding. In this matter, the advantage goes to the majority of *inheritors* (primarily Indian Hindus) who likely have some knowledge of at least one Indian language (if not Sanskrit) and are familiar with Hindu mythology. Inheritors may recognize some words and references to gods and goddesses in the Hindu pantheon in these prayers, but even so, without knowledge of Sanskrit these devotees rely on the translations into their native language almost as much as the *adopters*. Adopters (primarily American metaphysicals) rarely have facility in any Indian language.[69] Some ardent devotees may learn Malayalam and/or Sanskrit, but they are only a small minority in comparison to the numbers of devotees that have no facility in either language. The majority of adopters who recite these prayers frequently learn the Sanskrit sounds through repetition and by listening to their performance during darshan programs, satsangs, and audio recordings.

The strong majority of Amma's American devotees do not immediately comprehend more than a small portion of either of these prayers upon first reading them. Select lines that are simple, such as "*oṁ devyai namaḥ*" (n. 107, *Śata Nāmāvali*), are readily understandable even to nonadepts, while others, such as "*oṁ saṁsāra-paṅka-nirmagna-samuddharaṇa-paṇḍitāyai namaḥ*" (n. 880, *Śrī Lalitā Sahasranāmāvali*), are difficult at first glance even for devotees who are moderately proficient in Sanskrit. But when devotees recite these prayers, they are not seeing them for the first time. For many it is their hundredth, thousandth, or hundred thousandth recitation. The result is that even if devotees do not understand the meaning of every word or even every name, the Sanskrit prayers begin to roll off their tongues as if they were fluent. Devotees vary in the extent to which they spend time with the translations of the Sanskrit in order to learn the meanings of the prayers. Those adopters, for whom the Sanskrit impedes their devotion, read these prayers in English translation only while listening to the Sanskrit recited on audio recordings or by live audiences during satsangs and darshan programs. Ironically, devotees who are the least culturally competent often know the meaning of these prayers quite well because they so frequently read them in translation. While only a select group of devotees immediately comprehends the full meaning of the Sanskrit the first time it is recited, over time most devotees understand the particular intentions and meanings behind the *Śata Nāmāvali* and the *Śrī Lalitā Sahasranāmāvali* (the 108-fold list of the attributes of Amma and the 1,000-fold list of the attributes of Lalitā, respectively). Some devotees cherish these divine names and attributes; many have chosen names for themselves or for their children from these lists.

The *Śata Nāmāvali* begins by listing the transcendent qualities of Amma's self-realization (n. 1–19) and then shifts to the specifics of Amma's biography (n. 20, 22, 23, 24) and her early devotional and revelatory experiences with God (n. 33–55). Other aspects that are highlighted include her humanitarianism and social mission (n. 31–32, 86, 90, 99), her ascetic virtuosity (n. 76–78, 82–86, 89, 94, 95, 100–101), her commitment to her devotees in the guru-disciple relationship (n. 88, 91–93, 96–98), and her connection and dedication to the betterment of Kerala (n. 20, 27, 60, 103, 106). Amma is also compared to Ramakrishna and Sarada Devi (n. 56–59), Chaitanya (n. 74), Krishna (n. 64–67), and the Divine Mother (n. 69–72), and equally compared to Kanya Kumari (n. 102) and "the Great Divine Mother" (*oṁ devyai namaḥ*) (n. 107).

In chanting the *Śrī Lalitā Sahasranāmāvali*, devotees worship *Lalitā Mahātripurasundarī*, who is understood to be the supreme goddess, the union of Shiva and Shakti. Amma explains the importance and benefits of the prayer's recitation:

> Worship (arcana) using *Lalitā Sahasranāma* is of the utmost value for the prosperity of the family and for peace in the world. There will never be [a] shortage of food or clothing in the home where *Lalitā Sahasranāma* is chanted daily. In olden days, when giving Kṛṣṇa or Viṣṇu *mantras* to their disciples, gurus usually instructed them to do arcana with *Lalitā Sahasranāma* as well.[70]

Devotees recite this prayer as a devotional means to connect with the Divine Mother (Lalitā, but often visualized as Amma) in their daily lives. When they recite the *Śata Nāmāvali* and the *Śrī Lalitā Sahasranāmāvali*, they inscribe Amma with their faith in her claims to divinity. Even if they initially participate without full faith, the repetitious nature of these actions serves to acculturate them in the devotional ethos of the movement. During public programs and in their personal practices, they use song, prayer, and chanting to invoke the divine in their daily lives following in the bhakti traditions of India. Bhakti traditions emerged in the sixth and seventh centuries and emphasized devotion through the personal and direct experience of God. In a recent news article, Laurie Patton was quoted saying that Amma "personifies the bhakti tradition" and she is undoubtedly correct.[71]

With that said, Amma's organizational reliance on the *Śrī Lalitā Sahasranāmāvali* also suggests that we should locate Amma within the Śakta Tantric tradition, known as Śrī Vidyā, which derives from the Śrīkula Tantric texts composed before the eleventh century.[72] The Śrī Vidyā tradition focuses its devotion on *Lalitā Tripurasundarī*, the beautiful and benevolent (and independent) goddess. The earliest texts of the tradition are the *Vāmakeśvara Tantra* (consisting of the *Nityāṣodaśikārṇava* and the *Yoginīhṛdaya*) and the *Tantrarāja Tantra*. Later texts extol the beautiful and beneficent qualities of the goddess Tripurasundarī, highly popularized in the *Saundaryalaharī*, the *Tripura Upaniṣad*, and the *Lalitāsahasranāma*.[73] While there are right-hand and left-hand approaches to Śrī Vidyā, the tradition that developed in South India created its distinctive identity by adopting and expanding the Kashmiri canon and by assimilating the ethics and ideologies of South Indian brahmanical culture.[74] In South India, Śrī Vidyā aligned with orthodox Vedanta and with the Śaṅkarācārya of Śṛṅgeri and Kanchipuram.[75] The theology of Śrī Vidyā integrates devotional bhakti attitudes toward the goddess with the vedantic emphasis on nonduality and formless (*nirguṇa*) conceptions of God. Gavin Flood observes that in the Śrī Vidyā traditions, "Although visualized and praised in personal terms, the Goddess is also an impersonal force or power. She unfolds the cosmos and contracts it once again in endless cycles of emanation and re-absorption. This process is conceptualized as the manifestation and contraction of the Word, the absolute as primal sound (*śabda nāda*), or the syllable *oṃ*, identified with energy, light and consciousness."[76] Śrī Vidyā lineage is also known for the worship of the goddess in the form of a sacred diagram, or *yantra*, of nine intersecting triangles called the *śrīcakra*, symbolizing the cosmos and the union of Shiva and Shakti, and in the form of a fifteen-syllable mantra, the *śrīvidyā*, from which the tradition earned its name.[77]

Two ideologically disparate lineages, Vedanta and Tantra, unite in South Indian Śrī Vidyā by aligning their religious practices. Douglas Brooks explains, "By treating orthopraxy as orthodoxy, the Śaṅkarites diminish the significant differences between Śaṅkara's non-dualistic (*advaita*) Vedānta and Śrīvidyā's Kashmiri Śaiva-based monism. Despite serious philosophical differences, the two traditions connect by sharing imagery, worship (*puja*), and devotion (*bhakti*). Further, the traditional

Tantric disdain for renunciation, shared by most Śrīvidyā writers, is rendered moot by the Śaṅkarites' public embrace of a tradition that embraces both enjoyment (*bhukti*) of this world and ultimate liberation (*mukti*)."[78] The unified product is a religiosity dedicated to advaita vedantic philosophy blended with practical devotion to the goddess Lalitā. This impulse precisely characterizes Amma's movement.

Who is the goddess Lalitā in relation to Amma? In the *Lalitāsahasranāmā* (listed as the *Śrī Lalitā Sahasranāmāvali* in Amma's archana booklet), she is revealed in a litany of contrasting attributes that reinforce her status as the totalizing goddess of the universe; she subsumes and represents every other form of the goddess. She is both beautiful and violent, independent and auspicious (a chaste wife and mother), sensual and ascetic. Brooks observes, "Without the slightest sense of controversy or contradiction, Lalitā is made into a Tantric image of potency and power completely in control of herself and in conformity with the values of male-dominated brahmanism. She seeks to uphold the status quo but will not be bound to it; she gives life and fortune, but reserves the right to take it away; she embodies enjoyment (n. 293), sensuality (n. 321), and playfulness (n. 340) as well as restraint (n. 900) in her role as chaste wife (n. 128) devoted to her husband (n. 320)."[79] The first fifty-one names of the *Lalitāsahasranāmā* describe her beautiful form, yet quickly thereafter the liturgy turns to the mythology of her violent conquests on the battlefield in the slaying of Bhaṇḍāsura (n. 64–82), repeated in greater detail in the *Lalitopākhyāna*. Later, the *Lalitāsahasranāmā* identifies Lalitā as both Durga (n. 140) and Kali (n. 751), modeling closely the account of her victories in battle with the accounts of these two goddesses in the *Devīmāhātmya*.

The mythology of the goddess Lalitā also may suggest a foundation for why so much of Amma's organizational message centers on love. The *Lalitopākhyāna*'s account of the slaying of Bhaṇḍāsura, largely modeled on the *Devīmāhātmya*'s account of the slaying of Mahiṣāsura, begins with the destruction of Love (the god Kama) by Shiva, who resents the disturbance in his meditative yoga. Shiva then fashions a man, Bhaṇḍa, from Love's ashes, who over time becomes a powerful and fearsome demon strangling the world with his domination. Only the goddess can destroy him, but he attacks with the appropriated strength of the gods. The goddess fends him off and the gods are pleased. The goddess Lalitā marries Shiva but retains her independence. After many years Lalitā marches into battle against the demon Bhaṇḍa with an army of *śaktis* and *yoginīs*. Bhaṇḍa dismisses them in his mind, presuming them to be beautiful (and thus benign), as the meaning of the name Lalitā implies. He is sorely mistaken. Lalitā creates Ganesha (from her laugh), who kills Bhaṇḍa's entire family. She then creates Durga (from her laugh), who kills the demon Mahiṣa. Next she creates the various avatars of Vishnu and Prahlāda who kill the remainder of Bhaṇḍa's armies. Finally, Lalitā kills the demon Bhaṇḍa with a missile called *mahākāmeśvara* (the great god of love). She then revives the god of Love and he declares his undying gratitude.[80]

Thus Love (the god Kāma) plays a pivotal role within the central mythology from which the goddess Lalitā derives her exalted status. Love, translated into Hindu religious practice as *bhakti*, also becomes the central practice of the cult of Lalitā. "Both *Lalitopākhyāna* and *Lalitāsahasranāma* insist that love (*bhakti*) alone can bring the worldly enjoyments (*bhukti*) and the ultimate liberation (*mukti*)."[81] Recall that in the South Indian Śrī Vidyā tradition the disparate philosophical traditions of Advaita Vedanta and Tantra are unified through the orthopraxy of bhakti devotionalism. Amma has translated this complex historical tradition and theological juxtaposition into the simple statement "My religion is Love." Used as a noun instead of a verb in this statement, the English word "Love" is more than a bit deceiving here. Instead, if we translate "love" as the devotional practice of "bhakti," immediately the valorization of orthopraxy that unified Vedanta and Tantra in the South Indian Śrī Vidyā tradition is revealed. In making Lalitā and the 108 names in praise of her central to her theology and practice, Amma positions herself within the South Indian Śrī Vidyā lineage in which the goddess Lalitā is a beautiful and independent totalizing goddess. In this mythological account, Love is the pivotal character through which Lalitā gains exalted status. Here too, Advaita Vedanta and Śakta Tantra unite, and orthopraxy supplants orthodoxy.

CONCLUSION

Located firmly in the Śrī Vidyā tradition, Amma presents herself as an incarnation of Mahādevī, literally "the great goddess," but she is often imagined as Kali or Lalitā. In fact, her trajectory from village notoriety to global fame can be traced in her gradual transition from the goddess Kali to the goddess Lalitā. Initially, Amma's bhavas were playful performances of Krishna enacting his divine play (līlā). Her bhāvas transformed into Devī Bhāvas only when she was angered by the mistreatment of her devotees and thus needed to use "Her [Devī's] authority and Her omnipotence to protect her children."[82] In her rage she became the fearsome form of Kali, bhadra Kali, and began to take revenge against those who slandered her name, ridiculed her mission, heckled her devotees, and sought to harm her physically. During these early Kali bhāvas Amma's devotees sought to cool Kali's fiery and vengeful comportment through prayer, chanting, and singing bhajans. Here, Amma's actions were clearly rooted in South Indian goddess traditions that venerate Kali as a fearsome yet maternal goddess intricately linked to female power (śakti), heat, sexuality, violence, and blood sacrifice.

This imaginary of Amma as Kali has largely remained bound to its cultural context restricted to her devotees in Kerala, particularly to residents at her ashram at Amritapuri. But even there, secure in her regional cultural heritage, the goddess Kali is becoming "sweetened," as she is elsewhere in India. In popular mainstream depictions of Kali, she is often beautiful and even sensual.[83] In her contemporary mythology, Kali is often depicted as beneficent, but still a current of potential anger stems from her fierce maternality and raw female power (śakti). Amma's support for the ritual chanting of the *Śrī Lalitā Sahasranāmāvali* and her beautified depictions of the goddess during Devī Bhāva suggest that she has transitioned from the fierce goddess Kali to the beautiful, beneficent, and independent goddess Lalitā.

Selva Raj suggests that Amma has recently accentuated her persona as Lalitā through "the strong emphasis on the chanting and study of the tantra text *Lalitasahasranamam* with interactive CD, special *stotras* (hymns) composed to Amma as Lalita, and the direct claim that Amma *is* Lalitambika."[84] In my decade of ethnographic research, I have never heard or read of Amma herself overtly claiming to *be* any one particular goddess. The closest one gets to this type of overt pronouncement is Amma's statement, "Here is a crazy girl who puts on the garb of Krishna and after some time that of Devi, but it is within this crazy girl that both exist."[85] With that said, Raj is quite right that the devotional literature surrounding her actively promotes the equating of Amma and Lalitā. Amma also exhibits particular behaviors, most explicitly through Devī Bhāva performances, that aim to reveal the goddess that exists within her. Devotees react to these behaviors, and most commonly Amma's immediate spokespeople and the literature surrounding her present her as various forms of the goddess. "Hrim Kali," a song that one of Amma's senior devotees wrote, explains Amma's transition into the benevolent form of the goddess. "In the beginning my Mother became the Lotus-eyed One [Krishna]. Then She became Kali, Her actual Form. Kali became peaceful becoming Lalitambika, the Mother for Her children. She became the Refuge for the devotees, the Servant of the servants, the Guru for ascetics, and everything for lowly me. . . . O Mother Bhagavati, the gracious Amritanandamayi."[86] As the song says, Amma has transformed from Kali to Lalitā, in whose peaceful form she has become the mother for her children: the Divine Mother for her devotees.

Her form as Lalitā is often perceived as the most powerful of forms because Lalitā is a totalizing goddess that subsumes all other forms of the goddess. Douglas Brooks explains, "Śrī Vidyā asserts that Shakti in her supreme aspect (*parāshakti*) manifests as benign (*saumya*) and beautiful (*saundarya*), rather than as terrifying (*ugra*) and horrifying (*ghora*). Thus, Lalitā is deliberately contrasted with such figures as Kālī and Durgā. Lalitā Tripurasundarī, however, is a totalization of great goddess conceptions. In other words, Lalitā is identified with every aspect of the goddess in every possible form and mode of depiction. While primarily depicted as benign, she is also described as terrifying; similarly, she is both auspicious and inauspicious."[87] When we contextualize Amma within her Śrī Vidyā lineage, her transition from Kali to Lalitā becomes not a linear transition from one goddess to another but an assimilating move in which she adopts the form of the beautiful, benign, and totalizing goddess Lalitā who, according to Śrī Vidyā doctrines, both subsumes and exemplifies the terrifying goddess Kali.[88]

This transition from a terrifying to a beautiful goddess does not somewhat flatly suggest that Amma needed to reimagine herself in order to be more palatable to a diversity of audiences (particularly Western audiences). From a more nuanced perspective, we might also see this "beautification" as a transition that reflects her growing security in her established place of religious authority, particularly as a woman. What we have seen is that in Amma's early identity construction she assumed the vengeful and fierce role of Kali to forcibly claim her socioreligious power and establish herself as a religious authority. As her socioreligious position became more secure and definitively established, Amma began to embrace a more beautified form of the goddess Lalitā while still retaining her independence and authority.[89]

For women, physical beauty has long been a "weapon of the weak," in James C. Scott's terms, and while it has enabled some to procure some limited power over their husbands and lovers, it has rarely secured their institutional power in society.[90] Many early feminists sought to suppress their feminine beauty in order to facilitate their claims to institutionalized power. It was only after they had achieved positions of power in society and had established institutional changes that some feminists felt able to embrace their feminine beauty as well as their power. Women's claims to power (especially religious authority) are still contentious around the globe, and the relation between feminine beauty and power is still often (if unconsciously) imagined as oppositional. But in Amma's most crucial moments of claiming contentious religious authority, Devī Bhāvas, she appears as her most resplendent and beautified self. It would seem, then, that at these contentious moments her beauty and power coalesce, each in service of the other.

Devī Bhāvas enable beauty and power to merge through her revelation of the goddess Lalitā, who as per Śrī Vidyā theology, subsumes all other goddesses. Thus Devī Bhāvas always reserve the potential for the aspect of the goddess Kali to appear in place of Lalitā. Again I draw attention to the song "Hrim Kali," which says, "She became *Kali, Her actual Form*. Kali became peaceful becoming Lalitambika, the Mother for Her children."[91] The song asserts that Kali is Amma's "actual form," whereas she assumes the peaceful form of Lalitā in order to become a benevolent mother to her devotees. Thus the vengeful, fierce, and powerful bhadra Kali always lurks just under the surface of her beautiful veneer in the form of the goddess Lalitā during Devī Bhāvas. Kali's role on the front stage in Amma's global movement may have been eclipsed, but her role on the back stage is very much present. As Amma secured international fame and religious authority, she no longer needed Kali to be as overt, but Kali remains there covertly as a warning and as a reminder of the vigorous power of the goddess that devotees believe to be present in Amma.

CHAPTER 3

The Avatar-Guru and Ordinary Women

The Boundaries of Mimetic Behavioral Models

The essence of motherhood is not restricted to women who have given birth; it is a principle inherent in both women and men. It is an attitude of mind. It is love—and that love is the very breath of life.[1]

—Mata Amritanandamayi

capitalism?

Even a casual observer would be struck by the predominance of powerful female imagery represented in the multisensory extravaganza of Amma's *darshan* programs.[2] Amma's image on ephemera and specific Amma products is a constant reminder that she "stands alone" as an independent female religious authority without a connection to any established sect (*sampradāya*) or tradition (*paramparā*).[3] During *Devi Bhava* darshan programs, Amma overtly reminds her audiences of her superhuman status as she represents herself with the elaborate accoutrements of the goddess. While many of her senior swamis are men, one is a *why?* woman, and the majority of her *brahmacārīṇīs* (celibate renunciates) are women. They conduct and orchestrate the logistical aspects of the darshan programs, which visibly include laity of all kinds performing traditional Hindu rituals that are traditionally restricted to male brahman priests. Similarly, as discussed in previous chapters, Amma's darshan embrace publicly violates Hindu orthodox norms of purity and pollution and thwarts *brahmanical* orthopraxies that prohibit low-caste females from assuming positions of religious authority. As we will see in this chapter, Amma also performs the role of *pujāriṇī* (priest) within her temples and encourages her female and lay followers to do the same.

female empowerment

Within Amma's movement there exists a reimagining of the role of women in relation to divinity, religious leadership, and ritual. In each of these arenas, Amma's actions inscribe women with more power than they are often permitted in conventional forms of Hindu religiosity (and, one might argue, in most orthodox forms in the majority of religions). She justifies these actions with social advocacy to (re)awaken the "female principle" in the world and for all of humanity to embody what she determines to be the feminine qualities of "universal motherhood": unconditional love, compassion, asceticism, patience, sacrifice, reflection, and flow. Herein, the signifier of the feminine comprises a polythetic set of characteristics, the conception of which derives from Amma's interpretation of Devī as described in the *Lalitā Sahasranāma* and the Purāṇas. It also largely coincides with the Victorian ideal of femininity, which became popular among Indic elites in nineteenth-century constructions of Indian Hindu womanhood under colonial rule. This chapter investigates the practices and discourses within Amma's movement in relation to women and religious authority as well as their context within Hindu traditions in an effort to interrogate such visual representations of female predominance.

In 1949 Simone de Beauvoir boldly declared, "One is not born, but rather becomes, a woman."[4] De Beauvoir recognized the role of "civilization" in constructing the "true woman" as an "artificial product," though she retained the idea that it is the female body that "becomes a woman." She explains, "The chief misunderstanding . . . is that it is *natural* for the female human being to make herself a *feminine* woman: it is not enough to be heterosexual, even a mother, to realize this ideal; the 'true woman' is an artificial product that civilization makes, as formerly eunuchs were made. Her presumed 'instincts' for coquetry, docility, are indoctrinated, as is phallic pride in man."[5] Her critique rightly called into question the presumed relational confluence between female-sexed bodies and the societal construction of that which is deemed feminine. De Beauvoir undermined the artificial ascription of a certain set of qualities as *naturally* more feminine than others.

Since de Beauvoir, many scholars attending to gender issues across the spectrum of disciplines have argued that the concepts of sex, gender, femininity, and masculinity cannot stand apart as independent ontological categories. Instead we must consider them social constructs, defined and characterized through particular contexts and with specific motivations. Joan Wallach Scott argues that "gender is *the social organization* of sexual difference." Sexual difference is a "function of our knowledge about the body and that knowledge is not 'pure,' cannot be isolated from its implication in a broad range of discursive contexts. Sexual difference is not, then, the originary cause from which social organization ultimately can be derived. It is instead a variable social organization that itself must be explained."[6] Following contemporary impulses toward constructivist theoretical models, Irene Gedalof suggests that the signifier of the feminine comprises "those gendered, culturally and historically variable qualities and activities that are usually, but not necessarily, assigned to those persons identified as female."[7] Dominant strains of discourse in the academic theorizing of gender largely agree that the linguistic and cultural signifiers of what is considered feminine, and even female, are not ex nihilo signified actualities but, rather, historically and culturally mediated productions.

We owe much of this notion to Judith Butler's influential work that popularized the notion of gender construction and performativity. Butler successfully argued that the attributes of gender are socially constructed in words, acts, gestures, and desires. She reconceptualized gender identity "as an *effect*, that is, as *produced* or *generated*."[8] Conditioned by social norms that aim to reinforce the heterosexual matrix, people exact gendered identities. Thus gender is not an identity in itself but an *act/ion* that creates an identity. Gender is an act/ion; it is something that we do—an act/ion that we perform each day in each moment. It is not inherent in an individual but is a fluctuating performance of assumed norms and conditioned responses.[9] Similarly, Michel Foucault suggests that there is no independent conception of sex outside of the historical construction of sexuality; sex is "an imaginary point determined by the deployment of sexuality."[10] For these theorists, sex, gender, and notions of what constitutes the masculine and feminine cannot stand alone as independent ontological categories with universal applicability. Instead they must be deconstructed into their discursive elements within their particular sociopolitical and historical contexts of usage and, most importantly, recognized as ideologically driven constructions with significant consequences for the development of human subjectivities and their understandings of appropriate social ordering.

Shifting gears from the realm of theory to sociohistorical practices, modifications in cultural attitudes toward supposedly natural characteristics of masculinity and femininity warrant the claims of these theorists. For example, in marked contrast to American perceptions today, in the 1910s through the 1940s, pink (closer to red) was considered the more suitable masculine color for boys, while the more fragile pale

blue signified the gentility and delicacy of girls.[11] In the 1950s, the professional role of business executive or physician was largely deemed un-
natural for women; instead, women were funneled into a more socially
acceptable role, for example, housewife or secretary. Compare this to
today's statistics that reveal that women have higher college graduation
rates and academic excellence than men, though the employment arena
continues to reflect imbalances in remuneration and job placement in
accordance with more traditional gender hierarchies.[12] Normative roles
based on gender stereotypes change over time and through social context, demonstrating consistency with constructivists' arguments, which
recognize the artificiality within socially sanctioned gender norms.

still have More to do, ways to BE better

Thus conceptions of what constitutes the feminine are social constructions assembled from the discursive, social, cultural, and religious
contexts through which the very process of subjecthood is created. The
characteristics that Amma associates with the feminine are wholly dependent on cultural norms of sex and gender, which relate female-sexed
bodies and female gender to certain characteristics. This equation of the
feminine with a certain set of polythetic characteristics, which Amma
presents as normative, is instead a posited identification constituted by
a specific set of selected (not innate) characteristics. Their constitutive
elements of ideotypical femininity are conditioned by society, history,
culture, and politics. → *transnational feminism*

As a transnational guru, Amma must carefully navigate the terrain
between maintaining what devotees perceive to be traditional cultural
and religious authenticity and fostering a universal discourse that appeals to diverse global audiences. In the quagmire of multiple intersecting lines of intercultural translations and encounters, she must maintain
a precarious balance between garnering authority from her Hindu roots
to appeal to Indian Hindus and the palatability of her discourses to
resonate with non-Indian audiences.[13] Within such a delicate balance,
the rhetoric of feminism is a dangerous ally, and it is one that Amma
avoids. For as Geetanjali Gangoli reminds us, "In spite of the nuances
within feminist conceptualisations of Indian society, the rhetoric of
'westernization' has been used consistently as a charge to embarrass and
silence feminists."[14] Detractors overtly critique feminism in Indian society
as a form of neoimperialism imported from the West, particularly
when initiated through nongovernmental organization programs with
Western-derived funding sources. Such critics view feminism as an as-
sault against the sanctity of Indian womanhood, particularly women's

✓ cannot become Westernized

traditional roles as keepers of the family, household, culture, and religion.

But even female Indian activists who identify as feminists note the discrepancies between Western notions of feminism and Indian feminism, though they may agree on the overarching political aim of providing avenues for women's social equality.[15] Many Indian feminists object to the antagonistic impulses between the sexes, which serve as a foundation of much of Western feminism. Part of the discrepancy here lies in the differences between the historical trajectories of Indian and Western feminism. Whereas Western feminism largely developed through a history of women struggling against men for equal recognition and remuneration, Indian feminism began first as a campaign for the improvement of women's social and educational position that was championed and led by men. Social programs directed toward solving "the woman question" were initially conceived as programs of social "uplift" activated by men in support of women (one is uplifted by others). Women only developed leadership roles in India as feminists in the early decades of the twentieth century.[16] Thus, in Indian feminism, men became companions in the struggle for women's empowerment rather than adversaries.   *why not in USA!*

Furthermore, in Hindu religious thought, there runs a strong current of the complementarity of the sexes. Among Shaivites there is the balance of masculine and feminine energy embodied in Shiva and Shakti, and in Sāṃkhya philosophy there is the inherent balance between feminine action/matter and masculine thought/spirit found in the gendered dichotomy between *prakṛti* (feminine) and *puruṣa* (masculine). In the Hindu pantheon of gods and goddesses, nearly every male god has his female consort who complements his strengths, for example, Radha/Krishna, Lakshmi/Narayana, and Sita/Ram. Furthermore, the primary deities of the Hindu pantheon are often depicted in androgynous manners, the most prominent being the half-man, half-woman iconography of Shiva as Ardhanarishvara. These Hindu symbioses between male and female proliferate in the Indic context in material culture as well as in personal and communal understandings of an idealized interdependence between the sexes.

Additionally, the dominant Hindu philosophical ideals of the nature of the self and subjectivity challenge any assertion of an inherent antagonism between men and women. In Hindu metaphysics, as explicitly outlined in the Upaniṣads and the *Bhagavad Gītā*, the nature of the self is conceptualized as *ātman*, the individual essence of a person. It is this ātman that transmigrates through the cycle of birth-life-death-rebirth (*saṃsāra*). In Śaṇkara's Advaita Vedanta (nondualist philosophy), the ātman is recognized as being comprised of the same essence as *brahman*, the cosmic essence of the universe. Through religious practice and austerity, one aims to cultivate "self-knowledge or the discrimination of the self from what is not the self. . . . Inwardness leads away from exteriority towards knowledge and freedom [*mokṣa*]."[17] The practice of self-discrimination focuses on the processes of determining what is self from what is not self, distinguishing the ultimate self from the conventional self. Sex and gender, like other materialities particular to temporal bodily appearances, locate within the realm of the conventional self, that which must be transcended in pursuit of the ultimate self (ātman).

While these metaphysical turns do not translate into interdependence and equality among men and women in modern Indic society, they do provide significant culturally and socially sanctioned resources from which contemporary women can stake their claim to demand equal representation. Some contemporary female ascetics invoke advaita vedantic metaphysical arguments that claim the ultimate ephemerality and meaninglessness of gender and sex distinctions in order to justify their positions of religious authority.[18] But as Meena Khandelwal notes, "In spite of the advaitic rhetoric of transcending differences, gender differences play a more important role in the lives of male and female renouncers than any other social distinction."[19] Khandelwal argues that female renouncers (*samnyāsinīs*) do not renounce their femininity; instead, they identify as mothers.[20]

As mentioned, early ethnographic research intimated that female ascetics operated in a parasitic relationship to their male counterparts; it concluded that there were minimal differences between male and female styles of world renunciation in Hindu traditions.[21] More recent scholars have countered that "female ascetics move beyond normative renunciate paradigms/practices and create alternative traditions of asceticism." Namely, they create alternative traditions that "express continuity with traditional gender roles" and "are thought to be representative of female householders lives (e.g., compassion, nurturing, love, and selfless service)."[22] Thus female ascetics develop alternative ascetic modalities contiguous with householder roles of appropriate models of femininity. They most commonly represent themselves as maternal ascetics, motherlike celibate renunciates, who are dedicated to selfless service, sacrifice, and spiritual counsel. Importantly, these symbolically maternal ascetics understand their devotees to be their children.[23]

Many female ascetics are portrayed as, called by name, and understood to be ideal mothers, though they are usually celibate and have no biological children. Khandelwal explains, "It is the role of mother that offers them power and respect in Hindu society, desexualizes them, and is least threatening to their male peers; it is not so surprising that they emphasize maternal identities."[24] McDaniel similarly concludes that the title "Mā or Devī or Vīrā" so commonly used in Shakta circles "protects women from being looked on in sexual terms. . . . To call a woman 'mother' is a classic way for an Indian male to deflect a woman's hint at marriage or a courtesan's proposition."[25] Here we might recall A. S. Altekar's famous and often-quoted pronouncement that "the apotheosis of the mother has reached a greater height in India than anywhere else."[26] By constructing their self-identities in terms of maternality, female religious adepts protect themselves within an established and esteemed station in society and present themselves as emblems of the exalted aspects of femininity. Such positioning also distances them from the more dangerous or sexualized aspects of womanhood that are perceived to be antithetical to the conventions of brahmanical asceticism, for example, the prostitute. In a practical sense as well, their position as motherlike but not actually mothers enables them to develop relationships and counsel householders (particularly householder women), without the high stakes, fear, and potential biases associated with confiding in one's own mother or mother-in-law.[27] The majority of female ascetics have constructed their identities as maternal figures, through which they claim to embody the feminine, particularly maternal, ideotypical qualities of love, compassion, sacrifice, and service. Positioning themselves in this socially esteemed role facilitates their transition into the male-dominated world of Hindu asceticism. In so doing, female ascetics draw on the established and widely accepted cultural exaltation of the mother while simultaneously deemphasizing their female sexuality in order to minimize their perceived threat to the established norms of brahmanical asceticism.

In his comparative study of asceticism, Gavin Flood draws on the French sociologist Danièle Hervieu-Léger's work that describes tradition as a "chain of memory" that confers transcendent authority on the past. Flood builds on this premise to assert that "ascetic traditions are forms of collective memory enacted in the body through praxis and enacted in language through discourse," essentially, that asceticism is "the enactment of the memory of tradition."[28] If we accept that asceticism, in both its male and female formations, is constituted by "the enactment of the memory of tradition" then perhaps it is only logical that female ascetics represent continuities in their ascetic identity formations with both ideotypical roles for maternal self-sacrifice and ideotypical feminine virtues. They formulate their maternal ascetic identities not by identifying with their male ascetic counterparts but, rather, by enacting the virtues of culturally signified female characteristics, such as compassion, love, sacrifice, service, nurturing, and counsel. In short, their "memory of tradition" expresses a gendered solidarity with householder women over and above an ascetic solidarity with renunciate men.

There is also evidence suggesting that maternality is cross-culturally linked to ideals of self-discipline and self-sacrifice. Robert Thurman argues, "In a sense, the ordeal of self-denial, extra effort, and struggle involved in bearing children . . . is perhaps the primal ascetical act, as the common example of self-sacrifice of a mammalian mother for her offspring is the primal ascetical heroism."[29] This "ascetical heroism" of mothers often stands at the forefront of Hindu nationalism, wherein women gain exalted positions because of their supposed maternal capacity for self-sacrifice and their ability to "give birth to the nation" by literally birthing generations of nationalist citizens.[30] Within Hindutva organizations, the symbol of heroic motherhood also enables Hindu women to mediate the cultural anxieties and the threat that female political leadership entails for the gender status quo.[31] Similarly, celibate female gurus and ascetics generally cultivate their renunciate identities through conventional, culturally bound understandings of maternality, which wholly reinforce stereotypical, historically codified conceptions of the "feminine." Consequently, many female leaders in right-wing Hindu nationalist movements live their lives unconventionally while they simultaneously advocate for more subservient roles conforming to existing hierarchies for other women. Likewise, the majority of female ascetics are rebels but not revolutionaries.[32] The pervasive iterations of "do as I say, not as I do" dominate female renunciate discourses about the viability for ascetic paths for women. Scholars note a similar double standard that operates among right-wing women activists.[33]

But in Amma's movement, while she does not advocate for all women to undertake the vows of renunciation, she does implement what we might call a revolutionary impulse that aims to alter socially constructed normative behaviors for women. Like the Hindu nationalist women's movements, she invigorates the available cultural esteem of motherhood as a symbol of female power. She implements the "ascetical heroism" of maternality metaphorically as a mimetic model not only for women but for men as well. Amma presents an ideology venerating the archetypal feminine qualities of universal motherhood as a prescription for the ailments of humanity. Throughout her writings and speeches, she explains that many of the current crises facing our species and planet derive in part from gender inequalities extant in contemporary society; this gender imbalance propagates an impinging crisis affecting all sectors of society.[34] She says, "Women and men should join hands to save our society and the coming generations from a huge disaster. . . . Instead, the situation today is akin to two heavily loaded vehicles speeding towards each other from opposite directions, each unprepared to move aside to let the other pass."[35]

Amma's advocacy for women represents a matrifocal critique, a socially oriented platform that aims to create equality and balance between the sexes by privileging the idealized qualities of motherhood. Politically, she campaigns to raise awareness of gender-based oppression and injustices while modifying power structures in society to be more gender egalitarian. She argues that historically and currently, men have subordinated and oppressed women, which has resulted in the widespread assumed inferiority of women. In her view, this is not natural or divinely authorized but is instead a grievous injustice that men have enacted on women. In an effort to correct such injustices, she privileges the feminine in her discourses and uses her own religious authority, social power, and financial capacity to convey and enact her message. In practice, she situates her female renunciate devotees in positions of religious authority and laywomen in positions of social power through her humanitarian efforts.

Amma has implemented significant humanitarian and educational programs that reflect her commitment to bettering women's position in society, particularly in India. To this end, she has instituted numerous resources aimed at providing women with the social and economic resources to attain positions of greater power and autonomy in society. Her movement's humanitarian endeavors provide resources for both men and women through a variety of programs, but several projects offer much needed resources directed at improving the social lives of women in India. In the wake of the Indian Ocean tsunami in 2005, Amma established tailoring classes in which two thousand women participated; she also gave away three hundred sewing machines to enable women to supplement their family incomes through sewing work. In 1999, Amma established a monthly pension project for disenfranchised women and the physically and mentally challenged; this program has served one hundred thousand people since its founding. Hundreds of young women live in dormitories at Amritapuri and attend courses at educational institutions that Amma has established.[36]

More recently, her humanitarian outreach programs have highlighted the idea that when women are given seed monies and resources to improve their situations, they in turn direct their attention to the betterment of their communities. The headline "Empowering Women" leads the list of itemized activities of Amma's charitable organization Embracing the World (ETW). The website text reads, "Research has shown that empowering women with equal economic opportunity is one of the most effective ways to reduce poverty throughout entire communities."[37] Nearly two-thirds of the short films collected in the highly produced and marketed documentary of ETW charitable activities, called *Stories from the Field*, focus on female subjects who are "empowering" themselves and their communities through ETW scholarships and charitable activities. The short films, with titles such as *You Can Do This, Too: A Successful Woman Inspires Others,* highlight women engaging in microbusinesses (rubber tapping, mushroom farming, bamboo crafts, cocoa roasting, umbrella making, sari painting, and the like), orphanage work, and education and scholarship programs.[38] The programs largely emphasize their positive effects among women and children in particular. For example, *Slum Renovation, Mysore* invites the audience to witness a home building project's positive effects on two sisters and their mother. The opening address of the short film depicts smiling women and children and informs the audience "65 percent of [the] slum population are women and children."[39] In another clip, a young girl whose father is a cancer patient and whose brother is "not so sharp" explains, "I don't feel afraid anymore when I face difficulties. Before I used to feel powerless—what can a small girl like me do? Still, father is helpless and things are difficult, but with Amma's blessings I'm able to face all adversaries." In the short film *Renuka: A Quiet Heroine Shares Her Story,* the audience is presented with significant statistics about the far-reaching impact of ETW funds: $100,000 start-up capital for microbusiness and vocational training grants, free medical camps serving 300 people a month, 400,000 free homes built across India, 50 free occupational courses offered, and 2,400 people who receive vocational training in Idukki, Kerala.[40]

Amma centralizes the role of women in nearly every avenue in which she engages, whether it is social engagement, ritual officiation, scripture recitation, or mimetically inspired codes of conduct. As such, her interpretation of Hinduism is radically innovative, particularly in relation to the constructions of socially appropriate female behavior. Other contemporary female ascetics use the powerful Hindu motif of the veneration of the mother to secure their religious positions as autonomous and esteemed ascetics. But, as we have seen, Amma takes this one step further by presenting herself as an embodiment of the goddess through *Devī Bhāvas*. Emboldened as both a living goddess and a powerful female maternal ascetic, she has used her position to create a transnational religious institution wherein women hold both administrative and religious leadership positions and focus their energies on the improvement of women's conditions across the globe. In the following sections, I address specifically Amma's valorization of the feminine, rendered distinctly visible through her implementation of women as Hindu ritual authorities and her goddess-centric theology.

GENDERED INNOVATIONS OF HINDU RITUAL

It is after 3 a.m. as I make my way back to my suburban hotel room after the climax and conclusion of Amma's evening darshan program in July 2011. Bleary-eyed and exhausted, I optimistically set my alarm for less than two hours later, just in case I can pull myself together to attend the *homa* (fire sacrifice), which begins at 6 a.m. It seems that immediately after closing my eyes my alarm goes off. I turn it off and resign myself to missing the homa yet again, having been unable to resist seeing the close of the evening programs. At 5:20 a.m. there is a fire in my hotel, and nervous hotel employees bang on each door demanding that all sleepy occupants exit calmly and gather in the parking lot. I take it as a sign. Hurriedly attempting to draw some life into my overtired face, I gather the bare essentials and head out the door with the rest of the evacuees. But instead of pacing the parking lot with the crowd of pajama-clad hotel patrons, I move quickly to attend the homa.

Racing toward the eastward facing balcony of the hotel, I quickly toss the paper cup of gas station coffee that I had gulped and attempt to begin to present myself as peaceful and meditative in the early morning dawn. Out on the low balcony, I circumnavigate parallel sections of pre-arranged chair seating for fifty or so before securing a front-row floor seat adjacent to the three-tiered square structure of bricks in which the homa will be offered. A tall, languid brahmacāriṇī with pale-white skin and sari purposefully gathers assorted accoutrements in small copper and brass bowls next to the sacrificial fire altar and a heaping pile of rose petals that all but obscure the silver tray beneath them. A young Japanese man wearing a white dhoti assists her. He wears no sacred thread of the brahmans but instead a simple white T-shirt. I imagine that they are assistants who will soon make way for Br. Shantamrita, a white male renunciate who conducts most homas on Amma's tours and administrates the Asia Pacific regions of her organization. But instead the white brahmacāriṇī, Padmavati (Lynn), positions herself in the officiant space and draws the assembled audience together with collective chants of "Oṁ" and opening prayers in praise of the guru. I learn later that Br. Shantamrita is abroad, actively assessing the humanitarian needs of the 2011 tsunami-devastated regions of Japan.

Soon the sacrificial fire blazes as the hot sun rises over the suburban Chicago landscape. Padmavati conducts the homa in the style of what she later explains as the South Indian tantric tradition, implementing slight innovations according to Amma's direction. She conducts the homa in near silence, her lips moving with lightning-speed mantras with each offering. Later she tells me that tantric priests conduct this type of homa, having assumed a kūrma-pīṭha, the visualization of the ritual body as a tortoise, which symbolizes the internalization of the ritual as in when the turtle draws all of its appendages into its shell. Padmavati trained to learn the officiation of the homa at Amritapuri through an apprenticeship with Amma's pujārīs (male ritual officiants) there. After gaining competence as a pujārinī (female ritual officiant), she was directed by Amma to relocate to the San Ramon, California, ashram to perform homas and pujas for the ashram community, as well as to perform them in other parts of the United States (see figure 8).

Later, when I asked her about her unusual position as a white woman performing vedic homas, Padmavati responded with several different justifications, none of which was offered defensively. She emphasized, with reverence and humility, that she performed these vedic rituals traditionally reserved for male brahman priests only because of Amma's grace. She explained that she has always had a propensity for ritual. When her astrological chart was consulted, it showed that she was a brahman priest in a past life, and her planetary alignment revealed that she is suited to life as a pujārinī. She then added that in the vedic age women participated in ritual; it is only just recently that women have been disallowed from becoming ritual officiants. To solidify her case,

FIGURE 8. Padmavati performing vedic *homa* (© MA Center)

she then explained that "all great saints and prophets like Jesus and Śaṅkarācārya have seen beyond appearances" (notably here alluding to their analogy to Amma). She related the parable of when Śankara once bowed to a *śudra* who crossed his path while other brahmans shunned away from him to retain their purity.[41] In her view, the ability to see beyond the external body and treat all persons equally marks these religious adepts as exemplary and divine figures.

But despite Padmavati's confidence in her reasoning, she admitted that the night before she was to conduct the homa in Chicago she sought Amma's counsel. She asked Amma about the upcoming homa, particularly regarding whether her choice of a Japanese male assistant would be acceptable, or if she should offer the role to a brahmacāriṇī. Padmavati was particularly concerned because they (a white female lead and a Japanese male assistant) would be conducting the homa in a city like Chicago, which is home to such a significant population of immigrant Indian Hindus who would surely be in attendance. But Amma reassured her and reinforced her decision to conduct the homa with her Japanese male assistant as planned. Padmavati need not have been uneasy; the Indian Hindu devotees of Chicago likely would have voiced similarly reasoned justifications as Padmavati articulated. They would have done so because they too believe in the retooling of religious hierarchies to incorporate the inclusive democratization of ritual authority. They reiterate these ideals as Amma does, signifying their mimetic devotional relationship to their guru.[42]

Simply put, by their nature of being devotees they believe in Amma and they support her actions. Their unwavering faith tells them that what Amma does is right and in the interests of the good. If devotees disagree or fail to comprehend the guru's actions, it suggests a lack of awareness on their part, not hers. Despite all other innovations, contemporary devotees hold fast to the ancient tradition of the unwavering authority of the guru that defines the guru-disciple relationship. Disciples must not challenge the guru; rather, they must develop spiritually, in order to understand Amma's divinely inspired directions. Thereby, within her movement the guru maintains unchallenged internal support for her actions, including the radical revisioning and democratization of just who is empowered to be the ritual officiants (pūjārī/iṇīs). Devotees who find themselves in continuous disagreement with their guru largely separate themselves from the movement through attrition. Criticism of the movement, and of guru organizations more generally, tends to come in the form of external assaults rather than internal ones, the most vitriolic of which are often levied by ex-devotees.

Guru movements have a unique capacity for innovation, even when viewed through traditional historical codes of sanctioned Hindu behavior, the Dharmaśāstras. The Dharmaśāstras become sites of potential innovation because of the important caveat that one should also consider as dharma (right action) the exemplary behavior (sadāchāra) of righteous people, the ātma tushti or "conscience" of the righteous.[43] Such a formulation allows for considerable innovations to be coded as abiding within śāstric ideals of dharma. This is particularly prevalent within the field of modern gurus, wherein if they are regarded as righteous (or dharmic) individuals, their actions and behaviors themselves become a source for dharma—even when they may be contradictory to traditional interpretations of śāstric conventions. This cultivates a somewhat tautological argument: if the guru is dharmic and what dharmic people do is dharma, then what the guru does is dharmic and what the guru says is dharma. This logic reigns unquestioned among devotees and is only challenged among the general populace when its first proposition fails, that is, when the dharmic nature of the guru is challenged through public perception of offensive and non-dharmic (adharmic) behavior. We have seen this most recently with the media hype surrounding the Swami Nityananda scandal, the investigations debunking Sathya Sai Baba's miracles, and so on. In such cases, antagonists challenge the dharmic nature of the guru himself and thereby call into question the dharmic nature of his actions. But for those contemporary gurus who have managed to maintain somewhat dharmic (or at least inoffensive reputations), their innovative actions are subtly coded as new dharmas under the śāstric ideal of the exemplary behavior of the righteous. In this particular instance, the innovative practice of a white woman conducting a vedic homa becomes dharmic because Amma (who is believed to be of dharmic nature) says it is dharmic.

But the source of Padmavati's anxiety when faced with performing the vedic homa for large numbers of Indian Hindus in Chicago derives from the fact that Hindu pūjārīs are usually men. In fact, conservative Hindu conventions based in dharmaśāstric literature demand that this role be filled by only brahman men (men born into the highest class). Amma's instantiation of women as authoritative ritual officiants overtly and publicly thwarts conventional prohibitions against female ritual leadership. While Padmavati is the first white American female in Amma's organization to conduct vedic homas on American soil, she is not the first woman that Amma has instituted as a pūjārinī within her organization. Amma has also given her brahmacāriṇīs unprecedented levels of religious authority by establishing them as pūjārinīs in her temple at Amritapuri. In May 2009 I witnessed the routine event of a brahmacāriṇī performing the evening āratī (the waving of camphor lamps) and puja (ritual worship) in the Kali temple at Amritapuri.

At Amritapuri and in her various regional ashram temples, Amma alone performs the prāṇapratiṣṭha (the ritual act that infuses an inanimate object with life force, or prāṇa, of the image of the deity). However, in partial adherence to Hindu śāstric injunctions, Amma largely positions men (of any caste) as the principal pūjārīs in her temples in India. To comply with the expectations of the surrounding Indian community, Amritapuri has, over the years, separated the ashram spaces according to gender: a men's area and a women's area. As a result, women conduct the pujas offered at the Kali temple, which is (conveniently) located in the women's area. Male pūjārīs conduct the vedic homas at Amritapuri, but women (both Indian and non-Indian) have also learned to conduct homas and pujas under their direction, with Amma's sanctioning authority. Several of these women have taken up posts as principal pūjārinīs at branch locations outside of India, such as Padmavati in San Ramon and Jivamrita (Jeanne) in France.[44] One tract on the Brahmasthanam temple contains ambiguous language, as it reads, "In addition to the congregational pujas, daily pujas are conducted by the temple priests according to the injunctions of the Sastras. It is important to note that the worship in the Brahmasthanam temples is performed by Amma's brahmacaris, sincere sadhaks striving intently for God-realization, their lives dedicated to the welfare of humanity."[45] Herein there is no overt assertion of females performing the daily pujas at the Brahmasthanam temples or being trained to conduct vedic homas there, though they do so regularly in practice. The tract uses the inclusive masculine forms of the nouns "priests," "brahmacaris," and "sadhaks," though women perform each of these roles along with their male counterparts.[46]

There is quietude in the manner in which Amma asserts women's authority as viable ritual officiants. She does not advertise or radicalize her actions with vociferous or argumentative rhetoric; rather, she subtly makes alterations to gender and caste hierarchies while following all other śāstric injunctions. As Amritrashmi (Maribel), a senior devotee at Amritapuri, explained, "Frankly, as in the West, most women's roles are 'support roles'—women clean up the puja articles, make the garlands, light the lamps, etc. . . . However, Amma has pioneered having women as pujarinis, etc., something that used to hold true in ancient times but fell into disuse as India became more patriarchal. There is nothing in Hindu scriptural teaching barring women; there is no formal decree barring them; simply, it became 'a man's world' and men held onto their privileges and women stepped back. But Amma wants this to revert to the ways of the old days, and is doing her part towards that. She is not doing it in a big and splashy way, as that tends to entrench opposition; she simply does it, quietly, where it works smoothly, and lets the see[d] grow."

Amma's performance of the consecration ceremonies of the *murtis* (statues and images believed to embody divine presence) in her temples is even more radical than her sanctioning of brahmacāriṇīs as authoritative ritual officiants. Through these bold acts, which have drawn criticism from more orthodox Hindu onlookers, Amma challenges the gender conventions of Hindu religious traditions. To defend her inclusion of women as religious authorities operating in the inner sanctum of her temples, she invokes the often-repeated mythos of the Golden Age of the Vedas as a time when women supposedly shared equally in rituals with men (a sentiment Padmavati and Amritrashmi reiterated). Amma explains:

Until recently, women were not allowed to worship in the inner sanctum of a temple; nor could women consecrate a temple or perform Vedic rituals. Women didn't even have the freedom to chant Vedic mantras. But Amma [speaking of herself in the third person] is encouraging and appointing women to do these things. And it is Amma who performs the consecration ceremony in all the temples built by our ashram. There were many who protested against women doing these things, because for generations all those ceremonies and rituals had been done only by men. To those who questioned what we were doing, Amma explained that we are worshipping a God who is beyond all differences, who does not differentiate between male and female. As it turns out, the majority of people have supported this revolutionary move. Those prohibitions against women were never actually a part of ancient Hindu tradition. They were in all likelihood invented later by men who belonged to the higher classes of society, in order to exploit and oppress women. They didn't exist in ancient India.[47]

Justified with the aim of reviving the mythic gender egalitarianism of the Golden Age of the Vedas, Amma's organization installs women in positions of religious authority as sanctified ritual officiants. These nontraditional ritual actors either complement or usurp the position traditionally held by the male priest, who is the culturally and religiously designated appropriate mediator for Hindu rituals.

But Amma's organization is not alone in granting priestly authority to female adepts. While the field of scholarly literature on female priests is still developing, Laurie Patton has written on the śāstric precedents and justifications for female ritual leadership,[48] and Vasudha Narayanan has contributed a seminal article documenting the subculture of minority female ritual officiants in India. Narayanan cites location after location wherein "progressive groups" have instituted cadres of female priests to conduct domestic rituals. Temple rituals, on the other hand, are more restrictive within traditional caste and gender distinctions, for example, upper-caste men still comprise a significant majority of temple priests and students at seminary-type schools run by various *mathas* (religious organizations).[49] However, small regional temples and goddess temples often provide a counterpoint to this majority by supporting female priests, a dichotomy Narayanan relates to the freedom of the vernacular established appositionally to the conformity of the Sanskritic brahmanical tradition.

News media sources have also noted that female Hindu priests are becoming increasingly commonplace in India and in the United States. As *India Today* reported in 2000, "Though Hindu scriptures do not prevent women from performing religious rites, priesthood has always been dominated by men. However, breaking free from the shackles of tradition, these women have managed to shatter the glass panel."[50] While "crack" rather than "shatter" may be a more appropriate metaphor, still two institutes in Pune, the Shankar Seva Samiti (est. 1979) and the Dnyana Prabodhini Center (est. 1990), have trained over two hundred female priests since their founding.[51] Other ritual officiant trainers and their female apprentices operate in the private sphere, such as Mama Thatte, a Hindu priest and scholar of vedic literature, who began training women to become priests in 1970.[52] One optimistic journalist estimates that "approximately 700 women, most of them from Pune, a busy metropolis, 164-km south of Mumbai (previously Bombay), have undergone the necessary training since the seventies, and many of them are practicing."[53] While the most conservative Hindus reject the idea that a woman might function as a priest for rites such as marriages, death anniversaries, sacred thread investitures, and housewarmings, women priests are widely employed and supported by the "progressive Hindu who wants to break away from difficult ritualistic offerings" of which they find many supporters among the younger urbanite populations. In fact, Arya Joshi, the course coordinator at Dnyana Prabodhini, suggests that only 25 percent of the population opposes women priests, and those are largely representative of "the old and traditional families in the city."[54]

These largely urban-centered female priests are not accepted just because they are women. Many seek their services because they conduct rituals in a more democratic and inclusive manner than their male counterparts. Training for female priests is open to all castes, regardless of marital status (women may be single, married, widowed, or divorced); similarly, female priests offer their ritual officiant services to all patrons regardless of their gender, caste, or social status. This democratizing strategy runs through the campaign and is infused in the procedures of the ritual as well, wherein female priests pointedly explain aspects of the ritual to their commissioners. These egalitarian and educational components of women's ritual officiation appeal to many younger generations that seek to understand the meaning behind the practice. Arya Joshi explains, "At the Prabodhini we encourage everyone to participate and read from the text. A copy of the chants is given to everyone." Families who employ female priests often do so because they have had unsatisfactory experiences with male priests. Varsha Godgil explains as she relates her latest experience with a male priest, "He didn't explain anything and rushed everything."[55] In contrast, Manohar Mokashi, who commissioned a female priest for his mother's last rights, related,

"The rituals were explained to us. All family members were made a part of the rituals."[56] This explanatory aspect has become significantly more important to patrons in recent decades as they seek to find personal meaning in traditional ritual practices and to be competent in explaining ritual meanings to non-Hindus (an issue particularly important to diasporic Hindus). For many, the ancient tradition of sacred and thereby secret formulas of vedic mantras that are available only to specially trained, privileged classes of exclusively male religious exemplars is marked by an antiquated elitism that is not in step with the globalized, cosmopolitan, and democratic ideals of modern India.[57]

During Amma's darshan tours, teams of female brahmacāriṇīs instruct hundreds of male and female and Hindu and non-Hindu novices in cities across the United States in the pragmatic details of Hindu rituals. In so doing, Amma not only empowers her teams of young female brahmacāriṇīs to function as ritual adepts and teachers, but she is also democratizing the historically institutionalized hierarchies of traditional Hindu ritual. At Amritapuri Amma has also created an innovative type of ritual that she terms *congregational puja* (*samūha grahadoṣa śanti pūjā*), a worship ritual in which many devotees gather together to perform a puja themselves. In a tract on the Brahmasthānam temple, the authors explain that Amma teaches that "worship ceremonies performed by a large group are many times more powerful than individual worship," and that there are benefits to the devotees performing the ritual themselves rather than having a priest perform it for them.[58] Whether encouraging women to become pūjāriṇīs or encouraging the laity to perform its own rituals, Amma's interventions destabilize male brahmanical control over ritual activities.

In a similar vein, Nathan Hatch explains that the nineteenth-century democratization of American Christianity began first with the process of wresting complete power, authority, and control over rituals from a select order of men. Initiators transferred that ecclesiastical authority into the hearts and minds of all persons, not only priests. He said: "First, they denied the age-old distinction that set the clergy apart as *a separate order of men*, and they refused to defer to learned theologians and traditional orthodoxies . . . the fundamental impetus of these movements was to make Christianity a liberating force; people were given the right to think and act for themselves rather than depending upon the mediations of an educated elite."[59] Similarly, in the Hindu context, female pūjāriṇīs and lay ritual officiants challenge the supremacy of the male brahmanical priesthood as "a separate order of men" charged with mediating between humanity and the gods. Amma, her devotees, and the women priests of Pune are quietly and carefully "planting the seeds" that have the potential to develop into an innovative and substantive democratizing influence to modern Hinduism, particularly when coupled with the global cosmopolitanism of the urban and educated middle classes of modern India.

But what is the relationship to innovation here? Max Weber famously suggests that "the bearer of charisma enjoys loyalty and authority by virtue of a mission believed to be embodied in him; this mission has not necessarily and not always been revolutionary, but in its most charismatic forms it has inverted all value hierarchies and overthrown custom, law and tradition."[60] Following Weber's assertion, we might then suppose that a charismatic religious leader like Amma would challenge, if not wholly overthrow, "custom, law, and tradition" (an apt characterization of the combinative qualities of śāstric knowledge). But ritual action in particular tends to be presented as the recapitulation and continuation of ancient ways of doing things. Ritual actions "imply the legitimacy of age and tradition" and "present themselves as the unchanging, time-honored customs of an enduring community."[61] In the South Asian context, Sheldon Pollock has argued that although Indic cultural and intellectual history "is crowded with exciting discovery and innovation . . . these are not, however, perceived to be such; they are instead viewed, through the inverting lens of ideology, as renovation and recovery."[62] The commonly accepted and historically sanctioned a priori authority of śāstra militates against the possibility for "experience, experiment, invention, discovery, [and] innovation." He cites the ninth-century Kashmiri logician, Jayantabatta, who asks, "How can we discover any new fact or truth? One should consider novelty only in rephrasing the older truths of the ancients in modern terminology."[63] If authoritative knowledge is divinely created (*apaurusheya*) like the Vedas, then modern knowledge must recapitulate such sanctioned knowledge or risk being considered unauthoritative (adharmic), as that which contradicts or is not evidenced within the śāstras. How then are women able to become not only ascetic renouncers but also pūjārinīs while adhering to dharma in contemporary Indic society?

Vijaya Ramaswamy notes that while men "have social sanction for their renunciation, female asceticism was [in the medieval period], prima facie, a flouting of existing social conventions."[64] That is, the very existence of female ascetics is a transgression against traditional śāstric authorities. Still, female ascetics in the modern period carefully circumnavigate these treacherous territories between upholding śāstric injunctions of authoritative knowledge and challenging (or disregarding) misogynist śāstric rulings that prevent women from acquiring śāstric knowledge. While modern female ascetics often assert their rights to perform vedic sacrifice and rituals traditionally designated under male domain, they take care to remind audiences that there are no official śāstric injunctions against such female ritual activity.

In the early twentieth century, the Bengali saint Anandamayi Ma even commissioned a cadre of male brahman priests to investigate the śāstras to determine whether she and her brahmacāriṇīs who were conducting vedic homas violated any written śāstric principles. When the commission returned with a negative verdict that in fact there were no explicit regulations forbidding women from ritual officiation, she then initiated ritual performances in adherence to śāstric injunctions, but they were radically innovative in that they were performed by women independently. Her hagiographers exhibit the cultural importance of adhering to authorized śāstric injunctions in that they routinely take particular pains to remind audiences that "during Mā's [Anandamayi Ma's] life span, no violation of the *śāstric* tradition has been witnessed."[65]

More than half a century later, Amma exhibits a similar tension with śāstric injunctions. She rejects all prohibitions against women's participation in ritual leadership, arguing that such restrictions represent brahmanical misogyny rather than the ancient śāstric texts. She argues that over time Hindus devised a patriarchal structure that sought to destabilize women's roles in religious and ritual activity. Amma usually assigns these patriarchal interventions to the purāṇic period when she suggests that male brahmans wrongly interpreted the original śāstric injunctions in their efforts to prevent women's participation. In her view, then, it was the misogyny of the brahmans that devised unauthoritative (adharmic) interpretations of the authoritative śāstric texts. Thus Amma's contemporary revisions, which reinsert the authority of women as viable and effective independent religious and ritual actors, do not stand on the tumultuous ground of innovation but, rather, rest assuredly in the sanctified space of the renovation and recovery of the original and authoritative śāstric traditions.

Amma contends that brahmanical injunctions against women were not present in the texts but were merely social conventions that degraded women's once-powerful positions in Hindu society. She argues that modern society must restore itself to the more egalitarian social relations of the vedic period by augmenting the leadership and available roles for women, which will again bring balance to male-female relations. This restorative impulse in her theology protects her innovations from being perceived as adharmic radical changes to existing conventional ritual structures and instead engulfs them in the sanctimonious authority of the Vedas and Dharmaśāstras. As Vasudha Narayanan rightly notes, although the marked increase in female religious leadership within priestly traditions has changed the demographic of Hindu religious leadership, such changes are not coded as innovations. She says, "The reform itself is not understood as anything new or innovative; there are ample narratives in the more than three millennia of texts which provide precedents. These stories are retrieved, valorized and used as precedents for current changes."[66] In so doing, Amma's movement follows in the footsteps of many nineteenth- and twentieth-century Hindu reform movements (Arya Samaj, Brahmo Samaj, Ramakrishna Mission, Swaminarayan Hinduism, and so on) that justify their modernist innovations with claims to vedic and upaniṣadic authority.

However, the impulse to recode the new as ancient is not a tendency confined to modern Hindu religiosity; rather, it is often a defining characteristic of new religious movements in general. As Robert Ellwood explains, new religious movements are united by the subjective experience that "what they are participating in is not rightly understood by emphasizing the smallness, recentness, and marginality of the group. . . . They will . . . insist that their group is older and deeper than the more visible churches. Thus Spiritualism . . . calls itself 'the oldest religion in the world.' Theosophy speaks of its lore as 'the Ancient Wisdom.' Zen claims to be the essential but unspoken message of the Buddha, if not something even older than the Enlightened One."[67] Such formulations represent the phenomena that Hobsbawm and Ranger allude to as *"the invention of tradition."*[68] In short, effective claims to historicity and sociocultural precedent grant contemporary innovations an aura of authenticity, power, and authority.

As women insert themselves into traditionally restricted male spaces of ritual authority, their presence often initiates a democratizing process that easily elides with the elimination of caste and class hierarchies. The very existence of female priests not only transgresses conventional gender restrictions, but their presence often results in additional claims that all castes and classes of people should be able to actively participate in learning the intricacies of vedic ritual. In Amma's ashrams and in rituals conducted under her auspices across the globe, traditional Hindu caste restrictions simply do not apply. Amma authorizes women and men of all castes (and ethnicities) to perform vedic rituals, as long as they have been accorded adequate training in order to complete the rituals in compliance with śāstric stipulations. Training for pūjāriṇīs who will perform vedic homas includes a lengthy apprenticeship with a knowledgeable pūjārī, whereas training for specific pujas to Amma while she is on tour (pada puja, arati, and so on) usually comprises a one-hour or two-hour training session with Amma's touring brahmacāriṇīs.

Like her darshan embrace, Amma sanctions and mentors ritual officiants without regard for traditional caste and gender prohibitions. She also makes no distinction between Indian Hindus and foreigners, who are termed *mlecchas* in dharmaśāstric texts and categorized as śudras ("untouchables," or *dalits*, who occupy the lowest social position in Hindu India). Such inclusions stem from the fact that women and śudras are often equated and encompassed within the same knowledge restrictions in śāstric texts. Parallel opportunities deemed acceptable for women and śudras stem from śāstric injunctions that define women's status as equated with that of śudras: in many cases women are defined as śudras. Viewed in this light, we can recognize that Amma's actions ultimately validate the superstructures of śāstric injunctions, despite the fact that she is ultimately challenging their hierarchical restrictions.

Dharmaśāstric prohibitions often group women and śudras together, arguing that neither should access vedic learning, this despite the accounts of dozens of female sages in the Vedas, Gargi's influential role, and the necessity of female participation in household sacrifices. Dharmaśāstras, such as *Gautama Dharma Sūtra*, *Vāsiṣṭha Dharma Sūtra*, and *Baudhāyana Dharma Sūtra*, confirm the commonly iterated prohibitions against independent female activity (let alone ritual action) found in *Manusmriti*.[69] But relatively early on within the Hindu tradition, the *Bhagavad Gītā* issues *bhakti yoga* as a means for all persons to attain "the highest goal," or *mokṣa*. Verse 9.32 explains, "They who take refuge in Me, Son of Pṛthā [Arjuna], Even if they are born of those whose wombs are evil (i.e., those of low origin), Women, Vaiśyas, even Śudras, Also go to the highest goal."[70] The *Śrīmād Bhagavatam*, verse 1.4.25, explicitly links women and śudras under a singular rubric when it states, "For those unable to learn and recite the vedā [women and śudras], Vyāsa composed *Mahābhārata* which is considered the fifth vedā."[71] Sections in the *Śaiva Āgamas* (from which the Śaiva Siddhāntas of Tamil Nadu draw significant authority) indicate that only men of the twice-born classes should conduct Shivapuja, because only they are eligible to receive general initiation "with seed" (*sabīja*), which binds the ritual officiant to the "common code of conduct." Others, including "children, simpletons, elderly persons, women, hedonists, and disabled persons," are allowed to perform initiation, but they are permitted to do so only "without seed" (*nirbīja*), which is less fruitful.[72] Thus while there are prohibitions against women and śudras performing independent ritual action with the freedoms and authority of their male brahmanical counterparts, various scriptures that generate traditional śāstric authority allow for (and in some cases demand) their dependent participation, restricted participation, and/or subservient function within ritual contexts.

These limited allowances enable women in the modern period to justify their claims that women were never wholly prohibited from vedic knowledge and ritual function on the basis of dharmaśāstric evidence. They direct attention to the fact that in vedic times women were instrumental and necessary to the sacrifice, part of a husband-wife unit that conducted ritual action within the home. Vedic texts devote extensive attention to the problematic of ritual pollution incurred as a result of the menstruating or recently child-bearing wife.[73] If there are strict prohibitions against the presence of a menstruating wife, then it follows that a nonmenstruating wife was likely allowed to be present. In the modern period as well, vedic sacrifices for numerous occasions (such as the consecration of a new home) are routinely conducted by a husband-wife unit, along with a pūjārī/iṇī who jointly officiates the ritual.

The fissure with dharmaśāstric verifiability emerges when women claim independent authority to conduct vedic rituals autonomously, as pūjāriṇīs, without restrictions, limitations, or dependence on men. But once this dharmaśāstric slippage from women as joint participants to women as independent participants has been implemented, other hierarchies tend to dissolve as well. In the modern period, it is often the case that once the prohibitions against female participants are violated, similar effects apply to other categories of nonmale brahmanical authority (śudras, "friends of the twice-born," and even mlecchas). This is not only because of the weakening of hierarchies or a burgeoning democratic impulse of egalitarianism but also, because women and śudras occupy the same categorical sanction of allowed participation in religious actions.

The egalitarian impulses of medieval bhakti devotionalism also retain linkages between women and those of low-caste status by attempting to subvert brahmanical restrictions against both categories of people. Auvaiyar, a twelfth–thirteenth-century low-caste female saint (Viraśaivite), says, "There are no castes but two if you want me to tell / The good men who help the poor in distress / The other, that will not so help / These are the low born." Similarly, Akka Mahadevi, a twelfth-century female saint, says, "O Brothers, why do you talk to me / who has given up her caste and sex / having united with Chenna Mallikarjuna." Uttiranallur Nangai, a fifteenth-century female saint, says, "The revealed Vedas are lies, body and soul are lies. Are not all castes one?"[74] Such women were independent female devotional saints who implemented the egalitarian impulses of the bhakti movement to transcend brahmanical restrictions against low-caste and female religious adepts. But, again, these radical transgressions of caste and gender restrictions operate from within the overarching paradigm of dharmaśāstric reasoning, because they provide religious authority to those who are omitted from ritual activity without wholly subverting the existing paradigm. This is not a radical upheaval tradition but, like Jayantabaṭṭa, suggests a "rephrasing" of "older truths of the ancients in modern terminology." I propose that the "modern terminology" in question is the language of democracy and egalitarianism.

Amma is concerned with adhering to and (just as importantly) being perceived as adhering to śāstric injunctions that mandate the appropriate methods for authoritative and appropriate ritual action. Pujas and homas conducted under her auspices are largely traditional in form: Sanskrit mantras are recited, standard items are offered, and ritual purity is maintained in largely inherited ways that adhere to conventional śāstric injunctions.[75] However, Amma inverts commonly upheld value hierarchies by upsetting traditional understandings of who is qualified to be a ritual actor. Her movement sanctifies ritual action that is largely consistent with dharmaśāstric conventions, but sanctioned ritual actors are often women, laypersons of all castes, and non-Hindus. In fact, Amma emphasizes the importance of female and layperson leadership in the performance of ritual action, arguing that rituals performed by these particular populations serve as a restoration of dharma; they correct the gender and caste imbalances imposed by brahmanical male hierarchies. Her contention that the rituals are more efficacious when performed without priests as mediators suggests a democratic revisioning of ritual authority in Hindu religiosity. The irony here is that she does so by invoking that very śāstric authority that she aims to reform.

DISCOURSE: THE GODDESS SPEAKS
FEMINIST THEOLOGY

In her discourses, Amma positions the goddess as an exemplar for human women in order to argue for a necessary increase in women's power in society within and beyond the religious field. Amma presents herself as the Divine Mother to her devotees, and she uses the qualities of divine motherhood as an ideal typology for human behavior. Coupled with an advaita vedantic understanding of the nonduality of existence, Amma asserts, "The Atman or Self that is in me is also within you. If you can realize that Indivisible Principle that is ever shining in you, you will become That."[76] Thus, in principle, Amma explains to her devotees that, like her, all persons consist of the same essence of self (ātman), and as a result all persons are capable of recognizing their own unity with the essence of the universe (brahman). In practice, this ideology constantly reinforces her religious authority by encouraging her devotees to embody the ideal qualities that she herself epitomizes as the Divine Mother. Thus her theological project is intimately linked to her claims to religious authority. It serves to buttress those claims by staking out the parameters of the discourse and presenting devotees with an ideal, of which Amma is a living and perfected example.

It is from her position of power and religious authority, secured in part through the routinized performance of Devī Bhāvas, that Amma speaks of the conditions of human women in society. Her concern with the oppression of women in society is only one of many social issues that her organization tackles (other issues include homelessness, poverty, elder care, illiteracy, and lack of proper medical care). However, Amma routinely returns to topics regarding women's issues. Such issues directly relate to her own struggle to garner religious authority in a Hindu cultural system that largely restricts female leadership in religious institutions. Like many of her female ascetic/ecstatic contemporaries, Amma broke through this restriction initially by performing bhāvas, which set her apart from socially sanctioned behaviors for women. She exhibited a radical break with convention that signified her removal from marital markets and householder endeavors. Once situated in a relatively secure position of religious authority, she set about changing the established social and ritual status of women in Hindu traditions. Whether intentional or not, this conviction not only altruistically creates a path to achieving higher social status for other women but also serves to justify and reinforce her own position of authority.

In her most pointed critiques of the subservient status of women in society, her keynote addresses "The Awakening of Universal Motherhood" and "The Infinite Power of Women," Amma is careful to begin by explicitly saying that women and men are equal in her eyes.[77] In her social prescriptions for improving the position of women in society, Amma negotiates between the feminist impulse to recognize the very real power differences between men and women in society and her advaita vedantic ideology that obfuscates difference in favor of ultimate oneness. She refutes the belief that women should be subservient, arguing that gender hierarchies are not natural, preordained by God, or extant in the original unadulterated vedic injunctions. In a provocative, though commonplace, line of argumentation, Amma uses advaita vedantic nonduality to eliminate gender differences in an effort to assert the equality of men and women. She says, "For those who have realized God, there is no difference between male and female. The realized ones have equal vision. If anywhere in the world there exist rules that prevent women from enjoying their rightful freedom, rules that obstruct their progress in society, then those are not God's commandments, but are born out of the selfishness of men."[78] Thus Amma transfers the agent responsible for the subservience of women from the superhuman to the human and argues that both women and men need to work to improve the position of women in society.

In order to reconcile the nonduality of Advaita Vedanta with the necessary recognition of difference in feminism, Amma argues that the power imbalance between men and women is a social problem that stems from the disconnection of contemporary society from the philosophical truths of ultimate reality. She says, "There is a man in the inner depths of every woman, and a woman in the inner depths of every man. This truth dawned in the meditation of the great saints and seers eons ago. This is what the Ardhanariswara (half God and half Goddess) concept in the Hindu faith signifies. Whether you are a woman or a man, your real humanity will come to light only when the feminine and masculine qualities within you are balanced."[79] In other writings she repeatedly notes, "There is femininity in men and masculinity in women."[80] In these comments, Amma argues that both the singularity of gender and gender inequality are social constructions that signify a fundamental misinterpretation of the balance and equality between the masculine and the feminine that is divinely ordained.

Amma's most commonly iterated prescription for women (and men) is that they should embody the characteristics of "universal motherhood."

She claims that motherhood is a representative metaphor for the qualities of unconditional love, compassion, nurturing, austerities, and self-sacrifice, which both men and women can and should embody. In the majority of her discourses, she explains that motherhood does not mandate the actual physical birthing of children but, rather, represents ideal qualities that can be developed in all people. She says:

> Anyone—woman or man—who has the courage to overcome the limitations of the mind can attain the state of universal motherhood. The love of awakened motherhood is a love and compassion felt not only towards one's own children, but towards all people, animals, and plants, rocks and rivers—a love extended to all of nature, all beings. Indeed, to a woman in whom the state of true motherhood has awakened, all creatures are her children. This love, this motherhood, is Divine Love—and that is God.[81]

Here Amma explains that universal motherhood should be understood in its metaphorical sense as a taxonomy of ideal qualities. She assures her devotees that hers is not solely a women-centric theology that serves to exclude men, but that men can also participate fully by embodying the exemplary qualities of motherhood.

Amma suggests that men and women should reconstruct their own gendered identities to create a balance between the masculine and feminine within themselves. Though she advocates a balance between masculine and feminine qualities, she reasons that because the feminine has been suppressed and demeaned historically, in its current state of imbalance society must validate and develop the feminine in particular to achieve this balance. In so doing, she still advocates within essentialized notions of what masculinity and femininity connote. She argues that there are fundamental qualities that are masculine and fundamental qualities that are feminine, and that both men and women would be served well by embodying more of the feminine qualities. Amma strikes a delicate (or precarious) balance between idealizing maternal qualities, characteristics, and dispositions that are inherently present in women and those that both men and women can embody.

She sometimes shifts her emphasis from the veneration of maternality in a symbolic sense (that both men and women must develop) to the veneration of maternality that is intimately related to women's biological capacities. She says: "Women are essentially mothers, the creators of life. . . . The principle of motherhood is as vast and powerful as the universe. With the power of motherhood within her, a woman can influence the entire world."[82] Here Amma seems to implement the idea of motherhood not as a metaphor but through its physiological aspects. She argues that the rejection of motherhood is a rejection of a woman's true nature. Amma critiques the articulations of Western feminism circulating in India, that many Indians feel women are encouraged to be like men.[83] She expands on this problem with examples from the West, which she sees as fractured in part because of this tendency. Amma says:

> A woman should be respected and her feelings should to be [sic] given proper consideration. Her maternal qualities should be recognized and she should be given a higher, well deserved position in society, along with men. At the same time, she should know that the greatest gift God has bestowed on her is the gift of motherhood, the right to give birth and to raise a child with the proper care, love and affection. It is a unique gift, and it is hers alone. To give birth to the greatest people born on this earth, the divine incarnations, the great leaders, philosophers, and scientists—to give birth to all the eminent souls and to all of mankind—this is one of the greatest blessings of all. Why has God given women this wonderful gift? Because they alone have the capacity to express such qualities as love, compassion, caring, and patience, in all its [sic] fullness and beauty. Every woman should know this and try to comprehend the significance of this blessing. But it would seem that women are slowly forgetting this truth; and if they ignore this fundamental and indispensable quality within themselves, our society will be turned upside down. It is therefore vitally important that women recognize these qualities within themselves.
>
> It is mostly in western societies that women are forgetting their feminine qualities. In the name of equality, many women are disregarding this most priceless blessing they have been given. In the West, as opposed to Indian society, women are more aggressive and less yielding. As western women try to catch up with men in all areas of life, they do not realize that they are sacrificing an essential part of their nature. The result of this is total chaos and confusion, both in the outer and inner life. Amma [speaking of herself in the third person] is not saying that a woman shouldn't do the same things that men do—she can and she should, and women have an immense inner power—but it should never be done at the cost of sacrificing her essential being. Going against nature is destructive; it is dangerous for the person in question as well as for society as a whole.[84]

In this passage it is clearly the physiological process of birthing to which Amma refers with the word "motherhood," not a symbolic matrix of commendable maternal qualities. Here Amma essentializes women according to their physiological capacities as mothers; motherhood becomes a woman's "essential being."

From this physiological argument, Amma concludes that women are human embodiments of the goddess. She co-opts goddess imagery and mythology to argue that women should be given more authority in society because there is an inherent connection between human women and the Divine Mother. She explains:

> In India, the Supreme Being has never been worshipped exclusively in masculine form. The Supreme Being is also worshipped as the Goddess in Her many aspects. She is, for example, worshipped as Saraswati, the Goddess of wisdom and learning; She is worshipped as Lakshmi, the Goddess of prosperity; and Santana Lakshmi, the Goddess who gives new life within a woman. She is also worshipped as Durga, the Goddess of strength and power. There was a time when men revered woman as the embodiment of these very qualities. She was considered an extension of the Goddess, a manifestation of Her attributes on Earth. And then, at some point, because of the selfishness of certain men of influence and their desire for power and dominion over all, this deep truth was distorted and severed from our culture. And thus it was that people forgot or ignored the profound connection between woman and the Divine Mother. . . . Only love, compassion, and patience—the fundamental qualities of women—can lessen the intrinsically aggressive, overactive tendencies of men. . . . If women reject their feminine qualities and try to become like men, the imbalance in the world will only become greater. This is not the need of the age. The real need is for women to contribute all they can to society by developing their universal motherhood, as well as their masculine qualities.[85]

Herein Amma enacts a commonplace Indic argument for the "uplift of women," which lauds maternality and encourages respect for women because of their correlation with Hindu goddesses.[86]

Amma dislocates the contemporary subordinate position of women from divinely ordained prescriptions in dharmaśāstric literature and places the blame on "certain men of influence" who desired to oppress women for their own personal gain. She blames the oppression of women not only on men in antiquity but also on men in the present day. She says:

> It lies in their [men's] nature to belittle and condemn the achievements of women. Women are not decorations or objects meant to be controlled by men. Men treat women like potted plants, making it impossible for them to grow to their full potential. Women were not created for the enjoyment of men. They were not made to host tea parties. Men use women like a tape recorder, which they like to control according to their whims and fancies, as if they were pressing play and pause buttons. Men consider themselves superior to women, both physically and intellectually. The arrogance of men's mistaken attitude—that women cannot survive in society without depending on men—is obvious in everything that men do.[87]

She chastises men for their oppression of women and suggests that this attitude cripples not only women but also all of society and themselves in the process. She says:

Men have also suffered greatly as a result of the exile of the feminine principle from the world. Because of the oppression of women and the suppression of the feminine aspect within men, men's lives have become fragmented, often painful. Men, too, have to awaken to their feminine qualities. They have to develop empathy and understanding in their attitude towards women, and in the way they relate to the world.[88]

She further identifies the privileging of the "male principle" and the subsequent subordination of the "female principle" as a primary source of the continued destruction of the earth. She says, "There is also a deep connection between the way men destroy Mother Nature and their attitude towards women. Nature should be accorded the same importance in our hearts as our own biological mothers."[89] Amma and her organization frequently espouse this type of ecofeminist ideology, employing it readily to caution against immanent peril if humanity does not alter its destructive (overly masculine) impact on the planet.

At times, Amma's discourses on women essentialize women as mothers, with feminine qualities and "life-giving power." For example, in response to the recent horrific gang rape and subsequent death of a young female student on a moving bus in Delhi on December 16, 2012, Amma issued an earnest plea for a revaluation of women's position in society. She began her declaration by noting that the intensely violent event suggests a radical degradation from India's legacy of teaching "God as Mother, seeing God Consciousness in everything and showing tolerance." She then argued that a woman must take responsibility for her own empowerment, that it is "she alone—who has to awaken herself." Women must "break the shackles of the rules and conditioning that society has imposed upon them." They must recognize that "a woman's greatest strength lies in her innate motherhood, in her creative life-giving power," which "can help women bring about a far more significant change in society than men can ever accomplish." She concludes by urging women to "actualize the qualities of motherhood within themselves" and advises that the "forthcoming age should be dedicated to awakening universal motherhood."[90] The online comments to Amma's address celebrated it as a powerful assertion of women's rights and implored other social, political, and religious leaders in India to follow her example. It was quickly distributed through social media sites and the Internet among devotees as a welcome rejoinder against this most recent and gruesome example of sexualized violence against women.

However, it is somewhat distressing here that Amma locates responsibility with women themselves rather than directing her focus to sociopolitical institutional structures of inequity. When Amma encourages women to "awaken" and to create a new society for themselves by "breaking the shackles" of patriarchy, her rhetoric places significant responsibility on women who are routinely subjugated by systemic structures of inequality. Furthermore, here too her message vacillates between idealizing metaphorical qualities of motherhood and physiological prescriptions of women as essentially mothers. In this style of rhetoric, Amma is one among many religious leaders, politicians, and social commentators around the world who encourages audiences to respect women by reminding them of the respect that they have for their own mothers, wives, and daughters. These claims attempt to personalize women by invoking their important familial relations (to men). In response, one might argue that women should be respected because they are people, not because they have particular relationships to men, that is, mothers, wives, and daughters. But still, in a cultural climate wherein one of the most (in)famous "hyper-gurus," Asaram Bapu, responded to the Delhi gang rape by saying that the victimized woman was as guilty as her attackers, it is no wonder that Amma's message was lauded as a welcome rejoinder.[91]

Amma's contention that women's respectability intimately relates to their creative abilities to become mothers (often equated with the creatrix power of the mother goddess) echoes a dominant strain of the women's spirituality movement in the West.[92] Following Judith Ochshorn, I would argue that this assertion not only leaves us without answers about goddess religions in the past (humans in all cultures reproduce, but only some worship goddesses), but also it emblemizes a pernicious form of biological reductionism that further domesticates and restricts women to fulfilling their maternal functions. The valorization of women as mothers falsely equates women's innate value with their ability to reproduce. Such a move reduces women to their biological capacities and thereby does not develop egalitarianism between the sexes by validating and empowering women, regardless of their biological choices. Further, in times of crisis, food shortage, poverty, and illness, pregnancy and motherhood can be challenging and even life threatening to women, not empowering.[93] But advocates within the women's spirituality movement (who seem to echo Amma's sentiments) counter that it is precisely the biologically creative power of the female that supplies her cosmic power and warrants her universal reverence.

Leaving aside Amma's controversial physiologically oriented assertions, when Amma directs both men and women to embody the ideotypical feminine qualities of universal motherhood, she promotes overt gender essentialisms. Her developments on this theme suggest that, in her view, masculinity and femininity are substantive categories, defined by certain essential qualities, but not necessarily related to male- and female-sexed bodies. In her language, men can develop the feminine and women can develop the masculine. She illustrates this concept explicitly in her reprimand of women whose recent adoption of hypermasculinity in the name of feminism has eclipsed their purportedly innate feminine qualities. The fact that Amma maintains that certain qualities are naturally feminine and others are naturally masculine suggests that we cannot locate her discourses within the constructivist feminist positions, which posit sex, gender, and ideas about femininity and masculinity as sociocultural constructs divorced from any independent ontological status.[94]

Both the biological and metaphorical arguments for the equation of women with the goddess inhere in Amma's discourses about the need for women and men to embrace the feminine qualities of universal motherhood to (re)balance the gender composition of society. Amma argues that the feminine qualities that are natural to women must be awakened in both males and females. She urges her devotees to intentionally reconstruct their behaviors, attitudes, and dispositions to conform to the "feminine" qualities of universal motherhood.[95] This call for the feminization of humanity into the ethos of maternal self-sacrifice forms the nexus of her entreaty for ascetic discipline and the denial of the primacy of self-indulgence and personal gratification. As such, it constitutes a project of the reconstruction of the subjectivities of devotees, a project that molds the preexisting habitus of her disciples into new patterns of learned behavior and personal identity. All of this gains significance because of the fact that in the guru-disciple relationship devotees are eager to please their guru. If Amma wants devotees to identify with the purportedly feminine qualities of universal motherhood, they do. As they comply with her wishes, devotees develop new behaviors, attitudes, and dispositions that acculturate themselves to the maternal-ascetic habitus of the movement.

The ideotypical cultural esteem of the mother represents a soft and endearing form of asceticism; it is self-sacrifice performed as an outpouring of love. These discourses idealize and essentialize exemplary motherhood as an ascetic practice. Amma's prescriptions aim to infuse devotees with an ethos of self-sacrifice as their primary life purpose. The exemplary mother sacrifices for her children, thinks of her children's needs before her own, and showers them with unconditional love, compassion, and devotion. Thus we might conceive of Amma's appeal for universal motherhood as an entreaty for devotees to adopt practices that subordinate their own needs and desires to those of others. Devotees discipline their bodies and minds through their mimesis of the strong and self-sacrificial mother, embodied in Amma.

Within the context of Hindu asceticism, maternal qualities are often represented as the epitome of self-sacrificial behaviors, and they are sometimes attributed to both men and women. Meena Khandelwal references several instances in which devotees ascribed maternal names and identities to their male gurus because they believed them to exemplify the utmost "feminine" virtues of love, compassion, sacrifice, and service.[96] Generally, their attention, nurturance, feeding, clothing, care, concern, selfless love, and compassion for their devotees incite these devotees to refer to them as mothers, or to view the devotees' relationship with the guru as children in their mother's arms.[97] Likewise, Amma presents herself as a loving mother to her devotees, and her devotees understand themselves to be her children. Understood as the adoption of a particular ascetical disposition, the cultivation of maternality implements a gendered transformation that becomes disassociated from biological sex.

Amma expects her devotees to acculturate to her movement's maternal-ascetic habitus by mimetically conforming to a maternalistic ideal, of which she is presented to be (and presents herself as) a perfected example. While Amma invokes the goddess as the primary creative power and exemplar of female authority, she also positions herself as a tangible and intimate physical presence of the goddess in her devotees' lives. Her public performances of maternalistic self-sacrifice, unconditional love, devotion, and compassion to her devotee children during darshan programs signify her intentional presentation of a mimetic model. Discourses surrounding her (such as those given by her swamis during darshan programs) continually remind devotees to strive to witness and then emulate Amma's maternalistic unconditional love, compassion, and selfless service. Devotees engage in intense processes of mimetic emulation, watching the guru intently in an effort to train their bodies, minds, and dispositions in accordance with her example. They strive to emulate what they see as Amma's loving and self-sacrificial disposition in their own relationships, actively transforming their existing habitus to Amma's ideal of universal motherhood.

CONCLUSION

Despite her active instantiation of women in positions of power and authority, Amma eschews the term *feminism* because, in her interpretation, it evokes ideas rooted in Western feminism and largely subsists on a language of difference that invokes antagonism between the sexes.[98] She focuses on the feminine because of her belief that the world has become hypermasculinized, wherein the masculine dominates and subordinates the feminine. She sees this as the primary cause for ecological, economic, political, and spiritual crises in the modern world. This formulation depends on her culturally embedded essentialization of masculine and feminine qualities: masculine qualities are egoism, ambition, aggression, stagnation, and reactivity; feminine qualities are compassion, nurturing, love, selflessness, sacrifice, and virtue. Amma argues that we must awaken the feminine principle through the development of universal motherhood. In so doing, we will restore society to a balance between the masculine and the feminine principles, reclaiming the high status of women she believes occurred during the Golden Age of the Vedas.

But the presumption that the vedic period represented egalitarianism between the sexes largely falls short of historical verifiability. On the contrary, some scholars argue that indigenous India was largely matriarchal and goddess-centric only prior to the vedic period, when Aryans developed Sanskrit language, the Vedas, and patriarchal and class hierarchies in Indic society.[99] Whether a pre-vedic matriarchal goddess cult existed or not, vedic scriptures represent women as largely dependent ritual actors and only occasionally as religious adepts. Much of the dharmaśāstric literature that followed was much more restrictive and subordinating, to the point of excluding women from vedic ritual administration entirely. The mythos of the gender egalitarianism of the Golden Age of the Vedas must then be interpreted as a popular "invention of tradition," a new innovation that seeks to mask its newness with the cloak of established tradition and, in this case, authoritative śāstric injunctions.

In addition to using the authority of the Vedas (in this imagined Golden Age of gender equality) against the restrictions placed on women within the later Dharmaśāstras, Amma uses the nexus of advaita vedantic philosophy as ammunition against restrictions placed on women. She argues that not only were women equal to men during the vedic period, but that in ultimate terms there cannot be any real distinction between women and men. Both are comprised of the same ātman, and, as such, both are vital and valuable to society. She has an amusing anecdote in which she compares women and men to the various appliances in a kitchen, all performing an important function and powered by the very same electricity. To recognize ultimate truth is to transcend conventional differences of sex and gender.

Last, Amma sometimes uses the goddess as a symbol for female empowerment explicitly because women in particular can view themselves (and be viewed) as human reflections of her superhuman prowess. While devotees may find that the goddess seems too distant, nebulous, or impassioned for them to effectively emulate her in their everyday lives, Amma is not. Amma is present, temporal, and as intimate as a hug. In their intimacy with Amma, devotees witness and receive periodic tactile reminders of the behavioral ideals of her feminine universal motherhood, exemplified through selfless service, love, and compassion for all of humanity.

In the darshan process, and particularly during Devī Bhāvas, the goddess transforms from a distant, intangible imaginary to an unmediated, personal, physical being who folds devotees into her embrace amid the sensory explosion of blowing fans, stage lights, sandalwood and rose aromas, the crush of flower petal garlands, and the immense crowds, all of which are sustained through Amma's central expression of embraces. For devotees, Amma is a "river of love," and by watching her and sitting in her immediate presence they hope not only to be "showered" in her grace and infused with her spiritual energy, but also to learn through mimesis how to transform themselves into similar conduits for unconditional love, compassion, and selfless service. Love and compassion are at the core of Amma's teachings and her darshan rituals. These are the qualities that Amma suggests are fundamentally feminine, though they should be internalized and expressed by both sexes.

The internal nexus of her global movement subsists on the ideal that Amma is the mother to her many children around the world. If we recognize the mimetic relationship between devotee and guru, then it is perhaps less surprising that Amma encourages all of her devotees to become similarly symbolic universal mothers. Just as Amma as a maternal ascetic is not a physically birthing mother, her devotees need not be females who birth children either. But just as Amma embodies and exudes the care, compassion, unconditional love, and self-sacrifice of the ideal mother, so too should all of her devotees aim to embody and exude such idealized maternal qualities through active processes of self-transformation. Self-transformation develops mimetically in tandem with their acculturation into the maternal-ascetic habitus of the movement.

Instead of viewing Amma as an advocate of biological motherhood, it is more productive to conceive of such statements as a very Indic form of feminist argumentation, which draws on the culturally symbolic portrayal of the feminine as exalted and worthy of veneration, not as daughters and wives but as mothers, exemplified with powerful creatrix, fertility, and generative properties. The theology of the *Devī Māhātmya* (excerpts from which are recited at all of Amma's darshan programs) suggests that the feminine aspect of existence signified in all matter (*Prakṛti*) alone existed before creation and it was She (Prakṛti) who wished to create. To do so, she assumed the form of the Great Mother and then created the primary male deities (Brahmā, Viṣṇu, and Śiva) out of her own body.[100] This generative power of the feminine suggests the primordial importance of the female, without whom there would be no existence.

Amma evokes the primacy of female power in creation in order to demonstrate the injustice and irony when the spawn of such a creative power grows to subordinate and demean its own creator. She says, "Since women have given birth to and raised men, how can women not be equal to them?"[101] In highlighting the creative power of women as the progenitors of humanity, Amma calls on her listeners to contemplate the strongest bonds in Indic society, that of the immediate family, particularly the bond between mother and child. When Amma argues that all women should be respected as mothers (like the goddess), she effectively chastises men for their subordination of women. She demands that they think of their own mothers and apply those same feelings of respect, gratitude, and admiration to all women. Thus her discourses that emphasize the physical maternality of women should not be read primarily as a restriction of women to their physiological capacities to produce children, despite the fact that they reinforce such normative assumptions of women as childbearers. Instead, they aim to draw culturally embedded parallels between the power of the creator goddess and human women in order to demand recognition for women's essential roles in society. Simultaneously, they present a frequently employed and culturally familiar reproach to Indian men (but not only Indian men) who are prompted to remember the affection and respect that they have for their own mothers and the goddess and to hold all women in such esteem.

The majority of goddess worship in India is largely divorced from any feminist impulse or agenda. In fact, some scholars have argued that there is an inverse relationship between the veneration of superhuman goddesses and the conditions of ordinary women in society.[102] When Cynthia Ann Humes interviewed pilgrims on the way to Vidhyachal with the question "How does the goddess Vindhyavāsinī compare to the ordinary woman? . . . the single most common explanatory response was that there is an obvious, insuperable gulf between the nature of women and the Goddess." Again and again, pilgrims told her that between the goddess and women "there is as much difference as earth and sky."[103] But in Amma's milieu, this distance evaporates. The goddess shifts from a superhuman entity, distant from ordinary women's experiences, to an intimate physical being whom devotees embrace personally through devotion and physically, in her human form, as Amma. Believed to be a living avatar-guru, Amma supplies a physical conduit for the goddess as well as a mimetic ideal through which devotees are encouraged to develop an ascetic habitus of universal motherhood. The next chapter foregrounds the voices of devotees to show how such radical revisions are received and incorporated into their existing understandings of women, women's position in society, and women's relation to divinity.

CHAPTER 4

Culturally Situated Testimonies

Differing Interpretations of the Role of the Goddess

All over the World
All over the world Mother hears
her children's hearts calling.
She longs to soothe their painful yearnings
and lead them to eternal Light.
Mother does not distinguish among nations,
for She is everywhere—
all people are her darling children.
There are many petals on a flower but the flower
is one—
the world is a flower and every nation is a petal.
To Mother all are one.[1]

—Messages from Amma

The North American guru landscape fosters intense communal interaction between multiple generations of immigrant Indian Hindus and the metaphysicals, those Americans who seek out alternative spiritualities, like gurus. This prolonged cultural encounter between these internally diverse communities characterizes the negotiation of shared identity in contemporary guru movements. Maintaining doctrines, practices, and social environments that satisfy and inspire both of these internally diverse communities has proven to be one of the most difficult tasks for modern gurus as they transition into the United States. Some movements have given up such negotiations and tend to attract devotees from either immigrant Indian Hindu or metaphysical populations, but not both. A minority of movements identify with culturally distinctive, traditionalist, or conservative Hindu messages in order to appeal to immigrant

Indian Hindus, a strategic decision that often keeps the metaphysicals at bay (the International Society for Krishna Consciousness is a significant exception here). The majority, however, minimize their connections to Hindu religion by reframing their discourses and practices in the language of spirituality, health, wellness, love, compassion, and science. Such constructed universalisms obfuscate the particularities of Hindu religiosity and transform their ideals into generalized principles, which broadly appeal to non-Hindu audiences. Taken to the extreme, such rhetoric alienates more conservative immigrant Indian Hindus, and the movement becomes predominantly comprised of metaphysicals.

Amma has developed a precarious balance between these internally diverse demographic communities wherein she maintains Hindu discourses, cultural indexes, and religious convictions but generalizes them in an active process of cultural translation for her non-Hindu audiences. We might imagine this as a discursive heteroglossia, an organizational rhetorical and practical strategy of "for those who have the ears to hear." Immigrant Indian Hindus recognize her Hinduness because her discourses are interlaced with familiar parables and Hindu religious references despite their representation in a generalized language of spirituality. Metaphysicals recognize the generalized language of spirituality and, because of their unfamiliarity with Hindu references, they view Hindu cultural signifiers as secondary (or even inconsequential) to her universalistic message. These metaphysicals acknowledge that Amma comes from a Hindu context, but they dissociate her message from Hindu religiosity. Many Hindus would agree. They too favor the universalistic language of spirituality and contend that Amma's message transcends any one religion.[2]

Both of these internally diverse communities of believers resonate with a commitment to inclusivism and universalistic ideals that can be expressed through the polysemous language of spirituality. But the reasoning for such commitments differs. Like the metaphysicals, immigrant Indian Hindus contend that Amma's message transcends Hinduism, but they do so because of their conviction regarding the universalistic interpretation of *sanātana dharma*, the eternal religion of India before it was named an "*–ism*" by the West during the colonial period. Their modern (and often politicized) understanding of Hindu religiosity attempts to transcend all boundaries and categorical confines to become the underlying eternal philosophy applicable to all humanity. Among metaphysicals, many have turned away from Christian denominations and view religion as a negative signifier of all that is corrupt, hierarchical, condemning, exclusive, and antiquated. These metaphysicals look to a new paradigm of spirituality (a new age) that will usher in consciousness, awareness, expansiveness, inclusion, and personal growth. What is most interesting here is that although the means of constructing such universalisms are distinct—sanātana dharma and spirituality—the ends are the same. Both demographics suggest that Amma's message represents the eternal message of spirituality (defined through two different lenses), which includes all persons of all faiths. Immigrant Indian Hindus and metaphysicals unite despite their differences because of their devotion to Amma and their mutual conviction in the universalistic applicability of her message.

But despite the similarities of the ends, the divergent means determine that Amma's devotees vary considerably in their conceptions of exactly what or who Amma is in relation to (G)od or the goddess. For many Hindus she is simply an incarnation of the Divine Mother, envisioned primarily as Kali or Lalitā. Indian Hindus are familiar with the concept and the possibility of divine incarnations (avatar-gurus). They view Amma as exemplary and unique but also locate her within a long historical tradition of avatar-gurus who have traversed Indian soil for thousands of years. Many Hindus buttress their belief in Amma's divinity through their personal experiences as her devotees as well as their cultural reference points for similar guru-disciple relations in Hindu traditions, texts, and mythology. Amma's frequent references to Hindu religious texts and mythology and her routine enactment of Hindu ritual practices enable them to recognize her as a Divine Mother and avatar-guru operating from within the Hindu field. Though they are internally diverse, they locate Amma's discourses within the broad spectrum of Hindu religion, understood as the eternal indigenous spirituality of India, sanātana dharma.

American metaphysicals' conceptions of Amma's relationship to divinity are particularly diffuse because they were not raised within a cultural milieu that venerates avatar-gurus. As a result, American metaphysicals must define Amma's relationship to the divine individually, according to their dispositions, beliefs, and preexisting worldviews. In their theological worldviews and prayers, they often integrate and even conflate Amma with their other beliefs about divinity: for neo-pagans she becomes the great mother goddess of imagined matriarchal antiquity; for goddess feminists she becomes one of many exemplary goddesses or even *the* goddess; for new agers she becomes light, universal consciousness, and/or love; and for the searchers who have no spiritual or religious affiliation she is often simply "Mother."[3] American metaphysicals believe these variant concepts to be complementary because of their commitments to universalism and perennialism. Despite their conceptual differences, these diverse metaphysicals situate Amma either as a Divine Mother, some form of superhuman power incarnate, or a realized being. I met no one in the field who believed her to be as humanly fallible as the general populace. Even if devotees are unconvinced by her supposedly superhuman feats, miracles, or *bhāvas*, they still point to her physical ability to sit giving her *darshan* embraces[4] while emitting what they see as a constant aura of compassion and unconditional love without respite or sustenance for twelve to twenty-four hours, day after day, as evidence of her ability to transcend beyond the confines of human frailties and physical needs.

Surely Amma is an exemplary figure, in the sense that she represents at the very minimum an unusually devoted person leading a highly unconventional life. Even a staunch sociologist like Max Weber suggests that the exemplary prophet acquires the status of prophet through charismatic leadership qualities acquired "by virtue of his personal gifts," underscored by "definite revelations."[5] But are Americans drawn to Amma's movement solely on the basis of their attraction to her personal charisma? Certainly some aspects of personal connection to the guru substantiate much of devotees' experiences. But there are also distinct ways in which her message appeals to modern Americans, both inheritors and adopters, because of its compatibility with quintessential American ideals, such as democracy, equality, universalism, and individualism. In addition, throughout American history Protestant influences have routinely reinforced the privileging of a personal, internal experience of spiritual transformation enacted through unmediated contact with divinity. These core American ideals juxtapose fruitfully in Amma's movement.

This chapter aims to demonstrate how multiply diverse ideological trajectories from various fields come to an unlikely confluence among the devotees in Amma's movement. Whether they are immigrant Indian Hindus searching for representation of their native South Indian goddess traditions in the tumult of diasporic dislocations or goddess movement enthusiasts searching for a personal connection with women-centric religiosity, both find sanctity and solace in Amma's movement. Once again, their reasons for traveling to Amma differ, but the ends are the same. It is this unlikely coming together of widely divergent populations that creates the lively, bustling, and carnivalesque crowds at Amma's darshan programs.

DEMOGRAPHICS: WHO ARE AMMA'S AMERICAN CHILDREN?

In Amma's movement, there are two broad categories of devotees, which I categorize as *inheritors* and *adopters*. I implement these categories as a potential corrective to Jan Nattier's influential categories of "import," "export," and "baggage" Buddhism, which attempt to analytically locate the populations and practices of American Buddhists.[6] While Nattier's categories were a bold initial step to map the field of Asian religions in the United States, as the field has exponentially expanded and become more deeply problematized a space has opened up for a more nuanced categorical analysis. First, while the term *baggage* accurately describes the importing of Asian religions along with Asian immigrants, it has a dangerously negative connotation. In modern parlance, Americans speak of childhood baggage, emotional baggage, and psychological baggage, all with some sense that one could lead a happier and fuller life if one were to rid oneself of this baggage. Herein the underlying assumption suggests that baggage impedes the potential for a generalized sense of happiness and contentment. Even in the most mundane and literal interpretations, most travelers cannot wait to be rid of their baggage at the airport: baggage is heavy and cumbersome and often is an unwelcome reminder of our attachments to material things. Notably the religious freedom of the ascetic wanderer, the itinerant preacher, the vagabond, and the intentionally rootless is defined by the absence of baggage. The sociolinguistic connotations to the idea of cultural or religious baggage at best suggest a negative connotation of religio-cultural particularities and at worst a return to an assimilationist paradigm, meaning that Asian immigrants may arrive in the United States with religio-cultural baggage, but they, like all travelers, should quickly unpack and blend into their new environments. In short, the term *baggage* has a lot of baggage. While this negative connotation reveals the most problematic aspect of Nattier's tertiary stratification, the terms *import* and *export* also suggest complicated discontinuities.

Import Buddhism describes a consumer-driven model in which presumably non-Asian Americans get excited by Asian ideas, travel to Asia, learn of Asian religions, and then import those ideas and practices into the United States. But in our modern globalized world, cultural adoption can occur without travel. Non-Asians routinely adopt Asian-style dress, religious behaviors, ideas, routines, health practices, art, and so on without traveling to Asia. Also, the term *import* suggests a tangible and internally constant imported object, the underlying understanding here being that that object remains intact upon transmission from one geography to the other. In fact, this is not the case in the predominant modality of non-Asians adopting Asian cultural products, as even a cursory glance at the field reveals. Ethnographic studies of what would be termed *import* Asian religious forms repeatedly demonstrate that the American manifestation of such articles differs decidedly from its Asian counterpart. In many cases the American product transforms into an amalgam or a "Creole" religiosity to which there is no one cohesive Asian counterpart.[7] Material culture as well exhibits the reformulation of Asian goods into hybridized products. Upon import to the United States, Indian saris become throw pillows, curtains, tablecloths, shirts, skirts, dresses, and pants, which are sold at stores whose cachet depends on their exotic marketing strategies of mining the world for "authentic global treasures"[8] (World Market, Pier One, and so on). The relationship between the products of Asia and their American resemblances suggests not a stationary object of import but, rather, a process of appropriation and transformation. The seemingly neutral term *import* obfuscates the heated politics of cultural property rights, representation, appropriation, and the (mis)adoption of Asian religio-cultural products.

Like the term *import*, the term *export* too implies a geographical distance that does not reflect the contemporary globalized transmission of ideas. Export refers to the proselytizing techniques of missionaries, presumably Asian missionaries (of Asian religions) who export their religions outside of Asia. But the spread of Asian religio-cultural products does not subsist on a unidirectional flow from Asia to other geographies, certainly not in today's world of "vernacular globalization." Scholars of cultural flows of globalization have demonstrated repeatedly the transnational (and supranational) networking flows of information, commerce, and capital: the "scalar dynamic" of the "complex, overlapping, and disjunctive order" of the "new global cultural economy."[9]

The terms *inheritor* and *adopter* signify the *behavioral* differences between groups of people who exhibit aspects of Asian religio-cultural traditions. While these categories relate to race, ethnicity, cultural heritage, and geography, importantly, they are not defined solely through any of these lenses. Inheritors are those who were born into environments in which there were strong religio-cultural ties to Asian religions. Adopters are those who were not and only later adopted various religio-cultural behaviors, ideas, material environments, and habits of Asian societies. These terms are intentionally disassociated from race, ethnicity, cultural heritage, and geography, and within them one might imagine the transgression of the aforementioned categories as one often finds in Amma's movement. The categories of inheritor and adopter are not contingent on race or cultural ethnicity, as other frequently used categories tend to be, that is, Indian/non-Indian, Hindu/non-Hindu, and American Hindu/American spiritualist. While the majority of inheritors are Indian Hindus and the majority of adopters are whites of diverse, but non-Hindu, religious backgrounds, that is not always the case—African Americans and Latinas/Latinos demonstrate a significant and increasing presence in spiritual communities derived from Asian religions. African American Buddhists, such as Reverend Zenju Earthlyn Manuel, bell hooks, Faith Hill, Jan Willis, and Ralph Steele, to name just a few key figures, are beginning to assert their presence in American Buddhist communities that have been historically so racially exclusive to upper-middle-class whites that they are sometimes called "white Buddhists."[10]

In transnational guru movements with Hindu roots, likewise, the population demographics have often been divided between Indian Hindus and white non-Hindus. But today there are minority populations of whites who prefer to identify as Hindus, and there are many non-white and non-Indian people participating in forms of Hindu religiosity. As such, this historical population division is diversifying, with an influx of Latino and African American populations, as well as those who embody complex and multiethnic identities, to the guru scene. Times are changing, albeit slowly, as African Americans and Latinas/Latinos become more visibly active in transnational guru movements. As a result, the white/Indian orientalistic dichotomy may fade into history. Some fascinating moments of cultural hybridization have emerged through music, such as the African American musical artists C. C. White and Temba Spirit. White recently produced the hybrid devotional album, *This IS Soul Kirtan*, which blends R & B, Southern blues, soul, gospel, jazz, Latin, and Hindu devotional music (*kirtan*). Temba Spirit emerged from his previous life of gang violence and prison as a self-described "hip-hop humanitarian" who has created phenomenal fusions of rap and kirtan that bend and blend cultural boundaries. Both of these devotees have sung for Amma during her public darshan programs in the United States.

Still, it is useful to consider the reasons that Asian religions in the United States tend to attract both inheritors from within the Asian ethnic community and adopters who are largely white but only minority populations of African Americans and Latinas/Latinos. Significant works have shown how immigrants often participate in culturally and ethnically specific religious environments in an effort to develop and maintain communal spaces to express a religious, cultural, and ethnic identity.[11] White adopters participate for a variety of personal and social reasons, but I contend that many of the roots of their involvement stem from historical privilege that provided access and cultural capital based on knowledge of Asia. Upper-middle-class whites (the primary demographic involved in Asian religions in the United States) emerge from a legacy where European elites collected and exhibited worldly treasures, practices, and ideas in formidable displays of imperial capital. Second, historically, American and European elites (often connected to missionary or colonial enterprises) had access to Asia and thus encountered Asian religions. Last, despite travelogues and missionary accounts, it was often those who had the financial resources for travel who gained knowledge of Asia (or at least existed in a cultural context where that was commonplace).[12]

Compounding this, in the American context, it is a tenuous and even dangerous enterprise for disenfranchised individuals (minorities) to adopt a marginalized religion (Asian religions), an adherence to which might challenge relations with their existing religio-cultural communities of support.[13] But in contemporary practice, two major paradigmatic shifts have served to diversify the appropriation and spread of Asian religio-cultural products across various demographic populations. First, and most obviously, Asian religious ideas have become exponentially more accessible to multifarious populations through global flows of people, cultures, and ideas, the Internet, transnationalism, Asian immigration, and globally proselytizing religious figures. Second, some non-white and non-Asian citizens in the United States and Europe (particularly those of education and means) now participate in the formerly elite cultural domains from which they were initially excluded because of the contemporary structures of multiculturalism, global capitalism, and neoliberalism.

The Indian American devotees who attend Amma's Chicago satsangs, where much of this ethnography was conducted, are primarily

Hindu immigrants from India; the majority come to Amma as families. Many of these families are from South India, particularly Kerala, and they retain aspects of their cultural and religious heritage. They typically range from first- to third-generation immigrants and live in affluent suburban areas, with the exception of some of the upwardly mobile young career professionals who work and/or go to school in central urban areas. Due to contemporary U.S. immigration policy, the majority are skilled workers with advanced degrees in business or one of the social or biological sciences. They mirror the demographics of Chicagoland Indian Americans more generally; according to U.S. Census figures (2000), 25,000 Indians live in the city, while 113,700 live in the suburbs. Simply put, Indian Americans are wealthier and more educated than their American counterparts. Indians in Chicago have a median household income of $60,428, compared to $41,994 among all Americans. In the suburbs, Naperville is the most affluent, where the median Indian family income is $92,696. Nearly 65 percent of Indians in the country have college degrees and 34 percent have advanced degrees, compared to the national averages of 24 percent and 9 percent.[14] Amma's Indian American devotees are generally suburban, wealthy, educated, civic minded, family members, and Hindu.

Many of the Indian Americans who have become Amma devotees are Malayalees who have emigrated from the South Indian state of Kerala. Amma has become so famous in Kerala that her name and image are ubiquitous. Amma is wholeheartedly Malayalee: she speaks only Malayalam in all of her discourses, relying on multiple translators, and she references Keralan folklore, geography, and culture in her talks. She encourages her local Malayalee devotees to provide traditional cultural programs and culinary delights at her public programs in cities across the United States. Many Malayalee devotees enjoy the cultural connections and experiences that they gain from participating as Amma devotees.

Many Indian devotees may not have heard of Amma until coming to America. In the United States, Hindu temples often provide a singular Pan-Indian worship space for many different kinds of Hindus. The first wave of Hindu immigrants to the United States after 1965 minimized sectarianism and pooled their resources to create Hindu spaces that accommodated many of the different forms of Hindu traditions in one central location. Amma's first American programs were held in these kinds of Pan-Hindu temples. As the Hindu diasporic religious field became more sectarianized in the 1980s and 1990s, Amma moved her darshan programs into secular spaces, for example, hotel ballrooms and convention centers. Still, Amma's programs are heavily advertised through the local Hindu temple informational tributaries. Indian devotees also advertise her programs in spaces that Indian Americans frequent, such as restaurants, clothing stores, cultural events, and concerts, as well as in newspapers and periodicals. As a result, many North Indian immigrants, Vaishnavites, Shaivites, Muslims, and Sikhs learn about Amma as a Pan-Indian guru detached from her Malayalee Hindu heritage.

Whether Malayalee, Gujarati, or Tamilian, Indians living in the United States recognize something familiar in Amma's demeanor and her message. Even if they have not been a part of a guru movement in India or in the United States, most Indians are aware of famous gurus in Indian history—from Ramakrishna to Swami Vivekananda, from Shirdi Sai Baba to Sathya Sai Baba, and from Paramhansa Yogananda to Swami Muktananda. If they are Hindu, they will recognize the variety of Hindu rituals that she enacts, such as *puja* (worship), *homas* (fire sacrifice), and darshan. Indians, especially Indian Hindus, may already have a mantra (sacred words and phrases for use in ritual and prayer) and may already be familiar with many of the Sanskrit texts that Amma references. Many will be surprised that Amma physically embraces her devotees in her version of darshan, but the majority will understand the concepts of darshan and deities becoming incarnate on earth as avatars. Some may recognize Amma's movement to be a version of Hinduism that is both inclusive and ecumenical, qualities that tend to make the movement more palatable to cosmopolitan global audiences.

Most adopter (largely non-Indian) devotees learn about Amma through informational tributaries in the United States that disseminate metaphysical spirituality and advertise touring spiritual leaders, yoga, self-improvement seminars, concerts, and events. These venues include occult and new age bookstores, yoga centers, periodicals, health food stores, restaurants, and the Internet. But the majority of newcomers to Amma's darshan programs learn about Amma through word of mouth—from their friends. The United States has long been host to a variety of communities that engage in alternative spiritualities or metaphysical religion, which has had a distinct presence in the United States since the arrival of the first European settlers.[15] Participants in metaphysical religion vocally object to the concepts and restrictions involved in organized religion and instead supplant the term with spirituality. In fact, as Catherine Albanese notes, this group defines itself, in part, by its rejection of a congregation, a hierarchy, rules, consistency, and the literal bricks and mortar of organized religion.[16]

Instead, they use the term *spiritual* to signify the anti-institutional, the personal, and the alternative. The spiritual is a category of negation in that it exists only in opposition to its antecedent: religion. It signifies an eclectic combination of practices and beliefs, but also the recurring ideologies of personal growth and development toward the understanding of, the emulation of, and/or the unification with a superhuman power (variously conceived). In fact, for believers, the terms *spiritual* and *spirituality* are particularly useful because of their polyvalent qualities. Some use the category of spirituality explicitly because it is a signifier without a specific signified; it alludes to a supramaterial worldview without demanding definition of its distinct components. As such, it enables a certain freedom from dogma and traditional religious constraints. As a result, in classifying this group, I take Albanese's effective reference to the metaphysical but pair it with the spiritual to describe their practice as "metaphysical spirituality," and I find useful Courtney Bender's succinct word for the practitioners: the "metaphysicals."

Importantly, adopters tend to emerge from a very specific demographic. As Albanese explains, they are "mostly white, more female than male, often middle-aged, sometimes young, and frequently urban dwellers . . . middle class and upwardly mobile, better educated than average, and not especially alienated from society."[17] Jeffrey Kripal articulates metaphysical communities' difficulty in expanding their influence and clientele beyond this limited demographic in his historical narrative of Esalen, an experimental psychological and spiritual community, located in Big Sur, California.[18] In general, the hippie movement, its later incarnation as the new age movement, and its most recent incarnation as the metaphysical spirituality of the twenty-first century have struggled to diversify their audiences beyond white middle and upper-middle classes. Following this pattern, the adopters who follow Amma are 90 percent to 95 percent white middle-to-upper-middle-class educated urban dwellers; they have the leisure time, the discretionary income, and the desire to research, sample, and participate as consumers in a variety of alternative spiritual options in America.

Although those who would identify with the term *spiritual* are still a minority, there is evidence that this population is growing and exerting more influence in defining the architecture of American religiosity. In October 2012, a Pew Forum survey recorded the highest level of religiously unaffiliated Americans, or "nones," ever—one in five Americans and one in three Americans among those under thirty years old. Strikingly, 68 percent of these "nones" say they believe in God, and 37 percent classify themselves as "spiritual, but not religious."[19] A Pew Forum survey in 2008 found that 65 percent of Americans believe that "many religions can lead to eternal life" (including 37 percent of white evangelicals).[20] This sentiment in particular echoes the Hindu formulation expressed in the *Ṛg Veda*, that "Truth is One, but the sages speak of it by many names" (1.164.46), which led Lisa Miller, the *Newsweek* author, to title her now-famous 2009 article on the subject "We Are All Hindus Now."[21] This type of generalized universalism only furthers the American predilection toward a la carte religiosity. Based on a consumerist model, this impetus (often fueled with the facility of the Internet) encourages these "spiritual, not religious" populations to purchase and adopt only the spiritual goods that suit their dispositions. The ease and the rapid speed with which practitioners and corporations commodify spirituality into spirituality-enhancing and life-enchanting products suggest that Carrette and King may be on to something when they argue provocatively that "[s]pirituality has become the primary means facilitating the corporate takeover of religion."[22]

American metaphysicals do not often congregate in a defined singular forum, but they do operate in overlapping social circles. The longer one participates in any one of these circles, the more familiar faces resurface in surprising circumstances in other, related circles. What emerges is what Courtney Bender calls an "entangled," interconnected web of groups and organizations formed by those who are seeking something beyond that which they have experienced in mainline American religions. She argues that "what we think of as the spiritual is actively produced within medical, religious, and arts institutions, among others. It is not unorganized or disorganized, but rather organized in different ways, within and adjacent to a variety of religious and secular institutional fields that inflect and shape various spiritual practices."[23] "Spiritual" and "spirituality" are code words that such practitioners use to define themselves, signifying their rejection of the dogmatism of religion and their acceptance of multiple alternative paths and beliefs.

Metaphysicals design these multifarious forms of spirituality by adopting pieces from a variety of religious traditions throughout the world. They import very little in composite form, and instead, in a *bricoleur* modality, they compile aspects of different religious practices and beliefs to fashion their own unique spiritualities. Adopter devotees come from extremely diverse religious backgrounds, but they unite through their commonalities as spiritual bricoleurs. Lévi-Strauss popularized the term *bricolage* and its agent, the bricoleur, to describe the anthropological method that compiles various fragments, through the instruments at hand, to form a composite. While the engineer represents the logocentric view of the subject, its privileged reference, the bricoleur is its decentered reflection. The engineer creates with a sense of personal agency, plan, and intention, whereas the bricoleur adapts and acquires in reaction to and as a reflection of its environment and stimuli.[24] I use the term *bricoleur* to refer to the many adopter devotees who excerpt iconography, theology, mythology, and ritual from established religious traditions and combine them to form innovative and creative amalgamations of individualized spiritualities.

Few metaphysicals are loyal and exclusive to one religious figure or spiritual practice. In fact, often they reject that very demand to adhere, be loyal, and submit to any given religious tradition as a trademark of organized religion. Thus, for most adopters, Amma is one of many different spiritual resources on which they draw in order to create their individualized mosaic of metaphysical spirituality. Some emulate the types of borrowing practices that Cynthia Eller found in her seminal work among communities of spiritual feminists. Eller explains, "Spiritual feminists have created their religion out of the elements at hand, scavenging a twig here and a thread there, which along with the wares they carried from their previous homes, have formed the unique combination of elements that is feminist spirituality."[25] Many adopters are involved in Shamanism, Zen, Tibetan Buddhism, Goddess religions, Paganism, Wicca, energy work, crystal work, psychological seminars, and countless other permutations of alternative religious activities. Many extract Jesus's teachings from organized Christianity and create theologies centered on him as an exemplar of spiritually guided living. Many metaphysicals who are Amma devotees have also participated in other contemporary guru movements. Though many adopters would say that they believe in Hindu ideas and regularly perform Hindu rituals in their homes, most do not claim to be Hindu or frequent Hindu temples because of the implied ethnic requirements. Instead they find an expressive outlet for their adopted Hindu beliefs in gurus like Amma who accept their amalgamated spiritualities without demanding their participation in a congregation or their adherence to a particular practice or belief (see figure 9).

At Amma's darshan programs in the United States, inheritors are brought together with adopters along with swirling crowds of devotees

FIGURE 9. Eclectic altar, left to right: Pema Chödrön, Thai Buddha, St. Francis of Assisi/
St. Francis Peace Prayer, Amma, Mexican clay fish, Rosary necklace (author photo)

in white who are touring with Amma and awestruck and discombobu-
lated first timers. Cities with significant local Indian American populations (Chicago, Detroit, Dallas, Toronto) correlate to active local satsangs
and significant populations of Indian Hindu attendees at Amma's public
programs. These inheritor devotees are often highly embedded within the
local Indian American community and have lasting relationships with
local Hindu temples as well as Hindu political, financial, and cultural
networks. Chicago and its suburbs have one of the stronger, wealthier,
and more influential Indian American populations in the United States.
Between 2004 and 2013, nearly equal populations of Indian Americans
and non-Indian Americans attended Amma's public programs in Chicago (a ratio of approximately 45 percent to 55 percent), in contrast to
the 2008 public program in Coralville, Iowa, where Indian Americans
comprised only 10 percent to 20 percent of the public program audience. In Boston, in 2008, Indian Americans were approximately 35
percent of the public program audience.

In November 2006, at Amma's public programs at her ashram in San
Ramon, California, the demographic ratio was approximately 21 per-

cent Indian American and 79 percent non-Indian American.[26] In the following years that I attended Amma's San Ramon programs (2008, 2011), the audience was comprised of a similar demographic. Though there is a significant Indian American population in the San Francisco Bay Area, adopter devotees are numerically overrepresented at Amma's public programs, for two reasons: first, the San Ramon ashram is a pilgrimage site that draws devotees from across the United States; second, a significant population of metaphysicals resides in the Bay Area in order to surround themselves with the wide variety of spiritual ideas and organizations active there. Particular to San Ramon as well, Amma's message "My religion is Love" appears to have drawn a significant group of young white Rastafari sympathizers, a porous but somewhat cohesive group of dreadlocked, wildly dancing, closely embracing, deep-soul staring, blissed out, and intentionally "loose" folks[27] who regularly attend Amma's programs when she is in town. They exist in a somewhat liminal relationship to the ashram community there. Despite the fact that they are occasionally chastised for jumping too vigorously while dancing on the balcony during bhajans or severely reprimanded for smoking marijuana on ashram grounds (which Amma strictly forbids), they are largely welcomed within the community. As mentioned, this population is specific to the San Ramon ashram, though a select few also tour with Amma in the summertime. My interviews with them suggest that they are older than I had guessed (by twenty years in some cases), more drug free than I had imagined (many follow strict vegan, raw-foods, no illegal substances-type diet restrictions), and more homeless or alternately housed than I had anticipated. Their exuberant dancing, public displays of lengthy, warm embraces, and culturally unusual appearances often elicit curious stares and cautious glances from more conservative adopters and inheritors alike. But occasionally one can see young Indian children (even if dressed in their formal best for Amma's darshan) break from their families for a bit of impassioned dancing on the balcony among the dreadlocked in an explicit and genuine cultural encounter, united through the intensity of their devotion.

Devotees have many opportunities to socialize and interact with each other because of the sheer duration of Amma's darshan programs, the *sevā* (selfless service) shifts, and the significant free time involved. The fact that such a diverse group of devotees intermixes so fluidly speaks to the tamber and mood of the events. While there are certainly some intercultural faux pas and tensions, largely very disparate types of devotees work and socialize together without major incident and frequently with a warm sense of camaraderie and affection. All come together with a sense of joint purpose to experience Amma's grace and to share themselves through darshan: the bohemians and the formally dressed Indian families, the baby-boomer seekers and the young cosmopolitan staff members, the healthy and the sick, and the inheritors and adopters. They unite in their commonalities through Amma's universalist, humanistic message. Kind words and deeds are shared, people are respectful and accepting of differences, and conflicts are smoothed over; Amma's model behavior rings loudly in attendees' ears.

In fact, Amma's model behavior is very much like a stone thrown into a pond. The closer that devotees are to Amma both physically and temporally (the closer they get to her programs), the more they emulate her loving, compassionate manner of being. With that said, a lot of work has to be done in order to create the experience at Amma's programs, and there is certainly some fodder for argument when staff members are herding small armies of inexperienced volunteers. Different people organize and administrate various situations and challenges in different ways. In high-pressure situations, people do not always speak kindly, and sometimes feelings get hurt. Still, in the presence of Amma's example of love and compassion, most devotees are (to put it simply) on their best behavior. More than anything they are inclusive in their demeanor. They realize that it will take every willing volunteer to make these magnanimous programs a success. Young dreadlocked Rasta folks stand next to sari-clad Indian grandmothers where they communicate, work, and facilitate the programs whether in the kitchens slicing vegetables, working as a team to seat the audience, or in the flower stations stringing *mālās* (flower garlands) and plucking petals.

But how do these devotees imagine Amma and her message? Do inheritors and adopters view her in similar ways? The next section delves into conversations with the many devotees who involve themselves in Amma's movement in the United States. After hundreds of conversations, in formal interviews, satsangs, and sevā, I suggest that the perception of the relationship between ordinary women and the goddess is quite distinct in inheritor and adopter communities. Many inheritors (largely Indian Hindus) accept the mother goddess represented in Amma as their favored deity (*iṣṭadev*), but still as one divinity among many in the Hindu pantheon. For them, Devī, as she is embodied in Amma, looks upon women and men with equanimity and favors all with a mother's unconditional love, just as a mother loves her children. Adopters (largely American metaphysicals), on the other hand, emerge without the Hindu religious context of an indigenous pantheon of deities, and many have sought to construct one in bricolage fashion from various global sources. Many were raised as agnostics or in patriarchal religions, from which they actively sought out an alternative religious environment. A great many chose Amma's movement explicitly because they were attracted to the idea of a female guru or a feminine form of divinity in particular. Developing their devotions to Amma with such motivations, many adopters find in Amma not only affirmations of their goddess-centric worldviews but also the ability to commune with a living representation of a divinity whom they believe to be a powerful goddess incarnate. Like Amma, goddess feminists in the United States and some voices within Indian feminism emphasize that women were not always subordinated within patriarchal systems of religious authority. Each of these proponents claims that there once was a Golden Age in which women determined their own fates and were vital ritual actors, exalted in religious cosmology as living representations of the goddess. In so doing, they justify their adulation of Amma not only as a divine goddess but also as an exemplary human woman situated as a powerful religious leader and ritual officiant through a posited antiquity of prepatriarchal gynocentrism. They wholeheartedly ascribe to Amma's call to accentuate ideotypical feminine virtues and aim to develop a maternal ascetic habitus of love, compassion, and selfless service (sevā).

IN THE EYES OF DEVOTEES

As Amma traveled from India into transnational diasporic arenas, such as the United States, correspondingly her practices became more routinized and institutionalized. Her programs and attire became more focused on beautiful and pleasing images, scents, and sounds. Like her appearance, her rhetoric sweetened to become more palatable to diverse audiences. Similarly, she largely emphasized the sweetness of motherhood, signifying that she embodies the love, compassion, self-sacrifice, and devotion of a mother to her children. It is only the most proximate of her devotees who may see in Amma the anger and frustration of a mother forced to chastise her children when they are disobedient, wasteful, or otherwise challenging her guiding instructions.

The most devout inheritors largely see Amma as a mother and situate themselves as her little children. To them, she is not an ordinary mother but a cosmic, omnipresent, and omniscient one—a timeless representation of the mother goddess. Their reverence for Amma draws from a Hindu ideal of reverence for the Hindu goddess, with whom there is always the possibility of her incarnation on earth as an avatar. For these Hindu devotees, Amma is one such avatar-guru. The fact that she has become incarnate in a dark-skinned woman's body and that she advocates equality between the sexes signifies not feminism, but her transcendence of the material realities that bind humans within the continual cycle of rebirth (*saṃsāra*). Many inheritors believe that because Amma is divine she experiences the human condition in ultimate and transcendent terms and views all persons with equanimity. It is only because society often subordinates the female to the male that her equanimous vision is often mistakenly viewed as feminist. As Gayatri, a female Indian Hindu devotee, explained, "In Indian context explicitly and in western context latently, women are *still* considered inferior to men. However, Amma makes no difference. To Her, you and I are no different than a tree or a poisonous snake or the earth or moon. Amma is neither a feminist nor a male chauvinist. In a world where women are considered inferior, Amma gives equal status in word, deed, and action, thereby supporting feminists and discouraging male chauvinists." Thus, according to Gayatri, it is the unjust power imbalances of the human condition that make Amma's equanimity appear to be feminist, when in actuality it is not.

But the demographics of the Paloma *satsang*, a large biweekly congregational gathering comprised of inheritor devotees, may suggest a certain resonance between devotion to Amma and tendencies toward gender equality among Indian Hindu devotees. The strong majority of Indian Hindu women who attend the satsang are professionals with advanced degrees who work outside the home. In one family, the wife holds a major corporate managerial position that requires significant international travel, while the husband, who is retired, engages in part-time university course work. Another family, in which both husband and wife were actively employed, relocated due to the wife's major promotion. As a result, the husband stayed home with their young children for over a year in the new location while he looked for employment. The strong majority of these Indian Hindu wives and mothers are not only employed outside of the home, but they hold major positions as CPAs, corporate managers, scientists, engineers, and doctors. The fluctuating population of the satsang challenges exact percentage figures, but the approximate percentage of Indian Hindu wives who work outside the home in professional capacities and attend satsang is close to

85–90 percent. Compared to figures in India, wherein only 32.9 percent of women work outside of the home, this percentage is certainly striking.[28]

Perhaps we might attribute this unusually high percentage of women working outside of the home to the influence of American styles (or necessities) of dual-career households. But in 2009, only 59.2 percent of the general female American populace participated in the labor force.[29] It might also be tempting to suggest that there is something particular about the Indian diasporic population that supports dual-career households more than either its native-born American counterpart or its Indian counterpart. But telescoping on the Indian diaspora population in the United States in particular (unfortunately, figures are not parsed by religious affiliation), only 61 percent of married Indian women with present spouses participated in the labor force (though 80 percent of Indian women who were not married participated in the labor force).[30] These percentage figures are still significantly less than those of the Paloma satsang. In fact, it appears that the married Indian Hindu women of the Paloma satsang participate in the American labor force at similar or slightly higher levels than unmarried Indian women in the United States. This suggests that for Amma devotees marriage is not a significant contributing factor that decreases women's involvement in the labor force, a suggestive conclusion that effectively differentiates Amma devotees from both the general American and Indian populations.

Unfortunately, what these figures cannot reveal is the exact relationship between the augmentation of married Indian Hindu women's participation in the American labor force and their devotion to Amma. The majority of the older generation of female Indian Hindu devotees first attained education and professional careers and only later became Amma devotees. Some of the second generation, younger women in their thirties, were raised in families of Amma devotees and thus developed their educational and career credentials in light of their convictions about Amma and her message of female empowerment. The relationship between education and professionalism and devotion to Amma is much more ambiguous for many others. Regardless of such chicken-and-egg inquiries, which surely vary by individual circumstance and interlace more than neat categories allow, it is clear that many married Indian Hindu women in the United States find support rather than conflict between their devotion to Amma and their multiple roles as educated professionals, wives, and mothers. Similarly, their husbands (nearly all of whom actively participate in satsang) believe the community's and Amma's message to be reflective of their values, which they exhibit through active participation.

In Amma's milieu, the majority of Indian Hindu women would, like Gayatri, note that, in ultimate terms, gender difference is subordinate to the unifying essence (*ātman/brahman*) that comprises all existence. But many female devotees, who are also Indian Hindus, believe that Amma's message empowers women. Sujatha gets "inspired" when Amma "stresses on the fact that women are as strong as men, or perhaps even more strong mentally and emotionally . . . whatever men can do, women can also do." She finds such rhetoric of gender equality to be personally affective because she was raised in an Indian Hindu family in which it was clear if there had to be a choice regarding dessert portions or funds for higher education, boys, not girls, would receive the available share. She notes that in dominant Indian Hindu social hierarchies, "even the women have consciously started treating women as lower than men." Gayatri also recounts similarly endemic injustices in the treatment of boy children over girl children in India; she notes Amma's recollection that even Amma's mother used to feed her brothers thrice the amount she would give to her sisters.

But Gayatri also explains that Amma is subtly changing these paradigms. She says: "One example—In [an] Indian wedding, the bride falls at the groom's feet and as if this weren't enough, in some cultures such as mine, the bride's father falls at the groom's feet and 'begs' him to marry his daughter. In Amma's [D]evi [B]hava wedding the bride and groom fall at each other's feet. That is Her way of empowering women." Sujatha responded to such pervasive gender inequities in the family and society by saying, "[Amma says:] My girl children should be like little tigresses. . . . They should be so brave and bold and go out and make a really big fight to get what they need. Because society is not going to welcome the woman and give her it. Because it is power dominated by men, they will never give her that space. No, you have to go and demand. Get that respect from them. Earn that respect from them." From both of these perspectives, Amma has a particular message for women. Her view, articulated through both discourse and practice, attempts to eradicate the historical traditions of female subordination and endeavors to return women to their respected positions of importance in society.

But, notably, neither woman identifies Amma's message as feminist. Like many other Indian Hindu women and women's movements in India (particularly Hindu), Sujatha views feminism as a Western ideological infiltration that destroys the function of the family and society. While she noted that it is predominantly men who have attached such negative connotations to the term, she also suggests that feminism invokes the objective of fighting and struggle against men, an adversarial relationship that generates defensive attitudes toward feminism. Instead, like Amma, she suggests that the problematic should be framed in terms of empowering women. She says, "Empowering women has much more potential. Even men can relate to it. Men can relate to somebody who is not as fortunate as they are, whether they are men or women, and empowering them by giving them skills they need. . . . But the moment you differentiate it by gender or give it to only one group then there will certainly be the resistance from the other group." Such convictions resonate with the long history of Indian programs that were initiated to "uplift" women. Both uplift and empowerment suggest the collaboration between the sexes for the betterment of women, a historically acceptable strategy that has been widely implemented in India to achieve policy gains for women on the subcontinent.

Among inheritor devotees, many Indian Hindu women reference extant gender inequalities in Indic society and celebrate Amma's egalitarian message, but they do not relate her message of empowering women to the practice of goddess worship. Indian Hindus recognize that the conditions for women in India have changed over time, in their view from the high point during the Golden Age of the Vedas to the medieval decline and modern struggles for equality. But throughout all of this, the goddess has remained. From their perspective, it seems incongruous and reductionistic to directly relate the particular and variable social conditions for women to the veneration of the Hindu goddesses. Sujatha unwittingly echoed verbatim the devotees on a pilgrimage to the goddess Vindhyavāsinī (Durga) when she distinctly replied: "the goddess is one thing; humans are another."[31] There is also a sense that human women would not be so presumptuous to compare their social position to the omnipresent and omnipotent goddess: the gulf is too wide and too great. Furthermore, inheritors recognize that there are multiple gods and goddesses, each with his or her particular characteristics, habits, personalities, and practices. Thus creating parallels between all women and the goddess obfuscates this diversity, which is the hallmark of Hindu religiosity. Last, in Hindu cosmology, gender identity and physical form change between births in accordance with one's karmic attributes. Sujatha, following Amma, believes that "the connection we have for that deity in this birth is not only because you have ... developed this kind of [connection], but it is coming from several births before.... You cannot really feel that it is god versus goddess because it is man versus woman." If we accept Amma's suggestion that affinities for certain deities are formulated over multiple lifetimes, then one's current, temporal, and gendered body has little to do with the *longue durée* of the cosmic travel of the ātman along potentially infinite cycles of birth, death, and rebirth. As such, gendered bodies have even less relation to the connection between ātman and brahman, represented in material form through the connection of the individual with a particular deity. Thus while Amma represents both the living goddess and a message of women's empowerment, for Indian Hindus, even those most committed to Amma's emphasis on empowering women, the two have little connective tissue.

More than any other form, inheritors relate to Amma simply as mother. For some, the idealization of the symbolic maternal as represented in Amma can even supersede physiological motherhood in importance. Several years ago, at the San Ramon ashram, I was standing next to a young mother and her three-year-old daughter along the sides of a red-carpeted aisle through which Amma was about to pass after the completion of her darshan programs. We both craned our necks to look down the aisle as Amma approached, her hands gently outstretched to touch the fingertips of devotees who stretched and reached to gain closer proximity to her. As we did so, the mother turned to her daughter and, pointing to Amma, purposefully said, "Look. There is your *real* mother." Devotees imagine themselves to be Amma's children, quite literally, which exists in tandem with or even supersedes the importance of the physiological relationship to their own birth mothers.[32]

Some devotees may integrate their vision of Amma's omnipotence as mother with other maternal Hindu goddesses. But for many of these devotees, envisioning Amma as their mother serves to augment their intimate connection, to increase their devotion, and to enhance their ability to relate to her as a guru. Surya, an Indian Hindu *brahmacārī*, moved from South India to the United States as a skilled IT professional. Ironically, he met Amma in San Ramon and soon afterward he decided to become a renunciate. He now resides at Amritapuri. He explains:

> To have a spiritual master as a mother is a great blessing. It gives so much nourishment and support to us. I don't know if I could have done anything with a male guru who was strict and stern and, you know, in this modern day and age having Amma here is a double bonus—having mother's love

and compassion to pull you through. She can be strict and stern, but she can also be loving and kind. So that kind of combination only Amma can give. . . . I still love going to temples. I still love praying to deities, but actually, for me, Amma is all and all. She is my spiritual master. For me, as a disciple, she is everything to me. She is my master; she is my God. Even if I go to pray to a deity, actually it is Amma that I am praying to.

Surya's connection to Amma as mother, who is a physical embodiment of God, vividly portrays the commonplace apotheosis of mother and the esteem for the maternal ideal in Indic society.

But among adopters, particularly those who find solace in the goddess movement, a highly feminist theological reading of Amma as a living goddess surfaces. Many devotees have sought out goddess traditions explicitly because they believe them to be intimately intertwined with the political project of reclaiming women's spirituality. Others, less defined in their individualized religious convictions, are still searching for their own understanding of the divine and how Amma is connected to that vision. A pattern emerges in which the more committed individuals become, the more apt they are to formulate their understanding of divinity in terms of goddess devotionalism and Amma as a living embodiment of the goddess. Devotees not only conform to the maternal-ascetic habitus of selfless service (sevā) within the movement, they also adopt practices largely derived from devotional Hindu religiosity, such as *puja* (ritual worship), *archana* (prayers), and *bhajans* (devotional music). As such, the trajectory for devotees graduates from a polysemous conception of spirituality to direct worship of Amma as a living embodiment of the goddess.

Adopters with the slightest commitment often describe Amma in relation to their more nebulous conceptions of the divine, imagined as the cosmic order, universal consciousness, light, love, or energy. Many devotees who define themselves with the ideal of spirituality are overt about their indefinite understandings of exactly who or what God is. These devotees vacillate between a wide variety of ideas about the nature of divinity. They incorporate Amma into their individualized bricolage spiritual sensibilities by defining her in terms of that which they personally believe the superhuman to be. For many, Amma is a vortex of energy, consciousness, light, love, and/or compassion. They believe her to be superhuman, or at least an exemplary human (often iterated in terms of a realized being), but they do not emphasize her role as a goddess incarnation. As Brian explained,

I don't know what God is, so this is sort of a moot question for me until I know what God is. My view would be that somebody who could know what a thousand people is [*sic*] thinking at a given time probably is not thinking in their [*sic*] brain. So probably they are connected to a consciousness, and that is universal. And that consciousness that is universal would probably be called part of God. So my view is that Amma is not just this five foot two body that we see in front of us. . . . It is sort of a miracle that all of that consciousness can come through that. You can see that it is mind-blowing.

Marlene, who is heavily involved in energy work and crystal healing, said that Amma represents a heart energy that is increasing in the upcoming generations. She said, "I don't really hold Amma as a guru, I just hold her as this amazing light." For many American metaphysicals and casual devotees, this "light" that Amma embodies and exudes makes her darshan programs worth attending.

Other attendees at Amma's public programs believe that Amma is a realized being (one among many) who has perfected the extreme possibilities of human potential. They believe that she exhibits her self-realization during darshan programs in order to provide an example of what her devotees could become after significant "spiritual work." For example, Luke said:

Last year, after all of these years, she put my head on her belly and it was so like—cosmic vacuum. I could feel her heart beat in her belly and her belly didn't feel full; it felt like space. It was like I got energy rushes in my head and like my whole being melted from the depth of her being and how strong it is, you know, not needing much food and living on the pure light of the soul. Her body is sacred, beautiful, wonderful, living temple-like. We are so blessed to know that this can really happen with us.

For Luke, Amma is an exemplary being who represents the human potential of every individual. American metaphysicals, unwittingly or not, often draw on the capstone ideals of the human potential movement through their frequent references to the diffuse rhetoric of personal growth and spiritual development.[33] Many believe that they are on a spiritual path toward self-realization, which they can achieve through inner spiritual work accomplished through spiritual practice. For these metaphysicals, Amma is an exemplary being who has attained self-realization. She represents the physical embodiment of the formidable goal that they seek to achieve within their own personal development. They aim to emulate and replicate what they see as her boundless compassion and divine love through cultivating a mimetic relationship toward the guru.

This perspective, that Amma has achieved supranormal status, differs slightly from the more commonplace belief among Amma devotees that Amma is by her very nature supernatural. Trevor, a devotee who was raised as a Thai Buddhist, aptly explained this difference in views:

> There is nothing on earth like Amma. She is truly the only one of her kind that I have seen. You have the Dalai Lama, who is like a simple monk, he says. And a man who has done great, has gone through great training to be who he is. But then you have Amma who seems to be more than that, [she] seems to be sent, or something, different than someone who has achieved something. She just seems to *be* that something . . . she doesn't have a conventional human personality like everyone else does. She just is this unshakable wellspring of love like I have never seen in any other human. And that is worth coming back for, because love is so conditional in the human world, and to see it not be is truly remarkable.

In Trevor's view, the Dalai Lama is supranormal, whereas Amma is supernatural. While many devotees, like Trevor, do not specify exactly what that something is that Amma appears to be, it is clear that it transfers her to the realm of the supernatural in their conceptions. Because Amma's movement emphasizes a theology based in upaniṣadic scriptures that create litanies of lists of what the ultimate reality (brahman) is not—not this, not that (*neti neti*)—many devotees feel comfortable characterizing their ideas about the divine with these types of nondescript terminologies.

However, a significant segment of the North American adopter population purposefully interlaces Amma's identity and message of equanimity with a feminist politics. Like most inheritors, these adopters envision Amma as an incarnation of the omnipotent and omniscient goddess. But in contrast they often link her identity to a pantheon of powerful goddesses extracted not only from Hindu religiosity but from all of the religions of the world (Isis, Black Madonnas, Tara, Sara). From this perspective, Amma's identity as a female guru and her vision of equanimity among the sexes (attained through a privileging of the feminine) interlace to signify a spiritual alternative to the predominance of patriarchal religious institutions.

Some devotees openly position Amma as a goddess within their American goddess movement quests for female divinity in service of women's empowerment. As Celia explained:

> I was raised as a staunch Catholic, but it never fit for me. I mean I loved the ceremony of going to church; I was grateful that I learned about God. But I never believed the crap that women can't be priests, only nuns, etc. etc., all

of the patriarchy in the church I wasn't comfortable with. So when I turned eighteen, I explored many different religions and my affiliation is more Pagan. I believe in more of the earth based, you know, the Wicca, the goddess oriented, the Native American all of that; even Buddhism and Hinduism is considered Pagan in the Christian world [*sic*]. So that is what I felt fed me. And I always felt that—this is a mind-blowing thing for me because all of my life I spoke to a woman and I always thought it was Mary, the Virgin Mother, whenever I would say prayers. But as I got a little bit older . . . I started calling her Mata. I had never heard that word before. . . . And I knew that she was dark in my head and in my visions. . . . And then, when I met Amma and I knew that it was Mata Amritanandamayi, it just blew me away. And seeing her and meeting her, I instantly knew. . . . And I believe that I served her in the goddess temples, you know, way back when, when women were doing the goddess temples and the spirituality was more matriarchal. . . . I particularly feel that she is an avatar, which is a direct incarnation.

For Celia, and devotees like her, Amma fits well into their beliefs in neopagan goddess theology, cast broadly to include those traditions that Christianity historically deemed pagan or heathen (Celia includes Wicca, ecofeminism, Native American traditions, shamanism, Buddhism, and Hinduism). Celia also relates an account of past-life experiences with Amma, referencing the myth of matriarchal pre-Christian history often advocated within the women's spirituality and goddess movements.

In her devotional account of Amma, Judith Cornell repeatedly locates Amma within what she imagines to be the pan-global veneration of the Dark Mother. She says, "The Dark Mother is known by different names. Catholics call her the Black Madonna, the Buddhists call her Tara, and the Gypsies, who migrated to Europe from India, have called her by the name of Sara/Kali. And there are the ancient Dark Mothers: Sophia from the Old Testament, Artemis of Ephesus, the Roman Ceres, and Isis the Egyptian goddess. In fact the Dark Mother is venerated in some form all over the world."[34] For Cornell, Amma is a living embodiment of the "eternal" tradition of Dark Mothers who serve as protectors of the poor and oppressed. She finds significance in the temporal confluence of Amma's stay at the monastery chapel Estella in Spain, while the traveling Black Madonna icon, Notre Dame Du Puy, also resided in the small and remote chapel.[35] In her interpretation, Amma's dedication to the poor and oppressed integrally intertwines within the existing realm of devotion to Black Madonnas in the Catholic tradition, as well as the veneration of Dark Mothers throughout history in all corners of the globe.

Many adopter devotees, whether they believe in the credibility of a matriarchal goddess-centered pre-Christian history or not, believe that the times are ripe for revising the patriarchal godhead with a turn toward the feminine. Some interpret Amma as a positive female role model for women because she runs a powerful organization while maintaining her commitment to femininity. Maya explained:

> She [Amma] really does embody the universal feminine. . . . I think that's what's up right now, at this point in our existence. And she really helps shift more than just men's minds about looking at the feminine—it's really important to shift women's minds and their conditioning about what it means to be feminine. I think in the past it meant force, like bringing up our masculine sides was our place of power. And Amma runs a multinational corporation while she is hugging people and being present with every single person, and making sure that everything is running smoothly. Again, it is her example that makes her attractive to people. It's not really what she says. You see her running a business, being a mother. Kind of like a stay-at-home mom [laughs], she's always at one of her ashrams hugging people. But she is also a businesswoman. And she is doing it from a very feminine place.

Devotees like Maya take to heart Amma's women-centric prescriptions and find reinforcement for their feminism in Amma's exemplary behavior. Maya not only believes Amma to be "the embodiment of the divine feminine," but she also witnesses intensely her ability to juxtapose very maternal actions with her role as an executive female.

Other Amma devotees believe that humanity needs female leadership and a resurgence of the feminine because they blame men for the current conditions in the world. My roommates at the Michigan programs in 2007, two sisters, both middle-aged adopters, joked that:

> Instead of searching for WMDs (weapons of mass destruction), we should be searching for OWDs (old white dudes)! [raucous laughter] . . . Well, John Gray says that men are from Mars, and let me tell you what—Mars is a dead planet. No life. And you look at the leadership and the leaders of this country that can't stop invading and making war—the Earth will become just like Mars if we continue to keep these men, these OWDs in control!

This critique of the hypermasculinity of the political leadership of the time (President George W. Bush, and others) and male leadership in general reveals their mimesis of the layered ambivalences within Amma's teachings between privileging females or feminine qualities.

A similar ambivalence exists between her juxtaposition of advaita vedantic nondualism with the feminist recognition of gender difference. Amma's primary discourses invoke a universal similitude of divinity in all creatures, often annunciated with the repetitious rubric "We are all one." In a recent speech, she developed this idea, explaining, "Efforts at coexistence fail when we claim 'we are all one,' but we disrespect each other's ancient customs and traditions. . . . We have to acknowledge the fact that even though we are one in essence, externally we are different . . . an awareness of the need for coexistence amidst diversity is the only way to alleviate the suffering of others."[36] Herein we can discern Amma's careful balance between ascription to the advaita vedantic conception of the ultimate reality of universal oneness, while she addresses the practical realities of social injustice and differences in resource allocations.

Whether influenced by feminism or not, adopter devotees envision Amma as the Divine Mother and see her as a powerful role model for all of humanity. Like inheritors, many adopters also iterated the view of Amma as a loving mother goddess who enables them to relate to the divine as children would to their mother. Lyrics to the Goddess Jams' song "Dear AMMA" highlight Amma as an omnipotent and omnipresent mother goddess and her devotees as her children. The group, comprised of primarily female adopter devotees who live in the San Ramon ashram, sing: "Amma is the stars, Amma is the moon, Amma is the water, and the lunch at noon, Amma is the goddess of a million worlds and Amma is the Mama for this lil, lil, baby girl." Herein they envision Amma as their mother and simultaneously praise her as the supreme goddess who represents and encompasses all other forms. In true Hindu form, she embodies both immanence and transcendence, the intimate and the infinite.

It is often the case that the more ardent devotees become, the more likely they are to supplant their preexisting conceptions of divinity with Amma, envisioned as *the* divinity. Casual attendees often view Amma as one among many spiritual masters whom they believe to be realized beings conveying both an example for and a message to humanity. More committed devotees (exhibited by their active involvement in the movement and dedication to their personal spiritual practices) tend to incorporate Amma, often envisioned as divine, into their existing pantheons or bricolage spiritualities. Those who are even more committed (exhibited by various levels of asceticism, for example, touring with Amma, dedicating themselves to selfless service, implementing Amma's teachings, actively participating in satsangs, adopting considerable life-altering behaviors, or undertaking renunciation [brahmacārī/nīs]) commonly envision Amma as their primary connection to the divine. These most ardent devotees relate to the divine not *through* Amma but *as* Amma. For these devotees, Amma *is* the goddess.

In fact, the more devotees become ingrained into the mimetic model of the guru-disciple relationship, the more they are likely to attempt to reflect Amma's behaviors by disciplining their lifestyles and worldviews to conform to the maternal-ascetic habitus of the movement. The maternal asceticism of the guru provides a mimetic model for her followers, both as goddess (the reenvisioning of the self) and as maternal-ascetic (the disciplining of the self). French sociologist Emile Durkheim suggests that asceticism (what he calls *the negative cult*) is an essential component of religious life. He contends that ascetic virtuosos exist so that the laity might follow their example, albeit in a limited and restrained fashion. Thus the ascetic and the laity are not wholly distinct, but their behaviors signify the spectrum of prohibitions enacted in order to maintain distinctive spaces of the sacred. He explains, "Those certain individuals [ascetics] amount to so many living models that encourage striving. Such is the historical role of the great ascetics. . . . The contempt that they profess for all that ordinarily impassions men strikes us as bizarre. But those extremes are necessary to maintain among the faithful an adequate level of distaste for easy living and mundane pleasures. An elite must set the goal too high so that the mass does not set it too low. Some must go to extremes so that the average may remain high enough."[37]

Amma devotees routinely recounted how being in Amma's presence was enough to enact significant lifestyle changes in their personal habits. Devotees gradually conform their behaviors to those Amma deems best (listening to devotional music, wearing modest clothing, limiting indulgences, and so on). As devotees acculturate themselves to the maternal-ascetic habitus of the movement, they often say their indulgences dissipated without a concerted effort—just witnessing the extremities of Amma's asceticism curtailed their desires for worldly passions. As Patience explained:

> I feel like when I met Amma personally, I feel like I was born again. And everybody—all of my worldly friends—they looked at me and they were like, "You are not you. Who are you? I still like you and everything, but you're different. You're like . . . much more holy" . . . it's almost like I've been cleaned or baptized or something. . . . I [used to think] about stuff, worldly stuff like that [going to bars]. But now it's like I have no desire. . . . For example, I took hundreds of dollars of worldly music that I used to have and gave it away to friends . . . CDs and tapes and a lot of DVDs, you know like movies that had too much violence in them. . . . And now if I feel like watching something I'll watch a video of Amma, you know giving darshan. Or if I want to listen, I'll listen to bhajans of course. It opens my heart . . .

and I don't miss the other stuff at all. . . . I've had to weed some of my
friends out of my life and just love them and pray for them at a distance.

Although Patience claims a particularly intense singularity of focus,
many devotees related similar accounts that after being with Amma for
some time they simply no longer had the desire to indulge in their vices.
The most common examples were smoking cigarettes and drinking al-
cohol; many devotees explained that after years of smoking cigarettes
and trying multiple methods to quit (acupuncture, hypnosis, nicotine
patches, and so on) praying to Amma and inculcating themselves in devotions to her quickly eliminated their desires for the habit. The self-
sacrificing mother provides a poignant model that encourages devotees
in a compassionate, gentle, and loving way to develop ascetic behaviors.
It also provides the primary impetus for devotees' intense commitment
to humanitarian efforts through significant selfless service (sevā).

Durkheim also rightly suggests that it is the ascetic behavior of exemplary religious virtuosos that warrants their exaltation to those en-
cumbered within a material existence. He explains, "By the very act of
renouncing things, he [sic] has risen above things. Because he has silenced
nature, he is stronger than nature."[38] The ascetic may even become
"equal or superior to the gods."[39] In Amma's case, devotees frequently
ascribe the divine qualities of the goddess to Amma because they have
witnessed her devotional asceticism, her maternal ethos, and her self-
discipline and self-sacrifice while constantly embracing strangers during
countless hours of darshan programs that tax her physical body. Those
who are most deeply integrated into the movement have most likely
spent some time in India and at Amma's primary ashram, Amritapuri.
At Amritapuri, the equation between Amma and the goddess is palpa-
ble and ubiquitous, but it is not the more generalized idea of the goddess espoused by metaphysicals in the United States. Instead, many
devotees in India associate Amma with the fearsome yet maternal
Hindu goddess Kali. Structures in place at Amritapuri reinforce this
belief: the primary temple of the ashram is a Kali temple, wherein an
image of Amma in Devī Bhāva stands at the base of the goddess figurine
and another altar space houses the sickle and sword that Amma used to
wield during early Kali bhāvas. Amritapuri is located in the South Indian coastal state of Kerala, where Hindus have birthed and nurtured a
long historical tradition of Kali worship since antiquity, and Amma's
ashram is no exception.[40]

Critics of Amma's movement find this equation of Amma with the omnipotent mother goddess Kali to be the most repugnant aspect of the movement. One ardently critical blogger explained heatedly, "They do not all say she is god in [A]merica, but, most of them, between them selves [*sic*], and everyone living at [the] ashram [Amritapuri] 100 percent think she is kali mother of the universe." Though Amma's most vitriolic critics usually have their own personal axes to grind with her organization, I concur with this blogger's assessment that the idea that Amma *is* Kali in human form, which is ubiquitous at Amritapuri, has only vaguely made the transition to the United States.

In fact, Kali is not mentioned or visible in Amma's presentation of herself to her North American audiences. Amma represents herself to her North American audiences primarily as a global humanitarian. Second, she represents herself as a loving mother guru who gives hugs to anyone who desires one for free. She is widely popularized in the American press as "the hugging saint," and journalistic pieces about her in American newspapers and on television, of which there have been hundreds, emphasize her hugs, her humanitarianism, and her interfaith work ("My religion is love"). The language in Amma's darshan programs highlights her as a realized master (*satguru*), and Devī Bhāva performances reveal her in all of her splendor as a benevolent Divine Mother. While there are references to her as a goddess incarnation, they largely depict her as an incarnation of the beautiful, sweet, loving, and benevolent Hindu mother goddesses Lalitā, not the fearsome, vengeful, sexualized, and violent Hindu mother goddess Kali, popular in the backwaters of Kerala.

CONCLUSION

The term *feminism* holds an uncomfortable position in much of the Indic context. The impulses of second-wave feminism in particular, which sought to assign normative categories to gendered bodies, found that many women of color at home and abroad rejected the very characterization of appropriate womanhood disseminated within rhetoric meant to alleviate their presumed oppression. The tendency toward the essentialization of women became the Achilles heel of the movement, and women raised cacophonous voices regarding their different experiences about its monochromatic portrait of uninhibited womanhood. In India, many women viewed this feminism from the West as a movement that aimed to instruct non-Western women about their own oppression. It was often characterized as one more form of Western imperialism, meddling and dictating policy in areas where it should not have.

Prior to this influx of Western feminism, Indians had already developed their own social agendas of female empowerment and strategic uplift, which were enacted initially through male leadership and then later through male and female collaboration. Many resented this new Western feminism that they believed attempted to initiate a war between the sexes. Some argued that such antagonism would destroy women's traditional place in society and the family. This was coupled with a keen awareness of the history of British imperialistic projects, which used the status of Indian women to gain political favor back at home and to justify their claims to colonial authority.[41] Western condemnation of the status of Indian women was rife with political and historical memory.

Amma emerges through this discursive morass invoking existing religio-cultural formations of matrifocality to challenge routinized behaviors of male domination and female subordination. She recalls a mythic Golden Age of the Vedas in which women were honored, respected, and shared in religious ritual functions. She reminds Indian Hindus that all women should be received as embodiments of the goddess, to be revered and esteemed. She positions herself as one such goddess incarnation and demonstrates the actions of the self-sacrificing mother, one of the most pervasive cultural motifs in Hindu society, through compassion and love expressed through a maternal embrace. She calls for the revitalization of the feminine principle in a world that she sees as consumed with archetypal masculine attributes. She suggests that only the bolstering of feminine qualities of love, compassion, and self-sacrifice can heal the extensive global crises that have come about because of current embroilment in egoistic, ambitious, and destructive masculine tendencies. But despite her framing of the problem in gendered dichotomies, Amma largely dissociates gender from sex. Thus both men and women must develop their feminine traits of love, compassion, and self-sacrifice. In fact, the predominance that Amma gives to the feminine as a solution to contemporary crises stems from her assertion that we (as a civilization) have fallen so far down the rabbit hole of hypermasculinity.

On these socially critical points, both inheritors and adopters vigorously nod in agreement. Similarly, when they view Amma, the most devout from both demographics regard her as an embodiment of the goddess. But they sharply diverge when relating goddess worship to the practicalities of bettering women's socioeconomic status. Despite the diffuse arenas in Indic society in which the goddess is superimposed on Indian women, largely, Indian Hindu devotees do not mimetically relate to the goddess as a symbol for female empowerment. This dissociation between the lived realities of women and the goddess among Indian Hindus contradicts the conclusion of American women's spirituality and goddess movements, which assumes a causal connection between goddess worship and female empowerment. The reason for this ideological discrepancy stems from the chasm created between the complexities of lived reality and the simplicity of a romantic vision based on essentialisms.

In Indic society, Hindu women have been immersed in a cultural environment in which goddess worship is commonplace. They have witnessed their mothers offering puja to the goddess and then, with the same hands, turning to give their sons larger shares of food than their daughters. They have witnessed advocates for female empowerment as well as misogynistic policy makers who offer alms at the same goddess temple. They envision a historical trajectory that once respected women, then declined into female subordination, and is only now attempting to recover equal rights for women, and all the while people continued to give offerings to the goddess. They have walked the crowded streets in urban environments and stepped around roadside shrines to Sitala, Sita, Kali, and Radha/Krishna while passing the tall spires and open ponds of Durga and Lakshmi Narayana temples. They have lived in the tumult of modernity that every so often spawns a new goddess, like Santoshi Ma, who first made her appearance in a Bollywood film in 1975. More recently, in 2010, Angrezi Ma, the dalit Goddess English, was recently enshrined in her first temple in Uttar Pradesh. Local teachers in the Nalanda public school composed this song in her honor: "She hails from London, this Goddess English / She reigns over computers, she's everybody's goddess." The mantra chanted on the occasion was "A-B-C-D."[42] Hindu women recognize the inherent diversity in the names and forms of the goddess, each with her own specialty and function. They have seen men dressed as Kali in the streets begging for spare change. They have seen men acting and dancing dressed as the goddess on Keralan stages in elaborate epic dramatizations, knowing acutely that human women are forbidden to perform such roles.

Raised within such a religio-cultural environment, many of these women interpret the goddess as multifarious and unrelated to feministic aims. Goddesses are innumerable, with distinctive attributes that protest easy conflations into a singular, supposedly empowering entity. Goddesses continue to be exalted, while the social realities of women fluctuate throughout history. Goddesses can be both benevolent and malevolent. They have the power to support or squelch women's demands. They can be wholly co-opted by men, barring women from public identification with them. Goddesses are invented and reinvented at will according to those who would find them useful, culturally symbolic tools.

Indian Hindus also relate the idea of becoming a goddess in quite literal terms, having indigenous cultural reference points for those women (and men) who are overcome by the goddess through possession rituals. Generalities of popular opinion tend to derive from the foundational literature on possession that suggests that possessed individuals usually emerge from disenfranchised classes and rural village environments and their privileged access to the goddess enables them to establish microbusinesses of spiritual and healing entrepreneurship.[43] As Kathleen Erndl relates, "In reading about South Asia, one often gets the [false] impression that possession and related ecstatic behavior are part of the 'little tradition' and thus confined to the lower castes and the poor and uneducated in rural areas."[44] Isabelle Nabokov/Clark-Decès also complicates such commonplace assumptions, suggesting that her fieldwork among Tamil *cāmis* (swamis) confirms the anthropological conclusion that it is not socioeconomic status but, rather, "emotional afflictions or personal crises [that are] critical springboards for life-changing religious experiences."[45] Both scholars rightly note that sweeping generalizations about those who are vibrantly affected by the presence of the goddess possession in South Asia are contentious. But, still, there exists a commonplace cultural stigma of disenfranchisement or emotional instability attached to those individuals who exhibit the presence of the goddess. As such, the enterprise of becoming a goddess symbolizes a series of social attributes that Indian Hindu Amma devotees, who are largely educated, upper middle class, cosmopolitan, and mentally stable, do not find appealing or conducive to their lifestyles and worldviews.

The majority of American adopters have limited knowledge of such realities. They largely base their ideas about the Hindu goddess on romantic imaginings of spiritual India, goddess feminist ideology that still searches for matriarchal goddesses to alleviate patriarchy, and monothetic representations of Hindu traditions. The majority of the metaphysicals were raised within Abrahamic traditions with a patriarchal God or entirely without religion in secular households. Their encounter with goddesses often begins with the active seeking of alternative forms of religiosity. Devotion to the goddess incites the allure of the wholly other, that which likely was absent within the faith (or lack of faith) of their childhood. Furthermore, many who were raised Christians have imagined women's relation to divinity through their religious tradition's ambivalence between the virginal Mary and the failures of Eve. The failure of Eve has often been translated into the mapping of the deficiencies of women. The commonplace reading of Genesis 2:4–3:24, that God first made Adam and then made Eve from Adam's rib, is often used to justify man's supremacy over woman. The events of Genesis have been invoked from Aquinas to Luther and beyond to characterize women as subordinate. Central to Catholic tradition, the Virgin Mary also symbolizes qualities supposedly inherent in women, for example, kindness, compassion, piety, docility, and subordination.[46] Characterized as weak and sinful like Eve or pious and subordinate like Mary, many women have discarded Christocentric traditions in search of positive and agentive female divinities. When they encounter powerful and independent Hindu goddesses, they transpose the mimetic relationship between humanity and biblical events that is so powerful in Christian contexts onto their new religious persuasions and many imagine themselves to be similarly powerful and independent like Kali, Durga, or Lalitā.[47] While their religious tradition may have changed, their manner of approaching divine personas retains some of its internal scaffolding.

Additionally, second-wave feminism, goddess movements, and the latent orientalism extant in the search for spirituality in India coalesce to encourage Americans to posit India and its goddess traditions as a means by which to transform the self, to find meaning, to exalt the feminine, and to encounter alternative paradigms of experiencing the divine. Thus the metaphysicals' encounter with India rests on a foundation of perceived self-transformation by absorbing the material and religious cultures of India within the self. They are both consuming and consumed by the goddess, projecting and reflecting themselves in the light of the other, adopting and co-opting in the process of self-transformation. This is why many metaphysicals regard Amma as one who has perfected self-realization, but also as one who has completed a journey of self-transformation, for which they are also traversing the same path.

Because of their limited knowledge of Hindu traditions, many metaphysicals are unaware when they initially encounter Amma and her movement that there are multiple goddesses in Hindu traditions. While engaged within the movement, they frequently develop higher levels of Indic cultural competency. The most serious devotees learn Malayalam and Sanskrit and spend a considerable time in India. But the majority of adopter devotees have encountered underlying ideas of goddess feminism and women's spirituality much more frequently than they have been introduced to the thousands of different goddesses in the pantheon of Hindu divinities. Neither do they enter into the movement with a general historical knowledge of women's empowerment movements in India. It is much more likely that they have a general sense that women in India struggle for equality and that supporting the betterment of their social situation would be a positive contribution. Thus, unlike Indian Hindus, the metaphysicals do not enter into Amma's movement with the cultural inhibitions of equating women's everyday experiences with goddess worship. Instead they largely see the goddess as a powerful symbol for women, a symbol that has the potential to help them regain their self-worth and empower them to improve their social conditions. What they do not recognize is that the Hindu goddess, while new to them, has been in India for a long time, and all the while women's social positions have remained subordinate within a patriarchal religious system.

For the metaphysicals, feminism is largely considered a positive development. Few would balk at the term in the way that Indian Hindus often do, and fewer would recognize its imperialistic roots. But their diverse feminisms have much more in common with the women's spirituality movement, goddess feminism, and second-wave feminism than the deconstructivist strains of third-wave and postfeminism that offer more critical analyses. For many of these devotees, Amma's characterization of certain qualities as masculine and other qualities as feminine resonates with their foreboding sense that there *is* a crisis in the world today, for which Amma's seemingly simple solution, that there needs to be a resurgence of the feminine, is a welcome rejoinder. It is a solution that is tangible and possible to be implemented on a personal level, both of which supply devotees with a sense of individual control in their participation in the highly complex and constantly fluctuating globalized environment of postmodernity.

Despite the different attributes that adopters and inheritors inscribe on the goddess and her relationship to human women, both populations find precisely what they are looking for in Amma. Whether devotees express that they see her as Love, Light, Kali, Durga, Lalitā, or Devi, each time they say her name in prayers or in casual conversations they call her Mother. One poignant event occurs routinely at Amma's programs: a small child who speaks a South Indian language cries out to his biological mother. Regardless of whether the thousands in attendance are bustling about or silently meditating, he cries loudly, "Amma! Amma! Amma!" (Mother! Mother! Mother!), and usually there are then cheers from the audience and gleeful laughter regarding the young child who has such devotion to Amma. The laughter of the crowd is not intentionally malicious. The delightedly laughing devotees only resonate with the fact that they too approach Amma crying out her name, like little children who are crying out desperately for their mother.

CHAPTER 5

Congregational Dynamics

Growing Pains En Route from the Particular to the Universal

Westerners in the United States complain that the Indians get all the attention, Indians in the United States complain that a few Malayalam speakers get all the attention, Indians in India complain that the foreigners get special attention, women claim that Amma talks to men more, etc., etc.[1]

—Anonymous blog comment

To the Oriental, the world of spirit is as real as to the Occidental is the world of senses. In the spiritual, the Oriental finds everything he wants or hopes for; in it he finds all that makes life real to him. To the Occidental he is a dreamer; to the Oriental the Occidental is a dreamer playing with ephemeral toys, and he laughs to think that grown-up men and women should make so much of a handful of matter which they will have to leave sooner or later. Each calls the other a dreamer. . . . Therefore it is fitting that, whenever there is a spiritual adjustment, it should come from the Orient. It is also fitting that when the Oriental wants to learn about machine-making, he should sit at the feet of the Occidental and learn from him. When the Occident wants to learn about the spirit, about God, about the soul, about the meaning and the mystery of this universe, he must sit at the feet of the Orient to learn.[2]

—Swami Vivekananda

Even though the breeze blows everywhere, coolness will be felt more if we sit in the shade of a tree. In the same way, although God is all-pervading, His presence will clearly shine in certain places more than in others. That is the greatness of satsang. In the presence of a Perfect Master, one can experience God more than in any other place.[3]

—Mata Amritanandamayi

Amma's *darshan*[4] embrace attempts to transcend societal classifications by devaluing differences and accentuating commonalities between people, cultures, and religions. Her transnational movement bridges continents and religious traditions, and, most important, all regardless of race, gender, nationality, religion, wellness, hygiene, mental state, or morality, are welcome to attend Amma's darshan programs for free and receive Amma's embrace. At the social and organizational levels as well, both Amma and her devotees are aware of the diversity of the attendees at these programs. It is immediately striking, even to the most casual participants. Amma's darshan programs in the United States invoke a carnivalesque atmosphere in which people of different ethnicities congregate amid bright hotel ballroom lights, the hustle of the marketplace, the savory aromas of bustling kitchens, and the blaring bhajans and recordings of Amma's speeches.

Ripe with the excitement and anticipation of Amma's arrival, the darshan experience, pending marriages, and so on, a charged energy pervades the spiritually vibrant space. For months, many devotees anticipate attending Amma's darshan programs. This is particularly true for those devotees who have severe physical disabilities or illnesses and come to Amma (often in desperation) for what they believe to be her healing darshan embrace. Other devotees suffer from emotional and psychological traumas, which they lay at Amma's feet during their darshan experiences. While the majority of attendees come because of acculturated devotion, mere curiosity, the extraordinary atmosphere, or to ease what might be best categorized as "bourgeois suffering," the truly needy comprise a visible portion of the audience. Perhaps because of the intense anticipation of devotees, during darshan programs there are frequently moments when they are overcome with emotion and exhibit this through raucous laughter, frenetic dancing, hysterical crying, silent weeping, and/or zealous outbursts. These events color the general atmosphere of darshan programs because of their outward exhibition of moments of ecstatic jubilation and emotional release. The immensity and diversity of the crowds, compounded by the emotionally charged nature of the darshan experience, create a forum for potentially wild and sometimes dangerous behaviors.

Organizers are acutely conscious of this social reality because in a large crowd diversity can have both positive and negative valences. The diverse crowd at Amma's gatherings amplifies the festival atmosphere, but it can also be dangerous. During the 2007 Chicago programs, Sujatha warned me that the previous year they had to throw out a pedophile who was standing behind the little boys. A similar situation occurred in 2009 during the Chicago programs. A small population of mentally unstable and clinically mentally ill people also come to Amma for darshan. In 2011, the Chicago team worked with local police authorities to contain a mentally unstable Indian woman who was vigorously pushing through the crowd, knocking over small children along her way, and violently confronting unsuspecting attendees with shockingly obscene outbursts. In prior years the woman had been photographed and tagged as a possible offender in the large white binder reserved for senior *sevites* (selfless service volunteers) at the welcome desk. In this case, Chicago sevites contacted the local police authorities, who contained the woman, talked her through her rage, and escorted her safely into a waiting taxi cab. In 2012, a man who had recently been taken into police custody as a suspect in the recent vandalization of the newly purchased Chicago ashram site had the gall to attend Amma's public programs. Once again, as in the aforementioned cases, the vigilant local security team quickly demonstrated its skill and dedication in maintaining the safety and sanctity of the ashram space.

Such events stem from the fact that Amma welcomes all people equally. Unless these exceptional attendees are violent or abusive, they are welcome to receive what many believe to be Amma's healing embraces. When I noted the numbers of mentally challenged attendees at Amma's programs, Br. Dayamrita Chaitanya responded by explaining:

I see a lot of mentally deranged people, including me. [laughs] Yes, of course it is true because as I said, understand, why did they become mentally deranged? It was because of a lack of love that they had in their lives. If you take every mental patient and analyze it, [sic] you will understand that at some time or the other they did not get enough love in their lives and it made them who they are. And so, the fact that they are attracted to Amma is because of the love factor—the selfless love. Of course, because the love that they get from the world is always selfish and conditioned, but when they go to Amma they get this selfless love and that is what is attracting them, that is what is attracting everybody in fact.

Similarly, a senior ashram resident explained, "Mentally ill people come to Amma's programs because they are seeking mental peace." Another devotee, Kalyani (Danielle), explained, "A lot of those kinds of people [mentally ill people] follow Amma. Amma draws them in." So in such a heterogeneous environment, how does one make sense of such extreme diversity? Who are Amma's devotees? Who attends Amma's darshan programs and *satsangs* (congregational gatherings)? How are they interrelated? This chapter addresses these questions, situating Amma's devotees in their contemporary social context and acknowledging their historical antecedents in the American religious landscape.

All ethnicities, cultures, genders, castes, races, creeds, and classes of inheritors, adopters, and visitors are welcome to attend Amma's darshan programs, satsangs, special events, and service opportunities, and to participate broadly in the devotional community. In chapter 1 I argued that ideally a spirit of unity and mutual witnessing inheres within Amma's darshan experience. This chapter analyzes year-round devotional communities operating without Amma's physical presence and notes that devotees easily slip from mutual witnessing back into the politics of recognition. They often reify relations wherein the self and the other are recognized as distinct, furthering sometimes exclusive communal identities that may unwittingly substantiate and buttress cultural stereotypes. While the doors are open to all, in practice the movement's demographics tend to settle into traditional patterns of what Stephen Warner adroitly terms "de facto congregationalism," meaning the self-imposed binding of communities into exclusive and homogenous worship groups.[5] Satsangs fracture along the antiquated ethnic categories of Indian and white to form de facto congregations, with inheritors largely mapping onto Indian communities and adopters respectively mapping onto white communities.

In Indian de facto congregations Malayalee Hindus (from Kerala, Amma's home state) predominate, but there are also significant populations of North Indian Hindus and Sikhs, as well as a small minority population of non-Indians (less than 10 percent consisting of whites, Latinos, and African Americans). These de facto congregations signify their status as inheritors by routinely linking Hindu practices, festivals, food, gender segregation, and cultural norms to their ritualized biweekly

Amma worship services. The other de facto congregations consist of a majority white population of adopters, a population that is occasionally slightly diversified, with scattered attendance by Indians, Latinos, and African Americans. The adopters who attend these de facto congregations are linked religiously through their devotion to Amma, but little else. Their multifarious and individualized spiritualities overlap through the formation of a communal Venn diagram, with Amma as the central nexus of commonality and the various peripheries as quite disparate. These community members adopt Hindu-style devotional rituals, practices, and beliefs through their participation in Amma's movement, which often results in the rejection or at least the transformation of their religious upbringing. These two groups of inheritors and adopters interact during Amma's public programs, retreats, and satsangs.[6] Their beliefs, practices, interactions, and the communities that they build together create the tenor of Amma's organization in the United States.

Much of the current work on church segregation and de facto congregationalism in the United States focuses on relations between Caucasians and African Americans. It was likely Martin Luther King Jr., if not someone long before him, who famously noted "eleven o'clock on Sunday morning was the most segregated hour in America."[7] Even today, ethnic homogeneity still characterizes the majority of American congregations, despite significant efforts to integrate Christians into multiracial congregations. In this chapter I argue that as new religious movements and Asian religions establish their foundations in the United States, they too (like their Christian peers) conform to de facto congregationalism and exhibit similar preferences for communal homogeneity.[8]

American religiosity is often explained with economic metaphors: a bountiful market or bazaar of evermore particularizing sectarian opportunities. There appears to be a particular religious option perfectly catered to the shifting individual desires of every religious seeker. As R. Laurence Moore argues, "The American religious system may be said to be 'working' only when it is creating cracks in denominations, when it is producing novelty, even when it is fueling antagonisms." He elaborates that even supposedly mainline American religions define themselves in relation to sectarian minorities. Sectarian religious minorities, for their part, seek to establish themselves in a process of identity construction that demands homogenizing and particularizing structures. Citing the ideotypical case of Mormonism, Moore continues, "Nothing was more 'normal' or 'typical' of American life than the process of carving out a separate self-identification, a goal toward which all the early Mormon enterprise was directed."[9] The process of carving out a personalized communal space characterizes American religiosity, in which fractionalization and fragmentation dominate any pretense to overarching unity. Amma's American devotees assimilate into the American religious landscape similarly by adapting to this demand for communal self-identification.

Inheritors and adopters have different sites of communal continuity; one seeks opportunities to reinforce inherited traditions, while the other seeks opportunities to develop self-styled interpretations of tradition. Thus groups of inheritors and adopters often find difficulties in establishing multiethnic congregations that can sustain this process of self-identification and the practical mapping of tradition. As a result, in congregational gatherings, Amma devotees tend to separate into homogenous communities of inheritors or adopters. They retreat to their culturally inherited (and already constructed) subjectivities with which they are familiar in order to create a congregation with a unified self-identity. This is not only a matter of preference; it also signifies the need for viable and strong representation as a minority religious group in the American religious landscape. Put simply, it is difficult to create multicultural, multiethnic congregational communities that mandate the construction of new, integrated communal identities. It is much easier to rely on those self-identities already firmly embedded in their inherited sociocultural subjectivities. As a result, like their American congregational counterparts, Amma's satsangs exhibited homogenizing tendencies toward associating with only "like-minded" people, engaging in the "production of difference"[10] between their satsangs and others. In the following discussion, I offer analyses to explain why inheritors and adopters in the Chicagoland satsangs interacted closely during Amma's semiannual darshan programs but were largely segregated for the remainder of the year into what devotees often called "Indian" and "Western" satsangs.

Before proceeding, it is important to note that recently the Chicagoland communities have come together as never before in a joint purpose with their new ashram, the Mata Amritanandamayi Center of Chicago (MACC), purchased in April 2012. Establishing an Amma ashram had been a long-term dream for the devotional community in Chicago, primarily among many of the leaders of the Paloma satsang. On June 30, 2012, Amma consecrated the site, and she (along with Illinois governor Pat Quinn) celebrated the establishment of the 140-acre ashram site in the exurbs of Chicago.[11] When purchased, the multibuilding site was in desperate need of repair, but Amma likely knew that because of this the selling price would be less and she could rely on the boundless devotional labor of devotees to do the necessary work.[12] After the April purchase, devotees from around the region came together for countless hours of sevā, and, miraculously, the large auditorium (darshan hall) sparkled when it hosted thousands of devotees for Amma's July 2012 programs. The new ashram site also meant that one of Amma's principal *brahmacāris*, Br. Shantamrita, a relatively young white American, would now reside at the ashram and that frequent satsangs, sevā days, GreenFriends initiatives, and cultural and devotional programs would be held at the MACC, which would serve as the nexus for *all* devotees. As Mira, a veteran inheritor devotee explained, the new ashram has drawn in "so many new members" of "different strains" and Br. Shantamrita is "really putting us back to basics, that we're here for Amma. He really united us." In its first year, Chandan (Micah), an adopter devotee, transferred from another ashram to become the first full time lay-resident at the MACC. The constant presence of these two adopter devotees, who are both quite serious in their devotion, demands respect and immediately integrates all events held at the MACC, even if they draw primarily from the powerful and influential inheritor community.

Only a short walk from a Metra line, the exurban ashram provides a tranquil respite for many devotees, and its very existence has fostered a communal spirit among disparate and previously geographically segmented devotees. It has also drawn in a significant influx of excitement, support, and involvement from new people who diversify and integrate what were once individual bounded satsang communities. That is not to say that there is no longer any conflict within the Chicago devotional community; no community exists without some conflict. But the MACC signifies not only the fulfillment of a long-awaited dream but a fresh, new, ethnically and culturally neutral, and community-driven devotional space that is welcoming to all of Amma's devotees. More than anything else, the new ashram site provides a singular and institutional forum for satsangs that are now organized under the leadership of Br. Shantamrita, a brahmacārī with a direct connection to Amma who takes special care with the youth group and the daily management of the MACC, and also coordinates and leads satsangs (see figure 10).

The local satsang is the primary arena in which Amma devotees express their faith with other devotees throughout the year. Satsangs are devotional gatherings where devotees converge to express their love for Amma and share in a communal spirit; they occur weekly, bimonthly,

FIGURE 10. Entry sign, MA Center Chicago, formally consecrated
by Amma, June 30, 2012 (© MA Center)

or monthly, depending on the location. Recently, in Chicago devotees
have also instituted a daily virtual satsang organized as a communal
conference call. According to Amma's direction, satsangs should be operated with the guidance and instruction of the MA Center in San Ramon, California. The center instructs local chapters that the satsang
program should remain consistent and be composed of the following
elements, in this order: chanting *Oṁ* (three times), chanting the *Dhyāna
Śloka*, chanting the *Mātā Amṛtānandamayi Aṣṭottara Śata Nāmāvali*

(*The 108 Names of* Mātā Amṛtānandamayi), chanting the *Śri Lalitā Sahasranāmāvali* (*The 1000 Names of Śri Lalitā*), a recitation of Amma's message (excerpted from her texts), bhajan singing, chanting *Mahiṣāsura Mardini Stotram* (*Ayi Giri Nandini*), performance of the *arati*, and the partaking of *prasad*. Thus Amma's satsang programs are bound to Hindu ritualism. Through satsangs, inheritors reinvigorate their native religiosity, and adopters must adapt to Hindu ritual constructs. Devotees can access a regional listing of the more than eighty satsangs in the nation through Amma's U.S. website.[13]

But only a very small fraction of program attendees participates in monthly satsangs. While eight thousand to ten thousand people attended Amma's public programs in Chicago in 2008, usually it was the same sixty to seventy devotees who attended Chicagoland satsangs regularly; that is .0087 percent, rounded up to .01 percent at best.[14] Further, among those devotees who did participate in satsangs, the feeling of a joint purpose dissipated, and the multicultural unity often apparent during darshan programs became a challenge. Generally, devotees retreated to their separate corners, stayed in their cultural comfort zones, and sought to create comfortable congregational environments by surrounding themselves with like-minded people. Although satsang attendees consist of only a portion of darshan program attendees, they are a very important population in that they orchestrate and organize all of the local details and leadership necessary for the administration of Amma's tours. They also create a continuous base of support, devotion, and publicity for Amma and her teachings throughout the year through devotional and humanitarian service activities.

DE FACTO CONGREGATIONALISM

During the period of my consistent involvement with Chicagoland satsangs, Chicago was known to have one of the strongest satsangs in the nation: Paloma, the primary suburban satsang, drew in between thirty-five and fifty-five devotees regularly each month; usually 95 percent to 100 percent of the regular attendees were inheritors to Hindu traditions. In addition, Chicagoland hosted at various times a downtown satsang, a growing Day Creek satsang, an irregularly hosted and poorly attended Flora satsang, and an independent satsang held at a downtown yoga center. Periodic but informal satsangs occurred routinely in various locations. Except for Paloma, the remaining satsangs were all comprised of adopters and their demographics were usually 85–90 percent white with the remaining 10–15 percent including Indian, Latino, Asian, and African Americans. The Paloma satsang was the engine behind the administration of Amma's movement in Chicago; the remaining satsangs were less organized, less consistent, and less connected to the MA Center in San Ramon. They were also less involved with the finances, planning, and orchestration of Amma's annual darshan programs in Chicago. This section aims to explain the foundations of this unbalanced distribution of power and authority that divided Amma's community of devotees along ethnic lines.

Satsangs are an effective forum for ethnic groups to re-create culturally specific communities and religious environments.[15] Immigrant Indian Hindus aim to re-create a Hindu environment via two strategies: by celebrating and reenacting religious practice and by teaching children about the religion. For these devotees, Amma's movement provides an intimate experience with a Hindu guru (whom many believe to be an avatar) that augments their participation in more traditional Hindu religiosity. Not surprisingly, the Paloma satsang emphasized cultural programs, Malayalee food, language, festivals, and community events. In addition to founding a chapter of Amma's international youth group, Amrita Yuva Dharma Dhara (AYUDH),[16] it also began a *bālā kendra* (child education) program, both of which have become very active (see figure 11).

Adopters have very different aims. Instead of aiming to re-create a religious environment, they aim to create one. They are spiritual seekers who have left behind their religious (or secular) upbringing in search of new spiritual experiences. As spiritual seekers, they describe themselves with terminology that emphasizes movement; they speak of being "on the path," "on a spiritual journey," "seeking energy," "seeking enlightenment," and "seeking self-realization." This is also a highly personal notion of self-contained religiosity; people speak in individualistic language: "on my path," "in my spiritual journey," "my spiritual goals," and so on. Many make material choices in accordance with their spiritual goals, because they believe themselves to be on spiritual journeys. Often they have chosen less financially lucrative lifestyles than their skills and education would merit in efforts to align their careers (and the majority of their time) with their spiritual practices and beliefs. It is common to meet ex-lawyers who are massage therapists, ex-engineers who are artists, and computer specialists who work in society only as much as necessary.

FIGURE 11. Paloma satsang youth group (*bālā kendra*) presents maple tree saplings to Amma for her blessing as part of the GreenFriends initiative to plant trees, Chicago, July 2009 (devotee photo)

→ reminded of eat, pray, love (journey to find oneself) (tv shows, movies)

Adopters largely come to Amma as *individuals*. In his seminal work *The New Age Movement*, Paul Heelas calls this movement one of "self-spirituality."[17] Sarah Pike explains that the new age ushered in "a cultural shift towards understanding the self as a commodity to be created and presented" and "a search for individualized religion."[18] Because these spiritual travelers participate as individuals, they do not emphasize the transmission of religious values to the next generation. Steve Bruce argues that "liberal religion has a problem transmitting itself to subsequent generations, first, because there is no need for such transmission and, secondly, because there is no basis for agreement on what to transmit in detail."[19] Not surprisingly, in satsangs run by adopters, there is little impetus for youth religious education programs.

Some examples from the field of spiritual *bricoleurs* and their creations of unique spiritualities will help define the category of adopter devotees. During a Michigan retreat in 2007 I shared a room with two sisters (both white adopters) who were longtime devotees of Amma. In our conversations, one woman described herself as part Jesus-centered Christian and part Hindu; the other woman described herself as part Christian, part Hopi, and part Amma devotee. One of the women said that both she and her sister "must have had some past lives as Indians [Native Americans] in America, because we both love sweat lodges and feel a real power in the humility with which Indians [Native Americans] regard the Mother Earth." Many of these spiritual bricoleurs also retain their ties to established religious traditions while incorporating aspects of guru devotion and a variety of beliefs and practices into their spiritual dispositions. I encountered Muslims, Catholics, Protestants, Sikhs, and Jews, all of whom also described their devotion to Amma. One devotee, a longtime resident of the American Southwest, showed me his striking tattoo of Amma in the garb of the Virgin of Guadalupe, explaining with devotional affection, "Amma is *my* Guadalupe." At Amma's 2009 Chicago programs, I asked a bearded African American man with long nails, who wore a black turban, large silver pendants, and a long robe, what religion he was, only to find out that his unusual appearance was a self-created style that he had adopted after a series of epiphanies and dreams that convinced him that he should burn all of his "secular" clothes and wear only this spiritualized attire. He espoused religious beliefs that were as eclectic as his appearance, but he unified it all together with universalistic statements such as "everything is spirituality" and "love is the core of all spirituality" (see figure 12).

Perhaps recognizing the difficulties that many non-Hindu devotees experience when classifying their unique religiosities, Amma recently introduced the identity statement, "My religion is Love."[20] Many devotees echo this sentiment. Julia, the founder of the Day Creek satsang, often says that she does not believe in the categories of religion and tells people that she believes in love. Still she prays, practices Integrated Amrita Meditation, chants a Sanskrit mantra, practices energy healing, and fills her home with dozens of religious objects and images from Buddhist, Hindu, and Christian traditions. In a similar fashion, many devotees reject the act of classifying oneself into a particular religion. Instead they suggest variations on the perennialist themes: "We are essentially one; all religions point to the same truth; the globe is a whole; unity prevails within diversity."[21] In so doing, they extract a minimalist moral ethic common to the majority of religions and ascribe to it a universal Truth. Both Amma and her devotees place heavy emphasis on love in particular as the primary foundation of all religions and spirituality.

Because many Amma devotees (both inheritors and adopters) believe in these universalistic maxims, they often see no problem with traveling between various guru movements for spiritual inspiration. In this vision, spiritual teachers are only particularly fashioned conduits for the

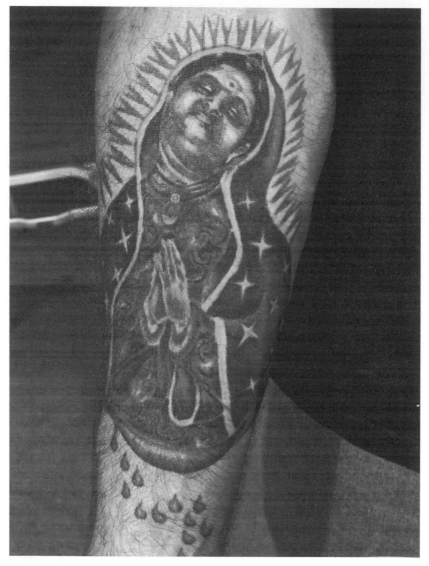

FIGURE 12. "She is *my* Guadalupe." Amma represented as the Virgin of Guadalupe in a devotee's tattoo (author photo)

one universal Truth; devotees follow the particular teacher whose style resonates with their personal dispositions at that moment in time. Still, the majority of devotees are loyal to Amma because of their preference for her style and particular teachings, though ultimately they espouse the universalist position that all paths (and spiritual teachers) lead to the same goal.[22] Many Amma devotees are ex-Sathya Sai Baba devotees, ex-Maharishi Mahesh Yogi devotees, or ex-Hare Krishnas; these devotees may retain affinities for their previous guru allegiances, but they have found something in particular that resonates with them even more deeply in Amma. Other devotees are habitual wanderers through the field of Hindu gurus. For example, Ivan is simultaneously involved (at some level) with the Vedanta Society, the International Society for Krishna Consciousness (ISKCON), the Ramakrishna Mission, Sathya Sai Baba, Mother Meera, and Amma.

Inheritors to Hindu traditions resonate with this universalizing rhetoric through their familiarity with advaita vedantic ideals, while adopters resonate with it through their belief in perennialism, the view that we should "go beyond traditions as normally conceived, going beyond the differences to find—by way of experience—the inner, esoteric core."[23] These de facto congregations unite in this universalist/perennialist philosophy (rooted in their respective cultural traditions) but retain their differences in terms of their cultural backgrounds and in their reasons for participating in Amma's movement. As a result, inheritors and adopters search for different kinds of congregational communities. Inheritors participate in congregations in order to reinforce their connections to Indian culture while simultaneously participating in the multicultural American religious landscape. Adopters are generally much less attached to the idea of congregation, but when they do participate, they do so to affirm their bricolage spiritualities in the company of other like-minded individuals. Both groups aim to reaffirm their faith by participating in communal religiosity. However, inheritors do so by enacting rituals that emphasize their roots in the Hindu tradition and India. Contrarily, adopters must adapt to Hindu ritual action in satsangs, but they also find solace in gathering with other devotees who have similarly created their own unique spiritualities from an amalgam of practices and beliefs from a variety of religious traditions.

In a seminal article on this subject, Rodney Stark, William Bainbridge, and Daniel Doyle divided Euro-Americans and Asians who participate in Asian religious traditions in America into members of "cults" and "ethnic churches." Written before such terms became taboo in academia, they explained that "cults" should be defined as religious groups that are a part of a "deviant religious tradition."[24] They included Asian religions in America within the category of cult, but they did so only when the adherents were primarily white. When Asian immigrants formed religious groups in America, they defined them as "ethnic churches."[25] Of course the negative connotation associated with the word "cult" renders it dysfunctional, however, the authors highlight an important distinction between the communities that inheritors and adopters create. Ethnic churches strive to support traditional culture, ethnicity, and religion, whereas adopters' congregations display a countercultural and non-traditional initiative.

In fact, the Paloma satsang functioned largely as an "ethnic church." It was hosted by Arnav and Durga Pillai, a wealthy Indian couple who immigrated in the 1960s and still have close family relations in Kerala, particularly in the areas surrounding Amma's birthplace and ashram headquarters. Prior to 2012, when the MACC was purchased and all satsangs began to be held there, the Pillais had been hosting the satsang for nearly twenty years in their suburban home. Their children and grandchildren are also Amma devotees. In 2010 inheritor attendees began to supplement the monthly Paloma satsang with an additional monthly one held at various attendees' suburban homes; both satsangs drew attendees from the same community of inheritors to Hindu traditions. The Paloma satsang community represented a close-knit group of Indian immigrants who sought to maintain connections to their shared culture and language through communal religious rituals, child education, meals, holidays, and the celebration of life-cycle events. Satsangs provided an opportunity for these inheritors to network within the Indian community, as well as for intergenerational mentoring. Youth education occurred through formalized initiatives (AYUDH and the bālā kendra) and on an intentional, but often informal, level. It was common for an older leader in the community to teach informal lessons to youth on the merits, ideals, and moral lessons in Hindu scriptures. Devotees also organized a book club that meets before the satsangs to read and discuss passages from Amma's publications.[26] After the purchase of the MACC, satsangs have changed in that they have unified devotees across what were once geographically specific, fragmented subsets of bounded communities. Still, while the leadership of the MACC has shifted and diversified, there is a continued reality that inheritor members of the retired Paloma satsang remain an active, traditional, and influential network.

Paloma satsang members referred to each other as family and supported each other significantly in times of hardship. Some families came to the United States for work and/or education and left their entire extended families in India. Thus the satsang family came the closest to an Indian-style extended family in the United States. The transition to complete self-reliance as a nuclear American-style family unit can be quite challenging for some Indians who are accustomed to living in more traditional-style Indian joint families.[27] The satsang family recognized this and responded to the difficulties a family may experience during this transition. Their familial solidarity stemmed from an inherent recognition of themselves in the other members. For example, when one of the core satsang families was involved in a severe automobile accident, the whole family stayed with the hosts of the satsang for three weeks until the parents recovered enough to be able return to work, cook meals, and tend to their children. When I asked Padmadevi if she would be having another wedding ceremony beside the one conducted by Amma during *Devī Bhāva*, she said, "This is it. My whole family is here and his whole family is here, and of course my *satsang family* is here. So, there really isn't any point to having an additional ceremony." The Paloma satsang developed a strong community forum in which inheritors could freely express themselves both culturally and religiously.

The ethnic church atmosphere of the Paloma satsang led many adopters to seek out and/or establish alternative satsangs in which they felt more culturally competent. Adopters participated in a community to support their nontraditional religious activities, but the impetus to connect in congregation with others was weaker without the need for buttressing cultural and ethnic ties. In fact, there was some resistance to the idea of organized religion in any form, including congregation. Thus the satsangs comprised of adopters struggled to organize and maintain members. They were fractional, splintering off in all directions. Adopters preferred to develop their own satsangs tailored to their own styles and at their own convenience because they were unwilling to pledge allegiance to one central community. These devotees, a spiritual network of individuals, did not connect enough to create a family of consistent attendees. Adopters tend to reject the notion of religion with its rules, dogma, and hierarchies, which will often lead to a rejection of any organized religious community. Additionally, the Hindu ritualized structure of the satsang program demands a cultural adaptation that many adopters are unwilling to perform. As a result, their numbers were considerably smaller and their administrative influence within the movement was considerably less.

Kalyani (Danielle), a white woman in her thirties, an adopter, used to run the Arcadia satsang. At the time she lived in the city and hosted the satsang in her home. Jivan, an Indian man in his thirties, used to attend her satsang, and "by Amma's grace" they fell in love and got married.

Kalyani was raised Jewish and her husband is Hindu. She once described her religiously eclectic wedding ceremony: they were married under a chuppah in front of a huge photo of Amma, and all the bridesmaids and the bride wore saris and all the groomsmen and the groom wore yarmulkes. In their daily practice, before each meal together, they first pray the "Brahma prayer," a Sanskrit verse from the *Bhagavad Gītā* [4.24], which Amma encourages, and then the Birkat HaMazon, the Jewish blessing for sustenance. Jokingly, she told me that they call themselves "Jew-Hoos" (Jewish Hindus). After she and her husband moved to the far-west suburbs, they commuted into the city to run the satsang in a downtown yoga studio for nearly four years. Kalyani said that she did this lengthy commute in part because she "doesn't feel much of a connection to the community in Paloma." She attended the Paloma satsang on some special occasions but often referred to it as "the Indian satsang." Kalyani said that she used to be very active in the Paloma satsang, but then she began to feel like her opinion did not really matter in the final decision-making processes. She explained that Paloma's exclusivity and fixity were "infamous" throughout Amma's national organization (a topic to which I will return), and that although she was treated respectfully when she participated, she also remained an outsider. Notably, her Indian Hindu husband often attended the Paloma satsang.

In 2008, Shanti (Sarah), also a white female adopter in her thirties, organized a group of her friends to hold informal satsangs, rotating among their houses. This roving satsang eventually replaced the fading Arcadia satsang. This satsang opened the hosting invitation to other participants; somewhat sporadically, adopter devotees hosted a monthly gathering in their urban or suburban domiciles. But this satsang eventually was discontinued due to lack of community involvement. When I asked Shanti why she did not attend the Paloma satsang, she responded, "I have just never felt really comfortable with the Paloma satsang." Again, I asked why, and she said, "Well you know . . . just the group." After a bit more prodding, she said, "Well, it doesn't matter, but [some of our friends] told us that they, the Paloma people, they were making fun of us in Malayalam on our wedding day!" Astonished, I said, "When you were being married by Amma?" She said, "Yes! Isn't that awful! So, since then, and in general, I just don't feel comfortable being around that kind of energy over there." Kalyani confirmed Shanti's story with a nod and a raised eyebrow to me and then quickly changed the subject.

Whether a real or an imagined event, the underlying tensions here signify both the apprehensions of adopters as they intercede into Hindu cultural arenas ("Am I doing it right?") and the defense mechanisms of inheritor devotees who use humor as an effective, but complacent, release for their uneasiness with the politics of cultural appropriation.

Julia, a white female adopter in her fifties, was the most overt about her reasons for starting her own satsang as an alternative to the Paloma satsang. She explained to me that when she asked Amma if she could start a satsang in her home, Amma said yes and that she should host a "Western" one. Soon thereafter, Julia began her satsang and altered the standardized format so that it was explicitly focused on English bhajans and English translations of the Sanskrit prayers. At the second satsang she held, she explained why her satsang would have a different emphasis than the Paloma one:

> Julia opened by explaining the purpose of this satsang and saying that although she has known Amma since 1999, she still does not know the "Sand-script" [Sanskrit] prayers or know the bhajans by heart. For her, the language differences create a communication barrier that is difficult to pass through. She explained that this was her primary motivation to start her own satsang. She said that there will be an emphasis on English bhajans during this satsang and only as much Sanskrit as is necessary to recite the 108 names of Amma. Even with this, she suggested that if people don't feel comfortable attempting to read out the 108 names of Amma in Sanskrit that they can just read the English translations silently along with the pace of the Sanskrit CD.

As Julia developed her satsang into something uniquely designed by the attendees, she suggested that every other month they read the 108 names in English instead of in Sanskrit. She also integrated videos of Amma's bhajans, readings from Amma's books, meditation tapes, and several community service projects into the mission and devotional program of her satsang. Several devotees related to me (privately) that they did not like Julia's satsang being designated as a satsang for Westerners. They felt that this overt segregation between ethnicities was "divisive" and ran counter to the spirit of Amma's movement. In my communications with senior ashram associates as well, they were careful to reinforce that "Amma is for all inclusiveness and not for segregation." They explained that Amma may have enabled Julia's satsang so that Julia would not have to adhere to Kerala-style conventions of the Paloma satsang without demanding that the Paloma satsang alter its culturally specific format.

Julia's account of her first encounter with the Paloma satsang demonstrates the depth of her feelings of alienation as she made her first entrée into a primarily Malayalee Hindu cultural environment.

> Julia said that when she first went to the Paloma satsang she was very apprehensive and insecure as to her culturally unfamiliar surroundings. So she sat in the satsang and prayed to Amma and told Amma [mentally] "Tell me, give me a sign. I was raised Catholic and here I am among all of these foreigners and I need a sign to tell me if I should be here and if this is what I should be doing." She said that she asked Amma to send her a sign of a rainbow to verify that she should be involved in the Paloma satsang and more generally in devotion to Amma. The next day . . . there was a huge rainbow arching across the evening sky. Julia took this as an immediate validation and proof that "Amma was showing me the way," that "by Amma's grace the rainbow had appeared," and that Amma was telling her that she should be doing what she was doing. She knew that "Amma was trying to send me a message," that it was proof that "Amma knows everything and is everywhere and is able to carry messages to people all over the world."

Julia still attended the Paloma satsang, but she was even more involved in the satsang that she hosted in her home monthly. With a flurry of activity, followed by a banquet of Indian takeout, Julia worked hard to create an environment in which she could worship Amma among friends while adapting the uncomfortably foreign aspects of the satsang ritual program to fit her American lifestyle.

Surabhi (Kerry), a white female adopter in her early forties, explained that she founded her own satsang because she usually works on Saturday, the day the Paloma satsang meets. She moved to Chicagoland from New York, where there is a different satsang every week. She said she misses the large community of Amma devotees of which she was a part there, and so she decided to start her own satsang every Sunday in Flora so that she could attend. However, her Flora satsang met sporadically and often had few attendees. In March 2007, Surabhi became discouraged about the lack of attendees and asked Br. Dayamrita Chaitanya whether she should stop holding her satsang.[28] In response, he told her that Amma is always present at her satsangs, so she is never alone. He said that Amma wants to have as many satsangs as possible, and that she should continue to host her satsang and try to recruit more devotees to attend. Despite this advice, Surabhi eventually discontinued her satsang.

Katrina, a white female adopter in her early thirties, moved to Chicago in 2007. She is a serious Amma devotee who spent months living at Amma's ashram in Amritapuri, Kerala. Katrina was aware of the various satsangs in Chicagoland, but instead of attending one of these extant communities, she chose to establish her own independent satsang in a downtown yoga studio. She advertised for her satsang among her clientele and conducted it as she saw fit, without the supervision of the MA Center, until she moved out of state several years later. Katrina's example demonstrates effectively the individualized essence of adopter populations that are contentedly designing their own particularized devotional environments while thwarting congregational ideals of community and consensus.

In general, the satsangs of adopters did not come together in tight familial groups, supported by large numbers of regular attendees. These devotees did not exhibit the desire to unite as an ethnocultural community because they did not share similar views or cultural commonalities aside from their devotion to Amma. Their complex amalgamations of spiritual beliefs and practices overlapped with each other only in limited ways and sometimes not at all outside of Amma devotionalism. These adopters usually arrive at Amma devotionalism as individuals without extended family members or children who provide additional impetus for their involvement in congregational gatherings. Even more fundamentally, many adopters may be alienated by the mandated satsang structure, which is organized solely around Hindu rituals. These Hindu rituals are largely foreign to adopters. Those who find spiritual comfort in them are willing to make the cultural adaptations and translations necessary to participate. During satsangs, adopters must conform to Hindu ritualism; there is little room for the spiritual innovation and bricoleur mentality through which they have arrived at their spiritual subjectivities. In short, independence and kaleidoscopic self-definition may have brought them to Amma's movement, but once situated therein, they must subordinate themselves to the Hindu ritual structures of the satsang. For many adopters, this is too heavy a price and instead they choose to design their personalized devotions in private and beyond the authoritative gaze of the satsang and institution. Throughout the movement there are significant populations of adopters who are ardent devotees, but only very rarely attend their local satsangs.

Because of their fragmentation, inconsistency, and tension within the suprastructure of the organization, the satsangs organized by adopters in Chicago had few, if any, unmediated interactions with the MA Center. In Chicago, the leaders and hosts of the Paloma satsang (inheritors) controlled all of the administrative communications with Amma and the MA Center. This secured their position of prominence in the guru community, where proximity to the guru easily translates into increased religious authority. Amma often visits the Pillai home when she makes her annual journey to Chicago for her summer tours. Paloma was the oldest of all of the satsangs, and before Amma became famous, she used to stay at the home of the Pillais whenever she came to Chicago. The Pillais are Malayalee and speak to Amma and her swamis in Malayalam; thus, at the highest levels of administration, non-Malayalam speakers are also excluded by a linguistic boundary. On a material level, inheritors are often wealthy. Many support Amma and other Hindu networks financially; for example, many of the core Paloma devotees organized a capital campaign to raise $100,000 for the deposit on the ashram site in the exurbs of Chicago.

In contrast, although many adopters make similarly significant financial contributions and feel comfortable knowing that money given to Amma supports her charitable endeavors, some devotees are more wary of giving money to gurus in general. The reasons for this are threefold: first, many adopters reject lucrative careers in favor of spiritually attuned labor; they focus explicitly on their spiritual development and in the process reject the materialism, which they see to be informing the decisions of the majority of Americans. In this manner, many view their rejection of the workaday world as a contemporary echo of Timothy Leary's famous adage: "Turn on, tune in, drop out."[29] Another segment of this population works only as much as is necessary to fund their ability to spend additional time with Amma. Many of the most ardent adopter devotees live on limited incomes or on their savings and credit cards in order to have the freedom to travel to and from Amma's ashrams (in India and in the United States) and to travel with her when she tours the United States. As a result, many in these populations rarely have the discretionary income to significantly contribute to capital projects.

Second, because of the negative stereotype of the Indian guru who swindles gullible Westerners, some adopters are reluctant to give money directly to any Indian guru. In America, anticult advocates often use the supposed financial motives of Indian gurus to defame guru movements.[30] Since gurus first made their entrée into American public life, cultural skepticism has abounded; critics often malign the guru as a dishonest Indian swami who dupes the innocent. Although these tropes aggravate their cause with inflammatory rhetoric to further this corrupt guru stereotype, sometimes therein lies a kernel of truth. For example, in 2009, Julia commissioned a *yajña* (fire sacrifice) to be done for her by a new company that was offering puja and yajña services (sold in the United States and performed in India). While relating this story to me she was crying and very disillusioned because after her yajña the swami spoke to her on the telephone for several hours and was very sexually suggestive toward her. He told her that their astrological charts were perfectly aligned, suggested that she move to India and consider marrying an Indian man, and demanded that their special relationship be kept secret from their mutual friend. Quite taken aback by his behavior, she gingerly asked their mutual friend (who had given her the referral) about her thoughts on this swami. At that point she was shocked to find out that her friend had been engaging in a sexual relationship with the swami for the past year. Hearing this, she was distraught not only because she felt that she had given thousands of dollars away to a fraudulent enterprise, but also because she had recommended his services to several other Amma devotees. She quickly ordered the other satsang members to stop payment on their checks to the swami and disassociated the entire community from his nefarious sexual behavior.

Third, their commitment to metaphysical spirituality instantiates their subsequent rejection of the brick-and-mortar projects of institutionalized religion. Many adopters are not interested in financially contributing to religious institutions in any form. With that said, the majority of adopters readily pay for services rendered. The metaphysical market is ripe with saleable products and services. In fact, one of the primary critiques of metaphysical spirituality asserts that the metaphysicals have rampantly commodified and corporatized religion.[31] Not only have they propagated the consumeristic self-as-commodity mentality, but also "inner spirituality has been put to work for the purposes of outer prosperity."[32]

Perhaps recognizing that the majority of adopters are much more apt to give money in exchange for goods and services rather than through straightforward donations, Amma tours the United States with a variety of goods and services available for purchase. During darshan programs, devotees can purchase a wide assortment of general goods from India and goods branded with Amma's logo and spiritual messages. Additionally, numerous touring staff members accompany Amma and voluntarily provide spiritual services such as massage, Ayurvedic consultations, Jyotish consultations, acupuncture, and radiance healing. Because these staff members volunteer their time but charge for their services, the money that devotees exchange for their services becomes a donation to Amma's organization. Products manufactured in India are imported and sold at American prices, and articles worn or used by Amma are sold for an exorbitant price (because of what we might call "proxemic value"). Displays and interactive exhibits at darshan programs enable attendees to learn more about Embracing the World's extensive humanitarian campaigns, including model replicas of housing developments that Amma has built. These tables prominently display donation forms and receptacles. As such, devotees who may feel uncomfortable with direct contributions to a guru assuage their fears in the belief that all donations will contribute to Amma's humanitarian activities. Thus without any major direct solicitation from American devotees, Amma's organization receives significant financial support as a result of her tours in the United States.[33]

This differential in spending preferences in part determines the social capital that each group possesses. Inheritors are eager to contribute financially to capital projects that will create communal spaces within which they will be able to transmit cultural and religious values to the next generation. Adopters, for the most part, are not interested in pledging allegiance to one community, and thus they are not ready contributors to capital campaigns. Importantly, inheritors and adopters may very well contribute similar amounts of money to Amma's organization. But instead of the direct donations of inheritors (often oriented around capital projects), adopters donate in exchange for goods and services and to support humanitarian programs. The net result of this materialist dichotomy is that inheritors reserve access to and maintain control over the capital campaigns and finances of Amma's movement. Their fiscal control correlates directly with their position of supremacy in administrative and organizational affairs. With that said, it was an adopter devotee who initially donated the land for the MA Center in San Ramon, which represents an important exception to this fiscal dichotomy.

While the Paloma satsang was always welcoming to newcomers, it did maintain a communal boundary, sometimes intentionally and sometimes accidentally. On the intentional side, some adopters were simply too wild or too culturally insensitive for the Paloma satsang, which maintained traditional Hindu cultural norms, such as gender-segregated seating. These devotees were quietly shunned or publicly asked not to return.[34] On the accidental side, even though the Paloma devotees were very welcoming to outsiders, there were moments when the majority of attendees slipped into speaking Malayalam or Hindi. Further, there were financial meetings, administrative concerns, and high-level communications with the MA Center to which only a select few families of seasoned inheritors were privy. Adopters easily felt excluded, even though everyone was very welcoming in demeanor, because of these private administrative meetings, the language barrier, the cultural programs, the specialized clothing, the culinary specificities, and the social regulations.

Before broadening this analysis based on this particular ethnographic data, I would like to address Kalyani's contention that Paloma was "infamous" on a national level for its inheritor exclusivity. Her contention was that Paloma was particularly unique in its self-construction as a culturally homogenous inheritor satsang, which subsequently fostered the de facto congregational tendencies of the remaining devotees who reacted to their exclusivity. Concerned with the possible implications of this, I questioned Br. Dayamrita about the particularity of the de facto congregational tendencies in Chicagoland satsangs. He said:

> I haven't had so much experience,[35] but I definitely feel that particular scenario in Chicago. Nowhere else have I ever felt it or seen it. . . . The point of what Amma teaches always is to go beyond all of these differences. So if people hold onto their identities, it is their fault that they have not imbibed the teachings of Amma properly, so what we need to do is to understand that.

Dayamrita is in a unique position, in that he travels across the country visiting the various satsangs regularly; thus I trust his observation that Chicagoland satsangs exhibited a particularly exacerbated form of congregational homogenization. Similarly, a senior ashram associate rightly pointed out that in most cities there is a core group of devotees who were instrumental in bringing Amma to that city. These original devotees often retain the closest proximity to Amma and positions of influence within the local operations of the organization. In Chicago, these devotes happened to be Hindu Malayalees (from Amma's home region of Kerala), whereas in other cities he claimed that this was not the case and other cultural groups occupied such positions.

So why are Chicagoland satsangs particularly prone to de facto congregationalism? It might be tempting to argue that they reflect the racial politics of the city of Chicago, which is annually reminded that it is among the top-ten most racially segregated cities in the United States. But we can effectively determine that this is not the case, because Milwaukee hosts a vibrantly diverse satsang and often tops the list of the most racially segregated cities in the United States. Instead, it is precisely because Chicago has one of the largest communities of Amma devotees in the nation that devotees have the capacity to separate into relatively homogenous subsets yet still achieve their communal goals. Smaller satsangs do not have the ability to separate into de facto congregations and still maintain the population density needed to organize Amma's programs, because of their limited numbers.

Chicagoland satsangs enacted de facto congregationalism *because* of the strong inheritor community there. Based on this theory, we might confirm that other large urban areas with strong inheritor populations also develop richly ethnocentric and culturally traditional satsang communities to reinforce the cultural identities of the immigrant Indian Hindu population. The strongest and most vibrant satsang communities in the United States are sustained and recommitted through inheritors' continued dedication to building a religious education for their children and cultural continuity with their homeland (India) in diaspora. These satsangs also increase their power within the broader organization because of their linguistic privilege, ethnic heritage, cultural affinities, and institutional connections to the epicenter of Amma's organization at Amritapuri. In many cities, immigrant Indian Hindus create, organize, and orchestrate the primary satsangs, developing their congregations into "ethnic churches." Adopters then either choose to adapt culturally, develop their own satsangs, or simply not attend.

Building on Tulasi Srinivas's term *proxemic desire*, which she used to define devotees' desire for proximity to the guru, I suggest that guru movements base their systems of social hierarchies on a similar system of proxemics. Proximity to the guru equates to power in the organization, and, reciprocally, power in the organization equates to proximity to the guru. The hierarchical system of authority within the movement radiates from Amma as the central charismatic authority toward the periphery, a hierarchy I call "proxemic authority." Those devotees who have been with Amma the longest often occupy higher positions of proxemic authority than those who are newer to the movement. Because the movement developed from the backwaters of Kerala and then gradually spread to the rest of the world, the gradation between those who have been with Amma for the longest amount of time to the shortest often parallels the categories of inheritors and adopters. Many inheritors were raised with Amma in their lives, whereas the majority of adopters developed their devotion as adults. To compound this authority of longevity, inheritors develop a proximity to Amma in an unmediated sense in that they speak directly to Amma in her native Malayalam, deal directly with the central administrative figures in the movement regarding institutional management, and solicit Amma's advice directly for major satsang action items. While adopters also have access to Amma, because of their lack of linguistic and cultural capital they usually organize through an inheritor, who translates, conveys, and relays Amma's message. The need for this intermediary (usually an inheritor fluent in Malayalam) fortifies their distance from Amma in the proxemic authority structure, which reinforces their subordinate status.

Any impediment to this proximity serves as a point of frustration in a system in which devotees vigorously exhibit a proxemic desire to be close to the guru (by rushing to touch her outstretched hands, relishing in bodily contact with her, purchasing items she has used, savoring food items that she has partially eaten, and so on). Many adopters are envious of inheritors who have greater access to Amma because of their sociolinguistic capital. Some recognize and resent the inheritors' presumed roles of intermediaries in administrative affairs. Conversely, some inheritors are protective of their religio-cultural traditions and communities and fear that adopters may misrepresent or malign them. While Amma routinely impresses upon her followers that they are all her children, sometimes there is tension among siblings. As in any conflict between children, a successful intervention must get to the root of the issue. Herein, I submit, the root reveals itself to be the continued repercussions of the legacy of romantic orientalism.

ROMANTIC ORIENTALISM IN THE NEW AGE

In 1997 I spoke to a Hindu Indian boatman, my lane neighbor in the boisterous gully mazes of Bengali Tola, Varanasi. I had known him for almost a year. I was close to his wife and children, and I considered them all good friends. He was telling me the story of how when the British first invaded Varanasi in the eighteenth century, they stabbed Nandi, Shiva's bull, who guards the entrance to Kedarnath temple. According to his story, blood began to gush from the wound in the marble stone and flooded the streets of Varanasi. Referring to the British invasion, he said, "When you people came" (*jab tum log āye*). Shocked at first, my young mind reassured my wounded heart that my nineteen-year-old white, female great-granddaughter of immigrants self carried neither the power nor the related guilt inherent in the colonial legacy of the British Empire. But for my friend, in some sense I did. Whiteness (whether American, European, South African, or Australian) is necessarily wrapped up part and parcel with the legacy of colonialism. Colonialism and its discursive antecedent, orientalism, were initiated and propagated (at least at the outset) by whites, who engaged in a racialized othering and paternalistic subordination of brown-skinned peoples.

It was only later (into the early nineteenth century) that Indians began to articulate orientalist statements in mimesis of their colonizers. Even as such, when orientalizing essentialisms emerge from unlikely mouths (those of the colonized), they often remain underscrutinized. Postcolonial theorists Frantz Fanon and Homi Bhabha have argued effectively that the colonized mimic the colonizer's perceptions of them, meaning that the colonizer creates an image of the colonized and, in response, the colonized absorb that image into their own self-perceptions.[36] This epistemological turn pervades the social dynamics of the dialectic between inheritors and adopters of Hindu spirituality. European romantic orientalists were the first to romanticize India as the spiritual epicenter of the world. In response, Indians appropriated the orientalist language of the colonizer and actively proclaimed India the spiritual epicenter of the world. As Peter van der Veer contends, "Vivekananda is probably the first major Indian advocate of a 'Hindu spirituality,' largely created by Orientalism and adopted in the anticlerical and anticolonial rhetorics of Theosophy. . . . His writings in English often compare the lack of spirituality in the West to its abundance in India."[37] Following Vivekananda's example, some contemporary Hindus depict themselves as spiritual guides to the wisdom of the East and the secrets to self-realization. This motif has become so commonplace today that even many Hindu nationalists believe India to be unique in the global community not because of the merits of its people and resources but because of its unique position as the guru to the world.[38] For instance, Ashok Singhal, the international president of the Hindu nationalist party, the Vishva Hindu Parishad, used the English term *spirituality* to explain in Hindi that "of all nations, India alone has spirituality."[39]

Inheritors and adopters of Hindu traditions operate within a language of self-orientalizing behaviors, depicting Indians as authentic cultural brokers for Hindu spirituality and American spiritual seekers as consumers, as per Swami Vivekananda's now-famous statement that appears at the beginning of this chapter. This romantic orientalism continues to inform the globally ubiquitous *imaginaire* of India as the guru to the world, a mystical treasure trove brimming with ancient secrets of enlightenment and spiritual power. "Asiatik" researchers and colonial attachés, for example, Sir William Jones, propagated this vision in the final decades of the eighteenth century. In the nineteenth century, Hindu reformers largely embraced such a positive, albeit essentialist, understanding of India wherein they found temporary solace from the onslaught of colonial and missionary critique. The first generation of global transnational gurus, led by Swami Vivekananda, engaged and forcefully proclaimed this cultural essentialism in the West. Therein contemporary Indophiles developed and expanded the notion of the supranormal spiritual proclivities of India to the emblematic nexus of India's contributions to humanity. Following in this wake were The Beatles, hippies, spiritual trekkers, and filmic *imaginaires*, from Fritz Lang's *Indian Epic* to the more modern *Eat, Pray, Love*. The figure of the guru operates center stage here, often profiting from such orientalist representations. The recent documentary film *Kumaré* (2012), in which a young Indian man fakes being a guru and garners numerous ardent devotees in American metaphysical communities, illustrates the ironic calamity of such ethnic stereotypes based on what Vijay Prashad calls "benevolent racism."[40]

In the culture of Amma's movement, adopters are attracted to this *imaginaire* of India as a vortex of exceptional spiritual possibilities. They appropriate select aspects of Hindu culture and customs to exhibit their access and affinity for India's potential for supranormal spirituality. Many meditate, place *bindis* on their foreheads, dress in Indian clothing, learn Sanskrit, join ashrams, and prostrate before their guru, often becoming "more Indian than the Indians." Others incorporate Hindu philosophy and culture as one of a number of religious sources that they meld together into their bricolage spiritualities. And still others emulate Hindu culture only superficially, with incorrect information and pronunciation, and with little regard for or interest in accuracy, particularly regarding the variations and nuances within Hindu cultures. In sum, many adopters appropriate Hindu traditions much in the same orientalist vein as did the scholars of the colonial era, with careful attention and an underlying love for Hindu culture. Others operate much like venture capitalists, collecting treasures and tropes from the Orient to build their own self-image, profits, and collections. When such appropriations are coupled with the consumerist impulses of the robust metaphysical spirituality marketplace, they have the capacity to change from cultural borrowings to cultural exploitation. Both tendencies toward romanticization and appropriation engage in an orientalist understanding of India. In so doing, they exoticize India into a land that is sexualized, mystical, effeminate, and spiritual.

Indians react to this in multifaceted ways. While gurus have existed in India since the beginning of religious documentation, the newer motif of proselytizing gurus traveling in the West is, in part, a reaction to the ever-increasing market of potential Western devotees. Herein, Indian gurus are eager to capitalize on the West to the extent that many develop what Joanne Punzo Waghorne calls a "de-ethnicized" spiritual modality of Hinduism in order to cater to Western constituencies.[41] Srinivas Aravamudan argues that the guru succeeds where the colonial *baboo* fails because of his [or her] ability to effectively mirror the values of other [read Western] cultures. He says, "[T]he bluster of the guru is that of the fraudulent super-baboo. . . . Unlike the self-effacing poltroonishness of baboos, gurus are authoritative, confident, and secure in their borrowings, translations, and pronunciamentos. Rather than apologizing for cultural bastardy and hybridity as baboos do, gurus perform their intercultural mimesis with impunity."[42] Aravamudan rightly situates contemporary gurus within the context of the Indian nationalist response to colonial critique. In the nineteenth century, gurus became cultural ambassadors par excellence, who were able to transcend the social limitations of the *baboo* and *bhadralok*[43] under the banner of promoting Hindu spirituality on a global scale. Codified by orientalists as the most coveted product of India, Hindu spirituality became a desirable export commodity among the elite in Europe and America. Gurus mobilized in response to this demand and began to proselytize globally, articulating orientalized notions of themselves as spiritual adepts explicitly because of their Indianness. The continuing echoes of this paradigm are rendered explicit when metaphysicals devalue white gurus explicitly because they equate Indianness with spiritual prowess and authenticity.

The romantic orientalism of India's (and Indians') proclivities and possibilities for attaining supranatural spiritual states thrives in the discourse of metaphysical spirituality in general, and in Amma's movement in particular. But, on the surface, most devotees allude to the institutional ideals that "we are all mother's children," or "there is no difference between us." For example, Laura, a devout, middle-aged, upper-middle-class adopter explained:

> At first seeing us [non-Indians] at the programs the Indians were like "why are you here?" and they were "real standoffish"—you could feel it. But now we have grown to be brothers and sisters with the same mother. Indians see the love that Westerners have for Amma and they recognize themselves in

that. Besides, Amma wouldn't allow it to be any other way; she wouldn't stand for it. Amma wants us all to be her children.

Br. Dayamrita explains a similarly idealistic view:

Here, mostly in San Ramon . . . people here don't feel the difference being black, white, brown, red, it wouldn't matter to them. I mean once we come, we are all Amma's children. We are the children of the Divine Mother, so who cares?

These sentiments represent the ideals of Amma and her organization, but everyday realities suggest that there are commonly recognized cultural chasms between inheritors and adopters, many of which follow from the legacies of romantic orientalism. Several years ago, on a nearly freezing blustery winter night after satsang, a somewhat uncomfortable conversation ensued between Dipesh, a middle-aged Indian American man, and me.

A: I have seen you before, right? Do you go to the Paloma satsang?

D: Yes, I go there. I have seen you there before. I have seen you *lots* of times before. I just saw you last week in Michigan [at Amma's darshan programs], but you were looking very different then.

A: You were in Michigan? I didn't see you.

D: Yes, I saw you; you were wearing a white sari. You were looking more Indian than the Indians.

A: (Laugh) Yes, I like to wear my saris when Amma comes to town.

D: *Why do you do this? Why do you wear white saris to see Amma?*

A: Well, I have saris at home that I never get to wear and I love to wear them. I can't really wear them around Chicago because people will think it is strange to see a white woman in a sari. (nervous laugh) So, I wear them when Amma comes to visit.

D: *But why do you wear them? Is this really the only reason?*

A: Well, I suppose it is also that Amma asks her devotees to wear white clothes, you know, for purity.[44] So I wear a white sari in order to respect her wishes. [We have put on our shoes and are walking outside by now. The cold and wind hit me like a truck; it is close to 10 degrees outside. Dipesh is going the opposite direction that I need to go, but I walk with him for a moment because he asks me the same question again.]

D: But you could wear white Western clothes. *Why do you choose to wear a white sari?*

A: Well, I really like to wear them and I miss wearing them. If I don't wear them when Amma is in town, I don't ever have the opportunity otherwise to do so. Well, I've gotta run—it is too cold out here to talk anymore! Have a great holiday! Bye!

D: Oh. All right. Bye.

Unfortunately the text does not convey the challenging tone with which he asked me the same question three times, each time demanding a better answer. I left the conversation flustered and understood his intention to be a not-so-subtle reproach directed to non-Indian devotees who "pose" as Indians. His point (a valid one that I thereafter adopted) was that Amma's darshan programs should not be an opportunity to play dress up; one need not pretend to be something that she is not in order to participate.[45]

But this dialogue also directs us to a deeper, more pervasive system of hierarchies and exclusivities that substantiates Hindu traditions. In 2011, I was out for an Indian dinner in Artesia, a "little India" neighborhood just outside of Los Angeles. My three-year-old daughter was along for the adventure, and she was gleefully wearing a $4 set of sparkly metal turquoise bangles that represented the culmination of all of her worldly desires at that particular moment. Walking and windowshopping, we paused at a traffic light alongside a young, well-dressed Indian Hindu couple, who showered my daughter with somewhat commonplace compliments ("Isn't she adorable," "Look how cute she is," and so on). Then the young woman turned to me and, commenting on my daughter's new bangles in particular, asked poignantly, "Is that [wearing bangles] part of *your* tradition?" Familiarly unnerved, I recounted to her how she had fallen in love with them at the previous store because they were so sparkly and concluded that "no," I suppose they are not "part of [*my*] tradition." The mood was jovial, and no offense was intended (and none was taken), but, given my academic field, I pondered for some time this brief, forgettable, and largely benign social exchange.

The politics of cultural appropriation and adoption frequently develops into an intense debate and defensive postures among participants. The vehement discourses surrounding such issues signify a great deal of latent anxiety about cultural and intellectual property, identity, and the historical reality of exploitation through colonialism and orientalism. In a particularly vitriolic essay, Laura Donaldson takes to task white women who appropriate Native American traditions for their own supposed empowerment. She claims that these "pop-culture feminists" are "false" feminists who operate as "kidnappers" and "benefit" from imperialism. They are complacent in "white supremacy" and "postmodern neocolonial" domination through their appropriations, which superficially extract Native American cultural objects and art forms from their local contexts in order to collect them into superficial *pastiche* conglomerations of a romantically imagined history that never was and is not their own.[46] Such a critique depends on the ideal that cultures are ethnically bounded authentic identities that individuals and communities possess, quite literally own. As Richard Handler explains, in the individualistic worldview "there is an almost mystical bond uniting the agent with the things he acts upon. Moreover, if on the one hand those things become his property, on the other hand the individual comes to be defined by the things he possesses."[47] In this extension of what C. B. Macpherson called "possessive individualism,"[48] cultural symbols, objects, and ideas are bounded entities that can be "recognized" and "classified" and thus are representative of a particular culture, ethnicity, or nation. That which "the nation possesses is often conceived to be part of it, so that cultural content becomes the very body of the nation."[49] Thus the appropriation of these "possessions" by others outside of a national, ethnic, or cultural community becomes tantamount to stealing (a view often represented in the contemporary controversies concerning museum collections); such actions should be critiqued, shamed, and punished. When representatives of the dominant imperialistic power appropriate cultural commodities from previously colonized minorities, the sting of cultural exploitation amplifies intensely.

The impulses that inform contemporary multiculturalism tangentially support such ideas of cultural property. Multiculturalism affirms fixed ethnic and cultural identities (based on untenable notions of cohesive and bounded subjectivity) that become representations of individual and communal identity. Ethnic and cultural communities that seek representation in multicultural societies are encouraged to embody and perform their distinctive qualities (those that conform with the ascribed attributes of others within their community) in the public sphere in order to be recognized. Thus the multiculturalist politics of recognition reinforces communal claims to cultural authenticity as particular, distinct, and thus recognizable participants in society. Such a politics of recognition can also correlate to cartographic projects that contain and define minority ethnic populations through this very gaze of recognition.

But the metaphysicals that Donaldson takes to task (who are often an easy target for such cultural property disputes) promote a very different understanding of the individual, cultures, and interpersonal relations therein. Their imagined revolution is communal at its heart. It attempts to dissolve boundaries between the self and the other, envisioning a world in which we might, as John Lennon so famously dreamed:

> Imagine there's no countries . . .
> And no religion too
> Imagine all the people living life in peace . . .
> A brotherhood of man
> Imagine all the people sharing all the world
> You, you may say
> I'm a dreamer, but I'm not the only one
> I hope some day you'll join us
> And the world will live as one.[50]

Such a vision may seem romantic from our contemporary perspective, but it was foundational to the American metaphysical movement. In *American Veda*, Phillip Goldberg explicitly argues that The Beatles and their spiritual adventures in India catalyzed the intersection of new age subculture and Indic spirituality, making mainstream not only ideas such as the mantra, Krishna, and yoga but an alternate vision for society and the aspirations of the individual.[51] In the contemporary subcultures of American metaphysicals, they not only imagine, but actively create, alternate ways of being. They aim to dissolve boundaries (national, cultural, and ethnic), replace religion with spirituality, offer humanitarian efforts to eliminate suffering, and create unity by promoting oneness among diverse peoples. In constructing an imagined utopian reality in which humanistic oneness pervades and informs all things, metaphysicals seek to create a global village. In such a unified global village, cultural and intellectual property rights are antithetical to its foundational ideology. Sharing and exchanging without boundaries in brotherhood and sisterhood and supporting all of humanity as one are the ideals of the new age.

For critics, such dreaming ignores (or, worse, obfuscates) the history of domination and exploitation through colonialism. The inherent dissolution of cultural boundaries, property, and ownership therein also provides a sense of entitlement for whites to continue to appropriate whatever they can grasp in their neocolonial gaze. In their view, such a fanciful understanding of cultural relations hides the fact that such "sharing" exchanges exist within unjust power relations, and often the supposed sharing operates in unidirectional patterns. The sharing is not mutual; rather, it is about whites appropriating the cultural symbols, artifacts, and objects of once-colonized peoples (Africans, Native Americans, Indians, and so on). Such disproportionate power relations transform the egalitarian ideal of sharing into the politics of appropriation based on the old adage, "Whites won't let blacks [or any other minority culture] have anything that they can't have." In Cynthia Eller's summation, "European-Americans are accused of practicing what Renato Rosaldo calls an 'imperialist nostalgia,' initiating the imperialist culture contact that leads to the destruction of whole cultures, and then mourning over the loss of these same cultures, and hungrily collecting their myths, rituals, and traditional crafts for use or preservation."[52] For these critics, of which there are many, the discourses of imagined unity and sharing between cultures obscure their demands to be recognized as minority ethnic and cultural communities with rights to self-possession on which the dominant culture should not encroach.

Adopter devotees acculturate through Indic dress, food, comportment, and so on because of the aforementioned hierarchies of the proxemic relations of authority and desire. The guru (an Indian woman wearing a sari) stands at the center of a large network of relations, increasing in authority and power based on their proximity to her. Juxtaposed with these proxemic relations, devotees are repeatedly encouraged to develop a mimetic relationship with the guru: to love unconditionally as she loves, serve tirelessly as she serves, and so on. Viewed in this light, it may be reasonable to imagine that devotees would choose attire that is culturally more similar to Amma than their native dress. In fact, to some extent, the MA administrative regulations restrict American cultural patterns of attire (no tank tops, no shorts, and so on) and simultaneously encourage the adoption of Indian cultural fashions through the wide assortment of Indian clothing and ephemera for sale at the rear of the darshan hall. Many adopters attempt to become culturally compliant by transforming their physical appearance into something more "Indian," which also increases their symbolic proximity to Amma.

But there is also a social stigma in the Western appropriation of Indian clothing, one that recalls the exploitative relationship between the West and India under colonialism and that views contemporary Western appropriations of Indian culture as neocolonialism or at least neoorientalism. Once, while I was lingering among Indian saleswomen at Amma's Michigan programs, a sixty-year-old Indian woman, who seemed to be of the professional upper middle classes, was browsing next to me. I was quiet as the stall banter intensified between middle-aged, sari-clad Indian women. The Indian Hindu woman shopping next to me was looking for a shawl for her daughter. While deciding, she picked up one of the shawls that was block printed with the mantra "*oṁ namaḥ shivāya oṁ namaḥ shivāya.*" Immediately the stall coordinator said, "No! You can't buy her that! That is the cheapest shawl that we have!" Another saleswoman devotee asked her which one, and she showed her. In response, she exclaimed, "That is the one that the hippies wear! That one is for hippies; you don't want your daughter to look like that! Try the other one, the one that you had before [a traditional Kashmiri embroidered shawl], *that* was a nice one. . . . All the hippies wear *those*. . . . 'Ooooh *Sūtāā Rāām Sūtāā Rāām Sūtāā Rāām*.' " She said this in a sardonic and melodramatic voice, while she imitated "hippie" devotional chanting. While this shawl incident was amusing, and notably performed in my presence (I was not dressed as a "hippie" but instead I was wearing a traditional-print everyday sari), the banter at the booth reflects the commonplace Indic disdain for Western "spiritual tourism," the "hippies" who are ubiquitous at ashrams and holy places in India, often wearing block-print shawls just like the one the woman thought about buying her own daughter. There are many reasons people might resent hippies (or neohippies). Even in the United States, they have often been objects of ridicule for the dominant culture and older generations. In Indic culture, however, they are not only frequently regarded as freeloaders, unclean, or morally corrupt, but also many upper-middle-class Indians sense the romantic orientalist underpinnings that have brought these bohemian "global nomads" on their spiritual journeys to India and its ashrams.[53] The echoes of the romantic orientalist encounter between India and the West continue to resound in these contemporary cultural dynamics, particularly within the domains of religio-cultural appropriation and spiritual tourism.[54]

At times, Indian Hindus quietly make fun of non-Indians' performances of Indian cultural practices within their closed circles of inheritors, as seen here and earlier in Shanti's remembrance of her wedding ceremony. Certainly, non-Indian (mis)appropriations of Indian Hindu culture can be wholly amusing for those who have the religio-cultural knowledge to recognize when adopters fail to appropriate with accuracy.[55] But the impulse among Indian Hindus to laugh, make fun of, or even silently chuckle or raise an eyebrow also marks their solidarity in the face of cultural encroachment. Such events support Donna Goldstein's suggestion that "Humor is a vehicle for expressing sentiments that are difficult to communicate publicly or that point to areas of discontent in social life. The meanings behind laughter reveal both the cracks in the system and the masked or more subtle ways that power is challenged. Humor is one of the fugitive forms of insubordination."[56]

These moments of laughter and of making fun of someone signify a process of social venting that acknowledges the cultural encroachment but neutralizes its potential threat through humor. In these instances, humor functions as a form of "everyday resistance," those common practices of passive subversion that critique without directly "contest[ing] the formal definitions of hierarchy and power."[57]

In such tumultuous waters, Westerners feel encouraged to adopt Indic behaviors, but then they are sometimes chastised for cultural appropriations or misappropriations. Similarly, many Indian Hindus view "hippies" as harmless, even if they do so with disdain, but they become incensed at other appropriations and misappropriations that offend their religio-cultural sensibilities (Kali on a lunch box, bikini, and so on). These cultural exchanges are certainly difficult in themselves, in the present circumstance, but they become catalytic sites of extreme tension when compounded by the histories of orientalism and colonialism. For those who maintain this historical lens, contemporary religio-cultural appropriations become salt in a wound, and one often hears the vehemence of Donaldson's critique of white appropriations. As a result of this underlying tension, Westerners isolate themselves into homogenous groups because they want to appropriate at will without being faced with Indian claims to authenticity or Indian critiques of their encroachment on Indian culture. Indians isolate themselves as a protective mechanism because they may feel uncomfortable, offended, or set apart because of Westerners' misinterpretations, exploitations, and/or romanticized orientalist visions of their culture. In both communities, orientalist essentializations are reified and buttressed: India is more spiritual and America is more materialistic, just as Swami Vivekananda explained to Chicago audiences in 1893.

But the romantic notion of India as the guru to the world is, as with all orientalism, a Western projection, an imagined reality that has little to do with modern India. As the emerging dominance of the middle class in modern India becomes enmeshed in global capitalism, there is some suggestion that middle-class Indians are now becoming increasingly driven by consumerism, just as many countercultural subgroups in the West are jumping off the consumerist bandwagon. At the San Ramon ashram, Gomukh, an inheritor (a single, friendly, middle-aged, middle-class Indian man), explained:

> I love a lot of mix . . . I love the Westerners even more than I love the Indian people. Because the Indian people, I am sorry to say, but they are so much about money money money money. . . . Like in India, as I was saying before,

I want to go to yoga, meditation; where are they, where are they? Is there any gathering here? I look like a fool when I ask them. . . . They say, "Are you serious?" And I tell them that here in America I go to ashram. I go to satsang. They don't believe it. But they don't have it there [in India] . . . but here in the Bay Area [there are] so many yoga schools, satsangs—all the Babajis [gurus] . . . they all come here . . . and with *sevā* [selfless service] projects, the Indians, they all want a special project. They don't want to get their hands dirty. Westerners, they don't mind. They will get their hands dirty and I will get my hands dirty. . . . I want them [Indians] to remember their roots and where they came from, so they can teach their children. If they don't respect that, their children won't respect that: doing *sevā* and respecting Mother Earth.

Gomukh sees this mission to help Indians "remember their roots" as one of Amma's primary services. For him, Amma's call for a resurgence and global return to love, compassion, selfless service, and spirituality resonates with the return to the romanticized understanding of India and Hindu values. Nearly a century after Vivekananda preached that India alone had spirituality and the West had materialism, from Gomukh's perspective it appears that the roles are now reversed: the West has co-opted India's spirituality, and India has co-opted the West's materialism. But lest we overdramatize, let us look at bit closer at the American religious landscape through a sociological lens to analyze the proportionality of this new movement of Hindu-inspired metaphysical spirituality.

THE AMERICAN RELIGIOUS LANDSCAPE

Despite the exponential population growth that occurred in the wake of the Immigration Act of 1965, Indian Hindus are still a very small minority in the context of the larger society, approximately 0.5 percent of Americans. Furthermore, because of their minority status as participants in a guru movement, both inheritor and adopter groups of Amma devotees operate in tension with the greater society. To compound this, guru movements have been received into the American religious landscape with skepticism and suspicion and have incited anticult critiques, lawsuits, the formation of deprogramming services, and investigations into sexual relations, the treatment of children, and financial contributions.[58] Inheritor devotees face particular challenges in that they often need to defend their Hindu beliefs to undereducated Americans, defend themselves as ethnic minorities in a land with a problematic racial history, and defend their devotion to Amma to the general populace and even to other Hindus. Adopter devotees are in the precarious position of having chosen a foreign religiosity often in the wake of rejecting Christianity. While the most conservative onlookers often view them as "brainwashed," their acquaintances, colleagues, friends, family, and spouses may call on them to explain, justify, and defend their beliefs and their devotion to Amma. In the process, devotees are often ridiculed, laughed at, and sometimes rejected and/or disowned. Thus in the face of such overwhelming odds, when they congregate, both groups of Amma devotees seek to create close and unified devotional communities of like-minded individuals who will support and affirm their particular religious convictions.

Many devotees recognize the tension between their devotion to Amma and their environments. Ivan responded to my husband's noninvolvement with Amma's movement as a crisis in my personal spiritual development:

> He told me to be very patient and to keep trying "to show him [my husband] the beauty of Amma and to get him on the spiritual path." He said that "the most important thing is your own spiritual progress" and that I was on an "evolutionary journey" to "spiritual realization" and that it was very important to have someone that I was on the "same level" with in my primary relationship. . . . Again and again he repeated himself that the most important thing is my "spiritual development" on the path and that if anyone was trying to hold me back from that, then I would have to eliminate them from my life so that I could grow.

His vehement reaction reveals his belief that devotees must surround themselves with like-minded individuals to minimize tensions with nonbelievers. Coterminously, the existence and influence of nonbelievers in devotees' intimate relationships sustain a particularly precarious environment that has the potential to destabilize devotees' faith.

Julia, also an adopter, recounted similar sentiments when she recalled the initial violent opposition of her own Catholic family to her involvement with Amma's movement.

> She [Julia] told us that when she first started "getting into Amma" her family wanted to call the priest and she joked that they even thought about calling in an exorcist. Her family actively protested her involvement. She said that to deal with this she used to call on Amma and seek her guidance to help her deal with the tension in her family that was developing from her involvement. She said that she would sit in the darshan hall and pray to Amma to help her make her family understand.

Julia believes that because of her prayers, Amma ultimately intervened and alleviated her familial tensions. Later, Julia was happy to report that her family has since accepted her devotion to Amma, and that some have "been to see Amma" and have "gotten darshan."

Because the majority of adopters are converts to the movement, they are accustomed to this tension between devotees and external family members. When Surabhi, a Euro-American satsang leader in her thirties, offered me extra Hershey's kisses as prasad and I said that I would take another one for my son, she then asked about my son and wistfully told me, "Any child is really lucky to be raised with Amma in his life." I asked if she had been raised with a guru in her life as a young child and she said "No, *not at all*!" (rolling her eyes), and that her devotion to Amma had been quite recent (only for the past ten years or so). In Milwaukee, I misunderstood Emily's comment that her husband had "grown up" with Swami Yogananda, to which she laughed, made a face, and quickly corrected my error, specifying that he had "grown up spiritually" with Swami Yogananda. On another occasion at the Arcadia satsang, when I told Ananda, a Euro-American devotee in his forties, that my husband does not come to satsangs, he gave me a smile of solidarity and reassured me, saying, "My wife doesn't come to these either." This tension between outsiders and devotees directly correlates to the devotees' desires to maintain satsangs as a supportive space in which to stabilize and affirm their devotion to Amma. This "circle the wagons" approach to the devotional community becomes exaggerated among Amma's adopter devotees who may face opposition not only from society but in their intimate relationships.

Inheritors also face challenges when explaining their devotion to Amma, even to other Hindus. Several devout and influential inheritors actively participated in the Paloma satsang, despite the fact that their spouses were not devotees and did not attend. In such a family-centric environment, this proved to be a significant challenge for these members, particularly when they longed for their spouses' involvement and were subsequently often disappointed. (Over time, several of these initially disinterested spouses became more involved with Amma's movement, a sequence of events that devotees attributed to "Amma's grace.") Young, single devotees also struggle to find potential partners from within the movement and face even more resistance when they attempt to introduce their outside romantic partners to their communities of Amma devotees (and to Amma). When I asked one young inheritor about how she came to marry a particular man (who was, like her, also a Malayalee Hindu Amma devotee), she explained how difficult it was to convey to outsiders her devotion to Amma:

I just got tired of the whole meeting new people game, the dating, and here is someone who truly knows me as a person, who I am, what I believe in. . . . Also, it is very hard to explain to new people about Amma. I have brought some friends to see Amma, but for the others . . . it is just something that you have to experience. You have to be here to understand. It is very hard to explain to people. They always end up saying, "So you think that she is God?" And I try to explain that, "No, it's not like that." But still, they don't really understand what this is all about, and this is a big part of my life and who I am.

Devotees from both inheritor and adopter communities of Amma devotees expressed similar sentiments about the difficulty in finding a romantic partner outside of Amma's community of devotees and then introducing them to Amma. Many devotees directly ask Amma to find them appropriate spousal partners from within the movement.[59] Their difficulties in introducing their outside romantic partners to the movement and their subsequent desires to find romantic partners from within the movement signify the gravity of the tension between Amma's movement and the external socioreligious environment.

Many Americans are still unfamiliar with Hindu culture and religiosity, let alone the nuances of a particular guru movement. As recently as 1995, on his widely watched Christian TV show *The 700 Club*, Pat Robertson denounced Hinduism as "demonic," made links between new age religions in America and Hinduism, and said, "We can't let that stuff come into America."[60] Surface understandings of basic Hindu tenets (like karma) are infiltrating the mainstream U.S. media; for example, a recent United Way billboard reads, "Giving is good karma," and in the video game *inFamous* (2009), players choose to attain good or bad "karma points" as they decide whether to be the hero or not. Nonetheless, Hindus are often under pressure to explain more difficult theological concepts like the relationship between multiple deities or *saṃsāra* (the cycle of rebirth) to their colleagues and acquaintances. As illustrated by the California textbook debates in 2006, school-age Hindu children are often under similar pressure in the classroom to justify and explain Indic cultural traditions, such as the caste system and arranged marriage, traditions about which they, as American-born children, may have limited knowledge.[61]

Satsangs provide inheritors with a community with whom they can discuss challenges that arise as part of the immigrant Indian experience. In the Paloma satsang, often the Malayalee women talked to each other about basic family issues, such as whose child was now driving, who had been sick, how family members in India were getting along, who got a new job, new Indian restaurants, and upcoming cultural events. If we understand this satsang first as an ethnic community dedicated to relieving tensions through sharing common immigrant experiences and only second as a religious community dedicated to Amma, these conversations appear not mundane but culturally productive. The religious dispositions of the Hindu Indian attendees are an implicit and inalienable aspect of their lives, part of their ethnic and national identity, whereas the daily challenges of being even a model minority in America can be infinitely more complex.

CONCLUSION

In conclusion I must address a salient question: Is the analytical reasoning and sociohistorical context supplied here simply an apologetic for institutionalized racism? As mentioned at the outset of this chapter, in 1958, Dr. Martin Luther King Jr. wrote, "It is appalling that the most segregated hour of Christian America is eleven o'clock on Sunday morning, the same hour when many are standing to sing 'In Christ There Is No East Nor West.'"[62] In 2010, a Hartford Institute for Religion Research survey suggested that, despite recent growth, still only 13.7 percent of congregations in the United States are mixed (meaning that more than 20 percent of members provide racial and ethnic diversity).[63] Often the politically correct rationales given for this institutionalized segregation reference the different styles of worship of black and white congregations, which are based on the preferences and dispositions of the congregants. So is there anything truly different occurring among Amma devotees who profess to simply prefer their own relatively homogenous communities?

Simply put, yes. Beyond all administrative and cultural specificities, the intended purpose of satsangs is to invoke the visceral feeling of Amma's presence that devotees experience during darshan programs. As referenced at the outset of this chapter, Amma says, "In the presence of a Perfect Master," satsangs can enable devotees "to experience God more than in any other place." Here she is referring to one conventional meaning of the term *satsang*, to be in the company of a realized master or guru. The satsangs hosted around the world in Amma's name implement the term *satsang* in a virtual sense, as congregational gatherings that invoke her presence through imagery and prescribed ritual action. Thus devotees' feelings of the presence of Amma during satsangs serve as the barometer for their efficacy. It may be that communal tensions and complex relations among the diverse ethnic groups of satsang attendees undermine the goal of the satsang ritual, which is the aura of maternal love, security, confidence, and the affirmation of faith created in the invocation of Amma's presence. In summation, I offer the following formula: When satsangs maintain a positive balance (presence > tension), then they remain multicultural and multiracial. But when the balance becomes inverted and the communal tensions complicate the invocation of Amma's presence (tension > presence), then satsangs segregate into relatively homogenous de facto congregations in order to preserve their efficacy. In Chicago, it very well may be the case that the energy and vibrancy inherent in the new MACC ashram and the year-round presence of a resident brahmacārī will invigorate Amma's presence among diverse community members enough to bring together the various subsets. Only time will tell.

Still, because there is a mandatory fixed format to satsangs, the style and content of worship in inheritor and adopter congregations are quite similar. Their dependence on Hindu ritual action demands that attendees conduct themselves as Hindus would, at least for several hours. This performative element enables inheritor devotees to reaffirm their native religiosity, whereas it demands cultural adaptation (if not wholesale appropriation) from adopters. Though the satsang community insists on this process of cultural adaptation, outside the satsang environment adopters are sometimes criticized as being exploitative of Indic culture by ascribing to this very same process. For some adopters, this is a double bind that makes satsang participation unappealing. But other adopters demonstrate their readiness to undertake the risks of cultural adaptation by embodying Indian-style comportments and Hindu religiosity; this minority population of devotees tends to attend satsangs regularly and participate with conviction. However, the fact that such a small population of adopters attends satsangs regularly speaks to their generalized disinterest in a fixed religious community that requires any significant commitment or conformity to a fixed Hindu ritual program. Instead, adopter devotees turn out en masse only when Amma comes to town and they are able to participate in the darshan experience as individuals.

Many inheritors who persevere year-round to promote and sustain the organizational infrastructure for the movement regard adopters with trepidation, at least initially. They function as an exclusive community of committed workers, not only often distracted by, but also sometimes resentful of, the lightweight dabbling and eclectic spiritualities of these adopters.[64] Inheritors often quickly presume what they imagine to be adopters' lack of commitment and transient nature. Contrarily, inheritors welcome other inheritor devotees without reservation, because they believe their common cultural and religious ties will bind them to a more lasting commitment to the satsang.[65] As a result, those adopters who actively participate in the organizational leadership of the inheritor satsang communities have earned their position there through their exhibition of sincere devotion, their willingness to commit totally, and their readiness to undergo the process of cultural adaptation despite the potential for critique.

The de facto congregationalism among Chicagoland satsangs signifies the tensions inherent in Amma's movement. Amma's movement has developed a unique religiosity—one that was initially rooted in the Hindu traditions but has since marketed itself in the form of a global movement with a universalist and ecumenical message of spirituality. The tension between these two populations of inheritors and adopters signifies the tension between the particular and the universal—the local and the global. It is symptomatic of natural growing pains as the movement expands from a Keralan phenomenon to a global phenomenon. Caught in the flow and flux of globalization, devotees navigate multiple cultures. They reside in metaphysical borderlands, which are both fecund grounds for interpersonal dialogue and dangerous spaces of intercultural conflict. Their tendencies toward homogeneity in congregational gatherings reflect not the American legacy of segregation policies but instead a history of orientalism and the quintessential American tendency toward denominational fragmentation. They also reflect the failures of the multiculturalist politics of recognition, wherein devotees recognize not the unbounded and indeterminate personal identities of individuals but essentialized communal identities rife with cultural stereotyping. The common practice to separate into homogenous congregations shows that satsangs emulate prototypical American patterns of fragmentation that is most American when exhibiting distinct and personalized communal identities.

In contrast, during Amma's public darshan programs, the tumult of identity politics recedes into the background. Instead, devotees foreground communal solidarity, sacrality, emotional enrichment, and the sharing in the communal amassment of collective energy in the spirit of love as they come together in Amma's embrace. Such feelings of connectivity among diverse community members build their foundation on the impending dissolution of the self into the other that is Amma's darshan. The spirit of witnessing and acknowledging the other supersedes the impulses toward the stultifying recognition of communal essences.

When speaking of various social conflicts in satsang communities, several devotees iterated a commonplace "rock tumbler" metaphor, one often repeated among Amma devotees. Kalyani explained, "It is like we are sharp stones and Amma is putting us all into a rock tumbler together to smooth out all of our rough edges and make us into beautifully polished gems." This sentiment suggests that Amma intentionally puts together people of different personality types and different social and cultural backgrounds to work in the community in an effort to use those differences inherent in such diversity to refine their character. As one senior ashram associate explains, "When people have the correct attitude, the various hard and sharp edges of our personalities, when put in Amma's 'rock tumbler community,' are worn off and smoothed away. Good qualities such as patience and kindness and mental equanimity are cultivated." Coming together as a community, in the tumult of interpersonal relationships, challenges even the best among us. It is quite commonplace for Americans to surround themselves with those who agree with their politics, worldview, and lifestyle choices wherein our rough edges are poignantly sharpened for razor-sharp attacks on our ideological opponents. In contrast, Amma encourages devotees to struggle against this cultural paradigm by bringing together cultural diversity in the community, advocating a utopian effort of unity.

Multiculturalism, Universalism, and Communal Identity

The Guru in the American Diaspora

A cool breeze ushers in the sweet smell of the desert blooms as the devotional music infuses the darkened landscape with ecstatic devotional cries to Hindu deities. Night descends on Shakti Fest 2012, A Celebration of the Divine Mother, at Joshua Tree in the high deserts of California.[1] C. C. White begins her set, arching her melodic voice into a phenomenal hybridized genre of music she calls "soul *kirtan.*" Her musical innovation synchronizes ancestral African rhythms of soul, R&B, Southern blues, gospel, jazz, and Latin with the lyrical poetry of Hindu devotional music. The call-and-response patterns endemic to both gospel and bhajans blend fluidly into a uniquely American amalgam of Hindu devotion. She is a beautiful young African American woman, affectionately known as "The Queen of Soul Kirtan." With her radiant presence and a flaming-red head wrap, she exudes love and immediate acceptance for her community of sisters and brothers, both on and off the stage. Her chant to the Mother begins with an amalgam of spoken words and a soulful, tender melody:

> We all come into the world through the Mother. She is our first guru. Her mantra.
> Her heartbeat. Her love, an ever-renewing source. Let us remember Ma.
> This chant is for the Mother. The Mother in us all. [repeat]
> When I think of Mother, I chant "Ma." [repeat]
> This chant is for the Mother.
> Remember Ma.

This chant is for the Mother. The Mother in us all. [repeat]
Take refuge as her sons and daughters. Ma.
When I think of Mother, I chant "Ma." [repeat]
Ma, Ma, Ma. [repeat]
We surrender and are renewed by Ma.
Ma, Ma, Ma. [repeat]
Ma is there. Ma is there.
Ma, Ma, Ma. [repeat][2]

As her heartrending chant amplifies into rhythmic choruses of "Jai Ma," she is vibrant on the stage, inviting the audience to join her in the raptures of devotion in traditional call-and-response form. She sensitively caresses each utterance of "Jai Ma," while the two immense screens on either side of the stage flash projected images of Mata Amritanandamayi. The images interlace in a pattern showing the smiling visage of Amma alternating with the serene image of a pale-blue Krishna. The pictorial display first shows Amma in a simple white sari, then giving *darshan*, and then in *Devī Bhāva*, replete with her brocaded silk sari and silver crown.[3] The optical menagerie and devotional fervor of the music build in intensity, culminating in rhythmic pictorial flashes between Krishna wearing a silver crown and Amma in her Devī Bhāva splendor. At the culmination of the chant, the flashing images merge into one. The eager and euphoric audience of metaphysicals absorbs the message of Amma's divinity as the mother goddess as devotees dance, sing, sway, gyrate, twirl, and revel in the emotive communal form of devotional musical worship that is kirtan.

The following morning the blazing sun heats the desert once more and still the ecstatic kirtan continues on the main stage, unabated. But in the cool shade of the sanctuary, Shiva Rae, the leading innovator in prana flow yoga, closes a Shakti circle with the ritual prayer offered at Amma's Devī Bhāva programs.[4] The assembled metaphysicals enfold themselves in a cosmic spiral surrounding the ritual officiants (Shiva Rae, Mirabai Devi, Sara Ivanhoe, Dawn Cartwright, and Laura Plumb) at the center of the sanctuary, while Shiva Rae leads them in a practice of "bathing in that divine flow that is Ma." The seated metaphysicals crowd closely around Shiva Rae, who invites them to perform a ritual practice that occurs during Amma's Devī Bhāva darshan programs. Each person revolves her hands in a forward motion away and then back toward the central core of her body in a process of circulating internal energies, all the while chanting "*Oṁ Parāśaktyai namaḥ*" (Oṁ Primordial Female Divine Energy). The chanting voices repeat in unison, ascending in monotones until the sanctuary reverberates with the vibrant pulsations of collective sound asserted again and again for several minutes—and then silence. Shiva Rae passes the microphone to another ritual leader, who closes the Shakti circle with the following prayer:

> We offer these prayers to you within our sacred heart, knowing that the Kingdom of Heaven dwells within our own hearts. We ask today that all of these prayers be answered, manifested, and brought into form in our lives, in the lives of our loved ones, and in the lives of all beings on Mother Earth. We ask today Divine Light, beloved Divine Mother, that your light be our light, that your divine love be our divine love, that your divine grace be our divine grace, that your divine healing be our divine healing. Please wrap us in your divine mother's mantle of peace and protection. Victory to your light. Jai Ma.

No chasm exists between these individuals and the Divine Mother in this prayer. Instead, this collective of metaphysicals prays fervently that they may emulate and embody the qualities of the Divine Mother. The mother goddess serves as a mimetic model for human behavior, so that in perfecting themselves they may recognize the "Kingdom of Heaven" within their own "sacred hearts." This mimetic interpretation of the relationship to the divine characterizes the metaphysical communities, whose members largely believe themselves to be on a spiritual journey of self-perfection.

Few immigrant Indian Hindus were in attendance at Shakti Fest, but the kirtan audiences, yoga classes, and spiritual workshops overflowed with crowds of metaphysicals eager for spiritual experiences entwined with recurring personal affirmations of their self-identification with the Divine Mother. The representation of Hindu religiosity within Shakti Fest alternated between such mimetic devotion to the Divine Mother (often envisioned as Amma or Kali) and a substratum of ecstatic devotion to Krishna in Hare Krishna styles of worship. The underlying presence of jubilant dancing in tune with recurrent refrains of "Hare Krishna, Hare Rama" (the *mahāmantra* for the International Society for Krishna Consciousness [ISKCON]) serves as a vital reminder of the continued importance of ISKCON in shaping the *bhakti* (devotional) sensibilities of Hindu-inclined metaphysicals in the United States.[5] The vibrant community of metaphysicals stood in stark contrast to the absence of immigrant Indian Hindus at such a festival dedicated to the Hindu goddess. Similarly, the majority of Hindu temples to the goddess on that same weekend would also represent a vibrant community of immigrant Indian Hindus and few (if any) metaphysicals.

The tendency toward both ethnic and cultural homogeneity revealed within these communities suggests that the de facto congregationalism of

Amma's movement is not site specific. Rather, the overwhelming predominance of internal communal homogeneity suggests that these metaphysicals make personal religious choices within larger social structures that continue to replicate the historical relations between Indian Hindus and the West. As discussed in the last chapter, such homogenizing tendencies reveal the power dynamics of cultural encounters inherent in orientalism, wherein Europeans discursively constructed India through their own fantasy regardless of the lived religiosities and realities of Indian Hindus. The corresponding protectionist impulses of the immigrant Indian Hindu minorities in the United States reflect their keen awareness of the complicated politics and power dynamics of cultural appropriations.

These communal tendencies toward internal homogeneity may at first seem incongruous with the American celebration of religious pluralism and multiculturalism. There is no question that, when taken as a whole, an intensely broad swath of fervent and diverse religiosities finds space in America. But religion in the United States has always been vibrantly multicultural only when viewed from an aerial perspective. In fact, in the first migrations from Europe to America, it was precisely the availability of ample space to separate into homogenous communities far removed from conflicting worldviews that enabled the largely peaceful proliferation of religious diversity in the American environment.[6] The on-the-ground realities suggest that "like-minded" (and often ethnically homogenous) people tend to isolate themselves in specifically oriented communities in pockets of particularity and self-affirmation. This suggests a quintessentially American style of denominationalism, wherein the centrifugal fragmentation of the religious into specifically tailored congregational communities of worship consistently challenges the posited ideal of a fixed center.[7] Disestablishment and the freedom to choose a religious community in which one is surrounded by "like-minded" individuals have not only created the vibrancy inherent in the architecture of American religions but also its tendency toward fragmentation and communal fissure.

Similarly, a historical interpretation may also shed light on the impulses behind Amma's privileging of the feminine. Why does Amma feel that this privileging is a necessary corrective to what she believes to be the hypermasculinization of society and religion? While at first glance it may appear to be a distant antecedent, Amma's privileging of the feminine germinates from historically gendered constructions of Hindu religiosity, which colonial governance reified and elaborated. Enlightenment ideals, substantiated by culture and the race theory of Darwinian

evolutionism, privileged the white adult male and his intellectual ratio-
nalist potential as the pinnacle of evolutionary advancement of scientific reasoning and rationality. When applied to the concurrent colonial
and missionary entrées into the East, such ideals privileged rationality,
science, monotheism, ethics, texts, and philosophy, which were equated
with masculine sensibilities. Their antitheses—magic, irrationality, idolatry, animism, devotion, experience, and ritual—were largely condemned
as effeminate expressions of childlike and backward peoples who had
not yet evolved into the personification of Enlightenment sensibilities.
Colonial governments justified their dominance with these types of
paternalistic rationalizations. European colonial interventionists in the
East believed they were assisting in human development and progress,
civilizing the rest of the world in their image.

Among orientalists operating in the Indic context, Hindu effeminacy
was envisioned as one of the most significant stalwarts that stymied cultural development along the evolutionary schema of Enlightenment progress. As early as the colonial project in 1770, Richard Orme's *History of
the Military Transactions of the British Nation in Indostan* suggested that
all natives showed "effeminacy of character." Hindus, particularly Ben-
galis, were singled out in the later discourses of James Mill, who argued
that they "possess[ed] a certain softness both in their persons and in their
address" that distinguished them from the "manlier races" of Europe.
Thomas Babington Macaulay, the law member for India in the 1830s,
famously argued, "The physical organization of the Bengalee is feeble
even to effeminacy," a characterization that would long haunt the Bengali
Hindu in the stereotype of the "effeminate Bengali *babu*."[8]

The first Protestant missionaries in India also imagined their own religiosity as a rational masculine savior of Hindus from the irrational
effeminacy of Hindu ritualism, idolatry, and superstition. The nineteenth-
century Protestant missionary William Ward equated Hindu effeminacy
with moral depravity and irrationality. In his view Hindu effeminacy
lacked any sense of the order or the rationality that characterized Protestant Christianity.[9] Ward understood the Hindu gods to be too effeminate to be efficacious, particularly Krishna, whose effeminacy he equated
with immoral lasciviousness. Even affectionate orientalist scholars, such
as William Jones, who held Hindu gods (including Krishna) in high esteem, still believed that the supposed effeminacy of the Hindus formed
a causal relation to their primitive state.[10] The perceived effeminacy of
the Hindus served to further justify the Protestant missionaries' active

endeavors to sculpt Hindus paternalistically to reflect the missionaries' masculine imaginary of themselves.[11]

Operating within the same orientalist framework, Hindu reformers such as Rammohan Roy also attempted to combat these gendered stereotypes by creating a form of Hinduism that was rational, ethical, scientific, and monotheistic—a masculine Hinduism that could fight toe-to-toe with the Protestantism of the colonizers and missionaries.[12] The first entrées of Hindu religiosity into the United States occurred in the midst of this nineteenth-century contestation. In the mid to late nineteenth century, limited information about Hindu religiosity was passed to the American public through the efforts of early Baptist and Unitarian missionaries, the celebration of Rammohan Roy, the eastward spiritual imaginings of the Transcendentalists, the esoteric affinities of the Theosophical Society, the publication of Max Müller's lectures on Vedanta, and Americans' general sympathies with, and even the emulation of, British colonial endeavors. But in 1893 the World's Parliament of Religions at the Columbian Exposition in Chicago brought Hindu thought center stage in American life through the charismatic speeches of Swami Vivekananda. Swami Vivekananda began his early religious engagement as a disciple of Ramakrishna (who was an ecstatic devotee of the goddess Kali) and with a significant engagement with the Brahmo Samaj, then led by Keshub Chandra Sen. Although he retained his devotion to the mother goddess in his lectures in India, the Hinduism that he presented to Americans during his tours there only rarely spoke of his devotion to the divine feminine. In fact, Vivekananda was quite fearful that Western audiences would misunderstand the Tantric elements of his own guru's (Ramakrishna's) devotion to the Hindu goddess Kali. Ramakrishna not only served as the *pūjārī* (priest) at the central Kali temple in Kolkutta, but he also worshipped his wife, Sarada Devi, as a living embodiment of the goddess Lalitā. However, Vivekananda encouraged his disciples to censor the sexual aspects of Ramakrishna's life and instead to portray him as a saint and prophet who espoused only advaita vedantic theology.[13] He followed his forebears in representing a form of Hindu religiosity that was imbued with the orientalist understanding of the masculine qualities inherent in Protestant Christianity. As such, he claimed that Hinduism was monistic instead of polytheistic, ethical instead of depraved, scientific instead of superstitious, rational instead of irrational, and philosophical instead of ritualistic. In his public representations of Hindu religiosity in the United States, he effectively erased the goddess.

In addition to this tendency to highlight the masculine qualities of Hinduism and suppress the feminine in the American context, his discourses on Indian nationalism in India even more overtly advocated a masculine Hinduism. Vivekananda buttressed orientalist claims of Hindu effeminacy when he chastised Hindus against such weaknesses and encouraged them to reclaim their masculinity in order to rise up and defeat the British. He argued for the creation of a class of warrior-monks, who would be required to test their manhood through spiritual prowess in order to protect the Hindu nation and to procure independence through spiritual and moral fortitude.[14] In his speeches on nationalism, he argued:

> We have wept long enough. No more weeping, but stand on your feet and be men. It is man-making religion that we want. It is man-making theories we want. It is man-making education that we want. And here is the test of truth—anything that makes you weak, physically, intellectually, and spiritually reject as poison.[15]

Vivekananda followed the orientalist condemnation of Hindus as effeminate. However, he argued that this effeminacy was not innate but a result of oppression and enslavement by the colonial government. He considered the effeminacy of the Hindus a superimposed state of being that they had to eradicate in order to use the inherent spiritual power of Hindu religiosity to become manly warrior-monks. He said:

> There is another defect in us . . . through centuries of slavery, we have become like a nation of women. You can scarcely get three women together for five minutes in this country or any other country but they quarrel. . . . Women we are. If a woman comes to lead women they all begin immediately to criticize her, tear her to pieces. . . . If a man comes and gives them a little harsh treatment, scolds them now and again . . . it is all right. . . . In the same way, if one of our countrymen stands up and tries to become great, we all try to hold him down, but if a foreigner comes and tries to kick us it is all right. We have been used to it, have we not? . . . So give up being a slave. For the next fifty years this alone shall be our keynote—this is our great mother India.[16]

Vivekananda's rhetoric of masculine Hinduism became an important narrative for the nationalist movement in India. During his lifetime and after his death, his message of Hindu manliness instigated the establishment of educational institutions within the Hindu nationalist movements that incorporate physical fitness regimens and religious education. Such institutions aimed to ensure that upcoming generations would fulfill Vivekananda's dream of a powerful and masculine citizenry, based in the inherent spiritual supremacy of a Hindu India.

In time, Vivekananda's masculinized ideal of Hindu religiosity became a paradigmatic keystone of the Sangh Parivar, the many branches of the Hindu nationalist movement. The diversely affiliated political groups that comprise the Sangh Parivar constructed masculinist narratives that sought to counter the gendered colonial justification for the British presence in India. This multifaceted masculinist narrative celebrated the Hindu soldier and the warrior-monk as two dominant representations of Indic masculinity juxtaposed with mythic figures drawn from indigenous tradition in an attempt to aggressively seize control of a burgeoning Hindu nation. Women participated in such masculinist constructions by aligning themselves with female images within the nation: nation as woman (Mother India), heroic mother, pure wife, and masculinized, celibate woman-warrior.[17] This hypermasculinization of Hindu nationalist politics has garnered strength and authority for the promise of a unified Hindu nation, but it has also generated extreme violence and deleterious consequences with regard to contemporary relations between Hindus and minority communities in India, Muslims and Christians in particular. Such hypermasculinized aggressive Hinduism permeated not only the subcontinent but also found eager adherents in the United States, where immigrant Indian Hindus often resonate with its foundational emphasis on a persecuted Hindu religiosity in the face of external threat.

Even prior to the late twentieth-century rise in Hindu nationalism, the United States had developed its own legacy in response to Vivekananda's brand of masculinized Hindu religiosity. The majority of Americans equated Vivekananda's neo-vedantic interpretation of Hindu religiosity with Hindu religiosity as a whole. In fact, the Vedanta Societies that he established were the primary representatives of Hinduism in the United States until the Immigration Act of 1965. It was only after this dramatic increase of immigrant Indian Hindus that the representations of Hinduism in the United States diversified exponentially. While these Hindus respected Vivekananda as a cultural icon and religious adept, their message differed from his in that they emphasized a multiplicity of the particular, practical, ritualistic, and devotional aspects of Hindu religiosity. They established hundreds of temples, organizations, cultural centers, and websites that supported their diverse understanding of Hindu religiosity. Their practical Hindu religiosity confronted the American imaginary of Hinduism that had stood in for the whole of Hinduism heretofore. Buttressed by en vogue multiculturalism and the American propensity for religion in general, these Hindus established themselves firmly as a successful, educated, affluent, and influential religious minority among American religions.

The Immigration Act of 1965 also opened America's doors to a wide gamut of gurus from India who began to proselytize to the American public with a variety of theologies and practices, all derived from within the diverse religious umbrella category of Hinduism. Often drawing their theologies and practices from an eclectic combination of Hindu ideas, they attracted followings of metaphysicals, who embraced similarly eclectic spiritual worldviews. The majority of these Hindu gurus who developed successful religious movements in the United States were men. As such, they incited the same critiques that Vivekananda had withstood at the turn of the century. Critics and wary observers often viewed these gurus as charlatans who were more interested in the pocketbooks of white women than guiding spiritual advancement. While early twentieth-century critics scoffed at the supposedly money-seeking charlatans masquerading under the pretext of religion, in the late twentieth century such scoffing turned to legal action. Few gurus were untouched by the skepticism and fears that arose in response to their charismatic authority, claims of divinity, sexual indiscretions, and financial demands on their followings. One by one the American guru movements of the 1960s and 1970s fell to financial scandals and sexual misconduct, many of which resulted in legal prosecution. The anticult hysteria of the 1970s and 1980s increased the market for deprogramming services and family support networks that attempted to rescue countercultural American youth from the clutches of secretive and isolationist guru movements. Many young devotees were drawn away from guru movements and reintegrated into society by the aggressive actions of their loved ones. Others left guru movements through voluntary attrition as they became increasingly skeptical in the wake of scandals and corruption. Their disillusionment engulfed them as they witnessed their utopian dreams and illustrious gurus shattered because of their susceptibility to human vices. The American media significantly influenced the gendered construction of these scandals by frequently framing such scandals within the historically pervasive tropes of charlatan male Indian gurus seducing women both financially and sexually.

In 1987 Amma entered into the guru scene in the United States. She was one of the first female gurus to speak to American audiences, though several others have followed in her wake. Amma's combination of advaita vedantic philosophy and bhakti devotionalism represents the juxtaposition of the two most popular movements derived from Hindu religiosity among Americans: Vivekananda's Advaita Vedanta–inspired Vedanta Societies and A. C. Bhaktivedanta Prabhupada's bhakti-centric ISKCON movement. In addition to drawing on the extant American affinities for these particular strains of Hindu practice, she introduced the aspect of goddess veneration to Americans in novel and innovative ways. In guru communities in which the desire for proximity to the guru reigns paramount in devotees' minds, Amma offered the ultimate boon: the frequent opportunity to physically embrace the guru. Furthermore, her veneration and personal representation of the goddess established itself just as increasing numbers of metaphysicals were turning toward feminine expressions of the divine and immigrant Indian Hindus were seeking more particularized representations of Hindu religiosity. Many of the disillusioned devotees of the 1970s and 1980s guru scandals turned to Amma's movement with cautious optimism, believing that a female guru would escape the sexual corruptions of her male predecessors.

At the outset, Amma's American followers and supporters consisted of a few key wealthy metaphysicals and communities of immigrant Indian Hindus. Her initial darshan programs were held in small living rooms and finished basements. But it did not take long for much larger populations from both demographics to be drawn to her movement. Her darshan programs soon overflowed with metaphysical sympathizers who saw the continuity between Amma and their spiritual turn toward the feminine. The similar ideological convictions evidenced in Amma's message and among advocates of women's spirituality ensured that her message would resonate in similarly inclined metaphysical communities. Amma and the goddess movement in America implement the goddess as a feminist symbol in strikingly similar ways. Both valorize a historical "Golden Age" when the goddess reigned and societies were more egalitarian. Both believe the goddess to be a vital feminine role model for female empowerment. Both argue for the increase of feminine influences in society. Both blame the masculinization of society (and occasionally human men) for the destruction of the earth. Both assert an inner spiritual core at the nexus of all religions. Last, both exhibit internal tensions regarding biological versus metaphorical conceptions of human roles in relation to the goddess. Indian Hindus largely agree with the majority of these contentions, but they articulate their politics with the term *female empowerment* instead of the term *feminism*. The majority of Indian Hindus also distinguish their veneration of the goddess from their practical concerns about the socioeconomic position of human women. As such, the metaphysicals more than Indian Hindus are susceptible to critiques issued by both Indian and American feminists who find their historical claims untenable, their spiritual claims detrimental to the materiality of feminist causes, and their essentialisms exclusionary, ultimately reinforcing heterosexual normativity. But despite the potential feminist critiques, more interesting are the large populations of Americans who find meaning here.

The increasing populations that continue to learn about and attend Amma's darshan programs suggest historic alterations in the American reception of Hindu religions and ideas. We can gain insight into the shifts in American views of Hindu religiosity by focusing more closely on the differences between Vivekananda and Amma and their similar and supportive (even ecstatic) reception from the majority of American audiences. Like Vivekananda, Amma's religiosity developed in an Indian environment of worship of the Hindu goddess Kali. But these two influential gurus who became Hindu missionaries in the United States, separated by one hundred years, differed in the ways in which they presented themselves to their American audiences. While Vivekananda largely suppressed his devotion to the goddess in order to appeal to American audiences, Amma proudly proclaims her devotion to the goddess, whom she presents to American audiences in a beautified and benevolent form. The transition from the suppression of the goddess to the valorization of a beautified goddess does not signify a change in Hinduism in India but, rather, an alteration that these gurus perceived in their American audiences. On the one hand, Vivekananda introduced Hindu religiosity under the pressures of the American assimilationist paradigm; as such, he curtailed his message to conform more closely to the imagined center of American religiosity: liberal Protestantism. On the other hand, Amma (re)introduces Hindu religiosity under the protected privilege of American multiculturalism. Vivekananda publicly erased his guru's commitment to the goddesses Kali and Lalitā fearing that the American public would not accept such devotions. In contrast, Amma tours the United States to crowds of devotee supporters who gather in the thousands to be embraced and transformed by a living embodiment of the goddess, envisioned as Kali and/or Lalitā. The irony is striking.

In the current multiculturalist paradigm, the demonstration of cultural ethnicity is celebrated, and it is often seen as a positive identity marker, the display of which assists in the project of becoming American. Many Americans celebrate multiculturalism as a beneficial and even a necessary attitude in the public sphere because of the swelling diversity of the American population. However, some aspects of multiculturalism may in fact stagnate and reify essentialized stereotypes of cultural ethnicity. The politics of recognition inherent in multiculturalism, which Charles Taylor introduced, in fact "acquiesces in a stifling model of the nature of agency and its relationship to culture, or to 'identity' more generally."[18] Patchen Markell convincingly argues that social identities should not only be constructed through the category of what is known but also that which is unknown. He argues that the politics of recognition fails to come to terms with the Arendtian premise of "the fact that our choices and our identities are constitutively open to an unpredictable future, whose unpredictability arises in substantial part from the fact that we do not act in isolation but as agents among others."[19] Despite the American multiculturalist valorization of ethnic identity, the demand for recognition tends to reify existing ideas about the known other. This blind spot in the multiculturalist politics of recognition suggests that to be recognized one must actively perform a situated and stagnated formulation of cultural identity. In practice, such performances buttress historical and often romanticized tropes of what it means to be Hindu, based in cultural essentialisms. Such reinvigorations of antiquated and romanticized ideals encourage contemporary actors to situate themselves within already existing representations of Hindu religion. This reasoning supplies a provocative rationale for why Amma's theology so closely echoes Vivekananda's neo-vedantic monism of a century ago. Notably both gurus presented similar messages of neo-vedantic ecumenism rather than theological particularities when they spoke at their respective Parliaments of Religions in 1893 and 1993.[20]

Vivekananda encouraged his followers to become strong and manly through Hindu spirituality. Amma encourages her followers to embrace their femininity to become compassionate mothers through Hindu devotional practices. Underlying both of these prescriptions and practicalities are essentialisms about gendered identities. In Vivekananda's view, masculine qualities are strength, physical prowess, courage, asceticism, morality, and spiritual fortitude. Feminine qualities are weakness, fickleness, quarreling, cowardice, patience, faith, and purity. In Amma's view, the feminine qualities of universal motherhood are unconditional love, compassion, asceticism, patience, sacrifice, reflection, and flow. Masculine qualities are ambition, aggression, reactivity, stagnation, and egoism. While each argues that gender balance is the ultimate goal, Vivekananda saw an increase in Hindu masculinity as necessary to achieve that balance, whereas Amma argues for a necessary increase in Hindu femininity. Both Vivekananda's and Amma's gender essentialisms reflect the social and political climate of their historical circumstances. Vivekananda was largely a successful advocate for a masculinized Hinduism through which to counterbalance the colonial gendered critique of Hindu effeminacy. Amma's reinsertion of the feminine aspects of Hindu religiosity aims to provide a corrective measure that introduces balance. Her adamancy with regard to the importance of validating the feminine suggests that the era that necessitated Vivekananda's hypermasculinization has eclipsed. It may also be read as a critique of the hypermasculinization of contemporary Hindutva politics that Vivekananda's masculine Hinduism partially spawned.

In the American context, Amma's goddess-centric theology and practices further diversify Hinduism as it is practiced in the United States. Still, the fact that Amma suppresses the more dangerous and provocative aspects of goddess devotion as it is practiced in India may suggest that multiculturalism is yet an ideal rather than a reality. It also illuminates the fact that a multiculturalism, which is based on a politics of recognition, demands conformity to existing conceptions of sovereign cultural identity and as a result tends to reify rather than challenge cultural essentialisms. Unlike Vivekananda, who felt pressured to hide his devotion to the mother goddess entirely, Amma overtly venerates the independent female power of the mother goddess. But she presents her audiences with the goddess in her most beautiful and benevolent form, as a compassionate mother who selflessly embraces her children. There is no sacrifice, no blood, no sexuality, and no violence in her representation of the goddess as Lalitā. Even Amma's early ecstatic bhāvas during which she wielded sickle and sword have transformed into institutionalized and heavily orchestrated beauteous rituals that leave little to chance. Although Indian trends also suggest iconographical shifts toward the beautification or "sweetening" of the goddess, this calculated and largely successful representation certainly ensures that Amma is palatable to her middle-class bourgeois audiences.

In fact, this transition has enabled her to reach the hearts of millions of people with a laudable message of love, compassion, and selfless service. Between Vivekananda and Amma, there has been a century of broadening acceptance in American attitudes toward religious difference, but still something must be suppressed in translation. Amma is wholly justified in her perception that American audiences are not quite ready for the fearsome goddesses of village India. Americans proudly espouse multiculturalism, but their acceptance of difference still stagnates within strict boundaries of socially acceptable behavior, much of which is still rife with proclivities toward liberal Protestantism.[21] True acceptance of difference must allow for disorder and conflict and the witnessing of the common humanity, even among radical others. Smoothing over these differences by necessitating a beautified veneer obfuscates the vibrant diversity of human religious expression.

However, we should not end our story there with the assessment that Amma is somehow insufficient for not doing what we might wish that she would do: reinventing gender paradigms or representing all aspects of South Indian goddess devotionalism. For if we ask "For whom is this a problem?" we must inevitably conclude that for the tens of thousands of Amma devotees such discussions are wholly irrelevant. What matters instead is the heart experience, the internal ecstasy, the intimate connection between devotees and Amma, and the dissolution of the self in the embrace of the other. In our egoistic world of postmodernity, such an experience of unconditional love, compassion, and acceptance made available to all persons regardless of gender, caste, religion, class, ethnicity, or behaviors suggests a radical revision of our habitual attitudes that routinely erect stark divisions between the self and the other. Amma's embrace offers the possibility of connection, an unmediated and intense interpersonal connection, the wholehearted witnessing of the self in the other and the other in the self. Amma has given over 32 million hugs worldwide. For many in her darshan queue, even the possibility of such an experience is worth the wait.

Current Literature Engaging the Field of Contemporary Gurus

The religious adepts of India have occupied a central location in the field of Indology since its inception. Alternately identified as sants, sadhus, swamis, *samnyāsīs*, mahants, acharyas, ascetics, yogis, renunciates, babas, matas, and gurus, such religious adepts have captivated scholars' attention with their radically alternative lifestyles and untethered charismatic authority. Throughout Hindu scriptures, since antiquity, there is ample narrative evidence of both men and women retaining authoritative roles due to their spiritual prowess, whether they existed in extra-social stations as wandering reclusive ascetics or through active social engagement as teachers and gurus. Historically, the reclusive ascetic also functioned as a guru for only the most dedicated of disciples who sought out the guru in his or her remote extra-social environment. Today, as increasing numbers of ascetics engage proactively in a variety of social arenas, many develop the persona of guru as they gain large numbers of followers and students. In fact, the presence of the student differentiates between the guru and the ascetic. Asceticism is often (but not always) the practice for which many Indic traditions demand a religious adept who will serve as a guide and a teacher to illuminate the proper path.

Some gurus present themselves as fully human learned teachers whose expertise and authority derive from their extensive experience in spiritual disciplines. Other gurus present themselves as divine incarnations (*avatar-gurus*), bridging the earthly and divine realms. In North Indian *sant* traditions, according to Daniel Gold, the guru "should ideally be embodied as a living individual," but he also "must seem to be more than an individual human person. Indeed, he must appear in certain ways as a source of supreme grace comparable to others known throughout the religions of the world."[1] In this sense, the successful guru may be recognized in Max Weber's characterization of the exemplary prophet whose mission "directs itself to the self-interest of those who crave salvation, recommending to them the same path as he himself traversed."[2] The decisive feature within these formulations is the guru as a means, a means to attain something else. The guru is a tool, and for many Indic traditions an irreplaceable one.

The list of scholarly texts that address and include gurus is too extensive to outline in this limited review. As a result, I must unfortunately omit literature that includes the study of gurus within broader investigations into various social phenomena (see, for example, Copeman 2009; Barrett 2008; Prentiss 1999). Also, I restrict this account by focusing only on gurus who locate their roots in Hindu traditions; the voluminous literature on Sikh and Sufi gurus remains outside the purview of this inquiry. Last, there are hundreds of thousands of "local" gurus in India whose scope and influence do not transmigrate into global arenas. While these are key developers of the field, this review focuses instead on the scholastic accounts of those gurus categorized by Jacob Copeman and Aya Ikegame as "headline-stealing hyper-gurus," those god-men and goddess-women who employ "vast resources" and "engage in high-profile development works and achieve hegemony in public discourse and representation."[3] The majority of these gurus and their messages do transmigrate, circulating broadly into global arenas. As such, they are particularly pertinent to the development of my own study of one such guru operating in transnational and diasporic contexts.

The scholarship on gurus has tended to be specific in nature, with studies focusing on select gurus in their sociohistorical contexts. Still, some seminal works have developed the foundations of the field, such as Daniel Gold's *The Lord as Guru* (1987) directed at Indologists, a book that introduces the complex relations between the yogic traditions (Buddhist, Hindu, Sant, and Sufi) and the religious adepts of Northern India who garner followers, that is, gurus. In his more theoretical follow-up work, *Comprehending the Guru* (1988), Gold aims to incite comparative dialogue among historians of religions. His comparative efforts seek to rectify the field, which he characterizes as rife with "a total lack of coherence," mainly because individual embedded scholars constantly reinvent the wheel instead of synthesizing and building on each other's work. Taking a sociological approach, in the penultimate chapter, "Religio-Historical Syntax," in *Comprehending the Guru*, Gold adroitly, if complexly, produces a schema (replete with extensive charts) that attempts to address the meta-question "What does the emergence of the idea of sant tradition say about the capacity of human religious perception to comprehend the holy man?"[4] In the midst of Gold's careful analysis therein, he productively suggests that the distinctive dynamic of the holy man "is to continually make hidden truths immediate, and mundane community divine . . . [while he] must remain at once true to his own possibly changing realizations and sensitive to his devotees' probably changing needs."[5] Unfortunately, beyond Gold's seminal attempts to unify the field, the remainder of single-author investigations tends to focus somewhat myopically on the details of particular gurus, perhaps fulfilling Gold's accusations concerning the lack of unifying analytics within the field. To my knowledge, the only other scholar who has attempted a synthesis of the guru field in a single-authored text is Marie-Thérèse Charpentier, the author of *Indian Female Gurus in Contemporary Hinduism* (2010), which attempts the Herculean feat of creating a table listing female gurus, their birth and death dates, birth state, caste, education, marital status, children, and lineages. While scholars may secretly desire to write a magnum opus of the guru, the depth, diversity, and constant fluctuations of the field have ensured that it has not yet been written.

With that said, some of the most theoretically probing works in the field emerge from edited volumes, many of which aim to present a cartography of the field and to crystallize modalities in an effort to provide analytical tools for other scholars. In *The Graceful Guru* (2004), Karen Pechilis insightfully engages the particularities of gender through an excellent collection of scholastic encounters with various female gurus. It is in this erudite volume that Pechilis suggests that women might be viewed as the "3rd wave" of gurus in the modern period. Vasudha Narayanan also reveals the key insight that because the majority of female gurus are "stand alone" figures, operating outside of any sectarian *parampara* (tradition), they "tap not into the orthodox lineages but into the themes of universality and neo-Vedanta."[6] Antony Copley also provides a useful historical inquiry into the guru movements of the colonial period in the Indian context with his *Gurus and Their Followers* (2000), wherein historians carefully engage the Brahmo Samaj, the Ramakrishna Mission, the Arya Samaj, the Ahmadiyya movement, Theosophy, and Aurobindo. In another insightful volume, *Gurus in America* (2005),

Thomas Forsthoefel and Cynthia Ann Humes grapple with the diasporic context. Here, in the epilogue, Daniel Gold again supplies a welcome systematization of the field as he characterizes various gurus in the Indic categories *nirguna* and *saguna*, wherein *nirguna* represents the transnational gurus who eradicate the majority of Hindu cultural markings within their movements (including Maharishi Mahesh Yogi, Osho, and Gurumayi), in what Joanne Punzo Waghorne calls "de-ethnicized Hinduism,"[7] and *saguna* represents those who retain and even augment Hindu cultural markings (i.e., the International Society for Krishna Consciousness [ISKCON] and Amma). We in the field also look forward to the forthcoming edited volume, *Gurus of Modern Yoga* (2013), edited by Mark Singleton and Ellen Goldberg. Even a cursory glance at its list of contributors promises that the volume will shed new light on the intersections of yoga, devotion, and guru communities.

Most recently, in their edited volume, *The Guru in South Asia* (2012), Jacob Copeman and Aya Ikegame suggest that gurus might best be understood through their "uncontainability," meaning their ability to operate, coterminously, in multiple spheres of influence. In an effort to accentuate the multiple domains of contemporary gurus, they divide their work into ideotypical categorical snapshots that highlight a particular domain and the gurus' operative structures within it, for example, the media guru, the literary guru, the political guru, and the female guru. This format seeks to draw attention to "the diversity of thematics and conceptual schema" signified by the guru, highlighting the manner in which the guru serves as a "vector between domains," simultaneously producing and occupying multiple domains. In presenting this thematic approach, Copeman and Ikegame suggest that the figure of the guru extends into and in fact produces such diverse territories, while she or he transgresses categorical boundaries to the extent that the guru is ultimately "uncontainable." This notation of the guru's "expansive agency" leads the authors to conclude that the guru closely resembles Levi-Strauss's floating signifier, "a meaning-bearing unit that nevertheless has no distinct meaning." As such, the guru, in his or her "uncontainability," is beyond all limiting categories.[8] Beyond these initial explorations in their most recent volume, the authors continue this line of reasoning in their coauthored journal article "Guru Logics" (2012).

Their nuanced theoretical approach is a welcome contribution to the field, particularly their interrogation of the category of the guru as an ideotypical figure who exists as a "vector between domains," pushing beyond the by-now classic, but somewhat stagnating, language of "charisma." However, I remain slightly uneasy with their terminology of the guru's "uncontainability" for the simple fact that it so closely aligns with many contemporary gurus' own rhetoric of their omnipresence and the stark reality of their expansive grasping for authority within such a wide variety of domains. I wonder if scholarship should be so willing to echo gurus' aggrandized self-conceptions, providing theoretical frameworks that complement rather than challenge the gurus' claims to superhuman expansivity and power. Instead of echoing gurus' self-conceptions of their expansive uncontainability as omnipresent divinities, scholars might be better suited to look to gurus' very real social constructions of actions and rhetoric that aim to produce such an image of uncontainability. Such presentations of uncontainability are constructed realities that scholars should parse as social actions in particular circumstances. By drawing the field toward the gurus' "uncontainability" as a "floating signifier" with "no distinct meaning," might we not obfuscate the very human, social, and constructed nature of the religious authority that gurus produce and wield in the material world?

Still, "Guru Logics" represents one of the highlights within the burgeoning theoretical interventions as the field further develops its internal analytical resources. In fact, many of the significant contributions in this vein arise from similarly styled academic journal articles, wherein scholars often trace one aspect of a contemporary guru movement juxtaposed with a central thematic or theoretical frame. In his foundational article "The Guru in the Hindu Tradition" (1982), Joel Mlecko provides a significant resource for situating the figure of the guru within the Hindu context from antiquity to the modern period. It is particularly strong in its tracing of the figure of the guru within religious texts and offers a cursory engagement with the social realities of contemporary practice. More recently, Hugh Urban's contributions encourage readers to imagine cosmopolitan celebrity gurus as exemplifying "the spirit of late capitalism," as they adroitly juxtapose the religious, the transnational, and the impulse toward profit margins and materiality (see Urban 2003a; "Osho, from Sex Guru to Guru of the Rich: The Spiritual Logic of Late Capitalism," in Forsthoefel and Humes 2005). In several articles, Maya Warrier also provides key analyses about the Indian context of Mata Amritanandamayi; her careful scholarship is particularly helpful in discerning precisely how the Indian middle classes choose and travel between gurus, as in her 2003 article "Guru Choice and Spiritual Seeking in Contemporary India." Joanne Punzo Waghorne offers a significant contribution with her chapter "Global Gurus and the Third Stream of

American Religiosity" in *Political Hinduism* (2010), edited by Vinay Lal. Therein, Waghorne not only provides a useful schematic of Hindu religiosity in the United States, separating it into liberal, conservative, and spiritual modes, but she also develops an innovative presentation of Swami Vivekananda and his theological legacy in the United States. Additionally, David Smith includes a useful chapter on gurus in his book *Hinduism and Modernity* (2003); also, the 2011 volume of the academic journal *Nova Religio* focused on scholarship on Hindu new religious movements, including articles by Gene R. Thursby (mapping the field), Karline McLain (Shirdhi Sai Baba), Jennifer B. Saunders (Arya Samaj and Sanatan Dharm), Helen Crovetto (Ananda Seva Mission), and Phillip Charles Lucas (Ramana Maharshi).[9] In many cases, too numerous to name here, article-length contributions are the only academic studies conducted with regard to a particular guru movement; as such, they become increasingly important because they signify the only representative investigations into a broad variety of guru organizations.

Indeed, careful scholarship on particular guru movements should not be overlooked as being without merit. Some of these scholars present their research on a particular movement as a rightful topic of study in itself, while others use the guru movement as a window into broader phenomena: gender, diaspora, humanitarianism, or a particular philosophical school of thought. Other studies become even more geographically site specific, with detailed accounts of particular gurus operating in site-specific regions. For example, Lisa Hallstrom's *Mother of Bliss* (1999) carefully develops the scholarly conversation through her detailed ethnographic analysis, wherein Anandamayi Ma's devotees and Anandamayi Ma herself entirely disavow the categories of guru and saint and male and female, claiming that Anandamayi Ma transcends all such worldly distinctions. Jeffrey Kripal became infamous for his provocative psychoanalysis of Ramakrishna Paramhansa with his book *Kali's Child* (1995), whereas Gwilym Beckerlegge's *The Ramakrishna Mission* (2000) and *Swami Vivekananda's Legacy of Service* (2006) investigate the later generations of the Ramakrishna Mission and Math with reference to the rise in the perceived importance of humanitarian activities in global guru movements. With *Radhasoami Reality* (1991), Mark Juergensmeyer draws suggestive conclusions about why the Radhasoami movement appeals to the Indian middle classes of Northern India. Similarly, in *Hindu Selves in the Modern World* (2005), Maya Warrier invites her readers to learn of processes of self-identity construction among the Indian middle classes through an analysis of their involvement with the Mata Amritanandamayi Mission. Therein, her careful ethnographic research suggests that the individuation, cosmopolitanism, and ecumenism of Amma's movement suit Indian upper- and middle-class constructions of self-identity through their desire for personal autonomy and freedom, as well as instrumental and rational approaches for cultivating "balance" in their lives. Her careful study demonstrates one "instance of 'Hindu' faith and practice adapting to change in contemporary India," the shifting of "Hindu selfhood" to re-imagine itself in terms compatible with "modernity." She proposes that Amma's movement, and the sanctity that Indian devotees find therein, signifies the potential for "new and alternative configurations that run contrary to what many scholars studying Hinduism in contemporary India see as the inevitable 'incompatibility' between Hinduism and the imperatives of modernity in a fast-paced and rapidly changing world."[10]

Striking a similar vein of the conditions of globalization, postmodernity, and cosmopolitanism among what we might call "celebrity gurus," Smriti Srinivas's *In the Presence of Sai Baba* (2008) serves as a model for an effective, multisited ethnography covering territories as distinct as Bangalore, Atlanta, and Nairobi. She carefully maps spatial transnational networks unified in "a common core of performances, beliefs, and local associations for their devotion" to their avatar-guru, Sathya Sai Baba. Also focusing on the globalized cosmopolitanism of Indic religiosity in the persona of the celebrity guru, Tulasi Srinivas's *Winged Faith* (2010) breaks new ground in the theoretical analysis of globalized guru phenomena as implementing an "engaged cosmopolitanism" and a "grammar of diversity" that enable the various participants in the Sathya Sai Baba movement congeal together, despite geographic and internal diversity. Importantly, Tulasi Srinivas reimagines charisma in the sense of magnetism, wherein devotees actively desire to be physically close to the guru. She codes this social dynamic with the effective and useful terminology "proxemic desire," a phrase I have employed and developed throughout my own work.

Similar to the aforementioned titles' emphasis on transnationalism and globalization, Raymond Brady Williams also investigates reasons specific religious organizations seem to be particularly suited to Indic modernity, as well as a transnational, globalized, and cosmopolitan contexts. His books *A New Face of Hinduism* (1984) and *An Introduction to Swaminarayan Hinduism* (2001) as well as several key articles by Hanna Kim provide fascinating accounts of Swaminarayan Hinduism, one of the most exponentially growing (and changing) global guru organizations in the world. Similarly, in his classic work *Redemptive Encounters* (1986), Lawrence Babb suggests that his study of three contemporary guru-centric movements (Radhasoami, Brahma Kumaris, and Sathya Sai Baba) may illuminate the "ordered diversity" of Hindu traditions. Among its many laudable qualities, Babb's contributions are particularly influential in his discussion of the practice of *darshan*, wherein he offers an insightful analysis of the transformative and tactile qualities of "seeing."

The manner in which contemporary guru movements negotiate space and place within the United States has also garnered fruitful conversations in the field, often with a keen eye toward the interactions of diaspora Hindus and American metaphysicals, as discussed in my own work. In her book *Transcendent in America* (2010), Lola Williamson analyzes three contemporary guru-led movements (Self-Realization Fellowship, Transcendental Meditation, and Siddha Yoga) in her provocative call to categorize such innovative structures of Hindu religiosity as Hindu-Inspired Meditation Movements (HIMMs). Similarly, Corrine Dempsey brings the diaspora into focus with her brilliantly successful ethnography in her account of a goddess temple and its charismatic temple priest in the United States with *The Goddess Lives in Upstate New York* (2006). Carl Jackson's *Vedanta for the West* (1994) proves a formidable resource for the institutional and theological legacies of Ramakrishna, Swami Vivekananda, and the Vedanta Society in shaping contemporary Hindu religiosity in the United States. E. Burke Rochford's significant engagement with ISKCON in the United States represents an outstanding and lasting contribution to the field, as exemplified in both *Hare Krishna in America* (1985) and *Hare Krishna Transformed* (2007). In many ways Rochford's ethnographic sociological approach succeeds with such equipoise because of his clarity on his relationship to the field, as a scholar among devotees for more than thirty years. While many authors have contributed to the corpus of work on ISKCON, J. Stillson Judah's classic, *Hare Krishna and the Counterculture* (1975), Steven Gelberg's *Hare Krishna, Hare Krishna* (1983), and Larry Shinn's *The Dark Lord* (1987) deserve particular mention as well.

Much of the literature summarized thus far attempts to investigate contemporary gurus, their organizations, and their devotees with a critical, yet relatively considerate, lens. In general, these authors aim to carefully investigate the contemporary phenomenon of transnational gurus with an analytical and often sympathetic gaze. Their aims are not explicitly, a priori, directed toward critique, in the sense of exposé.

However, there is a broad spectrum of intentions behind investigations into gurus and their organizations for which critical examination is their exclusive aim, and some have offered meaningful and insightful critiques. Srinivas Aravamudan's detailed analysis of the metalinguistics of the guru in *Guru English* (2005) suggests that where the *baboo* (of effeminate Bengali infamy) fails, the cosmopolitan guru succeeds.[11] He rightly accosts contemporary gurus for reenacting orientalist essentialisms in an effort to proselytize their messages to global audiences, speaking as patriarchal authorities despite their frequent claims of androgyny and representing advaita vedantic universalisms as the whole Hindu religion. In his seminal work *The Karma of Brown Folk* (2000), Vijay Prashad crafts a convincing argument that effectively lambasts the outrageous proportions of commodification and product placement as evidenced in contemporary celebrity gurus, such as Deepak Chopra. Lise McKean's book *Divine Enterprise* (1996) chastises the juxtaposition of religion, politics, and commodification among North Indian gurus in Rishikesh, but ultimately one wonders if such confluences are in any sense problematic or unusual beyond the fact that they offend the author's preferences toward romanticized, pure, and otherworldly articulations of religion. Other works are less scholastic in nature but still emphasize the attempted revelation of fraudulent enterprise and unconstrained authoritarian structures at the heart of guru-led communities; many of these texts are infamous for their scathing indictments of contemporary gurus, such as Kramer and Alstad's *The Guru Papers* (1993).

The study of contemporary guru movements, like the study of new religious movements, is fraught with the complications of the relationship of the scholar to the field. Some works effectively operate as scholar-practitioner narratives, such as John Allen Grimes's recent philosophical approach in his work *Ramana Maharshi* (2012). But, more generally, tensions are particularly heightened in fledgling guru movements that are often highly proselytizing as well as quite protectionist, aggressively guarding their boundaries from persecution and exposés from outside critics. Devotees fill the field of publications with glowing positive accounts, while ex-devotees do the same with their scathing critiques. As Eileen Barker reveals, the role of the isolated researcher acting within such contested discursive spaces is fraught with "loneliness, psychological and emotional discomfort, and the intellectual uncertainties of research." She rightly contends that very few scholars make it for the long haul occupying such a liminal position; many sway to one direction or the other, alternately joining the critics or the devout.[12] In surveying the field of the academic study of gurus, it appears that it is acutely susceptible to scholar-practitioners who blur the boundaries between the scholarship *about* and the scholarship *of* religion. Perhaps this represents the magnetism of the charismatic nature of the guru, which pulls otherwise academic scholars into his or her fold, or, more likely, it represents the continued ambiguity in the field of religious studies wherein the lines between practitioner and scholar are routinely violated, a practice that continues to threaten to eclipse the social scientific credibility of the field.

I find this tension not only in my knowledge of publications and scholars' relationship to them but also in the routinely posed question from fellow academics, sometimes boldly accusatory and sometimes furtively seeking solidarity, as if sharing a desperate secret: Are you a devotee? As a result of this dilemma, much of the scholarship of the guru field, much like the scholarship of new religious movements, is composed of hagiographical and supportive members or vitriolic and jaded ex-members. Only a minority percentage of the active voices in the field attempt to occupy liminal positions between these two polarities, though surely there are many that I have unwittingly omitted in this brief review. With that said, the aforementioned titles have joined this burgeoning field, and I hope that mine has also made some small contribution to the spaces in between.

Notes

INTRODUCTION

1. Canan 2004, 19.

2. *Darshan* is the act of seeing and being seen by God in Hindu traditions. Most commonly, the term is used when Hindus view (and are viewed by) the divine in the form of sacred objects, spaces, and people. See Eck 1998.

3. Some who arrive *very* late into the program may find that darshan tokens are no longer being distributed. At this point latecomers are invited to stay for the next program instead. Occasionally local volunteers and other devotees attempt to assist in securing tokens for the latecomers. In most circumstances when attendees secure tokens despite all odds, they attribute it to "Amma's grace."

4. Hindu traditions support multiple paths for asceticism, meaning the renunciation of the material world. Like other Hindu ascetics, Amma's swamis have taken vows that signify their initiation into a lifestyle of celibacy, poverty, discipline, and devotion. Their distinctive dress (in this case the traditional ocher robe) specially marks them as renunciates.

5. *Brahmacārī/iṇīs* are disciples of Amma, the majority of whom are celibate renunciates. The most novice wear white (sawar kamiz, saris, kurta pajamas, and kurta/dhotis), while the more senior wear yellow. They are subordinate to the swamis (also celibate renunciates who wear ocher, all of whom are subordinate to Amma.

6. See "Social Welfare Activities," http://www.amritapuri.org/activity/social, accessed May 28, 2012.

7. See "Disaster Relief and Rehabilitation," http://www.amritapuri.org /activity/disaster, accessed May 28, 2012.

8. In 2012, Amma did not include Coralville, Iowa, on her summer tour schedule, but she reinstated it in 2013.

9. See also Khandelwal 2004; Menon 2010; Bacchetta 2002; Hallstrom 1999; Sarkar 2001.

10. Although "Ammachi" was once her distinctive moniker, used predominantly both within and outside of her movement, the contemporary ashram now prefers "Amma."

11. Hodder 1988, 137.

12. From *The Letters of Ralph Waldo Emerson*, quoted in Hodder 1988, 134.

13. Gaustad and Barlow 2001, 270.

14. The fascinating story of the development of facets of Hindu religiosity in the United States has been iterated time and again by multiple authors. Instead of reiterating this history beyond the cursory summation offered here, I invite readers to read the following works: Pechilis 2004; Forsthoefel and Humes 2005; Aravamudan 2005; Kurien 2007; Williamson 2010; Huffer (Lucia) 2010; Vertovec 2000; Goldberg 2010.

15. Pechilis 2004, "Introduction," 3–50.

16. Ghurye 1964; Gross 1979; Olivelle 1992; Oman 1905.

17. *Brahmanical* refers to a class of people in Indic society, *brahmans*. Brahman men have transmitted and maintained vedic knowledge and fulfilled priestly responsibilities for Hindus from antiquity to the present. Over the centuries, brahmanical authorities guaranteed that orthodox Hindu scriptures were transcribed, interpreted, communicated, taught, and performed internally (and often with careful secrecy) within and among privileged classes of brahman men. See Flood 1996.

18. *Nāradaparivrājaka Upaniṣad*, v. 196–97, 156, 160; *Yājñavalkya Upaniṣad*, v. 315–16; *Bṛhat-Saṃnyāsa Upaniṣad*, v. 270; cited in Olivelle 1992, 76–78.

19. Denton 2004, 58.

20. Hausner and Khandelwal 2006, 25.

21. See Khandelwal 2009; DeNapoli 2009; Banerjee 2005; Pechilis 2004; Bacchetta 2002, 2004; Khandelwal, Hausner, and Gold 2006; Chitgopekar 2002; Erndl 1993; Pintchman and Sherma 2011; Humes and McDermott 2009; Hiltebeitel and Erndl 2000; Charpentier 2010; Sarkar 2001.

22. "[I]f constructed gender is all there is, then there appears to be no 'outside,' no epistemic anchor in a precultural 'before' that might serve as an alternative epistemic point of departure for a critical assessment of existing gender relations" (see Butler 1999, 51).

23. Ibid., 23, emphasis in original.

24. Copeman and Ikegame 2012b.

25. *Nyāya Mañjari*, introduction, verse 8, cited in Pollock 1985, 515.

26. Warrier 2005, 142.

27. Ibid., 18, emphasis in original.

28. Ibid., 142.

29. Ibid., 1.

30. See Sangari and Vaid 1990; Chaudhuri 2004; Gangoli 2007; Gedalof 1999.

31. See Peskowitz, in Castelli 2001; Sered 1994; also see the postmodern scholars of gender who have repeatedly argued for the constructivist position that womanhood, femininity, and even the idea of being of the female sex are not inherent in female bodies (and, by extension, female goddesses) but, rather, ideals and characteristics marked as feminine are posited there through social discourse and action. See, most foundationally, Foucault 1990; Butler 1999; see Haraway, in Castelli 2001, for a concise history of the construction of gender as a category and its corollary disciplinary field.

32. See Purkayastha, Subramaniam, Desai, and Bose 2003; also see Dehejia 1999.

33. See Christ 1997; Anderson and Hopkins 1991; Noble 1991; Amazzone 2010. For a detailed ethnography on the women's spirituality movement that produces much of this genre of argumentation, see Eller 1993.

34. Like every democratically inspired charismatic religious movement, the authoritarian leaders of such congregations stand in tension with their own ideologies. See, for instance, Hatch 1989.

35. Geertz 1973, 7.

36. Ibid., 9.

37. Ricoeur 1984.

38. Jackson 1990.

39. Burowoy 1991, 280–81.

40. Appadurai 1996, 196.

41. Marcus 1995, 96.

42. The darshan programs I attended were as follows: 2004: Chicago, 1; 2005: Chicago, 1; 2006: San Ramon, 14 (including retreat), Boston, 8 (including retreat), Chicago, 4; 2007: Dearborn, 8 (including retreat), Chicago, 4; 2008: San Ramon, 8, Coralville, 4, Boston, 8 (including retreat), Chicago, 4; 2009: Amritapuri, 1, Coralville, 2, Chicago, 6; 2010: Chicago, 6; 2011: Dallas, 1, Coralville, 2, Chicago, 4; 2012: Chicago, 8; 2013: Los Angeles, 1, Chicago, 5—an approximate total of 100 darshan programs.

43. Armed with stopwatches, timekeeper sevā coordinators are charged with assigning devotees with the task of monitoring the one-minute shifts of prasad assistants and prasad assistant assistants.

44. Darshan line front (DLF) sevā entails offering attendees tissues to wipe from their faces sweat and makeup, asking their primary language, and asking the number of people in their party with whom they wish to take darshan. The DLF assistant then relays this information to Amma's immediate attendees, who coordinate the darshan line and ensure that devotees have the appropriate translators on hand if necessary.

45. The Devī Bhāva stage monitor ensures that after attendees have had darshan they are invited to spend some time sitting on the stage with Amma. They are also charged with coordinating the movement of those who wish to receive mantras, ensuring that they connect with mantra coordinators and proceed in the proper line to accept their mantra from Amma.

46. In 2009 I asked Amma if I could interview her for this project. She declined, saying that I could find what I needed for my research within her published materials. But she invited me to interview Br. Dayamrita and informed

him of her request, likely because he is the director of the North American ash-rams and satsangs.

47. Peña 2011, 3.

48. Perec 1989, 1990.

49. Renato Rosaldo, cited in Clifford 1997, 56.

CHAPTER 1

1. As discussed, *darshan* is the act of seeing and being seen by God in Hindu traditions. In Amma's movement, free-to-the-public programs during which Amma embraces all attendees present are colloquially called "darshan programs" and the sanctuary in which Amma "gives darshan" is called the "darshan hall."

2. See "Ammachi," http://jasonbeckerguitar.com/jasons_words.html, accessed April 4, 2012.

3. Some critics of Amma focus particularly on the "infantilizing" aspects of her movement. While the mother and child relationship is particularly central to Amma's movement, their critiques are also applicable to most religious traditions wherein the devout are required to submit to a supernatural authority.

4. Modern interpreters often appropriately read such social hierarchies for power relations in terms of master/slave, domination/subordination, and the exploitation or infantilization of disciples for the benefit of the powerful (and sometimes rich, greedy, prideful and/or corrupt) guru. Even Ekalavya's famed narrative can be read in such a manner with a critique of his guru's (Drona's) ethically questionable demand.

5. Dozens of narrative examples emerged from my field research of devotees who first came to Amma after divorces, deaths, illnesses, rapes, violent victimization, or long periods of malaise, void, depression, and/or anxiety. While some devotees simply encountered Amma and "fell in love," the majority of devotees went searching for her (or a new religious influence more generally) because of some challenging event, negative emotion, or physical ailment.

6. Sociologist Dipankar Gupta suggests that we might compare these "god-men" to U.S. evangelicals, such as Billy Graham or Jerry Falwell (Gupta 2009, 260–61). While there is a fascinating parallel in modality here (Internet, TV, charismatic leadership, political involvement, and hypercelebrity status), I agree with Copeman and Ikegame that, like many comparative moves, this one can result in oversimplification (Copeman and Ikegame 2012b). Still, one can find strong resonances with the scholarly work of Susan Harding and Jonathan Walton, among others, as these hypergurus engage the American populace, taking a page from the historical tradition of Christian evangelism in the United States. See, in particular, Harding 2001 and Walton 2009.

7. Juergensmeyer 1991, 84.

8. Pinney 2004, 194.

9. Nabokov/Clark-Decès 2000, 9.

10. Fuller 1992, 73.

11. Babb 1986, 79.

12. Goodman 1998, 9.

13. Babb 1986, 78.

14. Srinivas 2010, 158.
15. Ibid., 167.
16. Ibid.
17. Pinney 2004, 9.
18. Srinivas 2008, 76.
19. Pinney 2004, 194.
20. Srinivas 2008, 76.
21. Ibid., 77.
22. The term *sevā* (selfless service) is used ubiquitously in Amma's movement. Those who perform sevā are colloquially called *sevites*, despite the linguistic loss of the long ā of sevā, contra Sanskrit grammatical rules.
23. Upon Amma's entrance, her swamis chant the second *śloka* of the *Kaivalya Upaniṣad*: "*na karmaṇā na prajayā dhanena tyāgenaike amṛtatvam ānaśuḥ*" ("Not by work, not by offspring, or wealth; only by renunciation does one reach life eternal" [2.2]). The second portion of this śloka, "*tyāgenaike amṛtatvam ānaśuḥ*," is also printed above a floating lotus flower and conch shell on the ashram logo (Radhakrishnan 1992, 927). This chant is also included as track 2 on the CD *Chants*, with the explanation "Chant welcoming Amma, taken from declaration of the Upanishads, which means 'Neither by ritual, nor by progeny, nor by riches but by renunciation alone one can attain immortality'" ("Chants," MA Center, 2004). Selva Raj notes that during the *pada puja* the *swamī/ṇīs* recite verses 157 and 87 of the *Guru Gītā*: "*vandehaṁ saccidānandaṁ bhāvātītaṁ jagatgurum / nityaṁ pūrṇaṁ nirākāraṁ nirguṇaṁ svātmasaṁsthitaṁ // saptasāgaraparyantaṁ tīrthasnānaphalaṁ tu yat / gurupādapayōvindōḥ sahasrāṁśena tatphalam //* ("I prostrate to the Universal Teacher, Who is Satchidananda [Pure Being-Knowledge-Absolute Bliss], Who is beyond all differences, Who is eternal, all-full, attributeless, formless and ever centered in the Self. / Whatever merit is acquired by one, through pilgrimages and from bathing in the Sacred Waters extending to the seven seas, cannot be equal to even one thousandth part of the merit derived from partaking the water with which the Guru's Feet are washed" [Amritaswarupananda 1994], cited in Raj, "Ammachi," in Pechilis 2004, 204).
24. During the summer tour of 2013, Amma requested that all audience members be seated in chairs. Tour staff members explained that Amma had three reasons for this new practice: 1) in Indian culture the guest is considered to be God and one should not make a guest sit on the floor, 2) Amma wishes all attendees to be comfortable, and 3) Amma wants to have a direct line of vision between her and her devotees from the raised stage.
25. In India, there are often separate darshan queues and/or seating arrangements for males and females as per cultural conventions.
26. Prakash 2004, 20.
27. Srinivas 2008, 307–17.
28. Emile Durkheim used the term *collective effervescence* to explain ecstatic communal revelry wherein collective experience leads to "such a state of exaltation" that a man [*sic*] "should no longer know himself." He continues, "Feeling possessed and led on by some sort of external power that makes him think and act differently than he normally does, he naturally feels he is no longer

himself. It seems to him that he has become a new being . . . . And because his companions feel transformed in the same way at the same moment . . . it is as if he was in reality transported into a special world entirely different from the one in which he ordinarily lives . . . the world of sacred things." Durkheim contends, "It is in these effervescent social milieux, and indeed from that very effervescence, that the religious idea seems to have been born." Durkheim 1995, 220.

29. Amma first began to give Hershey's kisses in 1987 during her initial U.S. tour and continues to do so. In India, Amma gives hard candies instead of Hershey's kisses because chocolate would melt in the high temperatures of her largely open-air darshan programs.

30. Willey 2010, 451–60.

31. Ibid.

32. Certainly only in the first darshan experience would a devotee be considered a stranger. While there are clear intimacies and even friendships between Amma and her long-standing devotees, nearly all devotees would claim that Amma showers unlimited affection and unconditional love on each person who approaches her for darshan.

33. For the "Free Hugs" video, see http://www.youtube.com/watch?v=vr3x_RRJdd4, accessed May 28, 2012. For more information on the "Free Hugs" campaign, see http://www.freehugscampaign.org, accessed October 30, 2009.

34. Foucault 1990, 1.

35. Sarah Kershaw, "For Teenagers, Hello Means 'How about a Hug?' " *New York Times*, May 27, 2009, http://www.nytimes.com/2009/05/28/style/28hugs.html, accessed October 30, 2009.

36. Douglas 2002, 178.

37. Willey 2010, 460.

38. Amritaswarupananda 1991b, 196.

39. Bynum 1998, 172. There are also specifically Keralan mythological inheritances regarding the licking and drinking of pus to cure smallpox. In the legend of Dārikavadham (the traditional Keralan theatrical performance of the goddess Bhagavati), Kali is cursed and then stricken with smallpox. For curing this smallpox, Ghaṇṭākarṇan (Kali's brother, born from Shiva's ear) licks Kali's entire body (but not her face). See Caldwell 1999, 20.

40. Amritaswarupananda 1991b, 197.

41. Frédérique Apffel, cited in Urban 2009, 55.

42. Raj, "Ammachi," in Pechilis 2004, 214.

43. Some travelers to Amritapuri have raised interesting critiques about how separate Indians and Westerners are at the ashram, noting their separate food, eating spaces, chores, dormitories, and so on. See, for example, Jenny Kleeman, "Amma, the Hugging Saint," *The Guardian*, October 23, 2008, http://www.guardian.co.uk/world/2008/oct/24/religion-india, accessed March 18, 2013. Maya Warrier also notes that "one of the most striking aspects of ashram life is the demarcation between its Western and Indian areas of operation. Besides the separate Foreign Office . . . and the separate Seva Desk, there is a separate Western canteen, a Western shop, separate dormitories for Western occupants and even separate (and faster-moving!) queues for Westerners when they await

their turn for the Mata's darshan . . . I noticed little or no interaction between the Mata's Western devotees and her Indian ones" (Warrier 2005, 130). In some caste conscious Hindu ashrams (for example, Anandamayi Ma's, see Hallstrom 1999) the intentional separation of Indians and Westerners derives from the orthodox Hindu belief that Westerners are *mlecchas* (foreigners) according to *śāstric* injunctions and should thus be considered as "untouchables" (the most impure and servile class of people). In such cases, Westerners are separated into distinct spaces so that they do not pollute the brahmanical purity of ashram kitchens, dining spaces, washrooms, and so on. However, this reasoning is not referenced in Amma's ashrams where caste restrictions are not enforced and the separation between Indians and Westerners appears to be more habituated convention than regulated policy.

44. Sri Devi, "Have You Given Prasad Yet?" http://www.ammaaustralia.org .au/Tour/Amma-Tour-2008/Amma_Tour2008_Stories.htm, accessed December 15, 2011.

45. I have met many people outside of Amma's devotional communities who vividly recounted their hug with Amma, despite that they characterized the experience with lackluster descriptions, such as "nice," "okay," and "like hugging my grandma," or they explicitly explained that they did not "feel anything."

46. As Amma says, "If carried on the head, spiritual knowledge is a burden; but the same knowledge is beautiful if brought into the heart." Notably, this often-iterated ideology serves the pragmatic function of minimizing the intellectual analysis of Amma's motivations and organizational intricacies. Common in the majority of guru movements, this type of recurring anti-intellectualist sentiment buttresses the stipulation that devotees should surrender to the guru, meaning that they should abide by the guru's wishes without question, understanding her to be greater or equal to God.

47. Noguchi 2003, 168.

48. "Amma singing bandalo," *eVoice of Amma, Amritavani*: 12, June 13, 2011, http://www.amritapuri.org/13003/11sr.aum, accessed July 6, 2011.

49. While my ethnographic research focused particularly on the North American context, much of this discussion of darshan and darshan in absentia applies globally to Amma's devotional communities. Amma's organization creates largely static structures for her darshan programs, which she reproduces in cities around the world. Each darshan program hosts the same format, order, items for sale, and services rendered for all of Amma's devotees, regardless of geographical location.

50. Benjamin 1969, 221.

51. Upadhyaya 2009, 32.

52. Raj "Ammachi," in Pechilis 2004, 215.

53. "Amma Doll," http://www.theammashop.org/books/children/dla.html, accessed May 28, 2012.

54. Copeman and Ikegame 2012b, 26.

55. Cornell 2001, 230, emphasis in original.

56. Doniger (O'Flaherty) 1986, 15.

57. Ibid., 17–18.

58. Swami Paramatmananda (Neal Rosner), cited in Upadhyaya 2009, 63.

59. Ramdya 2011.

60. Radha Hegde, "Digital Gurus, Online Classicism: Transnational Pursuits of Audible Authenticity," lecture presented at University of California, Riverside, February 1, 2012.

61. Gilmore and Pine 2007.

62. Baudrillard 1994.

63. Taylor 1994, 31.

64. Ibid., 25.

65. Appiah 1994, 162–63.

66. Kurien 2007, 215.

67. Oliver 2001.

68. Oliver's penchant for love as a relative quality of witnessing the relationship between the self and the other leaves her open to critique from other theorists who see no such connective tissue. See Markell 2003, 37.

69. Oliver 2001, 221.

CHAPTER 2

1. Amma's words, excerpted from Amritaswarupananda 1988, 195.

2. As discussed in chapter 1, *darshan* is the act of seeing and being seen by God in Hindu traditions. Most commonly, the term is used when Hindus view (and are viewed by) the divine in the form of sacred objects, spaces, and people. Amma innovates this traditional visual encounter by transforming darshan into an embrace. For more on darshan in Hindu religious contexts, see Eck 1998.

3. Program flier, Dearborn, Michigan, December 2, 2007.

4. McDaniel 1989, 231.

5. Hallstrom 1999, 91.

6. See Dimock and Stewart 1999; Haberman 2003; Olson 1990.

7. June McDaniel also notes the importance of the songs of Rāmprasād and the *Kathāmṛta* of Rāmakrishna Paramahaṃsa for Bengali Śakta devotees. See McDaniel 1989, 25.

8. Pechilis, "Introduction," in Pechilis 2004, 4.

9. For particular references to the *bhāvas* of these female gurus, see Anderson "Gauri Ma," in Pechilis 2004, 68; Hallstrom 1999 and "Anandamayi Ma," in Pechilis 2004, 87; McDaniel, "Jayashri Ma," in Pechilis 2004, 123–24.

10. Hallstrom 1999, 34.

11. Amma's words, excerpted from Amritaswarupananda 1988, 195.

12. Lincoln 1994, 4, emphasis in original.

13. Ibid., 10–11.

14. Haberman 2003, xxxvi–xlix.

15. "The term rasa originally meant 'sap,' 'juice,' or 'essence,' and by extension 'flavor,' 'taste,' and 'enjoyment.' It was used in the Upaniṣads to mean 'essence,' and is often associated with 'joy' (*ānanda*). . . . Although later aestheticians easily read their meaning back into these early Upaniṣadic texts, the concept of rasa inherited by Rūpa came out of the specific context of aesthetics, particularly out of reflections on the nature of dramatic experience." See Haberman 2003, xxxvi.

16. *Bhaktirasāmṛtasindhu* 1.3.6, Haberman 2003, 99.

17. With that said, nearly every one of the most ardent devotees that I encountered in Amma's movement believed her to be superhuman in some form (a goddess, an avatar, and so on). Br. Dayamrita's contention that Amma is foremost a guru probably derives from his understanding of the guru to be equal to or even higher than (G)od.

18. "Public Programs, Retreats and Devi Bhava," http://ammachi.tribe .net /thread/b7ee41d7-5dea-4211-88bf-1180e4614bde, posted May 16, 2008, accessed March 18, 2013.

19. Victoria Anisman Reiner, "Amma, the Hugging Saint," http://suite101 .com/article/amma-a18661, accessed March 18, 2013.

20. Moses Siregar III, "The Amma Story," www.gracefloweressences.com /amma.html, accessed March 18, 2013.

21. "Devi Bhava, Can It Be True?" http://ashramdiary.blogspot.com/2007 /04/devi-bhava-can-it-be-true.html, posted April 23, 2007, accessed March 18, 2013.

22. Swami Amritaswarupananda Puri published his personal accounts of these events as they occurred at Amritapuri. See Amritaswarupananda 1988, 138–39.

23. Ibid.

24. Ibid., 103.

25. Ibid., 143; Cornell 2001, 53.

26. Caldwell 1999, 242–43.

27. Amritaswarupananda 1988, 151; Cornell 2001, 70.

28. See McDaniel 1989; Erndl 1993; Caldwell 1999; Bloomer 2009.

29. However, it is important to note that not all women who exhibit goddess possession in India do so voluntarily. The Kumari Devi tradition (widespread in Nepal and Bengal and minimally present elsewhere in India) raises questions about female agency and self-determination. In this tradition, a virgin girl becomes a living goddess: she resides in the temple, dresses as the goddess, and is presented for worship to ardent devotees. The duration of her installation as the goddess varies: sometimes (more commonly in Nepal) she remains instantiated as the goddess until her first menses, while other times (more commonly in India) she is only temporarily instantiated as the goddess for special pujas and festivals, such as Navaratri. See Allen 1996 and Boulanger 2001, as well as the short film *Kumari: The Living Goddesses of Nepal*. Also, Satyajit Ray, in his film *Devi* (1960), adeptly portrayed one young girl's lack of agency when she is presumed to be a goddess incarnation.

30. McDaniel, "Jayashri Ma," in Pechilis 2004, 123.

31. *Bhagavad Gītā* 11: 9–12.

32. Caldwell 1999, 11.

33. Ibid., 24–25.

34. Brubaker 1978, cited in Caldwell 1999, 24.

35. See the documentary film of Amma's early years, *Vintage Scenes*, MA Math, 2004. For more on the fearsome aspects of Hindu goddesses in South India, see Caldwell 1999; Foulston 2002; Waghorne 2004; Mines 2005.

36. Amritaswarupananda 1998, 45. This sentiment bears a striking resemblance to the way in which Krishna terrifies and overwhelms Arjuna and his

mother when he reveals himself in his cosmic form (*viśvarūpa*). In both instances, Krishna grants a vision of his true self but soon returns to his more comforting and comprehendible human form. Krishna reveals himself to Arjuna in the eleventh chapter of the *Bhagavad Gītā* (see Miller 1986, 97–108) and to his mother in the *Bhagavata Purāṇa* (Doniger 1975, 218–21).

37. Amritaswarupananda 1988, 196.

38. Amritaswarupananda 1995, 95, emphasis added. See also Amritaswarupananda 1988, 138–39 and 1995, 93–107. But Amma's devotees still longed for Krishna bhāva. In compliance with their wishes, Amma performed it once a month until November 1985, when the last one took place at Amritapuri.

39. Amritaswarupananda 1991b, 8.

40. Joanne Punzo Waghorne discusses a similar process of "bourgeoisification" of goddess temples in Chennai, as they shift from blood-sacrifice-accepting, fierce village goddesses to gentrified, sanctified, and beautified representations of benevolent goddesses in ordered public spaces that are welcoming and suited to the urban middle classes. See Waghorne 2004, 129–70.

41. Weber 1978, 1139.

42. During Devī Bhāva programs in Chicago in 2009, one long-term devotee (a middle-aged Indian Hindu man) had made special arrangements for his sevā to be covered by others because he really wanted to attend the Ātma puja. But that night, when he went to the ballroom entrance and saw all of the chairs arranged in accordance with the new policy, he "got a bad vibe" and decided not to participate. Additionally, many Indian Hindu devotees disagree with the new policy that allows devotees to wear their shoes in the darshan hall, particularly during the Ātma puja. Because this is a relatively new policy (2008), and one that goes against the grain of Hindu customs, there is still some confusion surrounding it. For example, often attendees are told that they can wear their shoes, but then someone else (either a misinformed sevite or bystander) will tell them to remove them (sometimes scornfully). The new shoes-on policy has been implemented to accommodate Westerners unfamiliar with Indian customs and hotel policies that require patrons to wear shoes.

43. Devī Bhāvas are special darshan programs that Amma performs in the same manner, with the same format, ritual structure, apparatus, and accoutrements in cities (outside of India) across the globe. The following generalized account relates the structure and form of Devī Bhāvas as I participated in them in the United States between 2004 and 2013 (approximately twenty Devī Bhāva darshan programs in Chicago, San Ramon, Boston, Iowa, Dallas and Los Angeles).

44. Many devotees have told me stories of the healing properties of Ātma puja water; many scramble to obtain as much of it as possible, preserving it carefully in their bags or water bottles for later use.

45. Amma designed this guided meditation, but Swami Amritaswarupananda performs it in the United States because of his fluency in English. In Kerala, Amma herself leads this guided meditation in Malayalam. An ardent devotee at Amritapuri told me that Amma is currently learning other Indian languages so that she can perform it herself throughout India. A recording of Swami Amritaswarupananda's meditation is available for purchase in the bookstore at the

back of the darshan hall. It is a guided meditation that focuses on envisioning Amma as the Divine Mother (though at the outset he suggests that devotees should meditate on the form of the Divine with which they feel most comfortable). Much of it centers on the intake of breath with the cosmic sound "Oṁ" and the release of breath with the sound "Mā."

46. All meditations and spiritual talks close with the following Sanskrit prayers: "*asato mā sadgamaya / tamaso mā jyotirgamaya / mṛtyormāmṛtaṁ gamaya / oṁ śāntiḥ śāntiḥ śāntiḥ*" (Oṁ, lead us from untruth to truth, from darkness to light, from death to immortality, Oṁ peace, peace, peace). (The first three lines of this prayer are taken from the *Bṛhadāraṇyaka Upaniṣad* 1.3.28.) This prayer is usually followed by "*lokāḥ samastāḥ sukhino bhavantū / lokāḥ samastāḥ sukhino bhavantū / lokāḥ samastāḥ sukhino bhavantū / oṁ śāntiḥ śāntiḥ śāntiḥ / oṁ śrī gurubhyo namaḥ hariḥ oṁ*" (Oṁ let the whole world be happy / Oṁ peace, peace, peace / Oṁ praise to the Supreme Guru). Amma places great importance in the *śloka: lokāḥ samastāḥ sukhino bhavantū* (let the whole world be happy / may all beings in the world be happy). It appears repeatedly on her material goods (T-shirts and so on), and during her birthday celebrations in 2003 (*Amritavarsham50*, which took place in Kochi) she led the audience of 100,000 people in repeating it continually for more than forty-five minutes.

47. It is of interest that the current ashram (as directed by Amma) granted illustrations permissions, but refused photos of Amma in Devī Bhāva to be used for publication in this book. Interested readers can find the ubiquitous image of Amma in Devī Bhāva for sale at her public darshan programs, ashrams, satsang locations, and at the online Amma shop (www.theammashop.org), as well as with any search engine on the Internet.

48. As a maternal ascetic, Amma wears her hair tightly pulled back into a low bun. In contrast, during the brief moments when she chants to the goddess prior to Devī Bhāva, her hair flows loosely to her waist. Then, as Devī, Amma's hair still flows loosely but is tied back into a low ponytail. Patrick Olivelle aptly synthesizes the existing contributions to the analysis of hair and asceticism in religious traditions. His conclusions suggest that tightly drawn or shaved hair tends to signify celibacy and renunciation, whereas loose hair symbolizes sexuality and matted hair extra-social status. Thus if we were prone to such symbolic judgments, we might read Amma's loose hair during Devī Bhāva as a sign of her transition to a sexualized goddess as opposed to her maternal ascetic persona with pulled-back hair (Olivelle 1998, 203–8). With that said, as an all-encompassing deity, Devī embodies both sexual and ascetic impulses; she is known as consort and mother as well as *nitya-kanyā* (the eternal virgin).

49. Amritanandamayi 1994a, 178.

50. These three rituals are the primary life-cycle rituals that Amma performs regularly. However, during Devī Bhāva, she also has performed the *upanayana* (sacred thread) rites. Though the upanayana rites are traditionally reserved for brahman boys, Amma performs them for both boys and girls (of all castes), in response to parents' requests. Also, in Europe, Amma performs baptisms for infants, though she has not expanded this practice to her tours in the United States.

51. As at her regular darshan programs, Amma takes no rest during the lengthy Devī Bhāva programs. She does not sleep, use the restroom, or eat any food. Occasionally she will drink a bit of a yogurt shake or water. After witnessing approximately one hundred darshan programs, I have only seen her leave the darshan seat once while the programs were under way.

52. These are saris that Amma has worn during previous Devī Bhāva programs. They are all gold-brocaded silk saris that devotees believe to be infused with the spiritual power of Amma and the Devī Bhāva darshan program. They are sold at Amma's darshan programs and can cost anywhere from $500–$1,000. I spoke with one couple who wanted to have Amma marry them, but they found it to be cost prohibitive because of the suggested donation and the expenses of the Devī Bhāva sari, *kurta pajama*, flower garlands, and so on.

53. In the traditional Hindu context, the groom is not required to bow to the bride. Amma emphasizes in her marriage ceremony this unusual momentary subordination of the groom to the bride, sometimes even by lightly pushing the groom's head down further, which often incites chuckling from Indian Hindu family members.

54. On annual Guru Purnima celebrations there is a formal *pada puja* that the swamis perform for Amma. Although it occurs at variously scheduled times, sometimes it occurs after these life-cycle rituals. This lengthier pada puja involves recitations from the *Guru Gītā* and the anointing of Amma's feet with the five nectars: milk, sugar, honey, clarified butter [ghee], and yogurt.

55. The repeating refrain from this bhajan is *"Amma Amma Tāye, Akhilāndeśvarī Nīye Annapūrṇeśvari Tāye, Oh Ādi Parā Śakti Nīye"* (O Mother, Mother dear Divine Mother, Goddess of the Universe, Giver of food to all creatures. Thou art the Primal Supreme Power). Translation cited from the insert of the bhajan CD "Amma Remembrance: Celebrating 15 Years of Blessings in the United States" (San Ramon, CA: MA Center, 2002).

56. In fact, the brahmacārī/iṇīs began this process hours ago. Usually all sales cease at around 4 a.m. and the brahmacārī/iṇīs who are responsible begin to pack everything into boxes to load on two semitrucks. These trucks follow Amma's entourage to the next city on the tour. The brahmacārī/iṇīs do as much packing as they can until the program is officially over and then break down the stage and sell the remainder of the perishable food and prasad items.

57. Amritaswarupananda 1988, 196–97.

58. Bourdieu 1984, 253–54.

59. See "Mahisasura Mardini—Hymn on the Divine Mother: Slayer of Demons," http://www.nandhi.com/mahisasura_mardini.htm, accessed May 28, 2012. In 2003, Karunamayi Ma also published a chanting booklet of the *Mahiṣāsura Mardini Stotram*, though I have never heard it recited during her darshan programs (Karunamayi 2003).

60. The archana book is a small pocket-sized Sanskrit prayer booklet currently available with translations in English, Malayalam, Hindi, Tamil, and Telugu. See Mata Amritanandamayi Math 2008.

61. There are two primary renditions of the *Guru Gītā* in circulation, a short version containing 182 verses and a longer version containing 352 verses. The verse that Amma's devotees use closely replicates verse 32 of the short version

and verse 58 of the longer version; it matches neither of those exactly because it replaces "*eva*" with "*sākṣat*" in the third *pada*. Amma's version reads: "*gururbrahma gurur viṣṇuḥ, gururdevo maheśvaraḥ, guruḥ sākṣat paraṁbrahma, tasmai Śrīgurave namaḥ.*" For more information on the *Guru Gītā* see Rigopoulos 2005.

62. The verses listed in the archana book are the popular "peace mantras" used widely in advaita vedantic and yogic circles, often attributed to the *Iśavasya Upaniṣad*. The verses attributed to the *Iśavasya Upaniṣad* included in Amma's archana book are as follows: *oṁ saha nāvavatu saha nau bhunaktu, saha vīryaṁ kara vāvahai, tejasvi nāvadhītamastu mā vidviṣa vahai, oṁ śāntiḥ, śāntiḥ, śāntiḥ; oṁ sarvesam* [sic] *svastirbhavatu, sarveśām śāntirbhavatu, sarveśām pūrnambhavatu, sarveśām mangalambhavatu, oṁ śāntiḥ, śāntiḥ, śāntiḥ; oṁ pūrnamadaḥ pūrnamidaṁ, pūrnāt pūrnamudacyate, pūrnasya pūrnamādāya, pūrnam-eva-vaśiṣyate, oṁ śāntiḥ, śāntiḥ, śāntiḥ* (Oh Lord, protect us as one, nourish us Lord, as one. Let us flourish in Thy strength as one. Let our knowledge, O Lord, be changed to Light and change our hate to love. Om peace, peace, peace. May perfection prevail on all; may peace prevail on all; may contentment prevail on all; may auspiciousness prevail on all. Om peace, peace, peace. That is the whole, this is the whole; from the whole, the whole becomes manifest; taking away the whole from the whole, the whole remains. Om peace, peace, peace).

63. The most recent edition of the archana book also includes chapters fifteen and eighteen of the *Bhagavad Gītā*.

64. Although the *Śrī Lalitā Aṣṭottara Śata Nāmāvali* (*The 108 Names of Devī* [*Lalitā*]) is chanted during Devī Bhāvas, its translations are not projected for the audience, as they respond in unison with "Oṁ Parāśaktyai namaḥ."

65. Integrated Amrita Meditation is Amma's patented meditation technique for which there are routine trainings and refresher workshops held at darshan programs and hosted by local satsangs throughout the year. See http://www.iam-meditation.org, accessed April 8, 2013.

66. Śankara's commentary on the *Cāndogya Upaniṣad* 1.1.10, cited in Pollock 2006, 570.

67. Often told by Amma in her public discourses, this story can also be found in Amritanandamayi 2006, 52.

68. Amritanandamayi 1997, 199.

69. The terms *inheritor* and *adopter* will be explained and examined in detail in chapter 4.

70. Br. Brahmamrita Chaitanya, "Introduction," in Menon et al. 1996, xxiv.

71. Pashman 2013.

72. In making this assessment, I should note that it goes against the grain of Amma's message, which actively protests any sort of sectarian religious classification.

73. Authorship of the *Saundaryalaharī* and the *Lalitāsahasranāma* is commonly attributed to the advaita vedantic philosopher Śankara, particularly among those indigenous to the tradition. However, L. M. Joshi (Joshi 1998), borrowing heavily from Dr. B. Datta, argues convincingly that the *Lalitāsahasranāma* is more likely authored by a Śankarācārya or a competent Śankarācārya follower from Kanci in the eleventh and twelfth centuries.

74. Brooks 1992, xv.
75. Flood 1996, 184–85.
76. Ibid., 188.
77. Ibid., 187.
78. Brooks 1992, 73.
79. Ibid., 65.
80. This brief summary is based on a much lengthier and detailed account in Brooks 1992, 68–69.
81. Ibid., 70–71. Brooks's translations of both *kāma* and *bhakti* as love signify a significant slippage in terminology. Kāma is better translated as desire and bhakti as devotion. While both of these ideas may derive from love (though not necessarily kāma), it is fairly reductionistic to conflate all of these terms in this manner. Still, Brooks's interpretation is pertinent because it demonstrates the theological propensity to conflate these terms, a philosophical reductionism that Amma also enacts.
82. Amritaswarupananda 1995, 95.
83. See McDermott 1993.
84. Raj, "Ammachi," in Pechilis 2004, 216, emphasis in original.
85. Amma's words, excerpted in Amritaswarupananda 1988, 195. Notably, the Bengali saint Anandamayi Ma also frequently referred to herself in the third person as "this crazy girl." See Hallstrom 1999.
86. "Amma as Kali, Lalithambika," http://www.indiadivine.org/audarya /ammachi/220084-amma-kali-lalithambika.html, accessed May 28, 2012.
87. Brooks 1992, 60.
88. This is a common theological move in Hinduism, in which each sect (*sampradāya*) subsumes and subordinates other deities in the Hindu pantheon to their primary deity: for Vaiṣṇava bhaktas Shiva becomes subordinate to Krishna, and vice versa for Śaivites. In this case, in South Indian Śrī Vidyā theology, all other forms of the goddess, including Kali, are subsumed by the supreme goddess Lalitā.
89. As discussed previously, Amma has retained Kali's predominance more in Kerala than she has on her tours in the United States. However, Amma's darshan programs share a fixed liturgy and presentation, and her organizational emphasis and the public recitation of the *Śrī Lalitā Sahasranāmāvali* are consistently enacted with the same modality in India and abroad.
90. See Scott 1985.
91. "Amma as Kali, Lalithambika," http://www.indiadivine.org/audarya /ammachi/220084-amma-kali-lalithambika.html, accessed May 28, 2012.

CHAPTER 3

1. Amritanandamayi 2011, 28.
2. *Darshan* is the act of seeing and being seen by God in Hindu traditions. Most commonly, the term is used when Hindus view (and are viewed by) the divine in the form of sacred objects, spaces, and people. See Eck 1998. Like many contemporary global gurus, Amma hosts darshan programs for the general public and her devotees. However, Amma's darshan events differ in that she

innovates the traditional visual act of darshan into an embrace. Usually Amma dresses in a simple white sari during darshan programs, but outside of India she dresses as the goddess during special programs called *Devī Bhāvas*. See chapters 1 and 2 for discussions of darshan and Devī Bhāvas, respectively.

3. See Narayanan, "Deities and Devotees," in Pechilis 2004, 150.

4. Beauvoir 2010, 267, emphasis in original.

5. Ibid., 408.

6. Scott 1999, 2, emphasis in original.

7. Gedalof 1999, 13–14.

8. Butler 1999, 201, emphasis in original.

9. Butler 1999.

10. Foucault 1990, 155.

11. Paoletti 2012.

12. DiPrete and Buchmann 2006; U.S. Government GAO Report, "Women's Earnings," 2003, http://usgovinfo.about.com/cs/censusstatistic/a/womenspay.htm, accessed January 23, 2012.

13. While this study focuses on Amma's North American devotees, both Indian Hindu devotees living in the United States and Amma's tour staff of brahmacārī/iṇīs who grew up in the United States and now travel with Amma exist in transnational spaces. Indian Hindus tack largely between India and the United States, building lives in each of these spaces and maintaining contact (via Skype, e-mail, and the Internet) with their families and loved ones in both geographical locations. The U.S. citizens who tour with Amma live at Amritapuri for extended periods while maintaining communication with family and loved ones around the world through similar media outlets. In opposition, Amma's non-Indian and nontouring North American devotees do not exist in transnational spaces but identify with India, Hindu religiosity, and Amma as a global persona and as such develop what we might identify as a "transnational imaginaire." It is for this reason that Amma develops her discourses into what Srinivas Aravamudan calls "Guru English," a cosmopolitan rhetoric that can simultaneously appeal to Indic, Western, and transnational audiences. See Aravamudan 2005.

14. Gangoli 2007, 7.

15. For further relevant information on the diverse voices within Indian feminism, particularly with regard to women and Hindu religion, see Sangari and Vaid 1990; Chaudhuri 2004; Chitgopekar 2002; Lama 2001; Kishwar 2001, 2004; Purkayastha et al. 2003; Sarkar and Butalia 1995.

16. Talwar 1990.

17. Flood 2005, 76.

18. See also Khandelwal 2004; Denton 2004; Khandelwal, Hausner, and Gold 2005; Hallstrom 1999; Pechilis 2004.

19. Khandelwal 2004, 192.

20. Ibid., 201.

21. Denton 2004.

22. DeNapoli 2009, 863–65; also see Khandelwal 2004.

23. The motif of a symbolic maternal religious leader who imagines herself as a mother to her devotee children recurs frequently in female-dominant religions.

In the American context, Ann Lee, the eighteenth-century founder of the Shaker community, provides one the most famous examples of such a formulation. See Sered 1994, 75–76.

24. Khandelwal 2004, 192.

25. McDaniel 1992, 36, cited in Pechilis 2004, 8, and Khanna 2000.

26. Altekar 1959, 101.

27. Ibid., 186.

28. Flood 2005, 9.

29. Thurman 1998, 109–10.

30. See Chatterjee 1993; Sarkar 2001; Ramaswamy 2010; Menon 2010.

31. Bedi 2006, 64; Banerjee 2005.

32. Khandelwal 2004; Ojha 1981, 280.

33. Banerjee 2005; Bacchetta 2004.

34. This brief summation of Amma's positions derives from her public speeches given during evening darshan programs, which I recorded in field notes between 2004 and 2013. Of the approximately one hundred darshan programs that I attended, roughly two-thirds were evening programs wherein Amma gave public addresses. Amma's position on gender, "women's empowerment," and "universal motherhood" also courses throughout her published writings and speeches, but it is highlighted in Amritanandamayi 1995, 1997, 2002, 2003, 2004, 2005, 2007, 2008, and 2013, and particularly emphasized in Amritanandamayi 2003 and 2008.

35. Amritanandamayi 2008, 24–25.

36. These educational institutions accept both male and female students without discrimination. They include: Amrita University, AIMS College of Medicine, AIMS College of Pharmacy (ACPS), AIMS College of Nursing, Amrita Institute of Computer Technology (AICT), Amrita Institute of Advanced Computing (AIAC), Amrita Institute of Management (AIM), Amrita Institute of Technology and Science (AITEC), Amrita Software Training Center (ASTC), M.A.M.T. Industrial Training Center, and Primary and Secondary Education (Amrita Vidhyalayam). See "Humanitarian Activities—Educational," http://www.ammachi.org/humanitarian-activities/educational/index.html, accessed May 29, 2012.

37. See "Embracing the World—Empowering Women," http://www.embracingtheworld.org/what-we-do/empowering-women, accessed May 29, 2012.

38. *Stories from the Field*, Disk 2, Chapter 3, Embracing the World.

39. *Stories from the Field*, Disk 1, Chapter 1, Embracing the World.

40. *Stories from the Field*, Disk 3, Chapter 2, Embracing the World.

41. This commonplace parable of Śankara and the *cāṇḍāla* (the son of a śudra and a brahman woman, the most despised of all persons in orthodox Hinduism) can be found in Isayeva 1993, 81.

42. It is notable that in 2013 at the Chicago programs, Padmavati conducted the homa again despite that Br. Shantamrita was not only present, but also the host as the new resident administrator of the Chicago ashram.

43. Narayanan 2005.

44. I am grateful to Amritrashmi [Maribel] for her conversational candor in discussing with me these matters.

45. Amritanandamayi 1995, 9–12.

46. The tract is published in English for wide circulation, but also appears in Malayalam and many other languages (Indian and European). The terms in question are largely Sanskrit terms that are left untranslated in the English edition. In Sanskrit, the masculine form of any noun referring to a group can include a minority of female members. In some Indic vernaculars, it is also common practice to refer to women honorifically with masculine pronouns and nouns.

47. Amritanandamayi 2003, 40–41.

48. Patton 2005.

49. Narayanan 2005, 4.

50. Apte 2000.

51. Radhika 2002; Daliwal 2001; Warty 2009.

52. Sabnis 2011.

53. Warty 2009. Sabnis reports that Arya Joshi, the coordinator at Dnyana Prabodhini, claims that they have "trained over 1,000 women priests since 1990." See Sabnis 2011.

54. Sabnis 2011.

55. Daliwal 2001.

56. Warty 2009.

57. Female priests have also developed their services in diaspora as well, but for largely different reasons. Shashi Tandon, a respected female elder in the Hindu community, and Neelima Shukla-Bhatt, a South Asian studies professor at Wellesley College, have both conducted ritual services as needed for their communities primarily because of a shortage of male priests. Despite the occasional mocking of their pretenses toward ritual authority, the Hindu communities in the United States largely and gratefully accept female ritual authority as a functional necessity as men have been drawn to "enter more lucrative, secular professions." See Ramirez 2008.

58. Amritanandamayi 1995, 11–12.

59. Hatch 1989, 9–11, my emphasis.

60. Weber 1978, 1117.

61. Bell 1997, 210.

62. Pollock 1985, 515.

63. *Nyāya Mañjari*, introduction, verse 8, cited in Pollock 1985, 515.

64. Ramaswamy 1992, 138.

65. Srivastava 1993, 91; also available in English translation, Srivastava 1995.

66. Narayanan 2005, 9.

67. Ellwood 1979, 19.

68. Hobsbawm and Ranger 1983.

69. GDS, XVIII.1; VāsDS, verses 1–2; BDS, II.3.44–45, cited in Jamison 1996, 15. Also see Doniger and Smith 1991.

70. *Mām hi pārtha vyapāśritya ye 'pi syuḥ pāpayonayaḥ striyo vāiśyās tathā śudrās te 'pi yānti parāṃ gatim.* Sargeant 1984, 408.

71. *Strī śūdra dvijabandhūnāṃ trayī na śruti gocarā karma śreyasi mūḍhānāṃ śreya evaṃ bhaved iha iti bhāratam ākhyānaṃ kṛpayā muninā kṛtam*, Venkatesananda 1989, 5. Prabhupada's translation, though imbued with International

Society for Krishna Consciousness style passion for Krishna, explicitly defines "those unable to learn and recite the Veda," explaining: "Out of compassion, the great sage [Vyāsa] thought it wise that this would enable men to achieve the ultimate goal of life. Thus he compiled the great historical narration called the *Māhabhārata* for women, laborers [*śudras*] and friends of the twice-born." See "*Srimad Bhagavatam*, 1.4.25," Prabhupada 1962.

72. SP (*Somaśanbhupaddhati* of Somaśambhu), 3.1.9, cited in Davis 1991, 40.

73. See Jamison 1996.

74. Ramaswamy 1992, 144–45.

75. There are minor sporadic unconventionalities to Amma's homas, for example, donation offerings can be made in suggested amounts of $50, $108, $200, and so on, whereas in a more conventional homa donation amounts are usually given or requested in noneven figures ($51, $201, etc.). Also, Amma's homas and pujas involve a significant quantity of rose petals, which are offered to feet, murtis, the fire altar, and so on. The rose holds a particular significance in Amma's movement; it is much less important (or even absent) in more conventional pujas and homas, though it is sometimes used nonexclusively in garlands (*mālās*) and puja offerings. The particularities of Amma's homas are difficult to discern because Amma's pūjārī/iṇīs explain that they perform the South Indian tantric tradition of offering mantras during homas silently (internally), and the ritual methods are also shrouded in secrecy, shared only among ritual officiants. Note that while lesser rituals (pada puja, arati, and so on) are educational and democratic, the vedic homas are still reserved for an elite class of trained priests (men and women, Indian and non-Indian). Outside observers are not educated in the intricacies of the ritual, but lay participants are paying customers who receive limited instruction and act according to the instructions of the priests.

76. Amma's words, excerpted from Amritaswarupananda 1988, 195.

77. Amritanandamayi 2003, 33, 2008, 32.

78. Amritanandamayi 2003, 43.

79. Ibid., 49.

80. Amritanandamayi, "I Am Love, the Embodiment of Love," Amma's birthday message 1995, Amritanandamayi 2007, 70.

81. Amritanandamayi 2003, 45.

82. Amritanandamayi 2003, 44.

83. It is somewhat unclear here exactly to whom Amma is referring with this critique. In my judgment, she is critiquing a diffused trope of Western feminism circulating in India. I suggest that we might locate this tendency to encourage women to become like men in the first generations of women who often were forced to accentuate their masculinity in order to compete in heretofore exclusively male arenas, which is closely related to second-wave feminism in the West. I have not seen any evidence that Amma is engaging with any specific feminist figures, writers, or political positions in issuing this critique.

84. Amritaswarupananda 1995, 14–15.

85. Amritanandamayi 2003, 41–42, 50, 57.

86. In Premchand's classic novel *Godaan* (*The Gift of a Cow*), first published in 1936, one of the central characters, Mr. Mehta, gives a vibrant speech to the Women's League wherein he invokes existing cultural paradigms to define ideal behaviors for Hindu women and to chastise those who violate such norms. He depicts modern Indian Hindu women as physical embodiments of goddesses who possess the supposedly feminine qualities of love, sacrifice, sympathy, and devotion. Women exist in "sacred temples of child-bearing and family rearing," which are their "sacred duties." He admonishes the largely female audience at the Women's League regarding adopting male characteristics and behaviors, which have only "destructive tendencies," demonstrated by their "ungodly" actions that are "crushing," "trampling," "burning," and "desolating" our world. See Premchand 2002, 197–99.

87. Amritanandamayi 2003, 38.

88. Ibid., 49.

89. Ibid., 49–50.

90. Amritanandamayi 2013.

91. Reacting to the Delhi rape of December 2012, Asaram Bapu responded "A mistake is not committed from one side." ("*Galti ek taraf se nahi hoti hai.*") He also proclaimed that if the victim would have been chanting her Saraswati mantra she would not have entered the bus and that once attacked she should have "taken God's name and could have held the hand of one of the men and said I consider you as my brother and should have said to the other two 'Brother I am helpless, you are my brother, my religious brother.' Then the misconduct wouldn't have happened." Nelson 2013. Notably, Asaram Bapu's comments incited public and social media fury to which he responded with criticism for the media, arguing that his remarks had been misconstrued.

92. See Eller 1993.

93. Ochshorn 1997, 377–405.

94. See Butler 1999, 173.

95. Pierre Bourdieu coined the term *habitus*. He defines habitus as follows: "The conditionings associated with a particular class of conditions of existence produce *habitus*, systems of durable, transposable dispositions, structured structures predisposed to function as structuring structures, that is, as principles which generate and organize practices and representations that can be objectively adapted to their outcomes without presupposing a conscious aiming at ends or an express mastery of the operations necessary in order to attain them. Objectively 'regulated' and 'regular' without being in any way the product of obedience to rules, they can be collectively orchestrated without being the product of the organizing action of a conductor." See Bourdieu 1990, 53.

96. Khandelwal 2004. See also the fascinating examples of the biologically male gurus Sri Bangaru Adigalar of Melmaruvathur and Sri Narayani Amma. Both are known by the shortened title, "Amma," and both claim to be human incarnations of the goddess. See http://www.sakthiolhi.org, and http://www.narayanipeedam.org, respectively, accessed December 1, 2012. For a similar account of a male, Pankaru Atikalar, who is viewed as a modern incarnation of the goddess Mariyamman, see Harman 2004.

97. Khandelwal 2004, 190–91.
98. Amritaswarupananda 1995, 14–15.
99. See Bhattacharyya 1996.
100. Humes 2009, 315.
101. Amritanandamayi 2008, 29.
102. Doniger 2010; Caldwell 1999.
103. Humes 2009, 321.

CHAPTER 4

1. Canan 2004, 17.
2. See also Huffer (Lucia) 2011.
3. Though it is not as common, Sikh, Muslim, Jewish, Christian, and Rasta-farian devotees incorporate their devotion to Amma into their faith in these es-tablished religious traditions. Devotees who do so often subscribe to liberal in-terpretations of their faith and somehow reconcile them with their devotion to Amma. Theological conceptions of universalism and perennialism often assist these devotees in this reconciliatory process. However, many theological and practical differences remain unreconciled; many devotees come to see Amma for darshan while maintaining their involvement in religions that would not ap-prove of their doing so. Rather than being anomalous, these types of contradic-tions in behavior and ideology characterize much of human life, which is often resistant to classification.
4. *Darshan* is the act of seeing and being seen by God in Hindu traditions. Most commonly, the term is used when Hindus view (and are viewed by) the divine in the form of sacred objects, spaces, and people. See Eck 1998. Like many contemporary global gurus, Amma hosts darshan programs for the gen-eral public and her devotees. However, Amma's darshan events differ in that she innovates the traditional visual act of darshan into an embrace. Usually Amma dresses in a simple white sari during darshan programs, but outside of India she dresses as the goddess during special programs called *Devī Bhāvas*. See chapters 1 and 2 for discussions of darshan and Devī Bhāvas, respectively.
5. Weber 1991, 47.
6. Nattier 1997, 72–81.
7. See also Prothero 1996; Pike 2006; Cadge 2005; Goldberg 2010; William-son 2010.
8. Writing of material religion, David Morgan explains, "As an object moves from one person to the next, from one social setting or one culture to the next, it acquires different values and associations, negotiating differences and carry-ing with it veneers of significance that will tell us much about what objects do . . . it is more productive to study the response to objects as they are displayed, ex-changed, destroyed, and circulated in order to determine what they mean to people, that is to say, how they build and maintain lifeworlds." See Morgan, "The Materiality of Cultural Construction," in Dudley 2012, 101–2.
9. Appadurai 1996, 32.
10. See also Pintak 2001.

11. Kurien 2007; Warner and Wittner 1998; Cadge 2005; Tweed 2002; Orsi 2010.

12. Iwamura 2011; Lee 1999; Briggs 1988; Thomas 1991.

13. See also Unger 2000.

14. Stone 2007. Statistical figures are provided by the South Asian American Research and Policy Institute. Also see Pew Research Center 2012a.

15. See Butler 1992; Albanese 2008; Bender 2010.

16. Albanese 2008.

17. Ibid., 509–10.

18. Kripal 2008.

19. Pew Research Center 2012b.

20. Miller 2009, 70.

21. Ibid.

22. Carrette and King 2005, 123.

23. Bender 2010, 23.

24. Lévi-Strauss 1968, 16–38.

25. Eller 1993, 41.

26. In November 2006, at the ashram in San Ramon, California, the demographics were approximately 45 percent men and 55 percent women, and 20 percent Indian and 80 percent non-Indian.

27. Binkley 2007.

28. Srivastava 2011.

29. Maloney and Schumer 2010.

30. Allard 2011.

31. Humes 2009, 321.

32. This is a pattern quite common in many communally oriented new religious movements, wherein the charismatic leader is envisioned as a parental figure and fellow devotees are considered siblings. See Daschke and Ashcraft 2005, 139–204.

33. See Kripal 2008.

34. Cornell 2001, 171.

35. Ibid., 172–79.

36. Amritanandamayi 2012.

37. Durkheim 1995, 320–21.

38. Ibid., 320.

39. Ibid., 316.

40. See Caldwell 1999.

41. See Burton 1994.

42. "*London se chalkar āyī, ye Āngrezī Devī Maiyā / Computer-wālī Maiyā, hai Āngrezī Devī Maiyā / Hum sabki devī maiyā, jan-jan kī Devī Maiyā.*" Anand 2010.

43. See also Lewis 1971; Boddy 1989.

44. Erndl 1993, 109.

45. Nabokov/Clark-Decès 2000, 24.

46. There are some Catholic cultural contexts in which Marian devotion exalts the Virgin as the primary object of worship and reverence, nearly eclipsing

the role of God, the Father. But even within such communities, arguably Mary nevertheless officially serves as a mediatrix between God and humanity, interceding on behalf of devotees precisely because she is subordinate to God who is envisioned as male.

47. Although it is beyond the scope of this inquiry, one can also see the mimetic relationship in place in popular Christian Evangelical campaigns such as What Would Jesus Do? (WWJD) that developed from early twentieth century Christian socialism. See Sheldon 2013 and Rauschenbusch 1917. In Catholicism the laity has often been encouraged to imitate the exemplary behavior of both Jesus Christ and the Virgin Mary, see Kempis 2003 and 2005.

CHAPTER 5

1. Anonymous comment defending Amma, submitted on April 17, 2007, http://guruphiliac.blogspot.com/2007/04/ammas-sex-scandal.html, accessed August 15, 2013.

2. Vivekananda, "My Master," vol. 4, *Lectures and Discourses*, 2003.

3. Amma's words, in Amritaswarupananda 1991a, 117.

4. As discussed in chapter 1, *darshan* is the act of seeing and being seen by God in Hindu traditions. Most commonly, the term is used when Hindus view (and are viewed by) the divine in the form of sacred objects, spaces, and people. Amma innovates this traditional visual encounter by transforming darshan into an embrace. For more on darshan in Hindu religious contexts, see Eck 1998.

5. Warner and Wittner 1998.

6. Amma's devotees also interact while living or staying in her ashrams. Amma's North American ashrams currently include San Ramon, California (San Francisco); Redondo Beach, California (Los Angeles); Santa Fe, New Mexico; Homestead, Iowa (Iowa City); La Fox, Illinois (Chicago); Dearborn, Michigan (Detroit); Potomac, Maryland (Washington, DC); Boylston, Massachusetts (Boston); and Georgetown, Ontario (Toronto, Canada). Several of these ashrams were purchased as part of Amma's initiative to develop centers in the United States in the past five years. They are usually stand-alone buildings with acreage in the exurbs of major urban cities. Amma's North American headquarters, the San Ramon ashram, hosts five to ten full-time residents, whereas the remaining ashrams host one to three residents, if any at all. This book focuses on the general population of Amma devotees who retain their positions in society. Still, many American devotees aspire to (or actually do) visit or live in (or near) one of Amma's ashrams. Many American devotees also visit Amma's primary ashram headquarters, Amritapuri, in Kerala.

7. Emerson 2006, 5.

8. While this claim is broader than my particular focus here, my research suggests Amma's movement is not an isolated case in this regard and more general pervasive patterns of de facto congregationalism persist among new religious movements and Asian religions in the United States. Denominational fragmentation coupled with congregational homogenization becomes particularly exacerbated as metaphysicals adopt religious practices, but not the ethnic-

cultural identity of an Asian religious group thus creating divides between what have been termed previously as *white Buddhists/Asian Buddhists* or *white Hindus/Indian Hindus*. See for example Warner and Wittner 1998; Prothero 1996; Cadge 2005; Albanese 2008; Williamson 2010. Similar patterns may also emerge in other religious communities that attract and maintain significant adopter populations, such as African American Muslims or white Rastafarians.

9. Moore 1986, 208–9.

10. Gupta and Ferguson 1997.

11. See "Governor of Illinois Inaugurates MA Center Chicago," http://www .amritapuri.org/15272/12mac.aum, accessed March 9, 2013.

12. Amma followed a similar method in choosing the site for the Los Angeles ashram in Redondo Beach, California. There, devotees continue to provide intense hours of *sevā* (selfless service) in order to repair the purchased ashram site and make it available for public use. In contrast, however, the Washington, DC, ashram was nearly a "turnkey" operation when purchased.

13. See "Centers in the United States," http://www.amma.org/centers/united -states.html, accessed May 28, 2012.

14. As previously mentioned, I attended the majority of satsangs in Chicagoland between February 2006 and October 2008 (totaling 32 months). My reflections herein are based on my experiences during this period, as well as on my interviews and conversations with Amma devotees at her darshan programs (2004–2013). In addition to learning about Chicago satsangs, devotees also told me of their experiences with their local satsangs in New York, Portland (Oregon), Indianapolis, Atlanta, Santa Fe, Montreal, Toronto, Detroit, Boston, San Francisco, Dallas, Houston, and Los Angeles.

15. See also Kurien 2007.

16. See "Ayudh America: Youth In Action," http://ayudhamericas.blogspot .com; "Ayudh International," http://www.ayudh.eu, both accessed May 28, 2012.

17. See Heelas 1996.

18. Pike 2006, 74; see also Lasch 1991.

19. Bruce 2000, 180.

20. Recently, Amma's ashram has also produced consumer goods branded with this statement, including photos of Amma, superimposed on clothing items and ephemera (stickers, key chains, and so on). Notably this identity statement echoes Mohandas Gandhi's famous assertion of *dayā dharma* (the duty of compassion, which might also be translated as "the religion of love"). In *Hind Swaraj*, Gandhi cites Tulsidas, who said, "Of religion, pity, or love, is the root, as egotism of the body. Therefore, we should not abandon pity [*dayā*] so long as we are alive." (*Dayā* is better translated as *compassion* rather than *pity*.) Gandhi continues, "This appears to me to be a scientific truth. I believe in it as much as I believe in two and two being four. The force of love is the same as the force of the soul or truth." See Gandhi 1996, 69.

21. Heelas 1996, 219.

22. Many devotees freely seek the messages of a variety of gurus, but some experience a lurking guilt as a result of their attention to gurus other than

Amma. Several of these devotees recounted that when contemplating attending or actually attending other gurus' events (and presumably feeling some confusion or guilt), Amma communicated with them (in dreams and/or meditation) and assuaged their anxieties by reminding them of universalist theological maxims. Contrarily, many devotees are completely attached to Amma's physical form and view Amma alone as their chosen guru/God (*iṣṭadev*).

23. Heelas 1996, 28.

24. While early scholarship identified cults as deviant religious traditions, it did not necessarily intend the sociological terms *cult* and *deviant* to be used pejoratively. Stark, Bainbridge, and Doyle's (1979) distinction between the deviant religious tradition (cult) and the ethnic church signifies the division of the two groups—one that is deviating from its native religious tradition and one that is continuing it. Importantly, when the authors were writing, Asian "cults" were so new to America that all non-Asian members were necessarily converts. Today, some of these non-Asians have become inheritors because they grew up in communities of Asian religious movements and thus are raising their own children as they were raised. Of the non-Indian Hindus in Amma's movement, some young families are actively raising their children in the movement, but the parents are largely converts and thus adopters.

25. Stark, Bainbridge, and Doyle 1979.

26. The Day Creek satsang also began a book club based on Paloma's model, though it was not as consistently held or as regularly publicized.

27. Traditionally, in India, when a couple marries the woman goes to live with her husband's family. As a married couple they will then live with the husband's parents, paternal grandparents, and often the husband's brothers' nuclear families. Much has been written about the shift from joint family to nuclear family living arrangements that occurred in the latter half of the twentieth century in the wake of Partition (1947) and the passing of the Hindu Code Bill (1956). See Majumdar 2007, 223–40.

28. Br. Dayamrita is the primary disciple who is responsible for administrating the endeavors of Amma devotees in North America. He resides at Amma's primary ashram in San Ramon and travels to the largest satsangs around the country to give lectures and to offer a direct connection to Amma. In the spring of 2012, he began to reside part time at the new ashram in La Fox, Illinois, as well as at the MA Center in San Ramon. In the fall of 2012, he was replaced by Br. Shantamrita at the MACC and he returned to his duties at the MA Center in San Ramon.

29. Timothy Leary, speech given at a press conference, New York City, September 19, 1966, which he later developed into a book by the same title.

30. Eck 1990, 111–42.

31. Carrette and King 2005.

32. Heelas 1996, 202.

33. One website (notably an anti-Amma site) claims that, according to insiders' accounts, Amma's organization grosses $3 million during each of her summer U.S. tours. I find this to be a realistic estimate. In Bronte Baxter, "'Amma the Hugging Saint': Mother-Cult Leader, U.N. Globalist," http://

cultofhuggingsaintamma.wordpress.com, accessed October 12, 2009 (content no longer available).

34. Only one devotee has been asked not to return (because of his inappropriate behavior, that is, making sexual advances toward women and attempting to walk away with children). Notably he was banned from all Chicagoland satsangs at the request of numerous devotees and with the authority of the MA Center.

35. This should be recognized as modesty, characteristic of a *brahmacārī* rather than a statement of fact. In fact, one of Br. Dayamrita's primary duties as the director of the MA Center in San Ramon for the past five years has been to supervise and maintain close administrative interactions with all of the satsangs in North America.

36. Fanon 1986; Bhabha 2004.

37. Van der Veer 2001, 73.

38. Bhave 2000.

39. McKean 1996, xv, cited in Van der Veer 2001, 70.

40. Prashad 2000, 4.

41. Waghorne 2010.

42. Aravamudan 2005, 134–35.

43. The term *baboo* (sometimes *babu*) is a pejorative term that came into popular usage in the colonial period to reference the supposedly effeminate and dull-witted Bengali native who remained inferior despite his attempt to educate himself in English and clerical skills. The term *bhadralok* refers to a subset of the colonial Bengali citizenry who were educated and upper class. It also takes on a pejorative connotation as these classes of bhadralok are often read as being complacent in or even benefiting from British colonial rule. See Aravamudan 2005; Hatcher 2008.

44. Amma used to suggest that her devotees wear white clothing to her darshan programs as a symbol of mental purity. But in early 2011 (before the U.S. summer tour), she discontinued this practice and began to encourage her nonrenunciate devotees to wear color. She even insisted that some of the *mahasevites* who were accustomed to wearing white for years (and who were [mis]recognized by others as *brahmacārī/iṇīs* [celibate renunciates] because of their white clothing) begin to wear color if they were not truly celibate renunciates. This was a major shift in the culture of the movement, and no reason was ever given to the public. However, I had seen several critiques of the movement (mostly on individual blogs) that called the movement a "cult" or "cultish" and cited the appearance of all of the devotees in white as a sign of "brainwashing." This public image problem may have had something to do with the decision.

45. It is important to note that sari wearing is considered a skill and an art form that traditional Indian women master. Much like the kimono, it is a point of pride among many Indian women to be able to tie saris beautifully. Some modern Indian women relate saris to antiquated traditionalism in Indic culture. Many of these women prefer Western clothes and Punjabi suits and may not know how to wrap a sari. Some young Indian women also view wearing saris as a mark of an older tradition and an older generation.

46. Donaldson 2001, 237–56. Deepak Sarma recently expressed a similar position in his *Huffington Post* piece "White Hindu Converts: Mimicry or Mockery?" See Sarma 2012.

47. Herein, Handler is elaborating on the seventeenth-century English philosopher John Locke's labor theory of value. See Handler 1988, 153.

48. Macpherson 2011.

49. Handler 1988, 154.

50. John Lennon, "Imagine."

51. Goldberg 2010.

52. Eller 1993, 77.

53. For the term *global nomads*, see D'Andrea 2007.

54. On spiritual tourism in India, see also Strauss 2005; D'Andrea 2007; Norman 2011; Huberman 2012; Airault 2002.

55. Here I am thinking particularly of poorly tied saris, garbled Sanskrit on metaphysical ephemera, linguistically incoherent or irrelevant translations of Indic terms, and religious ritual behavior that violates Hindu norms (e.g., shoes on while doing puja) or demonstrates errors or mistaken understandings.

56. Goldstein 2003, 5.

57. Scott 1985, 33.

58. Most famous are the multiple lawsuits filed against ISKCON, the lawsuits against Ma Jaya Sati Bhagavati, and the criminal charges brought against Bhagvan Shree Rajneesh (Osho).

59. Although Amma's movement can certainly be viewed as expansionist, as Warrier (2005, 23–24) argues, it is a qualified expansionism that subsists largely without the proselytizing fervor and missionary activity evident in many other religious movements and traditions. For example, this type of default endogamy stands in contrast to Jacob Copeman's account of the "logic of expansion" of the Nirankaris who seek to "marry outside of the Mission in order to introduce their spouses to it." See Copeman 2009, 96.

60. Cited in Kurien 2007 and reported and discussed widely in *Hinduism Today* (July 1995) and the *India Post* (July 28, 1995).

61. Visweswaran et al. 2009.

62. King 1993, 27.

63. See http://religioninsights.org/articles/racial-diversity-increasing-us-congregations, accessed April 13, 2013.

64. It is of interest that in Chicago this reserved (and sometimes disdainful) view of adopters becomes wholly problematic during Amma's tours when Amma's tour staff (often international adopters), whose members supersede local inheritors in the institutional administrative hierarchy, attempts to direct, supervise, and control aspects of Amma's programs.

65. That is, assuming that those new Indian Hindu potential devotees exhibit a somewhat similar value system as the satsang community. Some Indian Hindus are not welcomed so readily into organizational leadership positions if they exhibit, for example, mental illness, aggressive behavior, or an ideology antithetical to Amma's movement.

CONCLUSION

1. Sridhar (Steven) Silberfein has been a devotee of Amma since the mid-1980s. He used to host her annual programs at his Center for Spiritual Studies in Topanga Canyon and even had the honor of driving Amma from the San Ramon ashram to Southern California in the initial years of her tours. He has been a significant presence in several *bhakti* communities in the United States and India. In 2009, he founded Shakti Fest and its larger counterpart Bhakti Fest, both of which have become major outposts in the transformational and yoga festival circuit. See www.bhaktifest.com, accessed July 29, 2013.

2. Kirtan performed by C. C. White, with spoken word written and performed by Shiva Rae. See C. C. White, *This IS Soul Kirtan*, Natural Flow Music/C. C. White (ASCAP), 2011, compact disc. See also www.soulkirtan.com, accessed May 16, 2012.

3. *Darshan* is the act of seeing and being seen by God in Hindu traditions. Most commonly, the term is used when Hindus view (and are viewed by) the divine in the form of sacred objects, spaces, and people. See Eck 1998. Like many contemporary global gurus, Amma hosts darshan programs for the general public and her devotees. However, Amma's darshan events differ in that she innovates the traditional visual act of darshan into an embrace. Usually Amma dresses in a simple white sari during darshan programs, but outside of India she dresses as the goddess during special programs called *Devī Bhāvas*. See chapters 1 and 2 for discussions of darshan and Devī Bhāvas, respectively.

4. See http://shivarae.com, accessed May 6, 2012.

5. The full *mahamantra* for ISKCON devotees is, "*Hare Krishna Hare Krishna, Krishna Krishna Hare Hare, Hare Rama Hare Rama, Rama Rama Hare Hare.*"

6. Noll 2002.

7. See Moore 1986.

8. Cited in Sinha 1995, 15–16.

9. Sugirtharajah 2003, 81.

10. Ibid.

11. This was also one of the aims of the colonial government. Recall T. B. Macaulay's "Minute on Indian Education" (1835) in which he encouraged the development of "a class of interpreters between us and the millions whom we govern—a class of persons Indian in blood and colour, but English in tastes, in opinions, in morals and in intellect" (cited in Bhabha 2004, 124–25).

12. See Jaffrelot 1998.

13. Lorilai Biernacki explains, "When the message of the Ramakrishna Mission came to America, however, it came in sanitized form. Excluding the messy idolatry of multiple deities, which were probably correctly deemed not palatable to the predominantly Protestant climate of turn-of-the-century America, the message of Ramakrishna was brought to America in Advaita Vedanta formlessness, not through the image of the wild, dark Kali, the Mother, that Ramakrishna communed with and adored his entire life, but rather as the transcendent attributeless *brahman*." See Biernacki, "Shree Ma of Kamakkhya," in Pechilis 2004, 195. See also Urban 2003b, 162.

14. Banerjee 2005, 61.

15. Quoted in Banerjee 2005, 59.

16. Ibid., 60.

17. Ibid., 72–73.

18. Markell 2003, 175.

19. Ibid.

20. Amritanandamayi 1994b; also see Vivekananda, "Addresses at the Parliament of Religions," vol. 1, 2003.

21. Fessenden 2006.

APPENDIX

1. Gold 1988, 16.

2. Weber 1978, 448.

3. Copeman and Ikegame 2012b, 5.

4. Gold 1988, 77.

5. Ibid., 88–89.

6. Narayanan, "Deities and Devotees," in Pechilis 2004, 150.

7. Waghorne 2010.

8. Copeman and Ikegame 2012b, 38.

9. *Nova Religio: The Journal of Alternative and Emergent Religions* 15, no. 2 (November 2011).

10. Warrier 2005, 142.

11. Aravamudan 2005, 134–35.

12. Barker 2003, 22.

Works Cited

Airault, Régis. 2002. *Fous de l'Inde: Délires d'Occidentaux et Sentiment Océanique*. Paris: Petite Bibliothèque Payot.

Albanese, Catherine L. 2008. *A Republic of Mind and Spirit: A Cultural History of American Metaphysical Religion*. New Haven, CT: Yale University Press.

Allard, Mary Dorinda. 2011. "Asians in the U.S. Labor Force: Profile of a Diverse Population." *Monthly Labor Review* (November). U.S. Bureau of Labor Statistics.

Allen, Michel. 1996. *The Cult of Kumari: Virgin Worship in Nepal*. Kathmandu: Mandala Book Point.

Altekar, A. S. 1959. *The Position of Women in Hindu Civilization*. Delhi: Motilal Banarsidass.

Amazzone, Laura. 2010. *Goddess Durgā and Sacred Female Power*. Lanham, MD: Hamilton Books.

Amritanandamayi, Mata. 1994a. *For My Children: Spiritual Teachings of Mata Amritanandamayi*. Amritapuri: Mata Amritanandamayi Mission Trust.

_____. 1994b. *May Your Hearts Blossom: Address to the Parliament of World Religions 1993, Chicago*. Amritapuri: Mata Amritanandamayi Mission Trust.

_____. 1995. *The Brahmasthanam: An Epoch-Making Temple*. Amritapuri: Mata Amritanandamayi Math.

_____. 1997. *Eternal Wisdom*. Vol. 1. Amritapuri: Mata Amritanandamayi Mission Trust.

_____. 2002. *Lead Us to the Light*. San Ramon, CA: Mata Amritanandamayi Center.

_____. 2003. *The Awakening of Universal Motherhood*. Amritapuri: Mata Amritanandamayi Mission Trust.

_____. 2004. *Man and Nature*. Amritapuri: Mata Amritanandamayi Mission Trust. Originally published (Amritapuri: Mata Amritanandamayi Mission Trust, 1994).

_____. 2005. *Eternal Wisdom*. Part 2. San Ramon, CA: Mata Amritanandamayi Center. Originally published (San Ramon, CA: Mata Amritanandamayi Center, 1999).

_____. 2006. *The Eternal Truth*. Amritapuri: Mata Amritanandamayi Mission Trust.

_____. 2007. *Lead Us to Purity: A Selection of Sri Mata Amritanandamayi's Speeches, 1990–1999*. Amritapuri: Mata Amritanandamayi Math.

_____. 2008. *The Infinite Potential of Women*. Address delivered at the Global Peace Initiative of Women, Jaipur, India. Amritapuri: Mata Amritanandamayi Mission Trust.

_____. 2011. *Being with Dying*. Amritapuri: Mata Amritanandamayi Mission Trust.

_____. 2012. "Coexistence and Engagement between Cultures." Speech addressing the United Nations Alliance of Civilizations (UNAOC) Regional Consultations for Asia-South Pacific, November 29–30, Shanghai, China. *Amritavani* 69. http://www.amritapuri.org/15989/12china.aum, accessed December 1, 2012.

_____. 2013. "Women, Break Your Shackles and Awaken." *The New Indian Express*. January 6. http://newindianexpress.com/lifestyle/spirituality/article 1407336.ece, accessed March 15, 2013.

Amritaswarupananda, Swami. 1988. *Mata Amritanandamayi: A Biography*. Kollam: Mata Amritanandamayi Mission Trust.

_____. 1991a. *Awaken Children! Dialogues with Sri Sri Mata Amritanandamayi*. Vol. 2. San Ramon, CA: Mata Amritanandamayi Center.

_____. 1991b. *Awaken Children! Dialogues with Sri Sri Mata Amritanandamayi*. Vol. 3. San Ramon, CA: Mata Amritanandamayi Center.

_____. 1994. *Awaken Children! Dialogues with Sri Sri Mata Amritanandamayi*. Vol. 6. San Ramon, CA: Mata Amritanandamayi Center.

_____. 1995. *Awaken Children! Dialogues with Sri Sri Mata Amritanandamayi*. Vol. 7. San Ramon, CA: Mata Amritanandamayi Center.

_____. 1998. *Awaken Children! Dialogues with Sri Sri Mata Amritanandamayi*. Vol. 9. San Ramon, CA: Mata Amritanandamayi Center.

Anand, S. 2010. "Jai Angrezi Devi Maiyya Ki." *OPEN Magazine*. May 8. http://www.openthemagazine.com/article/nation/jai-angrezi-devi-maiyya -ki, accessed May 6, 2012.

Anderson, Sherry Ruth, and Patricia Hopkins. 1991. *The Feminine Face of God: The Unfolding of the Sacred in Women*. New York: Bantam Books.

Appadurai, Arjun. 1996. *Modernity at Large: Cultural Dimensions of Globalization*. Minneapolis: University of Minneapolis Press.

Appiah, K. Anthony. 1994. "Identity, Authenticity, Survival: Multicultural Societies and Social Reproduction." In *Multiculturalism*, edited by Charles Taylor and Amy Gutmann, 149–164. Princeton, NJ: Princeton University Press.

Apte, Kanchan. 2000. "Womantra." *India Today*. May 1. http://archives.digi
taltoday.in/indiatoday/20000501/offtrack.html, accessed May 29, 2012.

Aravamudan, Srinivas. 2005. *Guru English: South Asian Religion in a Cosmopolitan Language*. Princeton, NJ: Princeton University Press.

Babb, Lawrence A. 1986. *Redemptive Encounters: Three Modern Styles in the
Hindu Tradition*. Berkeley: University of California Press.

Bacchetta, Paola. 2002. "Hindu Nationalist Women Imagine Spatialities/Imag-
ine Themselves: Reflections on Gender-Supplemental-Agency." In *Right-
Wing Women: From Conservatives to Extremists around the World*, edited
by Paola Bacchetta and Margaret Power, 43–56. New York: Routledge.

———. 2004. *Gender in the Hindu Nation*. New Delhi: Women Unlimited.

Banerjee, Sikata. 2005. *Make Me a Man! Masculinity, Hinduism, and Nationalism in India*. Albany: State University of New York Press.

Barker, Eileen. 2003. "The Scientific Study of Religion? You Must be Joking!"
In *Cults and New Religious Movements: A Reader*, edited by Lorne L. Daw-
son, 43–56. Hoboken, NJ: Wiley-Blackwell.

Barrett, Ron. 2008. *Aghor Medicine: Pollution, Death, and Healing in Northern
India*. Berkeley: University of California Press.

Baudrillard, Jean. 1994. *Simulacra and Simulation*. Translated by Sheila Faria
Glaser. Ann Arbor: University of Michigan Press.

Beauvoir, Simone de. 2010. *The Second Sex*. New York: Knopf. Originally published (Editions Gallimard: Paris, 1949).

Beckerlegge, Gwilym. 2000. *The Ramakrishna Mission: The Making of a Modern
Hindu Movement*. New Delhi: Oxford University Press.

———. 2006. *Swami Vivekananda's Legacy of Service: A Study of the Ramakrishna Math and Mission*. New Delhi: Oxford University Press.

Bedi, Tarini. 2006. "Feminist Theory and the Right-Wing: Shiv Sena Women Mobi-
lize Mumbai." *Journal of International Women's Studies* 7, no. 4 (May): 51–68.

Bell, Catherine. 1997. *Ritual: Perspectives and Dimensions*. New York: Oxford
University Press.

Bender, Courtney. 2010. *The New Metaphysicals: Spirituality and the American
Religious Imagination*. Chicago: University of Chicago Press.

Benjamin, Walter. 1969. "The Work of Art in the Age of Mechanical Reproduction."
In *Illuminations*, edited by Hannah Arendt, 217–52. New York: Schocken Books.

Bhabha, Homi. 2004. *The Location of Culture*. New York: Routledge.

Bhattacharyya, Narendra Nath. 1996. *History of the Śakta Religion*. New
Delhi: Munshiram Manoharlal.

Bhave, Onkar. 2000. "Sadhvi Shakti Parishad—The Background of the Ori-
gins." In *Mātṛmāhāśakti: A Commemorative Volume*, edited by the Sadhvi
Shakti Parishad, 9–10. New Delhi: Vishva Hindu Parishad.

Binkley, Sam. 2007. *Getting Loose: Lifestyle Consumption in the 1970s*. Durham, NC: Duke University Press.

Bloomer, Kristen. 2009. "Making Mary: Hinduism, Catholicism and Spirit Possession in Contemporary Tamil Nadu, South India." PhD diss., University of
Chicago.

Boddy, Janice. 1989. *Wombs and Alien Spirits: Women, Men, and the Zār Cult
in Northern Sudan*. Madison: University of Wisconsin Press.

Boulanger, Marie-Sophie. 2001. *Le Regard de la Kumari: Le Monde Secret des Enfants-Dieux du Népal*. Paris: Presses de la Renaissance.

Bourdieu, Pierre. 1984. *Distinction: A Social Critique of the Judgement of Taste*. Cambridge, MA: Harvard University Press.

———. 1990. *The Logic of Practice*. Stanford, CA: Stanford University Press.

Briggs, Asa. 1988. *Victorian Things*. Chicago: University of Chicago Press.

Brooks, Douglas Renfrew. 1992. *Auspicious Wisdom: The Texts and Traditions of Śrīvidyā Śākta Tantrism in South India*. Albany: State University of New York Press.

Bruce, Steve. 2000. *Choice and Religion: A Critique of Rational Choice Theory*. New York: Oxford University Press.

Burowoy, Michael, ed. 1991. *Ethnography Unbound: Power and Resistance in the Modern Metropolis*. Berkeley: University of California Press.

Burton, Antoinette. 1994. *Burdens of History: British Feminists, Indian Women, and Imperial Culture, 1865–1915*. Chapel Hill: University of North Carolina Press.

Butler, Jon. 1992. *Awash in a Sea of Faith: Christianizing the American People*. Cambridge, MA: Harvard University Press.

Butler, Judith. 1999. *Gender Trouble: Feminism and the Subversion of Identity*. New York: Routledge. Originally published (New York: Routledge, 1990).

Bynum, Caroline Walker. 1998. *Holy Feast and Holy Fast: The Religious Significance of Food to Medieval Women*. Berkeley: University of California Press.

Cadge, Wendy. 2005. *Heartwood: The First Generation of Theravada Buddhism in America*. Chicago: University of Chicago Press.

Caldwell, Sarah. 1999. *Oh Terrifying Mother: Sexuality, Violence and Worship of the Goddess Kālī*. Delhi: Oxford University Press.

Canan, Janine. 2004. *Messages from Amma: In the Language of the Heart*. Berkeley, CA: Celestial Arts.

Carrette, Jeremy, and Richard King. 2005. *Selling Spirituality: The Silent Takeover of Religion*. New York: Routledge.

Castelli, Elizabeth A., ed. 2001. *Women, Gender, Religion: A Reader*. New York: Palgrave.

Charpentier, Marie-Thérèse. 2010. *Indian Female Gurus in Contemporary Hinduism*. Åbo, Finland: Åbo Akademi University Press.

Chatterjee, Partha. 1993. *The Nation and Its Fragments: Colonial and Postcolonial Histories*. Princeton, NJ: Princeton University Press.

Chaudhuri, Maitrayee, ed. 2004. *Feminism in India*. London: Zed Books.

Chitgopekar, Nilima, ed. 2002. *Invoking Goddesses: Gender Politics in Indian Religion*. New Delhi: Shakti Books.

Christ, Carol P. 1997. *Rebirth of the Goddess: Finding Meaning in Feminist Spirituality*. Reading, MA: Addison-Wesley.

Clifford, James. 1997. *Routes: Travel and Translation in the Late Twentieth Century*. Cambridge: Harvard University Press.

Copeman, Jacob. 2009. *Veins of Devotion: Blood Donation and Religious Experience in North India*. New Brunswick, NJ: Rutgers University Press.

Copeman, Jacob, and Aya Ikegame. 2012a. "Guru Logics." *HAU: Journal of Ethnographic Theory* 2, no. 1: 289–336.

_____, eds. 2012b. *The Guru in South Asia: New Interdisciplinary Perspectives.* New York: Routledge.

Copley, Antony. 2000. *Gurus and Their Followers: New Religious Reform Movements in Colonial India.* New Delhi: Oxford University Press.

Cornell, Judith. 2001. *Amma: Healing the Heart of the World.* New York: HarperCollins.

Daliwal, Lovejit. 2001. "Hindu Women Spread the Word." *BBC News.* April 26.

D'Andrea, Anthony. 2007. *Global Nomads: Techno and New Age as Transnational Countercultures in Ibiza and Goa.* New York: Routledge.

Daschke, Dereck, and Michael Ashcraft. 2005. *New Religious Movements: A Documentary Reader.* New York: New York University Press.

Davis, Richard. 1991. *Worshipping Śiva in Medieval India.* Princeton, NJ: Princeton University Press.

Dehejia, Vidya. 1999. *Devi: The Great Goddess.* New Delhi: Mapin.

Dempsey, Corinne. 2006. *The Goddess Lives in Upstate New York: Breaking Convention and Making Home at a North American Hindu Temple.* New York: Oxford University Press.

DeNapoli, Antoinette. 2009. "Beyond Brahmanical Asceticism: Recent and Emerging Models of Female Hindu Asceticism in South Asia." *Religion Compass* 3, no. 5: 857–75.

Denton, Lynn Teskey. 2004. *Female Ascetics in Hinduism.* Albany: State University of New York Press.

Dimock, Edward C., and Tony K. Stewart, trans. 1999. *Caitanya Caritāmṛta of Kṛṣṇadāsa Kavirāja.* Cambridge, MA: Harvard University Press.

DiPrete, Thomas A., and Claudia Buchmann. 2006. "Gender Specific Trends in the Value of Education and the Emerging Gender Gap in College Completion." *Demography* 43: 1–24.

Donaldson, Laura E. 2001. "On Medicine Women and White Shame-ans." In *Women, Religion, Gender: A Reader,* edited by Rosamond C. Castelli, 237–56. New York: Palgrave.

Doniger (O'Flaherty), Wendy. 1975. *Hindu Myths: A Sourcebook Translated from the Sanskrit.* New York: Penguin Press.

_____. 1986. *Dreams, Illusion, and Other Realities.* Chicago: University of Chicago Press.

_____. 2010. *The Hindus: An Alternative History.* New York: Penguin Press.

Doniger (O'Flaherty), Wendy, and Brian K. Smith, trans. 1991. *The Laws of Manu.* New York: Penguin Books.

Douglas, Mary. 2002. *Purity and Danger: An Analysis of Concept of Pollution and Taboo.* New York: Routledge.

Dudley, Sandra H., ed. 2012. *Museum Objects: Experiencing the Properties of Things.* New York: Routledge.

Durkheim, Emile. 1995. *The Elementary Forms of Religious Life.* New York: The Free Press.

Eck, Diana. 1990. "'New Age' Hinduism in America." In *Conflicting Images: India and the United States,* edited by Sulochana Raghavan Glazer and Nathan Glazer, 111–42. Glen Dale, MD: Riverdale Publishers.

_____. 1998. *Darśan: Seeing the Divine Image in India.* New York: Columbia University Press.

Eller, Cynthia. 1993. *Living in the Lap of the Goddess: The Feminist Spirituality Movement in America.* New York: Crossroad.

Ellwood, Jr., Robert S. 1979. *Alternative Altars: Unconventional and Eastern Spirituality in America.* Chicago: University of Chicago Press.

Emerson, Michael O. 2006. *People of the Dream: Multiracial Congregations in the United States.* Princeton, NJ: Princeton University Press.

Erndl, Kathleen M. 1993. *Victory to Mother: The Hindu Goddess of Northwest India in Myth, Ritual, and Symbol.* New York: Oxford University Press.

Fanon, Frantz. 1986. *Black Skin, White Masks.* London: Pluto Press.

Fessenden, Tracy. 2006. *Culture and Redemption: Religion, the Secular, and American Literature.* Princeton, NJ: Princeton University Press.

Flood, Gavin. 1996. *An Introduction to Hinduism.* Cambridge: Cambridge University Press.

_____. 2005. *The Ascetic Self: Subjectivity, Memory and Tradition.* Cambridge: Cambridge University Press.

Forsthoefel, Thomas A., and Cynthia Ann Humes. 2005. *Gurus in America.* Albany: State University of New York Press.

Foucault, Michel. 1990. *The History of Sexuality: An Introduction.* Vol. 1. New York: Vintage Books. Originally published (New York: Random House, 1978).

Foulston, Lynn. 2002. *At the Feet of the Goddess: The Divine Feminine in Local Hindu Religion.* Portland, OR: Sussex Press.

Fuller, Christopher. 1992. *The Camphor Flame: Popular Hinduism and Society in India.* Princeton, NJ: Princeton University Press.

Gandhi, M. K. 1996. *Hind Swaraj or Indian Home Rule.* Ahmedabad: Navajivan Trust. Originally published (Ahmedabad: Navajivan Publishing House, 1938).

Gangoli, Geetanjali. 2007. *Indian Feminisms: Law, Patriarchies and Violence in India.* Hampshire, UK: Ashgate.

Gaustad, Edwin Scott, and Philip L. Barlow. 2001. *New Historical Atlas of Religion in America.* New York: Oxford University Press.

Gedalof, Irene. 1999. *Against Purity: Rethinking Identity with Western and Indian Feminisms.* London: Routledge.

Geertz, Clifford. 1973. *The Interpretation of Cultures.* New York: Basic Books.

Gelberg, Steven J. 1983. *Hare Krishna, Hare Krishna.* New York: Grove Press.

Ghurye, Govind Sadashiv. 1964. *Indian Sadhus.* Bombay: Popular Prakashan.

Gilmore, James H., and B. Joseph Pine. 2007. *Authenticity: What Consumers Really Want.* Cambridge, MA: Harvard Business School Press.

Gold, Daniel. 1987. *The Lord as Guru.* New York: Oxford University Press.

_____. 1988. *Comprehending the Guru: Toward a Grammar of Religious Perception.* Atlanta: Scholars Press.

Goldberg, Phillip. 2010. *American Veda: From Emerson and the Beatles to Yoga and Meditation: How Indian Spirituality Changed the West.* New York: Harmony Books.

Goldstein, Donna M. 2003. *Laughter Out of Place: Race, Class, Violence, and Sexuality in a Rio Shantytown.* Berkeley: University of California Press.

Goodman, Martin. 1998. *In Search of the Divine Mother: The Mystery of Mother Meera*. New York: HarperCollins.

Grimes, John Allen. 2012. *Ramana Maharshi: The Crown Jewel of Advaita*. Boulder, CO: Albion-Andalus Books.

Gross, Robert. 1979. "Hindu Asceticism: A Study of the Sadhus of North India." PhD diss., University of California, Berkeley.

Gupta, Akhil, and James Ferguson, eds. 1997. *Culture, Power, Place: Explorations of Critical Anthropology*. Durham, NC: Duke University Press.

Gupta, Dipankar. 2009. *The Caged Phoenix: Can India Fly?* New Delhi: Viking.

Haberman, David L., trans. 2003. *The Bhaktirasāmṛtasindhu of Rūpa Gosvāmin*. Delhi: Motilal Banarsidass.

Hallstrom, Lisa Lassell. 1999. *Mother of Bliss: Anandamayi Ma*. New York: Oxford University Press.

Handler, Richard. 1988. *Nationalism and the Politics of Culture in Quebec*. Madison: University of Wisconsin Press.

Harding, Susan. 2001. *The Book of Jerry Falwell: Fundamentalist Language and Politics*. Princeton, NJ: Princeton University Press.

Harman, William. 2004. "Taming the Fever Goddess—Transforming a Tradition in Southern India." *Manushi: A Journal about Women and Society* 140 (January–February): 2–16.

Hatch, Nathan. 1989. *The Democratization of American Christianity*. New Haven, CT: Yale University Press.

Hatcher, Brian A. 2008. *Bourgeois Hinduism, Or the Faith of the Modern Vedantists: Rare Discourses from Early Colonial Bengal*. New York: Oxford University Press.

Hausner, Sondra L., and Meena Khandelwal. 2006. "Introduction." In *Women's Renunciation in South Asia: Nuns, Yoginis, Saints, and Singers*, edited by Meena Khandelwal, Sondra L. Hausner, and Ann Grodzins Gold, 1–36. New York: Palgrave Macmillan.

Heelas, Paul. 1996. *The New Age Movement: Religion, Culture and Society in the Age of Postmodernity*. Oxford: Wiley-Blackwell.

Hiltebeitel, Alf, and Kathleen M. Erndl, eds. 2000. *Is the Goddess a Feminist: The Politics of South Asian Goddesses*. New York: New York University Press.

Hobsbawm, Eric, and Terence Ranger, eds. 1983. *The Invention of Tradition*. Cambridge: Cambridge University Press.

Hodder, Alan D. 1988. "Emerson, Rammohan Roy, and the Unitarians." In *Studies in the American Renaissance*, edited by Joel A. Myerson, 133–48. Charlottesville: University of Virginia Press.

Huberman, Jenny. 2012. *Ambivalent Encounters: Childhood, Tourism and Social Change in Banaras, India*. New Brunswick, NJ: Rutgers University Press.

Huffer (Lucia), Amanda. 2010. "Darshan in a Hotel Ballroom: Amritanandamayi Ma's (Amma's) Communities of Devotees in the United States." PhD diss., University of Chicago.

⸻. 2011. "Backdoor Hinduism: A Recoding in the Language of Spirituality." *Nidān: International Journal for the Study of Hinduism* 23 (December): 53–71.

Humes, Cynthia Ann. 2009. "The Power of Creation." In *Breaking Boundaries with the Goddess*, edited by Cynthia Ann Humes and Rachel Fell McDermott, 297–333. New Delhi: Manohar.

Humes, Cynthia Ann, and Rachel Fell McDermott, eds. 2009. *Breaking Boundaries with the Goddess*. New Delhi: Manohar.

Isayeva, Natalia. 1993. *Shankara and Indian Philosophy*. Albany: State University of New York Press.

Iwamura, Jane. 2011. *Virtual Orientalism: Asian Religions and American Popular Culture*. New York: Oxford University Press.

Jackson, Carl T. 1994. *Vedanta for the West: The Ramakrishna Movement in the United States*. Bloomington: Indiana University Press.

Jackson, Jean E. 1990. "I Am a Fieldnote: Fieldnotes as a Symbol of Professional Identity." In *Fieldnotes: The Makings of Anthropology*, edited by Roger Sanjek, 3–33. Ithaca, NY: Cornell University Press.

Jaffrelot, Christophe. 1998. *The Hindu Nationalist Movement in India*. New York: Columbia University Press.

Jamison, Stephanie W. 1996. *Sacrificed Wife/Sacrificer's Wife: Women, Ritual, and Hospitality in Ancient India*. New York: Oxford University Press.

Joshi, L. M. 1998. *Lalitā-Sahasranāma: A Comprehensive Study of One Thousand Names of Lalitā Mahā-tripurasundarī*. New Delhi: D.K. Printworld.

Judah, J. Stillson. 1975. *Hare Krishna and the Counterculture*. Hoboken, NJ: John Wiley and Sons.

Juergensmeyer, Mark. 1991. *Radhasoami Reality: The Logic of a Modern Faith*. Princeton, NJ: Princeton University Press.

Karunamayi Vijayeswari Devi, Sri. 2003. *Sri Mahishasura Mardini Stotram*. Oak Brook, IL: Sri Matrudevi Viswashanti Ashram Trust/SMVA Trust.

Kempis, Thomas. 2003. *The Imitation of Christ*. Translated by Aloysius Croft and Harold Bolton. New York: Dover.

———. 2005. *The Imitation of Mary*. Translated by Matthew J. O'Connell. Edition and Introduction by Romolo Sbrocchi. New Jersey: The Catholic Book Publishing Corp.

Kershaw, Sarah. 2009. "For Teenagers, Hello Means 'How about a Hug?'" *New York Times*, May 27.

Khandelwal, Meena. 2004. *Women in Ochre Robes: Gendering Hindu Renunciation*. Albany: State University of New York Press.

———. 2009. "Research on Hindu Women's Renunciation Today: State of the Field." *Religion Compass* 3, no. 6: 1003–14.

Khandelwal, Meena, Sondra L. Hausner, and Ann Grodzins Gold. 2006. *Women's Renunciation in South Asia: Nuns, Yoginis, Saints, and Singers*. New York: Palgrave Macmillan.

Khanna, Madhu. 2000. "The Goddess-Women Equation in Śakta Tantras." In *Faces of the Feminine in Ancient, Medieval, and Modern India*, edited by Mandakranta Bose, 109–23. New York: Oxford University Press.

King, Coretta Scott. 1993. *Martin Luther King Jr. Companion*. New York: St. Martin's Press.

King, Ursula. 1984. "The Effect of Social Change on Religious Self-Understanding: Women Ascetics in Modern Hinduism." In *Changing South*

Asia, edited by K. Ballhatchet and D. Taylor, 69–83. London: School of Oriental and African Studies.

Kishwar, Madhu. 2001. "Yes to Sita, No to Ram." In *Questioning Ramayanas: A South Asian Tradition*, edited by Paula Richman, 285–308. Berkeley: University of California Press.

_____. 2004. "A Horror of 'Isms': Why I Do Not Call Myself a Feminist." In *Feminism in India*, edited by Maitrayee Chaudhuri, 26–51. London: Zed Books.

Kleeman, Jenny. 2008. "Amma, the Hugging Saint." *The Guardian*. October 23. http://www.guardian.co.uk/world/2008/oct/24/religion-india, accessed March 18, 2013.

Kramer, Joel, and Diana Alstad. 1993. *The Guru Papers: Masks of Authoritarian Power*. Berkeley, CA: Frog Books.

Kripal, Jeffrey J. 1995. *Kali's Child: The Mystical and the Erotic in the Life and Teachings of Ramakrishna*. Chicago: University of Chicago Press.

_____. 2008. *Esalen: America and the Religion of No Religion*. Chicago: University of Chicago Press.

Kurien, Prema A. 2007. *A Place at the Multicultural Table: The Development of an American Hinduism*. New Brunswick, NJ: Rutgers University Press.

Lama, Stephanie Tawa. 2001. "The Hindu Goddess and Women's Political Representation in South Asia: Symbolic Resource or Feminine Mystique?" *Revue Internationale de Sociologie* 11, no. 1: 5–20.

Lasch, Christopher. 1991. *The Culture of Narcissism: American Life in an Age of Diminishing Expectations*. New York: W.W. Norton & Co.

Lee, Robert G. 1999. *Orientals: Asian Americans in Popular Culture*. Philadelphia: Temple University Press.

Lévi-Strauss, Claude. 1968. *The Savage Mind (Nature of Human Society)*. Chicago: University of Chicago Press.

Lewis, I. M. 1971. *Ecstatic Religion: A Study of Shamanism and Spirit Possession*. New York: Routledge.

Lincoln, Bruce. 1994. *Authority: Construction and Corrosion*. Chicago: University of Chicago Press.

Macpherson, C. B. 2011. *The Political Theory of Possessive Individualism: Hobbes to Locke*. New York: Oxford University Press. Originally published (New York: Oxford University Press, 1962).

Majumdar, Rochona. 2007. "Family Values in Transition." In *From the Colonial to the Postcolonial*, edited by Dipesh Chakrabarty, Rochona Majumdar, and Andrew Sartori, 223–40. New York: Oxford University Press.

Maloney, Rep. Carolyn B., and Sen. Charles E. Schumer. 2010. "Women and the Economy 2010." 1–12, Report by the U.S. Congress Joint Economic Committee. August.

Marcus, George. 1995. "Ethnography in/of the World System: The Emergence of Multi-Sited Ethnography." *Annual Review of Anthropology* 24: 95–117.

Markell, Patchen. 2003. *Bound by Recognition*. Princeton, NJ: Princeton University Press.

Mata Amritanandamayi Math, trans. 2008. *Amritapuri Archana Book*. Kollam, Kerala: Mata Amritanandamayi Mission Trust.

McDaniel, June. 1989. *Madness of the Saints: Ecstatic Religion in Bengal*. Chicago: University of Chicago Press.

———. 1992. "The Embodiment of God among the Bauls of Bengal." *Journal of Feminist Studies in Religion* 9, no. 2: 27–39.

McDermott, Rachel Fell. 1993. "Evidence for the Transformation of the Goddess Kālī: Kamalākānta Bhaṭṭācārya and the Bengali Śakta Padāvalī Tradition." PhD diss., Harvard University.

McKean, Lise. 1996. *Divine Enterprise: Gurus and the Hindu Nationalist Movement*. Chicago: University of Chicago Press.

Menon, Kalyani. 2010. *Everyday Nationalism*. Philadelphia: University of Pennsylvania Press.

Menon, T. V. Narayana, comm., M. N. Namboodiri, trans., K. V. Dev, ed. 1996. *The Thousand Names of the Divine Mother: Śrī Lalitā Sahasranāma*. San Ramon, CA: Mata Amritanandamayi Center.

Miller, Barbara Stoler, trans. 1986. *The Bhagavad-Gita: Krishna's Counsel in Time of War*. New York: Bantam Classic.

Miller, Lisa. 2009. "We Are All Hindus Now." *Newsweek*, August 14, 70.

Mines, Diane P. 2005. *Fierce Gods: Inequality, Ritual, and the Politics of Dignity in a South Indian Village*. Bloomington: Indiana University Press.

Mlecko, Joel D. 1982. "The Guru in the Hindu Tradition." *Numen* 29, fasc. 1 (July): 33–61.

Moore, R. Laurence. 1986. *Religious Outsiders and the Making of Americans*. New York: Oxford University Press.

Nabokov/Clark-Decès, Isabelle. 2000. *Religion against the Self: An Ethnography of Tamil Rituals*. New York: Oxford University Press.

Narayanan, Vasudha. 2005. "Gender and Priesthood in the Hindu Tradition." *Journal of Hindu-Christian Studies* vol. 18, art. 8: 22–31.

Nattier, Jan. 1997. "Buddhism Comes to Main Street." *Wilson Quarterly* 2, no. 2 (Spring): 72–81.

Nelson, Sara C. 2013. "Late Gang Rape Victim 'Was Equally Responsible for Attack.'" *Huffington Post*. July 1. http://www.huffingtonpost.co.uk/2013/01/07/asaram-bapu-indian-guru-gang-rape-victim-equally-responsible_n_2424739.html, accessed August 15, 2013.

Noble, Vicki. 1991. *Shakti Woman: Feeling Our Fire, Healing Our World: The New Female Shamanism*. San Francisco: Harper Collins.

Noguchi, Mituko. 2003. "Mother of All (Japan)." In *My First Darshan: A Collection of Stories from around the World*, vol. 1. Amritapuri: Mata Amritanandamayi Math.

Noll, Mark. 2002. *The Old Religion in a New World: The History of North American Christianity*. Grand Rapids, MI: Eerdmans.

Norman, Alex. 2011. *Spiritual Tourism: Travel and Religious Practice in Western Society*. New York: Continuum Press.

Ochshorn, Judith. 1997. "Goddesses and the Lives of Women." In *Women and Goddess Traditions*, edited by Karen L. King, 377–405. Minneapolis, MN: Fortress Press.

Ojha, Catherine. 1981. "Feminine Asceticism in Hinduism: Its Tradition and Present Condition." *Man in India* 61, no. 3: 254–85.

Olivelle, Patrick. 1992. *Saṃnyāsa Upaniṣads: Hindu Scriptures on Asceticism and Renunciation.* Oxford: Oxford University Press.

———. 1998. "Deconstruction of the Body in Indian Asceticism." In *Asceticism*, edited by Vincent L. Wimbush and Richard Valantis, 188–210. New York: Oxford University Press.

Oliver, Kelly. 2001. *Witnessing: Beyond Recognition.* Minneapolis: University of Minnesota Press.

Olson, Carl. 1990. *The Mysterious Play of Kālī: An Interpretive Study of Rāmakrishna.* Atlanta: Scholars Press.

Oman, John Campbell. 1905. *The Mystics, Ascetics, and Saints of India: A Study of Sadhuism, with an Account of the Yogis, Sanyasis, Bairagis, and Other Strange Hindu Sectarians.* London: T Fisher Unwin.

Orsi, Robert. 2010. *The Madonna of 115th Street: Faith and Community in Italian Harlem, 1880–1950.* New Haven, CT: Yale University Press. Originally published in 1985.

Paoletti, Jo B. 2012. *Pink and Blue: Telling the Girls from the Boys in America.* Bloomington: Indiana University Press.

Pashman, Manya Brachear. 2013. "Renowned 'Hugging Saint' Opens Her Arms to the Needy." *Chicago Tribune.* July 4.

Patton, Laurie L. 2005. "Can Women Be Priests? Brief Notes toward an Argument from the Ancient Hindu World." *Journal of Hindu-Christian Studies* vol. 18, no. 7: 17–21.

Pechilis, Karen, ed. 2004. *The Graceful Guru: Hindu Female Gurus in India and the United States.* New York: Oxford University Press.

Peña, Elaine A. 2011. *Performing Piety: Making Space Sacred with the Virgin of Guadalupe.* Berkeley: University of California Press.

Perec, Georges. 1989. *L'Infra-Ordinaire.* Paris: Seuil.

———. 1990. *Tentative d'épuisement d'un lieu Parisien.* Paris: Bourgois.

Pew Research Center. 2012a. "Asian Americans: A Mosaic of Faiths." *Pew Forum Report.* July 19. http://www.pewforum.org/asian-americans-a-mosaic-of-faiths.aspx, accessed December 1, 2012.

———. 2012b. "'Nones' on the Rise: One-in-Five Adults Have No Religious Affiliation." *Pew Forum Report.* October 9. http://www.pewforum.org/Unaffiliated/nones-on-the-rise.aspx, accessed November 6, 2012.

Pike, Sarah M. 2006. *New Age and Neopagan Religions in America.* New York: Columbia University Press.

Pinney, Christopher. 2004. *"Photos of the Gods": The Printed Image and Political Struggle in India.* New Delhi: Oxford University Press.

Pintak, Lawrence. 2001. "Something Has to Change: Blacks in American Buddhism." *Shambala Sun.* September.

Pintchman, Tracy, and Rita D. Sherma, eds. 2011. *Women and Goddess in Hinduism: Reinterpretations and Re-envisionings.* New York: Palgrave Macmillan.

Pollock, Sheldon. 1985. "The Theory of Practice and the Practice of Theory in Indian Intellectual History." *Journal of the American Oriental Society* 105, no. 3: 499–519.

_____. 2006. *The Language of the Gods in the World of Men: Sanskrit, Culture, and Power in Premodern India*. Berkeley: University of California Press.

Prabhupada, A. C. Bhaktivedanta, trans. 1962. *Srimad Bhagavatam*. http://srimad-bhagavatam.com, accessed July 29, 2013.

Prakash, Om. 2004. "Phenomenal." *Immortal Bliss* (First Quarter).

Prashad, Vijay. 2000. *The Karma of Brown Folk*. Minneapolis: University of Minnesota Press.

Premchand. 2002. *Godaan (The Gift of a Cow)*. Translated by Gordon C. Roadarmel. Bloomington: Indiana University Press.

Prentiss, K. P. 1999. *The Embodiment of Bhakti*. New York: Oxford University Press.

Prothero, Steve. 1996. *The White Buddhist: The Asian Odyssey of Henry Steel Olcott*. Bloomington: Indiana University Press.

Purkayastha, Bandana, Mangala Subramaniam, Manisha Desai, and Sunita Bose. 2003. "The Study of Gender in India: A Partial Review." *Gender and Society* 17, no. 4 (August): 503–24.

Radhakrishnan, S., trans. 1992. *The Principal Upanishads*. New York: Prometheus Books.

Radhika, V. 2002. "Her Holiness: Overcoming the Gender Barrier to Priesthood." *India Together*, April.

Ramaswamy, Sumathi. 2010. *The Goddess and the Nation: Mapping Mother India*. Durham, NC: Duke University Press.

Ramaswamy, Vijaya. 1992. "Rebels—Conformists?: Women Saints in Medieval South India." *Anthropos*. Bd. 87, H 1./3: 133–46.

_____. 1997. *Walking Naked: Women, Society, and Spirituality in South India*. Shimla, India: Indian Institute of Advanced Study.

Ramdya, Kavita. 2011. *Bollywood Weddings: Dating, Engagement, and Marriage in Hindu America*. Lanham, MD: Lexington Books.

Ramirez, Margaret. 2008. "Hindu Women Filling Priest Shortage." *Chicago Tribune*. October 13.

Rauschenbusch, Walter. 1917. *A Theology for the Social Gospel*. New York: MacMillan.

Ricoeur, Paul. 1984. "The Model of the Text: Meaningful Action Considered As a Text." *Social Research*. 51:1/2, 185–218.

Rigopoulos, Antonio. 2005. "The *Guru-Gītā* Or 'Song of the Master' as Incorporated in the *Guru-Caritra* of Sarasvatī Gaṅgādar." In *Theory and Practice of Yoga*, edited by Knut A. Jacobsen, 237–92. Leiden: Brill.

Rochford, E. Burke. 1985. *Hare Krishna in America*. New Brunswick, NJ: Rutgers University Press.

_____. 2007. *Hare Krishna Transformed*. New York: New York University Press.

Sabnis, Vivek. 2011. "Pune's Women Priests Spur Filmmaker to Make Documentary." *Mid Day*. July 9. http://www.mid-day.com/news/2011/jul/090711-News-Pune-documentary-women-performing-Training-Suhasini-Mulay.htm, July 9, 2011, accessed May 28, 2012.

Sangari, Kumkum, and Sudesh Vaid, eds. 1990. *Recasting Women: Essays in Indian Colonial History*. New Brunswick. NJ: Rutgers University Press.

Sargeant, Winthrop, trans. 1984. *The Bhagavad Gītā*. Albany: State University of New York Press.

Sarkar, Tanika. 2001. *Hindu Wife, Hindu Nation: Community, Religion, and Cultural Nationalism*. Bloomington: Indiana University Press.

Sarkar, Tanika, and Urbashi Butalia, eds. 1995. *Women and the Hindu Right*. New Delhi: Kali for Women.

Sarma, Deepak. 2012. "White Hindu Converts: Mimicry or Mockery?" *Huffington Post*. November 14. http://www.huffingtonpost.com/deepak-sarma/mimicry-or-mockery-white-_b_2131329.html, accessed April 5, 2014.

Scott, James C. 1985. *Weapons of the Weak: Everyday Forms of Peasant Resistance*. New Haven, CT: Yale University Press.

Scott, Joan Wallach. 1999. *Gender and the Politics of History*. New York: Columbia University Press.

Sered, Susan Starr. 1994. *Priestess Mother, Sacred Sister: Religions Dominated by Women*. New York: Oxford University Press.

Sheldon, Charles M. 2013. *In His Steps: What Would Jesus Do?* Chicago: Moody Press. Originally published (Chicago: Chicago Advance, 1896).

Shinn, Larry D. 1987. *The Dark Lord: Cult Images and the Hare Krishnas in America*. Philadelphia: Westminster Press.

Singleton, Mark, and Ellen Goldberg, eds. 2013. *Gurus of Modern Yoga*. New York: Oxford University Press.

Sinha, Mrinalini. 1995. *Colonial Masculinity: The 'Manly Englishman' and the 'Effeminate Bengali' in the Late Nineteenth Century*. Manchester: Manchester University Press.

Smith, David. 2003. *Hinduism and Modernity*. Malden, MA: Blackwell.

Srinivas, Smriti. 2008. *In the Presence of Sai Baba: Body, City and Memory in a Global Religious Movement*. Leiden: Brill.

Srinivas, Tulasi. 2010. *Winged Faith: Rethinking Globalization and Religious Pluralism through the Sathya Sai Movement*. New York: Columbia University Press.

Srivastava, Mehul. 2011. "Keeping Women on the Job in India." *Bloomberg Businessweek*. March 3. http://www.businessweek.com/magazine/content/11_11/b4219010769063.htm, accessed April 4, 2013.

Srivastava, Premlata. 1993. *Yā Devī Sarvabhūteṣu Śrī Śrī Mā Ānandamayī*. New Delhi: National Book Organization.

———. 1995. *The Divine Mother: Shri Shri Ma Anandamayee*. New Delhi: National Book Organization.

Stark, Rodney, William S. Bainbridge, and Daniel P. Doyle. 1979. "Cults of America: A Reconnaissance in Space and Time." *Sociological Analysis* 40: 347–59.

Stone, Emily. 2007. "Chicago's Indians: A History." *CRAIN'S Chicago Business* 30, no. 48 (November 26): 25.

Strauss, Sarah. 2005. *Positioning Yoga*. New York: Bloomsbury.

Sugirtharajah, Sharada. 2003. *Imagining Hinduism: A Postcolonial Perspective*. New York: Routledge.

Talwar, Vir Bharat. 1990. "Feminist Consciousness in Women's Journals in Hindi 1910–1920." In *Recasting Women: Essays in Indian Colonial History*, edited by Kumkum Sangari and Sudesh Vaid, 204–232. New Brunswick, NJ: Rutgers University Press.

Taylor, Charles. 1994. *Multiculturalism*. Edited by Amy Gutmann. Princeton, NJ: Princeton University Press.

Thomas, Nicholas. 1991. *Entangled Objects: Exchange, Material Culture, and Colonialism in the Pacific*. Cambridge, MA: Harvard University Press.

Thurman, Robert A. F. 1998. "Tibetan Buddhist Perspectives on Asceticism." In *Asceticism*, edited by Vincent L. Wimbush and Richard Valantasis, 108–118. New York: Oxford University Press.

Tweed, Thomas. 2002. *Our Lady of the Exile: Diasporic Religion at a Cuban Catholic Shrine in Miami*. New York: Oxford University Press.

Unger, Rhoda K. 2000. "Outsiders Inside: Positive Marginality and Social Change." *Journal of Social Sciences* 56, no. 1: 163–79.

Upadhyaya, Bhavana. 2009. "Amma's Daughters." PhD diss., University of New Mexico.

Urban, Hugh. 2003a. "Avatar for Our Age: Sathya Sai Baba and the Cultural Contradictions of Late Capitalism." *Religion* 33: 73–93.

———. 2003b. *Tantra: Sex, Secrecy, Politics, and Power in the Study of Religion*. Berkeley: University of California Press.

———. 2009. *The Power of Tantra: Religion, Sexuality, and the Politics of South Asian Studies*. London: I.B. Tauris.

Van der Veer, Peter. 2001. *Imperial Encounters: Religion and Modernity in India and Britain*. Princeton, NJ: Princeton University Press.

Venkatesananda, Swami. 1989. *The Concise Srimad Bhagavatam*. Albany: State University of New York Press.

Vertovec, Steven. 2000. *The Hindu Diaspora: Comparative Patterns*. London: Routledge.

Visweswaran, Kamala, Michael Witzel, Nandini Manjrekar, Dipta Bhog, and Uma Chakravarti. 2009. "The Hindutva View of History." *Georgetown Journal of International Affairs* (Winter/Spring): 101–12.

Vivekananda, Swami. 2003. *The Complete Works of Swami Vivekananda*. Vols. 1–9. Hollywood, CA: Vedanta Press and Bookshop, www.ramakrishna vivekananda.info/vivekananda/complete_works.htm, accessed August 8, 2013.

Waghorne, Joanne Punzo. 2004. *Diaspora of the Gods: Modern Hindu Temples in an Urban Middle-Class World*. Oxford: Oxford University Press.

———. 2010. "Global Gurus and the Third Stream of American Religiosity." In *Political Hinduism*, edited by Vinay Lal, 122–49. New Delhi: Oxford University Press.

Walton, Jonathan. 2009. *Watch This! The Ethics and Aesthetics of Black Televangelism*. New York: New York University Press.

Warner, R. Stephen, and Judith G. Wittner, eds. 1998. *Gatherings in Diaspora: Religious Communities and the New Immigration*. Philadelphia: Temple University Press.

Warrier, Maya. 2003. "Guru Choice and Spiritual Seeking in Contemporary India." *International Journal of Hindu Studies* 7, no. 1/3 (February): 31–54.

———. 2005. *Hindu Selves in the Modern World: Guru Faith in the Mata Amritanandamayi Mission*. London: RoutledgeCurzon.

Warty, Daksha. 2009. "Women As Hindu Priests Have an Edge." *Inter Press Service*. November 24.

Weber, Max. 1978. *Economy and Society: An Outline of Interpretive Sociology*. Vols. 1 and 2. Edited by Guenther Roth and Claus Wittich. Berkeley: University of California Press.

_____. 1991. *The Sociology of Religion*. Boston: Beacon Press.

Willey, P. Kamala. 2010. *Earth Ethics: Of M. K. Gandhi with Teachings from Holy Mother Amma: An Introduction*. Mumbai: Wise Earth.

Williams, Raymond Brady. 1984. *A New Face of Hinduism: Swaminarayan Religion*. Cambridge: Cambridge University Press.

_____. 2001. *An Introduction to Swaminarayan Hinduism*. Cambridge: Cambridge University Press.

Williamson, Lola. 2010. *Transcendent in America: Hindu Inspired Meditation Movements as New Religion*. New York: New York University Press.

Index

Swami Abhedananda, 13
Abrahamic traditions, 178–79,
    272nn46,47
Adigalar, Sri Bangaru, 269n96
adopter devotees, 24–25, 34; beliefs about
    Amma of, 160–61, 167–72, 177–81,
    193–95, 235–39; cultural borrowing
    (orientalism) of, 209–10, 212–17,
    275nn44,45, 276n55; de facto
    congregationalism among, 186–87,
    222–25, 228–29; definition of, 151–52;
    demographics of, 154–57, 271n26;
    financial support by, 202–4, 274n33;
    individual spiritual focus of, 191–95;
    language skills and limitations of, 99,
    199, 205, 207; mimesis of Amma by,
    172–75, 228, 272n47; satsangs of,
    197–202, 223; at Shakti Fest 2012,
    226–28; traditional religious back-
    ground of, 218–22, 236. *See also*
    devotees in North America
advaita vedantic nondualism, 20, 23, 35,
    141–42, 195, 234–35; of Amma as
    Divine Mother, 132–40, 171–72; female
    asceticism in, 112–14; interpretation of
    darshan in, 42. *See also* women's
    empowerment
Ai Giri Nandini, 96–97
Akka Mahadevi, 131
Albanese, Catherine, 154–55
Alstad, Diana, 249
Altekar, A. S., 113

alternative religious activities.
    See spirituality movements
American devotees. *See* devotees in North
    America
American religious traditions, 186–87,
    218–22; liberal Protestantism in, 148,
    229, 236, 239, 272n8, 277n13;
    Marianism in, 27, 179, 272nn46,47
American Veda (Goldberg), 214
Amma, 1–12, 40*fig.*, 51*fig.*, 234–39;
    Amritapuri ashram of, 7, 9*fig.*, 10,
    174–75; background of, 6–7; clothing
    and appearance of, 33–34; darshan
    embrace of, 40*fig.*, 42–50, 70–71,
    254n1, 264n2; devotees in India to,
    246–47; divine authority of, 4, 18,
    21–25, 33–34, 65, 76–77, 79–82, 95–96,
    104–6, 117, 172–75, 235–39, 259n17,
    264n85; globalizing movement of,
    22–23; humanitarian and educational
    projects of, 8–10, 21, 34, 46, 51,
    115–16, 175, 203–4, 266n36; imagery
    of, 60–68, 107, 158*fig.*; international
    communities of, 7–8, 10; male advisors
    (senior swamis) of, 107; maternal ascetic
    habitus of, 5–6, 12, 15, 20, 34–35, 38,
    117, 254n3, 261n48; names and titles
    of, 12, 252n10; North American
    ashrams of, 8, 12, 46, 187–88, 189*fig.*,
    196, 204, 223, 272n6, 273n12; priestly
    role of, 107; revision of caste and gender
    hierarchies by, 24–25, 34–35, 50–60,